Kentucky Cooks

Kentucky Cooks

Favorite Recipes from *Kentucky Living*

Linda Allison-Lewis

THE UNIVERSITY PRESS OF KENTUCKY

Copyright © 2009 by Linda Allison-Lewis

Published by the University Press of Kentucky
Scholarly publisher for the Commonwealth, serving Bellarmine University, Berea
College, Centre College of Kentucky, Eastern Kentucky University, The Filson
Historical Society, Georgetown College, Kentucky Historical Society, Kentucky
State University, Morehead State University, Murray State University, Northern
Kentucky University, Transylvania University, University of Kentucky, University
of Louisville, and Western Kentucky University.
All rights reserved.

Editorial and Sales Offices: The University Press of Kentucky
663 South Limestone Street, Lexington, Kentucky 40508-4008
www.kentuckypress.com

13 12 11 10 09   5 4 3 2 1

Library of Congress Cataloging-in-Publication Data

Allison-Lewis, Linda, 1948–
    Kentucky cooks : favorite recipes from Kentucky living / Linda Allison-Lewis.
      p. cm.
    Includes index.
    ISBN 978-0-8131-2537-4 (hardcover : alk. paper)
    1. Cookery, American. 2. Cookery—Kentucky. I. Kentucky living. II. Title.
    TX715.A44292 2009
    641.59769—dc22   2008049876

This book is printed on acid-free recycled paper meeting the requirements of the
American National Standard for Permanence in Paper for Printed Library Materials.

∞ ❀

Manufactured in the United States of America.

 Member of the Association of
American University Presses

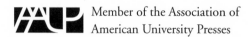

To my editor, Anita Travis Richter,
for helping me believe I really could
come back after my stroke

Contents

Acknowledgments

I want to thank my great kids and their spouses—Christian and Andrea Lewis, Scott Lewis, and Noélle and Eric Lang—for being in my life—My mom, Jean, who still inspires me with her great meals—My grandchildren, Nick and Meredith Lewis, who provide me with unspeakable joy every day—My sister, Tammy Ricketts, who not only helped me with this book but is always full of just the right ideas—My nephew, Bo Ricketts, computer whiz and typist extraordinaire—My boxers—Lola, Sophie, and Rox—who always sit adoringly at the stove, never letting on when they sense a flop coming—Laura Sutton, Leila Salisbury (I'll miss you), Mack McCormick, and the great staff at the University Press of Kentucky.

The *Kentucky Living* staff: Paul Wesslund, Anita Travis Richter, Ellie Hobgood, Paula Sparrow, Lynne Christenson, Monica Pickerill, Kate Wheatley, Arlene Toon, Kathy Wade, Tammy Simmons, Carol Smith, Nick Gatens, and Curt Smith.

I also want to acknowledge the writers and contributors who make *Kentucky Living* such a quality magazine: David and Lallee Dick, Teresa Bell Kindred, Shelly Nold, and all the others who provide me with great reading each month and great pride in this publication.

Most of all—my readers of fourteen years and the greatest audience I could have.

Introduction

It has been ten years since *Kentucky's Best: Fifty Years of Great Recipes* was published. It is a collection of not only recipes that have been in my family for years, but also my favorite recipes from Kentucky chefs, restaurants, and bed and breakfasts, as well as those that are truly traditions in the Bluegrass State.

For many years, I have dreamed of publishing a collection of the best recipes from my column, "Kentucky Cooks." I receive so many requests for recipes featured in my column and have been asked by readers where they can find the best of *Kentucky Living*. One day while reading an e-mail from a reader requesting such a book, I decided that it was time to pull that title and make it a reality. Now my readers do not have to take the time to write and wait for a reply. The best of *Kentucky Living* is in this collection.

I'm often asked about my job and the photos. Jim Battles is my photographer, and he not only does the food shots, but also takes photos on many topics for the magazine. He makes the food look so appetizing, and, surprisingly, there have been only a few mishaps. The most memorable was a beautiful scoop of ice cream melting under the lights. We plan our shots for the year and set up three or four months at a time, cooking the dishes in my home or Jim's studio. Besides being a great photographer and a talented drummer, he loves to eat our food as much as I do. We have to be *Kentucky Living*'s official foodies. Many times, I have the good intention of sending his wife, Nancy, and his kids a dish we prepare, but Jim and I usually manage to polish it off. I consider us a great team, and we have a wonderful time. Remember—first and foremost, we're foodies!

Throughout the years, my work at *Kentucky Living* has been hard to think of as a job. While I love signing books, judging food events, giving cooking demonstrations, and receiving everything from food products, cookbooks, recipes, and cooking gadgets to proposals (really), I love interacting with my readers more than anything. I feel like I know them and enjoy answering their letters and e-mails. One sweet lady has sent me an Easter card every year since I started to write my column in 1995.

I often call a reader to ask her opinion about an upcoming column or to congratulate him on a food accomplishment. I enjoy working with Kentucky State Fair winners and finalists and hearing about all their food contributions. I open the *Kentucky Living* Web site to learn about great recipes, such as Sour Cream Pound Cake from Marilyn Gay and those from so many other talented Kentucky cooks who share their favorites each month. More than anything, I love to laugh and chat with my readers, knowing that I'm in the company of the greatest cooks in the South: Kentucky cooks!

Can you tell that I'm proud of my magazine? Does this really sound like a job? Does it get any better than this? I don't think so!

Kentucky Cooks

Appetizers, Savory Snacks, and Spreads

Appetizers, Savory Snacks, and Spreads

"What she didn't realize was that she was wearing the evidence."

 I've never met a boxer I didn't love, and my own three girls—new baby Rox and Lola and Sophie (high-maintenance sisters and inseparable)—provide me with all the love and amusement one person can handle. Although they are big-time foodies, I never give them treats except for an occasional ice chip. I don't care to know what Noélle feeds them. Lola loves sweets and sticks of butter, while Sophie prefers finding medicine and eating Noélle's expensive makeup. The fact that they have attended school regularly and do not beg at the table does little to prevent them from dreaming and sneaking around to look for their favorites.

My cousin Kim comes from Florida every year the day after Christmas to celebrate the New Year with me. She loves to have a pot of my Bean Soup and my Coconut Cream Pie waiting when she gets here. On December 26, 2006, I was waiting when she called on her cell phone to tell me that she was getting off the interstate. I told the girls to sit at the door and wait for Aunt Kim while I walked outside to watch for her car. Something told me to place the pie high up at the back of the counter, just in case. In no more than a minute, I walked back into the house with the counter in full view through the dining room. SHEER HORROR! The pie plainly had no front or center. Sophie shot up the stairs, fearful that she would be blamed, while Lola sat perfectly still and looked at me, as if to say "WHAT?" I screamed "STAY!" and ran upstairs to grab Sophie's face and swing around all sixty-five pounds of her to smell her breath to make sure that she was innocent. She was. I ran back downstairs, to find Lola still sitting with coconut cream extending from her mouth to her eyebrows and covering the top of her head. It was evident that the funny fawn face with a black mask had thrown herself face first into the pie.

What she didn't realize was that she was wearing the evidence.

I enjoy entertaining, especially in the summer. Last year, I put in a patio with an outdoor kitchen and spent many nights serving snacks and light meals to friends and family. I even installed television, so we could spend entire nights not having to make trips to the kitchen. I've served many satisfying meals out there, consisting of no more than appetizers and snacks.

I celebrate Halloween in a big way. Lola, Sophie, and Rox dress up, and we invite friends over for a chili-and-snack block party. This year, we all sat around a fire pit and enjoyed watching kids of all ages get their treats. It's tradition on this holiday for us to serve White Chili and Pumpkin Crunch (both featured in *Kentucky's Best*), but any of the snacks in this chapter make for a great time spent with neighbors and friends.

Fresh Green Onion Butter is a wonderful topping for bruschetta and grilled vegetables. And Boursin Cheese, which tastes so good on crackers, will not break the bank when you make it yourself. A great idea for pulling parties inside when the weather gets cool is to serve chicken wings and Western Party Caviar. So start planning and come up with an occasion to celebrate in a laid-back way. It's all about family, friends, and food, right?

✑ SAVORY HERB CHEESECAKE ✑

1 cup Italian-style bread crumbs

3 tablespoons butter, melted

3 tablespoons finely chopped fresh basil

2 cloves garlic, chopped

½ cup light mayonnaise

1 pound ricotta cheese

1 ounce blue cheese, crumbled

1½ cups grated Parmesan cheese

½ cup toasted and finely chopped almonds for garnish

3 tablespoons slivered almonds for garnish

2 tablespoons snipped fresh chives for garnish

Lightly grease 8- or 9-inch springform pan. In bowl, combine bread crumbs and butter. Press into bottom of springform pan. Refrigerate.

In food processor or blender, combine basil, garlic, and mayonnaise until smooth. Set aside.

In mixing bowl, beat together ricotta, blue, and Parmesan cheeses until well blended. Beat in basil mixture. Spread cheese mixture over bread-crumb crust, pressing and smoothing top. Refrigerate for at least 8 hours or overnight.

When ready to serve, remove sides of pan and place cake on a platter. Press chopped almonds onto sides of cheesecake, if desired. To garnish top of cheesecake, make a "flower" with slivered almonds and chive stems, if desired. Serve with assorted crackers and toast points.

Yield: 12 servings

❧ ALL-SEASON TOMATO SALSA ❧

6 Roma tomatoes, chopped

¾ cup peeled and chopped jicama

½ cup chopped red onion

2 fresh jalapeño peppers, seeded and finely chopped

3 tablespoons chopped fresh cilantro

1 (6-ounce) can tomato paste

¼ cup honey

3 tablespoons red wine vinegar

2 tablespoons fresh lime juice

2 tablespoons vegetable oil

1 teaspoon salt

½ teaspoon dried oregano, crushed

In large bowl, combine ingredients and mix well. Refrigerate for 3 hours or longer, to blend flavors. Spoon into jar with tight-fitting lid. Store in refrigerator for up to 2 weeks.

Yield: 3 cups

∽ SHRIMP TOAST ∽

12 large shrimp, shelled and deveined, with tails

1 egg

2 ½ tablespoons cornstarch

¼ teaspoon salt

Dash of pepper

3 slices white sandwich bread, crusts removed and quartered

1 slice cooked ham, cut into ½-inch pieces

1 hard-boiled egg yolk, mashed

1 green onion, finely chopped

Vegetable oil

Cut deep slit down back of each shrimp. In large bowl, beat egg, cornstarch, salt, and pepper until blended. Add shrimp and toss to coat well.

Place 1 shrimp, cut side down, on each bread quarter and press shrimp gently into bread. Brush small amount of egg mixture over each shrimp. Place 1 piece of ham, small amount of egg yolk, and ¼ teaspoon green onion on top of each shrimp. Press lightly.

In large skillet, heat oil over medium-high heat and add 3 or 4 bread quarters at a time. Cook until golden and gently turn, cooking 1 to 2 minutes on each side. Drain on paper towels.

Yield: 12 servings

∽ BOURSIN CHEESE ∽

⅓ cup heavy cream

1 (8-ounce) package cream cheese

⅓ cup sour cream

3 tablespoons snipped fresh chives

2 cloves garlic, minced

Zest of 1 orange

1 tablespoon orange juice

Salt and pepper to taste

Whip cream until soft peaks form. Whip together cream cheese and sour cream until smooth and a little fluffy. In bowl, combine cream with cream cheese mixture. Fold in remaining ingredients. Cover and refrigerate for at least 2 hours, to allow flavors to develop.

Yield: 2 cups

✂ CORNED BEEF SPREAD ✂

2 cups corned beef, cooked

1 teaspoon Dijon mustard

2 teaspoons horseradish

2 teaspoons chopped fresh dill

½ cup mayonnaise

Salt and pepper to taste

In food processor, combine ingredients and pulse to blend. Do not puree. Mixture should still be chunky. Cover and refrigerate overnight. Serve with cocktail-size rye bread or crackers.

Yield: 24 servings

✑ HEAT'S-ON HOT WINGS ✑

3 pounds chicken wings

½ cup (1 stick) butter or margarine

⅓ cup Louisiana Hot Sauce (or your favorite brand)

1 teaspoon crushed red pepper

½ teaspoon cayenne pepper

Salt and pepper to taste

Cut off tips and separate wings at the joint. Arrange in a layer in a microwave-safe dish. Cover with plastic wrap and raise a corner to vent. Microwave at medium-high setting for 7 to 10 minutes. (Microwaves vary, so check for doneness every 2 or 3 minutes, rotating the dish and cooking longer if necessary.)

In microwave-safe bowl, melt butter or margarine, and add remaining ingredients. Heat until just bubbly, about 3 minutes. Set aside. Drain chicken on paper towels and toss with sauce. Wings are great when served with blue cheese dressing for dipping.

Yield: 6 servings

✑ CORN RELISH ✑

1 cup water

1 cup vinegar

½ cup sugar

½ teaspoon salt

1 teaspoon celery seed

1 teaspoon mustard seed

1 teaspoon turmeric

½ teaspoon Tabasco (or other hot pepper) sauce

1 green bell pepper, diced

1 red bell pepper, diced

4 green onions, sliced crosswise

4 cups fresh corn kernels (8 ears of corn)

1 tablespoon chopped fresh cilantro

1 tablespoon chopped fresh parsley

In large, nonreactive pot, combine ingredients, except cilantro and parsley. Bring to a boil, reduce heat, and cook at a low boil, uncovered, for 10 minutes. Add parsley and cilantro, and increase heat, cooking until most of the liquid is evaporated. Cool and refrigerate overnight, to allow flavors to blend. Serve as a relish or a vegetable.

Yield: about 3 cups

❧ HOT PEPPER AND PECAN JELLY ❧

1 cup water

2 teaspoons Tabasco (or other hot pepper) sauce

⅓ cup lemon juice

3 cups sugar

3 ounces liquid pectin

Red food coloring

½ cup toasted and crushed pecans

In large saucepan, combine water, Tabasco sauce, lemon juice, and sugar. Bring to a boil, stirring constantly. Add pectin and a few drops of red food coloring. Let mixture come to a rolling boil and continue to boil for 30 seconds. Add pecans. Remove from heat and skim off foam.

Pour into three 8-ounce canning jars, leaving ¼-inch headspace. Wipe rims of jars and put lids on. Process for 5 minutes in a boiling-water bath. Tighten lids.

Yield: 3 jars

❧ SWEETLY SPICED ❧
MANGO CHUTNEY

2 large (1½-pound) mangos, peeled and coarsely chopped

1 cup chopped red onion

⅓ cup cider vinegar

⅓ cup honey

1 tablespoon finely chopped crystallized ginger

1 clove garlic, finely chopped

1 teaspoon mustard seed

½ teaspoon ground cumin

½ teaspoon salt

In large saucepan, combine ingredients. Bring to a boil, stirring occasionally. Reduce heat, partially cover, and simmer for 1 hour, stirring occasionally, until thickened.

Yield: about 3 cups

❧ GREEN ONION BUTTER ❧

½ cup (1 stick) butter

¼ cup finely minced green onion

1 tablespoon minced fresh parsley

1 teaspoon freshly ground pepper

½ teaspoon dry mustard

In small bowl, combine ingredients and blend well. Serve on hot bread or baked potatoes.

Yield: ¾ cup

ເ∿ WESTERN PARTY CAVIAR ເ∿

When I was a restaurant critic, I fell in love with this great snack food, commonly called Texas Caviar. I tweaked the recipe a little bit, and I serve it with tortilla chips or watch my daughter, Noélle, eat it with a spoon.

1 (15-ounce) can black-eyed peas, drained

1 (15-ounce) can shoepeg corn, drained

1 medium tomato, chopped

2 jalapeño peppers, chopped

1 green bell pepper, chopped

3 green onions, chopped

1 (8-ounce) bottle Italian dressing (I use Wishbone)

In large bowl, combine ingredients and cover tightly. Refrigerate overnight, to blend flavors. Serve with tortilla chips, as you would salsa.

Yield: 4 cups

❧ OYSTER SPREAD ❧

2 (8-ounce) packages cream cheese, softened

¼ cup milk

2 to 3 tablespoons mayonnaise

1 tablespoon lemon juice

1 tablespoon Worcestershire sauce

Dash of hot sauce

Salt to taste

2 cans smoked oysters, finely chopped

Paprika

Chopped fresh parsley

In bowl, combine ingredients, except oysters, paprika, and parsley. Blend well. Stir in oysters and refrigerate for several hours. Sprinkle with paprika and parsley, and serve on cocktail-size rye bread.

Yield: 3 cups

❧ HONEY-MUSTARD ❧ SANDWICH SPREAD

1 cup whole fresh basil leaves, loosely packed, or 1½ tablespoons dried basil

¼ cup honey

¼ cup nonfat mayonnaise

2 tablespoons Dijon mustard

1 clove garlic, minced

Salt and pepper to taste

In food processor or blender, combine basil, honey, mayonnaise, mustard, and garlic. Process until smooth. Season with salt and pepper, and refrigerate. Store in refrigerator for up to 2 weeks.

Yield: ¾ cup, enough for 4 sandwiches

Soups and Salads

Soups and Salads

"Pigs' feet were hanging from the kitchen ceiling."

 My mother and her cousin Kitty were as close as sisters, and when pressure cookers first came out in the 1950s, they both couldn't wait to get one. My mother used hers all the time and produced some wonderful meals from it. Cousin Kitty, not so much.

Kitty's husband liked pigs' feet, and one Saturday, Kitty decided to cook them in her new pressure cooker. At that time, you could tell that the food inside the cooker was finished when a button popped up in the center of a weight that fit into the cooker's lid. You were supposed to keep an eye on that button.

In addition to pigs' feet, Kitty's husband liked "the ponies." While Kitty cooked, he was looking forward to watching the races on his brand-new television. Television was new at the time, and people would come from all around a neighborhood to sit in someone's living room (where they otherwise might never have been invited) to marvel at a new set. Kitty was soon lured out of the kitchen by the novelty.

When the button on the pressure cooker popped, she didn't see it. When the weight began to whistle, she didn't hear it. Eventually, of course, disaster. As my family tells it, the explosion was heard all over the neighborhood, there was grease on everything in the house, and pigs' feet were hanging from the kitchen ceiling.

Sadly, Kitty's husband died not long after that.

Kate Wheatley, *Kentucky Living* staff

Who doesn't love the idea of a wonderful soup simmering on the stove and a crisp garden salad full of fruits, fresh herbs, meats, and gorgeous greens? I often begin a pot of soup with a rich stock or broth that I have prepared at an earlier time and frozen just for soup days. I add wine, garlic, and herbs and make up my mind what it will become after it has simmered for a while. I love to be creative with soups. And nothing complements a great soup more than an out-of-the-ordinary salad. I've offered lots of exciting choices in this chapter.

If you are strictly an iceberg or a romaine individual, step outside your comfort zone when selecting greens. There are few greens better than a buttery Bibb or arugula. You'll be amazed at the difference it adds to your favorite salad dressings.

Enjoy this combination of great food choices for an exciting dinner tonight. Can I interest you in Avocado Bisque accompanied by Poppy Seed Turkey Salad? Surprise your family and listen to the raves.

∽ ALPHABET CHICKEN SOUP ∽

This is great soup to cook for kids when they're feeling under the weather. They'll appreciate the ABC's.

1 (3- to 4-pound) stewing chicken

3 quarts water

¼ teaspoon poultry seasoning

1½ cups alphabet pasta

1⅓ cups sliced carrots

1 cup finely chopped celery

1 medium onion, finely chopped

Salt and pepper to taste

In a large Dutch oven, combine chicken, water, and poultry seasoning. Bring to a boil. Cover and cook over low heat for 1 hour or until chicken is tender. Remove chicken and skim fat from broth. Cut meat from bone and return to soup. Add pasta, carrots, celery, and onion. Cook, covered, over medium heat for 20 to 30 minutes or until pasta is tender. Season with salt and pepper.

Yield: 8 servings

❧ CHILLED CREAM OF LEMON SOUP ❧

⅓ cup fresh lemon juice

Lemon rind, cut into 2½-inch strips

3 cups plus 2 tablespoons homemade or canned chicken broth

1½ teaspoons cornstarch

½ cup heavy cream, well chilled

½ cup crushed ice

Salt to taste

Snipped fresh chives for garnish

In saucepan, combine lemon juice, lemon rind, and 3 cups broth. Bring to a boil, boil for 5 minutes, and discard rind. Stir cornstarch into 2 tablespoons broth and then whisk it into broth mixture. Cook over moderately high heat, stirring until thickened. Remove pan from heat. Stir in cream. In blender, mix soup with crushed ice until smooth. Transfer to metal bowl, skim froth off top, cover with aluminum foil, and refrigerate. When ready to serve, season with salt, ladle into chilled bowls, and garnish with chives.

Yield: 2 servings

❧ AVOCADO BISQUE ❧

4 very ripe avocados

⅓ cup fresh lime juice

1 clove garlic, finely crushed

1 tablespoon mayonnaise

1 teaspoon curry powder

1 cup heavy cream

1½ cups canned chicken broth, brought to a slow boil and chilled

2 tablespoons chopped fresh parsley

1 tablespoon chopped fresh cilantro

½ teaspoon Tabasco (or other hot pepper) sauce

In blender, mix in batches avocados, lime juice, garlic, mayonnaise, and curry powder. Process until smooth. Transfer to large bowl and stir in remaining ingredients. Cover and refrigerate. When ready to serve, stir well and ladle into chilled bowls.

Yield: 4 servings

ço STRAWBERRY SOUP ço

1 pound strawberries

1 (15-ounce) container sour cream

2 teaspoons grenadine

1 teaspoon vanilla extract

1 tablespoon plus 1 teaspoon powdered sugar

¼ cup half-and-half

Sour cream for topping

Mix strawberries and sour cream. Beat slowly until well mixed. While blending strawberry mixture in a food processor, add grenadine, vanilla extract, and sugar. Blend until smooth, add half-and-half, and mix only until well blended. Refrigerate. When ready to serve, top with a dollop of sour cream.

Yield: 4 to 6 servings

ᴄꜱ CHILLED DILL SOUP ᴄꜱ

2 pints half-and-half

2 (16-ounce) containers plain yogurt

4 cucumbers, peeled, seeded, and diced

4 tablespoons chopped green onion

1 teaspoon salt

½ teaspoon white pepper

Sprigs of fresh dill

Sliced cucumber for garnish

Combine ingredients, except cucumber slices, stirring well. Chill thoroughly. When ready to serve, stir and garnish with cucumber.

Yield: 16 servings

ᴄꜱ FRENCH ONION SOUP ᴄꜱ

1 pound onions, sliced

3 tablespoons vegetable oil

2 (14-ounce) cans beef broth

1 teaspoon Worcestershire sauce

Pinch of pepper

6 slices French bread, toasted

⅔ cup shredded Swiss cheese

In large saucepan, cook and stir onions in oil over medium heat for 20 minutes or until golden brown. Stir in broth, Worcestershire sauce, and pepper. Bring to a boil and remove from heat.

Place bread on baking sheet and sprinkle with cheese. Broil 4 to 5 inches from heat for about 1 minute or until cheese is melted and golden. Serve soup topped with bread.

Yield: 6 servings

ℰ ROASTED CARROT AND ℰ ORANGE SOUP

10 to 12 large carrots

4 tablespoons (½ stick) butter

2 cups chopped yellow onion

5 cups chicken stock or broth

1 cup fresh orange juice

Zest of ½ orange

Salt and freshly ground pepper to taste

Grill or roast carrots, turning frequently, until tender. Cool and then chop carrots. In saucepan, melt butter and add onion. Cover and cook over low heat until tender and light brown. Add carrots and stock or broth, and bring to a boil. Reduce heat and cook until carrots are very tender.

Pour soup through a strainer and reserve the liquid. In a food processor or blender, puree the solids. Add 1 cup of the reserved liquid, orange juice, and orange zest. Process quickly until well blended. Add remaining reserved liquid. Pour back into pot and simmer for 10 minutes. Season with salt and pepper.

Yield: 6 servings

∾ HOT GERMAN POTATO SALAD ∾

This is a great Oktoberfest dish!

5 or 6 medium potatoes, peeled and boiled

5 or 6 strips bacon

1 medium onion, thinly sliced

1 tablespoon flour

⅓ cup cider vinegar

⅓ cup water

½ cup sugar

1½ teaspoons celery seed

Salt and pepper to taste

Cut potatoes into thin slices. Fry bacon until crisp. Remove from pan, crumble, and set aside. Add onion to bacon fat, cook until wilted, and add to bacon. Drain bacon fat, reserving about 2 tablespoons. To bacon drippings, add flour, vinegar, water, and sugar. Cook until thickened, stirring constantly. Pour over potatoes, add celery seed and onion mixture, and season with salt and pepper. Toss lightly. Adjust seasoning to taste.

Yield: 6 servings

∾ HOT SLAW ∾

Also a great dish for your own Oktoberfest!

½ pound bacon, chopped

½ cup cider vinegar

3 tablespoons sugar

½ teaspoon salt

½ teaspoon dry mustard

1 small head red cabbage, thinly sliced

Fry bacon until crisp and pour off all fat except ¼ cup. To bacon drippings, add vinegar, sugar, salt, and mustard. When ready to serve, pour hot dressing over cabbage, toss, and top with bacon.

Yield: 6 servings

✑ SUNDAY-BRUNCH MARINATED ✑ MUSHROOM SALAD

½ cup salad oil

¼ cup olive oil

1 tablespoon plus 1 teaspoon Worcestershire sauce

Scant teaspoon salt

1 teaspoon freshly ground pepper

2½ tablespoons lemon juice

2 cloves garlic, chopped

⅓ cup red wine

2 (15-ounce) cans or 1 (30-ounce) can button mushrooms, drained

In saucepan, combine ingredients and cook over medium heat for about 15 minutes. Cover and refrigerate for several hours.

Yield: 8 servings as an appetizer

❧ AMBROSIA ❧

This is another great southern ambrosia recipe!

6 navel oranges

1 (8-ounce) can crushed pineapple, drained (reserve juice)

¾ cup flaked sweetened coconut

2 teaspoons sugar

1 cup heavy cream

1 tablespoon plus 1 teaspoon powdered sugar

½ cup maraschino cherries, drained

Section oranges into a bowl. Add pineapple, coconut, sugar, and pineapple juice. Cover and refrigerate overnight.

When ready to serve, whip cream with powdered sugar until soft peaks form. Fold in fruit mixture and add cherries. Arrange on individual serving dishes.

Yield: 4 to 6 servings

❧ POPPY SEED TURKEY SALAD ❧

1 cup uncooked rice

2 cups chicken broth

2 cups cooked turkey breast slices, chopped

1½ cups unpeeled and diced apple

1 cup chopped celery

⅓ cup toasted and chopped pecans

⅓ to ½ cup poppy seed dressing

Salt and pepper to taste

4 large lettuce leaves

In saucepan, combine rice and broth. Bring to a boil, reduce heat, cover, and simmer for 15 minutes without disturbing, until liquid is absorbed. Let stand, covered, for 5 minutes. Cool and refrigerate.

When ready to serve, combine rice with remaining ingredients—except lettuce, salt, and pepper—in a medium bowl and toss with a fork. Season with salt and pepper, if needed. Serve on lettuce leaves.

Yield: 4 servings

❧ AVOCADO SALAD ❧

2 (3-ounce) packages or 1 (6-ounce) package lime gelatin

1 cup mayonnaise

2 avocados, mashed

1 (8-ounce) and 1 (3-ounce) package cream cheese

1 small jar pimientos, drained

2 cups chopped celery

1 small onion, grated

Dash of Worcestershire sauce

Garlic powder to taste

Salt and cayenne pepper to taste

Lettuce leaves

Bring 2 cups water to a boil and mix in gelatin. Add remaining ingredients, except lettuce, adjusting seasoning to taste. Pour into lightly oiled 4- or 5-cup mold. Refrigerate for several hours until well set. Serve on lettuce leaves.

Yield: 6 servings

∾ BLACK BEAN AND CORN SALAD ∾

2 cups corn kernels, fresh or frozen

1 (15-ounce) can black beans, drained

1 cup halved cherry tomatoes

½ large red onion, chopped

2 tablespoons chopped fresh cilantro

½ green bell pepper, chopped (optional)

Juice of ½ lime

Olive oil

Salt and pepper to taste

1 avocado, thinly sliced, for garnish

In bowl, combine corn, beans, tomatoes, onion, cilantro, and green pepper. Sprinkle with lime juice and drizzle with oil. Toss and season with salt and pepper. Arrange avocado across top.

Yield: 4 to 6 servings
Note: To prevent browning, brush avocado with lime juice.

∾ PRETZEL SALAD ∾

This remains one of my favorite holiday dishes.

2 cups crushed pretzels

1¼ cups sugar

½ cup plus 2 tablespoons (1¼ sticks) margarine or butter, melted

1 (8-ounce) container whipped cream cheese

1 cup whipped topping

2 cups pineapple juice

2 (3-ounce) packages strawberry gelatin

2 (10-ounce) packages frozen strawberries

Lettuce leaves

Whipped topping

Preheat oven to 350 degrees. Coat a 9 × 13-inch baking pan with cooking spray.

Mix pretzels, ¼ cup sugar, and margarine or butter. Spread pretzel mixture in baking pan. Bake for 10 minutes. Allow to cool completely.

Mix cream cheese, 1 cup sugar, and whipped topping, and spread over pretzel mixture. Heat pineapple juice and dissolve gelatin in it. Add strawberries and cool until gelatin just begins to set. Spread over cheese layer and refrigerate until solid.

When ready to serve, cut into squares, arrange on lettuce, and top with a dollop of whipped topping.

Yield: 8 servings

❧ BIBB LETTUCE SALAD ❧ WITH MANDARIN ORANGES AND POPPY SEED DRESSING

3 cups torn Bibb lettuce

1 celery stalk, thinly sliced

1 tablespoon chopped red onion

1 large carrot, peeled and shredded

½ cup mandarin oranges, drained

1 tablespoon toasted and sliced almonds

1 (8-ounce) bottle poppy seed dressing

Place lettuce on two salad plates and arrange remaining ingredients, except dressing, on lettuce. Drizzle with dressing.

Yield: 2 servings

❧ BLACKBERRY VINAIGRETTE SALAD ❧

1 tablespoon plus ½ cup olive oil

1 tablespoon minced green onion

3 cloves garlic, minced

1 pint blackberries

⅔ cup balsamic vinegar

1 teaspoon sugar

1 tablespoon chopped fresh mint

2 teaspoons chopped fresh tarragon

½ teaspoon salt

½ teaspoon freshly ground pepper

6 cups mixed salad greens, washed and dried

¼ cup toasted and slivered almonds

4 ounces feta cheese, crumbled, for topping

1 avocado, seeded and thinly sliced, for topping

12 blackberries for garnish

In large skillet, heat 1 tablespoon oil over medium-high heat. Add green onion and garlic. Sauté, stirring, for about 1 minute. Add blackberries, reserving about 12, and cook, stirring, for about 2 minutes. Add vinegar and deglaze pan by scraping the bottom with a spatula and allowing to cook until the vinaigrette is reduced by half. Remove from heat and put blackberries into a blender. Add sugar, mint, and tarragon, and process to a smooth paste. Add salt and pepper. While blender is running, add ½ cup olive oil through the feed tube and process until smooth. Strain through a fine sieve into a clean bowl and refrigerate until dressing has cooled completely, at least 1 hour.

When ready to serve, combine greens with almonds and toss with vinaigrette. Check seasoning and add salt or pepper to taste. Divide salad among 4 plates, top with cheese and avocado, and garnish with blackberries.

Yield: 4 servings

∾ HONEY-LIME DRESSING ∾

National Honey Board

This dressing makes a delicious salad when used on radicchio. Add grated lime zest sprinkled on top of salad for a refreshing taste.

1 cup sugar

½ cup honey

2 teaspoons dry mustard

⅓ cup lime juice

⅓ cup pineapple juice

2 cups salad oil

In blender or food processor, mix sugar, honey, mustard, lime juice, and pineapple juice. Blend briefly, slowly adding oil. Continue to mix until all oil is added and well incorporated. Pour into 1-quart container with a tight-fitting lid, and store in refrigerator for up to several weeks.

Yield: 4 cups

∾ SPINACH AND ∾ WATER CHESTNUT SOUP

5 cups chicken stock

3 cups fresh spinach, torn into bite-size pieces (unless baby spinach)

1 (8-ounce) can water chestnuts, drained and thinly sliced

1 teaspoon light soy sauce

4 green onions, cut at angle into ¼-inch slices

1 tablespoon chopped garlic

Salt and freshly ground pepper to taste

1 tablespoon fresh chives, or 1 teaspoon dried chives

In medium saucepan, bring stock to a gentle boil. Add spinach, water chestnuts, soy sauce, green onions, garlic, and salt and pepper, and simmer for about 3 minutes. Stir in chives and ladle into bowls.

Yield: 4 to 6 servings

❧ SPLIT PEA AND SAUSAGE SOUP ❧

1½ cups split peas

1 teaspoon salt

½ teaspoon pepper

1 pound smoked sausage (such as kielbasa), thinly sliced

3 celery stalks, diced

1 cup evaporated milk

Bring 5 cups water to a boil, add peas, and cook for 1 hour. Add salt, pepper, sausage, and celery. Simmer for 1 hour. Add a little boiling water if necessary (a few tablespoons at a time) to maintain consistency. Just before serving, add evaporated milk. Blend well, and adjust seasoning to taste.

Yield: 4 to 6 servings

❧ COLORFUL ITALIAN SALAD ❧

This salad is great to serve at potlucks.

2 medium red bell peppers, thinly sliced

2 medium yellow bell peppers, thinly sliced

1 banana pepper, cut into rings

1 green bell pepper, thinly sliced

1 red onion, thinly sliced

6 Roma tomatoes, thinly sliced

1 cup grated Parmesan cheese

¾ cup fat-free Italian dressing

1 tablespoon chopped fresh basil

1 tablespoon snipped fresh chives

Toss together ingredients. Serve immediately or after refrigerating for a few hours.

Yield: 6 servings

❧ NUTRITIOUS POTLUCK ❧ FRUIT SALAD

Sugar substitute equal to ⅔ cup sugar (I use Splenda)

2 tablespoons flour

⅓ cup orange juice

2 tablespoons lemon juice

1 (20-ounce) can pineapple chunks, drained (reserve juice)

Egg substitute equal to 1 egg

2 cups light whipped topping

3 pints strawberries, sliced

4 cups green seedless grapes

6 kiwifruits, peeled and sliced

1 pint raspberries

1 pint blueberries

6 medium bananas, cut into ½-inch slices

In saucepan, combine sugar substitute and flour. Stir in orange, lemon, and pineapple juices. Bring to a boil and remove from heat. Stir small amount of juice mixture into egg substitute, stir, and add to pan, stirring constantly. Bring to a boil and cook over medium heat, stirring constantly, for 2 minutes. Cool to room temperature, stirring occasionally. When cooled, fold in whipped topping. In large bowl, combine all ingredients and toss lightly to coat. Serve immediately or refrigerate until ready to serve.

Yield: 14 to 16 servings

✂ CHICKEN NOODLE SOUP ✂

2 tablespoons vegetable oil

1 medium onion, chopped

2 cloves garlic, minced

3 carrots, shredded

2 celery stalks, cut into ½-inch slices

1 bay leaf

½ teaspoon dried thyme

2 quarts chicken stock or broth

1 (8-ounce) package wide egg noodles

1½ cups shredded cooked chicken

Salt and freshly ground pepper to taste

¼ cup chopped fresh parsley

In large pot, combine oil, onion, garlic, carrots, celery, bay leaf, and thyme. Cook over medium heat, stirring constantly, for about 6 minutes, until vegetables are tender but not brown. Pour in stock or broth, and bring to a boil. Add noodles and cook for about 6 minutes, until tender. Add chicken, salt and pepper, and parsley. Cover and simmer for 10 minutes.

Yield: 4 servings

ೞ QUICK-AND-EASY ೞ MINESTRONE SOUP

1 cup pasta (tubetti, penne, macaroni, or any shape that holds sauce well)

Extra-virgin olive oil

5 cloves garlic, minced

1 cup finely chopped yellow onion

1 cup small-diced celery

1 cup small-diced carrots

1 tablespoon finely chopped rosemary or thyme leaves

1 (14-ounce) can cannelloni or kidney beans, drained and rinsed

1 (14½-ounce) can diced tomatoes

3 cups green beans (canned are fine)

6 cups chicken stock or broth

Salt and freshly ground pepper to taste

1 cup freshly grated Parmesan cheese

In large pot, bring salted water to a boil. Add pasta and cook according to package directions until al dente. Drain pasta and transfer to a baking sheet. Toss with a little oil to prevent sticking.

In medium saucepan drizzled with a small amount of olive oil, cook garlic over medium-high heat, stirring occasionally, until it begins to brown, about 1 minute. Reduce heat to medium and add onion, celery, and carrots. Cook, stirring occasionally to prevent browning, until vegetables are soft, 8 to 10 minutes. Add rosemary or thyme. Raise heat to high. Add beans, tomatoes, green beans, and stock, and bring to a boil. Reduce heat and simmer for 12 to 15 minutes, skimming off foam from the top. Season generously with pepper, and add salt to taste. When ready to serve, add pasta. Serve warm with cheese and olive oil for sprinkling.

Yield: 6 to 8 servings

↩ FRESHEST GARDEN ↩ VEGETABLE SALAD

4 cups fresh young spring salad greens (arugula, frisée, baby red-leaf lettuce, and/or Bibb lettuce)

1 pint cherry tomatoes

1 large red bell pepper, cut into long strips

1 yellow bell pepper, cut into strips

1 orange bell pepper, cut into strips

1 cup thin wax beans

1½ cups baby bella, shiitake, and crimini mushrooms

1 cup fresh spinach leaves

1 large red onion, cut into thin strips

½ cup snow peas, ends trimmed

Juice of ¼ lemon

In large bowl, combine greens. Add remaining ingredients and sprinkle with lemon juice or top with a light vinaigrette.

Yield: 10 to 12 servings

Breads

Breads

"And watch those chickens dance"

 Tammy Ricketts was a conscientious mother, to say the least. Her only child, Bo, was destined to learn healthy eating habits from infancy. I love and appreciate my sister now, but admit that I thought she was strange when Bo and my Noélle were growing up—first cousins and only a month apart.

Tammy would put them in high chairs and give each one tiny portions of a zillion different foods so they would try everything. At Easter, Noélle would get a basket of chocolate and bunnies, and Bo would get fresh, long carrots with leafy stems on them (so the Easter Bunny would eat healthy too) and fruit—only fruit. Her conscientiousness carried over into other areas as well. We lived in Cincinnati when Bo was very young, and my sons, Christian (aged fifteen) and Scott (aged nine), were going to baby-sit both Noélle and Bo when Tammy was visiting us. When we returned, she checked the diapers for Bo and Noélle to make sure that the boys had changed them often enough. She also checked the food jars to make sure that Bo and Noélle had eaten all she thought they should. She told my sons when they asked why she always brought so much luggage that she tried to anticipate Bo's every need. They bought that, but they had a hard time understanding the diaper caper.

Tammy wanted Bo to like chicken and turkey. She began to make chickens dance for him when he was a toddler. She would clean the chickens until they passed her inspections and sit Bo in front of her and make them dance. She would sing songs for the birds to dance to and then plop them in the oven. As Bo got older, he would get impatient waiting for dinner so he could eat his chicken. One particular Thanksgiving, he kept coming into the kitchen wanting to know when he could eat turkey. She would always let him look through the glass and ask if he could see the bird dancing. When the bird finished dancing, it was time to eat. He learned that day that the best way to find out if dinner was ready was to ask if the chickens had finished dancing. He's grown and ready to finish college now, and I wonder if he still thinks of that. I always expect his chickens to break out into a dance when he visits the colonel.

This is an exciting chapter for me because it includes great cornbread, Cheddar Muffins, and Spinach and Cheese–Stuffed Bread. My favorite addition was working with Charlotte White and members of her family (all Kentucky State Fair winners and finalists) on her Sourdough Light Rolls. Charlotte has won ribbons for her Sourdough Loaf Bread, Banana Bread, Mother's White Yeast Bread, and Sourdough Cinnamon Rolls. She has five grandchildren, who are the real judges. Of course, they win her heart no matter what, but to hear them brag to other children about how "Mimi makes the best rolls" is as good as it gets for her. This family can cook, and these breads are proof. Charlotte White's grandchildren say it best when they tell their friends, "You have to try one!"

You'll see a little of the old and a little of the new. The best thing I can think of when sampling the breads is that your kitchen will smell wonderful. Baking bread just may be my favorite aroma.

❧ SPINACH AND ❧ CHEESE–STUFFED BREAD

1 (1-pound) loaf frozen bread dough, thawed according to
  package directions

2 teaspoons olive oil

1 medium onion, finely chopped

8 ounces fresh mushrooms, sliced

2 cloves garlic, minced

1 (10-ounce) package frozen chopped spinach, thawed and
  squeezed dry

2 cups shredded reduced-fat Cheddar cheese or part-skim
  mozzarella cheese

½ cup grated Parmesan cheese

Let bread dough rise until doubled in size. Meanwhile, in skillet, heat oil and sauté onion, mushrooms, and garlic until tender. Stir in spinach.

Preheat oven to 350 degrees. Coat baking sheet with nonstick cooking spray.

On a lightly floured surface, roll dough into a 10 × 14-inch rectangle. Combine spinach mixture, Cheddar or mozzarella cheese, and 6 tablespoons Parmesan cheese. Spread mixture to within ½ inch of edges of dough, and sprinkle with 2 tablespoons Parmesan cheese. Roll up as a jelly roll, starting with a long side, and pinch seam to seal. Place seam side down on baking sheet and tuck ends under.

Bake for 25 to 30 minutes or until golden brown. Remove to a wire rack and let stand for 10 minutes before slicing. Serve warm.

Yield: 1 loaf

❧ CHEDDAR MUFFINS ❧

1¾ cups flour

⅓ cup cornmeal

1 tablespoon baking powder

½ teaspoon salt

¼ teaspoon pepper

1¼ cups shredded sharp Cheddar cheese

1 cup milk

1 egg

3 tablespoons grainy mustard

6 tablespoons (¾ stick) butter, melted

1 tablespoon chopped fresh mixed herbs, or 1 teaspoon dried mixed herbs

Preheat oven to 350 degrees. Line cups of muffin tin with paper or grease with butter.

In large bowl, mix flour, cornmeal, baking powder, salt, and pepper. Add 1 cup cheese and toss. In small bowl, whisk milk, egg, and mustard. Add to flour mixture with butter and mixed herbs. Mix just to blend.

Spoon into 10 2¾-inch muffin tin cups. Sprinkle tops with ¼ cup cheese. Bake for 20 to 25 minutes, until springy to the touch and a toothpick inserted into the center comes out clean.

Yield: 10 muffins

❧ CHEDDAR BRAID ❧

2 cups water

2 teaspoons salt

¼ cup sugar

½ cup nonfat powdered milk

2 tablespoons butter

3 cups shredded Cheddar cheese

1 tablespoon dry yeast

6 cups bread flour

½ cup sliced green olives

In saucepan, gently heat water, salt, sugar, powdered milk, butter, and 2 cups cheese until cheese is melted. Add yeast, flour, 1 cup cheese, and olives.

In bowl, mix with dough hooks until smooth and let dough rise until doubled in size.

Preheat oven to 350 degrees.

Divide dough into three balls. Roll each portion into a 12-inch strip and braid the three strips, tucking each end of the finished braid under. Bake on a greased baking sheet for about 30 minutes or until golden.

Yield: 1 loaf

✑ PITA BREAD ✑

1 teaspoon dry yeast

2 ½ cups warm water

2 cups whole-wheat flour

4 cups bread flour

2 teaspoons salt

2 tablespoons olive oil

In large bowl, sprinkle yeast over water and stir to dissolve. Add whole-wheat flour, 1 cup at a time, and 1 cup bread flour. Stir for 1 minute in the same direction to activate the gluten. Let mixture rest for 30 minutes.

Sprinkle salt and oil over dough and mix well. Add remaining bread flour 1 cup at a time. When dough becomes too stiff to stir, begin kneading on a lightly floured board. Knead for 8 to 10 minutes, until dough is smooth and elastic. Return dough to a lightly oiled bowl and cover with plastic wrap. Let dough rise until doubled in size, about 90 minutes. Punch down lightly. Dough may be made to this point and stored in the refrigerator for up to 5 days. To store, place dough in a large plastic bag secured at the opening to make room for expansion. Any smell of fermentation after a few days only improves the flavor of the bread. Dough should always be brought to room temperature before baking.

Preheat oven to 450 degrees.

If baking all at once, divide dough into 16 portions and roll out into 8-inch circles. Place cast-iron skillet, griddle, or quarry tiles on a rack in the bottom third of the oven. With lightly floured hands, flatten each circle and place on baking surface. Bake for 4 to 6 minutes, until bread has "ballooned" or turned slightly golden. If bread fails to balloon on the first try, don't worry. This takes practice, but the bread tastes great and is worth the effort. Remove from oven, let cool for about 5 minutes, and wrap in kitchen towels. Repeat with remaining dough.

Yield: 16 pitas

✂ FRY BREAD ✂

3 cups flour

1 tablespoon baking powder

½ teaspoon salt

1½ cups warm water

Vegetable oil

Fruit jam, butter, powdered sugar, honey, or molasses for
  topping

In large bowl, mix flour, baking powder, and salt. Add water and
stir until dough begins to form a ball. On a lightly floured surface,
knead dough lightly, for 2 to 3 minutes. Do not overwork. Place in
a bowl and refrigerate for 45 minutes.

Heat oil to 350 degrees in a large kettle or Dutch oven. On a
lightly floured surface, roll or pat dough into 2½-inch rounds about
¼ inch thick. Cut a hole or slit in the center of each round, so dough
will fry flat. Fry until golden brown on both sides, about 3 minutes,
depending on thickness of dough and temperature of oil. Serve with
your choice of toppings.

Yield: 8 to 10 breads

ဢ BUTTERMILK CHIVE BISCUITS ဢ

This is a different chive biscuit with an Italian-cheese twist.

2 cups flour

1 teaspoon salt

2 teaspoons baking powder

¼ teaspoon baking soda

⅓ cup vegetable shortening, chilled

¾ cup buttermilk

½ cup grated sharp Cheddar cheese

¼ cup grated Parmesan or Romano cheese

1 cup snipped fresh chives, or ½ cup dried chives

Milk

Preheat oven to 450 degrees.

Sift together flour, salt, baking powder, and baking soda. With pastry blender or fork, cut in shortening until mixture resembles coarse cornmeal. Make a well in the center and pour in buttermilk, Cheddar and Parmesan or Romano cheeses, and chives. Blend well until mixture holds together.

On lightly floured surface, knead dough 5 or 6 times. Do not overwork. Pat dough to ½-inch thickness and cut with floured biscuit cutter. Place on ungreased pan and brush tops with milk. Bake for 10 to 12 minutes or until browned.

Yield: 18 biscuits

❧ CHIVE CORN FRITTERS ❧

Vegetable oil

3 cups fresh corn kernels (6 ears of corn)

2 eggs, lightly beaten

2 tablespoons milk

2 tablespoons snipped fresh chives

½ teaspoon baking powder

½ cup flour

½ cup cornmeal

Salt and pepper to taste

Heat oil to 340 to 350 degrees.

Combine ingredients and fry by tablespoonful. Fritters will turn golden brown and rise to top of oil.

Yield: 3 dozen fritters

↢ CHARLOTTE WHITE'S ↣ SOURDOUGH LIGHT ROLLS

These are the great rolls that "Mimi" makes, according to her five grandchildren. Charlotte credits her sister-in-law, Jeanne Kemper, for her celebrated Kentucky State Fair success in winning so many first-place ribbons. If she had entered any contests before 2005, she probably would have had to build a ribbon room in her home.

Make Starter

1 package dry yeast

1½ cups warm water

¾ cup sugar

3 tablespoons potato flakes

Dissolve yeast in ½ cup water and set aside. In bowl, mix sugar and potato flakes, add 1 cup water, and stir. Combine yeast with sugar mixture and leave at room temperature all day. Refrigerate starter for 3 to 5 days.

Feed Starter

¾ cup sugar

3 tablespoons potato flakes

1 cup warm water

Remove starter from refrigerator and feed it.

Morning

Mix well sugar and potato flakes, and add water. Add to starter. Mix and put starter in glass jar with a hole punched in the lid to breathe, and let stand all day in warm area to sour.

Night

Stir starter well and take out 1 cup. Place the rest back in the covered jar and refrigerate for 3 to 5 days, when it will be fed again.

Make Dough

½ cup sugar

1 teaspoon salt

6 cups bread flour

⅓ cup corn oil

1 cup starter

1½ cups warm water

After removing 1 cup starter, set it aside and mix sugar, salt, and bread flour. Add oil, starter, and water. Mix well, using wooden spoon.

Put dough in a very large plastic container sprayed with cooking spray. Turn dough over and cover with towel. (I use a large plastic ice cream bucket with lid, and it works wonderfully.) Let stand overnight (12 hours) in a warm place.

Make Rolls

Next morning

Punch down dough lightly on floured surface. Divide dough into 3 parts. Stretch or roll each section of bread on floured surface and roll from shortest end. Pinch off 10 pieces from each roll. Shape each piece into a ball, pulling edges under to make a smooth top, and place in pan (about 20 rolls will fit in a 9 × 13-inch pan, and 9 or 10 rolls in a 9-inch round pan). Brush lightly with melted margarine. Place in warm spot and let rise for 6 to 8 hours, covered with a towel.

Night

Preheat oven to 325 degrees.

Remove towel and bake rolls for 25 to 30 minutes, until golden brown. Remove from oven and brush with melted margarine.

Yield: 30 rolls

❧ CHIVE BISCUITS ❧

2 ½ cups flour

2 ½ teaspoons baking powder

½ teaspoon baking soda

½ teaspoon salt

⅓ cup vegetable shortening

1 ¼ cups buttermilk

½ cup shredded sharp Cheddar cheese

2 tablespoons chopped fresh chives

2 tablespoons margarine or butter, melted

Preheat oven to 450 degrees.

In large bowl, combine flour, baking powder, baking soda, and salt. With pastry blender or two knives, cut in shortening until mixture resembles coarse crumbs. With fork, stir in buttermilk, cheese, and chives just until blended.

Drop by heaping tablespoons onto large ungreased cookie sheet, 1 inch apart. Brush with melted margarine or butter. Bake for 10 to 12 minutes or until golden. Serve warm.

Yield: 12 biscuits

❧ CRACKLIN' CORNBREAD ❧

½ cup cornmeal

½ cup flour

2 teaspoons baking powder

½ teaspoon salt

1 egg, beaten

1 ½ cups milk

¼ to ½ cup cracklings (crisp bits left in meat fat after it

is rendered), or 4 to 6 strips bacon, crisply fried and crumbled

Preheat oven to 400 degrees.

In bowl, sift together cornmeal, flour, baking powder, and salt. In another bowl, combine egg, milk, and cracklings or bacon. Add to dry ingredients and beat well. Pour batter into a hot, greased iron skillet. Bake until golden brown, approximately 25 to 30 minutes.

Yield: 6 to 8 servings

✄ ROLLS IN A JIFFY ✄

2 packages dry yeast

1 cup warm water

⅓ cup salad oil

1½ tablespoons sugar

2 teaspoons salt

1 egg, well beaten

3 to 3½ cups flour

Melted butter

In medium bowl, dissolve yeast in water. Stir in oil, sugar, salt, and egg. Stir in flour, 1 cup at a time, until dough is soft.

Turn out onto lightly floured surface and knead until smooth, adding a small amount of flour as needed to keep dough from getting sticky. Cover with towel and let dough rest for 20 minutes.

Preheat oven to 400 degrees. Grease cups of a muffin tin with butter.

Roll out into rectangle and brush surface with melted butter. Roll up as a jelly roll and cut into 1-inch slices. Place each piece in a muffin tin cup, cover, and let rise for 30 minutes. Bake for 10 to 12 minutes. Remove from oven and brush with melted butter.

Yield: 2 dozen rolls

GREEN CHILI AND CHEDDAR CORNBREAD

1 (about 7½-ounce) box cornbread mix

1 green chili, roasted, skinned, seeded, and diced

1 small jar pimientos, drained and finely chopped

¾ cup grated Cheddar cheese

Grease a baking dish or Dutch oven.

Mix cornbread batter according to recipe on the box. Some mixes may require an egg, plus milk or water. Stir in chili, pimientos, and half the cheese.

Pour batter into baking dish or Dutch oven, and bake according to package directions until golden brown. Remove from oven and sprinkle immediately with remaining cheese. Let sit for 5 minutes before slicing and serving.

Yield: 4 to 6 servings

Entrées

Entrées

"She forgot to remove the bags of 'pieces and parts.'"

 Back in the day, when my mother was in her prime, nobody had air-conditioning, so she liked to refresh herself with a beer or two when the kitchen got overheated. Maybe that's why she was never able to successfully pull together a turkey dinner. One Thanksgiving, all the side dishes were ready, but the turkey wouldn't be done for another four hours. Another Thanksgiving, the "part of the bird that goes over the fence last" exploded because she forgot to remove the bags of "pieces and parts." Yet another Thanksgiving, after preheating the oven, she pulled out the rack and out came gooey strings of melted plastic that had been my brother's fleet of toy cars. And so it went. Not surprisingly, she never attempted to teach me how to cook a turkey, and it all seemed so mysterious and failure-fraught to me that I've never had the courage to try it on my own.

Mom may have felt a little guilty about not sending me out into the world properly turkey-wise, because she once had a dream that I was dying. She was at my bedside, and in her dream, she was telling me, "Now honey, you're not going to die. You just can't die until you've learned to cook a turkey!"

Kate Wheatley, *Kentucky Living* staff

Aside from meals on holidays and for special occasions, entrées are the main focus of a meal. I get just as excited about side dishes, breads, and salads as I do for the main attraction. But I love to serve a variety of entrées and rarely cook the same one often. It seems that the older I get, the more I like to experiment with entrées. I love to make Shepherd's Pie, trying out different meats and fillings. And seafood is an excuse to wow them with dishes like Pecan-Crusted Orange Roughy with Fried Bananas. My son-in-law, Eric, is a big fan of shrimp, so I surprised him on his birthday a few years ago by serving shrimp served four ways, accompanied by a fresh salad topped with my own ranch dressing—his favorites!

Even if you're not a big fan of wild game, it can surprise you in an Italian or a Mexican dish spiced just right. And while I'm not a fan of my own fried chicken, I find new recipes to use or ask my sister to make it for me when the kids want fried chicken for Sunday dinner. Don't be afraid to try new twists on your own dishes. Experiment with entrées and find new ways to fix old favorites. Your family just might love it.

❦ CHILI-ROASTED SALMON ❦

4 (4-ounce) salmon fillets

Salt to taste

1 tablespoon balsamic vinegar

1 tablespoon honey

1 teaspoon chili powder

Preheat oven to 400 degrees. Place salmon on lightly greased baking sheet or broiler pan, and season with salt. In small bowl, combine remaining ingredients. Mix well. Spread mixture evenly over fish. Roast for 10 to 15 minutes or until fish flakes when tested with fork.

Yield: 4 servings

❦ FISH TACOS ❦

My daughter and I had dinner recently at a trendy new restaurant in Louisville. Noélle ordered the fish tacos and loved the restaurant's version. A week or so later, I was forced to come up with my own take on the dish after over-sautéing two large cod fillets and watching them flake in the pan instead of on the plate. Noélle loved it!

2 (6- to 8-ounce) cod fillets, cooked and flaked in pan

6 taco shells

1 cup shredded lettuce

1 cup chopped fresh tomatoes

½ cup finely shredded Monterey Jack cheese

Sour cream for topping

Guacamole for topping

¼ cup bottled fruit salsa (I use mango salsa)

1 (15-ounce) can black beans, drained

Evenly divide flaked cod among taco shells. Repeat with lettuce, tomatoes, and cheese. Top with sour cream and guacamole, if desired.

Combine salsa with black beans and serve on the side.

Yield: 3 servings

ൟ BOW-TIE PASTA WITH MUSHROOM ൟ RAGOUT AND BAKED CHEESE CRISPS

Ragout

2 large tomatoes, peeled and seeded

6 large mushrooms, sliced

Olive oil

¼ cup snipped fresh chives

2 cloves garlic, chopped

Salt and freshly ground pepper to taste

¼ teaspoon dried basil

4 ounces bow-tie pasta, cooked al dente

Whole chives for garnish

Cheese Crisps

½ cup finely grated Parmesan cheese

Coarsely grated Romano cheese

Preheat oven to 350 degrees. To make ragout, sauté tomatoes, mushrooms, chives, garlic, and salt and pepper in a small amount of oil. Add basil in the last few minutes of cooking. When reduced to a ragout consistency, toss with pasta and garnish with a few whole chives.

To make cheese crisps, during last few minutes of cooking the ragout, coat cookie sheet with nonstick cooking spray and sprinkle small rounds of Parmesan cheese on sheet. Bake until golden brown, and allow to cool for a few minutes. Sprinkle with Romano cheese.

Yield: 3 or 4 servings

✌ PECAN-CRUSTED ORANGE ✌ ROUGHY WITH FRIED BANANAS

4 bananas, not quite ripe and very firm

4 tablespoons (½ stick) butter

2 tablespoons olive oil

4 (6-ounce) orange roughy fillets

1 teaspoon ground cumin

1 egg, beaten

½ teaspoon salt

¼ teaspoon freshly ground pepper

1½ cups finely chopped pecans

2 tablespoons fresh lime juice

Cut bananas lengthwise into ¼-inch slices. In large ovenproof skillet, heat 2 tablespoons butter and oil over moderately high heat until foaming stops. Sauté banana slices for 1 minute on each side or until golden. Drain on paper towels.

Preheat oven to 450 degrees. Pat fish dry and sprinkle with cumin. In shallow dish, combine egg with salt and pepper. Dip each fillet in egg mixture and dredge in pecans. Add remaining butter to the skillet and heat until foaming stops. Sauté fillets for 2 to 3 minutes. Turn them over and top with banana slices. Sauté for 2 minutes. Drizzle with lime juice and transfer skillet to oven. Bake for 6 minutes. Serve immediately.

Yield: 4 servings

↜ SALMON PATTIES ↝

1 (15-ounce) can salmon, drained and cleaned

1 egg, lightly beaten

½ sleeve saltines, finely crushed

1 teaspoon flour

½ teaspoon freshly ground pepper

1 (15-ounce) can cream of celery soup

Vegetable oil

Combine ingredients (except oil) and shape into patties. In heavy skillet, heat oil. Fry patties until golden brown on each side. Drain well on paper towels.

Yield: 4 to 6 servings

↜ SOUTHERN FRIED CHICKEN ↝

Southerners love their fried chicken. Many differ about preparation and technique, preferring to soak the chicken pieces in salted water rather than buttermilk. I prefer the buttermilk method and find that a minimum of ingredients allows the wonderful flavor of fresh chicken to fully come through. Actually, I love to give the job to my sister, Tammy, who bore the brunt of cooking jokes at a young age, only to surprise us all by making the best fried chicken in the family. Guess who the joke is on now!

1 (3-pound) frying chicken, cut into 8 pieces

2 cups buttermilk

2 cups flour

1 teaspoon salt

½ teaspoon freshly ground pepper

2 teaspoons paprika

Peanut or canola oil

Gravy

¼ cup pan drippings and crust

¼ cup flour

1½ cups warm water

1½ cups milk

Salt and pepper to taste

Cover chicken with buttermilk and refrigerate for several hours or overnight.

In large wide-mouth bowl, combine flour, salt, pepper, and paprika. Heat enough oil to fill half of a large chicken fryer or deep skillet. Oil should be 350 degrees before adding chicken. (Do not crowd pieces in pan to maintain frying temperature.) Drain chicken and coat with seasoned flour. Place chicken in skillet and fry, turning once, for about 8 minutes for white meat and 10 to 12 minutes for dark meat, until golden brown. Drain on paper towels. Serve hot or cold.

To make gravy, heat pan drippings and crust left over from frying chicken. Gradually add flour, stirring well, until mixture just begins to turn brown. Slowly add water and milk, and stir until gravy thickens. Season with salt and pepper.

Yield: 6 servings

✌ PORK SHOULDER WITH ✌ STIR-FRIED VEGETABLES AND PLUM SAUCE

1 head garlic

2 tablespoons plus 1 teaspoon kosher salt

2 tablespoons distilled white vinegar

2 tablespoons fresh lemon juice

1 tablespoon pepper

1 (5-pound) pork shoulder or Boston butt, with skin

1 cup broccoli florets

1 cup sugar snap peas

1 cup julienned carrots

1 cup green beans

1 cup red pepper strips

½ celery stalk, chopped

1 cup baby cob corn

1 cup water chestnuts

1 small jar plum sauce

Using a mortar and pestle or the side of a large heavy knife, mash garlic to a paste with 2 tablespoons salt, and stir in vinegar, lemon juice, and pepper.

Pat pork dry. Using a small sharp knife, cut a wide pocket at large end of roast to separate skin from fat, leaving skin attached at sides and stopping before roast narrows to bone. Make 1-inch-deep slits in pork under skin and on all sides of the meat, twisting knife slightly to widen openings, and push some of garlic mixture into slits with fingers. Rub any remaining garlic mixture over roast (not skin). Wipe skin clean and rub with 1 teaspoon salt (to help it crisp). Place pork in a shallow glass or ceramic dish and refrigerate, covered, for at least 8 hours.

Put pork, skin side up, in flameproof roasting pan. Discard marinade and bring pork to room temperature, about 1 hour. Preheat oven to 350 degrees, with rack in middle. Cover pork with parchment paper and then tightly with foil, and roast for 2½ hours. Discard foil and parchment. Add ½ cup water to pan and roast, uncovered, adding more water when liquid evaporates (about every half hour) for 2 to 2½ hours, until skin is brown and crisp and meat is fork-tender. Transfer to cutting board or platter, and let stand for 30 minutes. Cut into small pieces.

Lightly steam vegetables and quickly stir-fry in a hot wok until done but still crisp. Pour plum sauce over vegetables and combine with pork.

Yield: 8 to 10 servings

❧ GRILLED CHIPOTLE ADOBO ❧ PORK TENDERLOIN

2 (1-pound) pork tenderloins

½ teaspoon salt

⅛ tablespoon pepper

3 tablespoons finely chopped chipotle chilies

⅓ cup plain yogurt

2 tablespoons adobo sauce

3 cloves garlic, minced

1 tablespoon olive oil

Place tenderloins in a shallow dish. Make a slit down the middle of each one without cutting through it. Season with salt and pepper, and fill each slit with chipotles. Press tenderloins so that chilies will not slide out. Set aside.

In medium bowl, mix yogurt, adobo sauce, garlic, and oil until well combined. Pour mixture over tenderloins and let stand for 15 to 20 minutes.

Preheat grill for medium-high heat. Place tenderloins on oiled grill rack and cook for 10 to 12 minutes a side. Baste occasionally with yogurt sauce. When internal temperature of tenderloins reaches 150 degrees, remove from grill and let stand for 5 minutes.

Yield: 6 to 8 servings

♋ BLACK BEAN CHILI WITH ♋ CILANTRO AND SERRANO SALSA

Chili

1 pound dried black beans, soaked overnight and drained

1 medium onion, thinly sliced

4 cloves garlic, minced

4 serrano chilies, finely chopped

Salt and pepper to taste

Salsa

4 medium tomatoes, diced

½ medium cucumber, diced

1 bunch cilantro, coarsely chopped

1 medium red onion, diced

2 serrano chilies, finely chopped

1 clove garlic, minced

½ cup fresh lime juice

To make chili, place beans in large stockpot with enough water to cover. Add onion, garlic, and chilies. Turn heat to high and skim foam off top as beans heat. When beans come to a boil, turn heat to low and simmer, covered, until tender, about 1¼ hours. Season with salt and pepper.

To make salsa, combine ingredients in glass bowl and cover. Refrigerate for at least 30 minutes for flavors to combine. Serve chili in bowls with a large spoonful of salsa.

Yield: 8 servings

ᘒ CHARLIE BRATCHER'S ᘒ DEER FRITTERS

Charlie Bratcher and his wife, Jolene, own a beautiful farm in Breckinridge County where game and southern dishes are always being served. My brother, Ronnie Allison, says that Charlie is the go-to man whenever a neighboring farmer in Garfield needs a helping hand—or a great dish.

1 (¾-pound) venison roast or shoulder

1 egg, lightly beaten

½ cup milk

½ cup flour

1 to 2 teaspoons garlic salt

1 teaspoon chopped fresh parsley

1 tablespoon meat tenderizer

5 green onions, bulb only

Vegetable oil

Cut venison into pieces 2½ × 3 inches and ½ inch thick. Place in bowl with salt water and refrigerate for 24 hours.

Rinse venison in cold water. In bowl, combine remaining ingredients, except oil, and dip meat into batter. Spread on large platter and refrigerate for 4 hours.

In large skillet, fry venison in ¼ inch of oil over medium heat until golden brown on both sides. Drain on paper towels. Serve immediately.

Yield: 3 or 4 servings

✍ VENISON ITALIAN ✍

2 pounds venison, cut into strips

¼ cup olive oil

½ onion, chopped

1 celery stalk, chopped

1 tablespoon butter

1 (25-ounce) can chopped tomatoes, undrained

1 (6-ounce) can tomato paste

1 tablespoon sugar

Salt and pepper to taste

1 teaspoon dried oregano, crushed

1 teaspoon dried thyme, crushed

1 teaspoon chopped parsley

Pasta

Grated Parmesan cheese

In Dutch oven, cook venison in oil over high heat. Drain on paper towels.

In oil left in pan, sauté onion and celery until transparent. Add butter, tomatoes, tomato paste, sugar, salt and pepper, oregano, thyme, and parsley. Cook over medium-high heat for 15 minutes. Reduce heat to medium and cook until liquid is reduced and sauce is very thick. Add venison, cover, and simmer for 30 minutes. Serve over pasta and sprinkle with cheese.

Yield: 4 to 6 servings

↜ JANICE'S VENISON SWISS STEAK ↝

My sister-in-law, Janice Allison, isn't particularly fond of cooking wild game, even though she's chosen a winner with this recipe. My brother, Ronnie, spends endless hours mapping out and planting deer plots to feed his venison. So the old Kentucky adage—"I'll catch 'em and you cook 'em"—is alive and well in Garfield, Kentucky. Janice draws the line at rabbit.

1 (2-pound) venison shoulder, roast, or ham

1 tablespoon olive oil

2 large onions, cut into strips

¾ cup dry red wine, such as a Cabernet

1 (6- to 8-ounce) can tomato paste

1 (15-ounce) can tomato sauce

2 cloves garlic

Pinch of dried rosemary

Pinch of dried thyme

Hot sauce to taste

Salt and pepper to taste

1 bay leaf, crumbled

1 tablespoon seasoned salt

1 teaspoon meat tenderizer

Cut venison into strips about 3 inches long and ¾ inch thick, trimmed of fat and tendons. In oil, brown meat.

In slow cooker, combine venison with remaining ingredients and cook on high setting for 2 hours. Reduce heat to low and cook for 8 hours.

Yield: 6 to 8 servings

↬ SHEPHERD'S PIE ↬
WITH VENISON

1 carrot, cut into wide strips

1 medium onion, chopped

½ cup finely chopped celery

1 tablespoon shortening

1 (14-ounce) can beef gravy (I use Franco-American)

3 cups ground venison, cooked

1 cup peas, cooked

Salt and pepper to taste

3 cups prepared mashed potatoes

In small saucepan, steam or cook carrots with a small amount of water until fork-tender. In medium skillet, sauté onion and celery in shortening until transparent. Add carrots, gravy, venison, and peas, and simmer for 3 to 5 minutes.

Preheat oven to 400 degrees. Pour meat mixture into 2-quart casserole dish. Season with salt and pepper, and top with potatoes. Bake for about 20 to 25 minutes or until brown on top.

Yield: 4 servings

↬ SHRIMP JULEP WITH ↬
PEAR SALAD

Chef Anoosh Shariat—Park Place on Main, Louisville

Anoosh Shariat is one of the most talented chefs in Louisville and a genuinely nice guy. The day he cooked at Park Place for Jim Battles and me was memorable. Chefs can be a little intimidating with their ingredients and instructions, but don't let that stop you. Anoosh is totally accessible and loves to share his culinary gifts.

Shrimp

1 tablespoon olive oil

12 jumbo shrimp, shelled

Salt to taste

1 tablespoon chopped shallots

¼ cup bourbon or chicken broth

2 tablespoons cane syrup (substitute cane syrup by boiling 1¼ cups sugar and ⅓ cup water until syrup consistency and measuring out 2 tablespoons)

1 tablespoon chopped fresh mint

½ cup (1 stick) butter

Pear Salad

2 pears, peeled and julienned

1 red bell pepper, julienned

1 yellow bell pepper, julienned

1 tablespoon chopped fresh mint

Juice of ½ lemon

2 tablespoons chopped fresh chives

Salt to taste

To make shrimp, heat oil in pan. Season shrimp with salt and add to pan. Sear. Turn shrimp, add shallots, and sauté for 1 minute. Remove from heat and add bourbon and cane syrup. Return to heat and add mint. Reduce liquid by half and swirl in butter.

To make pear salad, combine ingredients in bowl and marinate. Divide salad into four servings, and top each with shrimp.

Yield: 4 servings

✥ BLACK ANGUS TENDERLOIN ✥ AND JUMBO SHRIMP WRAPPED IN APPLE SMOKED BACON BROCHETTES

Chef Jim Gerhardt—Limestone Restaurant, Louisville

Among all the talented chefs in Louisville, Jim Gerhardt has to be my favorite. When he was developing his fabulous Kentucky Fine-Dining Menu at the Seelbach, I had the pleasure of experimenting with his Sourmash Bourbon Bread in my home. Limestone, his newest restaurant, is everything you would expect a great Jim Gerhardt dining experience to be. Someday I may give him the secret to my Derby Grits. Mmm . . . maybe not . . .

Marinade

½ cup soy sauce

½ cup balsamic vinegar

1 clove garlic, minced

½ bunch green onions, minced

½ cup olive oil

Juice of 1 lemon

Grated lemon peel

Brochettes

6 strips applewood-smoked bacon, halved

1 (12-ounce) beef tenderloin, cut into 12 squares (1 ounce each)

12 jumbo tiger shrimp, shelled and deveined

12 bamboo skewers (soaked in water)

Juice of 3 lemons

To make marinade, combine ingredients in flat baking dish. Prepare grill. To make brochettes, par-cook bacon in oven for about 5 minutes. Set aside. Wrap a tenderloin square with bacon and place on skewer. Wrap a shrimp with bacon and add to skewer. Place brochettes in marinade until time to grill. Grill over hot coals until shrimp is pink, about 4 to 6 minutes. Arrange brochettes on platter and squeeze lemon juice onto each.

Yield: 6 servings

᥍ BISON TENDERLOIN WITH ᥍ ROASTED ASPARAGUS AND STONE-GROUND CHEESE GRITS

Chef Anoosh Shariat—Park Place on Main, Louisville

The bison in this dish is so tender and delicious. Jim Battles and I fought over it the day the chef cooked it for our photo shoot.

Grits

1 cup stone-ground grits

2 cups milk

2 tablespoons chopped fresh rosemary

½ cup shredded smoked Gouda cheese

Salt and pepper to taste

Asparagus

2 bunches asparagus

3 tablespoons olive oil

2 tablespoons chopped shallots

2 tablespoons chopped garlic

Salt to taste

Bison

1 cup marsala wine or plum juice

½ cup dried cherries

5 cups veal stock

Salt and pepper to taste

4 (6-ounce) bison tenderloins or beef fillets

Olive oil

To make grits, combine grits and milk in saucepan. Bring to a boil and reduce heat to simmer. Cook, uncovered, for 25 to 30 minutes, stirring constantly to avoid clumping, until grits are soft and milk has been absorbed. Stir in rosemary and cheese. Season with salt and pepper. May be made in advance. To reheat, bring ½ cup milk to a simmer, add grits, and stir until hot.

To make asparagus, trim 1 inch off cut ends of asparagus stalks. Combine remaining ingredients to make marinade. Add asparagus, and marinate for 1 to 2 hours. Preheat oven to 400 degrees, and roast asparagus for 15 minutes.

To make bison, combine wine, cherries, veal stock, and salt and pepper in a heavy saucepan. Cook over medium heat until mixture comes to a boil and then until sauce is reduced and coats the back of a spoon. Rub bison with olive oil and season with salt and pepper. Place on hot grill and cook to desired temperature. For medium, cook for 7 minutes a side. Drizzle sauce over bison and serve each tenderloin over a mound of grits, with asparagus on the side.

Yield: 4 servings

❧ BEEF TIPS WITH MUSTARD ❧ CREAM SAUCE OVER RICE

1 (1-pound) pound top sirloin or rib-eye steak, cut into pieces

Seasoned flour, such as Kentucky Kernel

6 tablespoons (¾ stick) butter

¼ cup dry white wine

1 teaspoon minced onion

⅓ cup heavy cream

2 tablespoons Dijon mustard

White pepper to taste

2 cups cooked rice

Dredge beef in flour. In skillet, sauté beef in butter until well browned on both sides. Transfer to platter and keep warm.

Add wine and onion to the skillet, and simmer for 2 minutes. Stir well to deglaze the pan. Add cream and cook until thickened. Stir in mustard and pepper. Arrange beef tips on rice and pour sauce over beef.

Yield: 4 servings

❧ OLD-FASHIONED HAM ❧

½ (6- to 8-pound) fully cooked ham, with bone

20 whole cloves

½ cup light brown sugar, packed

3 tablespoons dry mustard

8 canned pineapple rings, drained (reserve juice or syrup)

Maraschino cherries

Preheat oven to 325 degrees. Score surface of the ham with shallow, diamond-shaped cuts and insert cloves evenly in cuts over top and sides. Combine sugar, mustard, and pineapple juice or syrup to make a thick paste. Spread paste over ham and decorate top and sides with pineapple rings and cherries, held by toothpicks. Bake for 20 minutes a pound or until internal temperature of ham reaches 140 degrees. I like to baste ham with pan juices several times while it cooks.

Yield: 12 to 14 servings

⁓ GLAZED HAM FOR ⁓ THE HOME SMOKER

1 (5- to 7-pound) fully cooked ham, with bone (shank or butt)

1⅓ cups maple syrup

1 teaspoon ground ginger

¼ teaspoon ground nutmeg

½ teaspoon ground allspice

12 to 16 whole cloves

8 canned pineapple rings, drained

Maraschino cherries

Score surface of the ham. Combine maple syrup, ginger, nutmeg, and allspice to make a paste. Place ham in large dish and brush with syrup mixture. Set aside for 2 hours or until ham reaches room temperature, basting frequently with syrup mixture.

When ready to smoke, remove ham from dish, stud with cloves, and place on smoker grid. Baste with syrup at least twice while smoking. Right before the last hour of smoking, decorate with pineapple rings and cherries. Baste again. Smoke until internal temperature of ham reaches 130 to 140 degrees.

For charcoal smoker: use 7 to 8 pounds of charcoal, 3 quarts of hot water, and 3 or 4 wood sticks, and smoke for 2½ to 3½ hours.

For electric smoker: use 3 quarts of hot water and 3 or 4 wood sticks, and smoke for 2 to 3 hours.

For gas smoker: use 4 quarts of hot water and 3 or 4 wood sticks, and smoke for 2 to 3 hours.

Yield: 12 to 16 servings

✌ COFFEE-PECAN-GLAZED HAM ✌

1 (7-pound) fully cooked smoked ham

½ cup light brown sugar, packed

¼ cup crushed pecans

¼ cup maple syrup

2 tablespoons cider vinegar

1 tablespoon Worcestershire sauce

1 tablespoon instant-coffee granules

1 cup water

1 tablespoon dry mustard

Preheat oven to 325 degrees. Cut rind off ham to expose fat. Place ham in shallow roasting pan, cover loosely with foil, and bake for 1¼ hours.

Combine remaining ingredients to make glaze, stirring until coffee granules dissolve. Brush glaze on ham. Bake, uncovered, for 40 to 50 minutes, basting with glaze every 15 minutes, or until internal temperature reaches 140 degrees in thickest part of ham. Let stand for 15 minutes.

Yield: 14 to 16 servings

❧ GLAZED CORNED BEEF ❧

1 (3-pound) corned beef brisket

1 cup orange marmalade

5 tablespoons Dijon mustard

¼ cup plus 1 tablespoon light brown sugar

Place corned beef in large pot and cover with water. Bring water to a boil and reduce heat. Cover partially and simmer for about 3 hours or until very tender.

Preheat oven to 350 degrees. Combine remaining ingredients and set aside. Remove beef from pot and drain. Place meat in ovenproof casserole and pour marmalade mixture over it. Bake for 30 to 40 minutes, until glaze is crisp and brown. Slice against the grain and serve immediately.

Yield: 8 servings

ᴄᴏ CHICKEN BREASTS MARSALA ᴄᴏ

2 chicken breast halves, with skin and bones

1½ teaspoons paprika

½ teaspoon salt

¼ teaspoon pepper

6 tablespoons (¾ stick) butter

1 (15-ounce) can artichoke hearts, drained and rinsed

½ pound mushrooms, sliced

½ teaspoon dried tarragon

Salt and pepper to taste

3 tablespoons flour

⅓ cup cream sherry or sweet marsala wine

1½ cups chicken broth

Pat chicken dry and rub paprika, salt, and pepper on both sides. In heavy skillet, melt 2 tablespoons butter and brown chicken, over medium heat, until golden brown, about 2½ to 3 minutes a side. Transfer to 2-quart shallow baking dish or casserole. Place artichoke hearts around chicken.

In skillet, melt remaining butter over medium heat. Add mushrooms, tarragon, and salt and pepper. Cook until liquid is evaporated, stirring constantly. Add flour and cook, stirring constantly, for 2 to 3 minutes. Add sherry or wine and broth, and bring to a boil, stirring constantly. Reduce heat and simmer, stirring, for 4 to 5 minutes. Pour sauce over chicken.

Preheat oven to 350 degrees. Cover casserole with lid or aluminum foil, and bake for 40 to 45 minutes or until chicken is thoroughly cooked.

Yield: 2 servings

❧ CHICKEN CACCIATORE ❧

1 (3-pound) chicken, cut into 8 pieces

1 tablespoon seasoned salt

1 cup flour

Olive oil

1 (28-ounce) can or 2 (14½-ounce) cans peeled tomatoes, undrained

½ cup chopped onion

½ cup red wine

½ teaspoon celery seed

1 teaspoon dried oregano

1 teaspoon dried thyme

1 teaspoon basil

½ teaspoon salt

½ teaspoon pepper

4 cups cooked rice

Parsley for garnish

Pat chicken dry. Mix seasoned salt and flour, and dredge chicken in mixture. In large Dutch oven, heat a small amount of olive oil and brown chicken. Set aside.

To pan drippings, add tomatoes, onion, wine, celery seed, oregano, thyme, basil, salt, and pepper. When mixture begins to simmer, add chicken and cover. Simmer for 30 minutes, stirring occasionally. Check seasoning and add salt and pepper to taste. Serve over rice and garnish with parsley.

Yield: 6 to 8 servings

✎ SHERRIED STEAK AND RICE ✎

Elaine Diener

1 (1½-pound) round steak, tenderized and cut into strips
1½ teaspoons vegetable oil
2 large onions, sliced
1 (15-ounce) can cream of mushroom soup
½ cup dry sherry
1 (4-ounce) can sliced mushrooms, drained (reserve liquid)
1½ teaspoons garlic salt
3 cups cooked rice

In large skillet, brown steak in oil over high heat. Add onions and sauté until tender but slightly crisp. Blend soup, sherry, mushroom liquid, and garlic salt. Pour over steak. Add mushrooms. Reduce heat, cover, and simmer for 1 hour or until steak is tender. Serve over rice.

Yield: 6 servings

❧ CROUTON AND WALNUT CATFISH ❧

3 tablespoons canola or sunflower oil

1½ cups cubed French bread

½ cup walnut pieces

2 tablespoons butter

2 tablespoons olive oil

½ teaspoon salt

½ teaspoon freshly ground pepper

6 (6-ounce) catfish fillets

4 cloves garlic, crushed and finely chopped
    (about 1 tablespoon)

¼ cup chopped chives

¼ cup water

Fresh parsley for garnish

Red wine vinegar

In large skillet, heat oil, add bread and walnuts, and sauté for 4 minutes or until brown. Set aside.

In same skillet, heat butter and oil. Sprinkle salt and pepper on both sides of fillets and place them in one layer in skillet. Sauté for 1½ minutes per side, until fish is just cooked in the center. Arrange on a platter.

Add garlic and chives to skillet drippings and cook over low heat for 30 seconds. Add water and stir to dissolve all bits in bottom of pan. Pour pan sauce over fish, top with croutons and walnuts, garnish with parsley, and sprinkle with vinegar. Serve immediately.

Yield: 6 servings

ও TOM AND LOIS ESREY'S ও
HIGH ON ROSE BANANA PEPPER
MUSTARD AND PINEAPPLE JELLY
PORK TENDERLOIN

Tom Esrey is one of my favorite people. He and his wife, Lois, are as enthusiastic about cooking as I am, and he keeps me up to date on all of the great Kentucky products sold at A Taste of Kentucky—also a favorite of mine!

1 tablespoon olive oil

1 tablespoon butter

1 (1½-pound) pork tenderloin

½ teaspoon onion powder

1 clove garlic, minced

8 to 10 large spinach leaves

¼ cup High on Rose banana pepper mustard

¾ cup pineapple jelly

In heavy sauté pan, heat oil and butter. Add pork and cook over high heat until brown on all sides. Remove meat from pan, set aside to cool a little, and sprinkle with onion powder and garlic.

Add spinach to boiling water and cook for 1 minute until wilted. Drain and rinse in ice-chilled water to stop spinach from cooking. Drain again and pat dry. Lay spinach leaves on work surface to form a rectangle that will wrap around tenderloin.

Combine banana pepper mustard and pineapple jelly, and brush entire surface of meat with half of the mixture. Wrap pork with spinach and place in covered baking dish. Preheat oven to 375 degrees.

Bake for 15 minutes and baste meat with remaining jelly mixture. Return to oven for 20 to 30 minutes. Allow to set, covered, for 10 minutes after removing from the oven. Cut into thick slices and serve over rice if desired.

Yield: 4 servings

Note: High on Rose banana pepper mustard can be found at many specialty shops or ordered from A Taste of Kentucky in Louisville.

∾ MESQUITE-MARINATED ∾ FLANK STEAK WITH BLACKBERRY SALSA

This was definitely a winner for us. I love to experiment with making salsa, and this version turned out to be both delicious and beautiful. I saved the Kentucky Living *photo on my fridge for many years.*

Steak

1 (1½- to 2-pound) flank steak

¼ cup olive oil

4 cloves garlic, crushed

3 tablespoons dry mesquite seasoning

Salsa

1 cup blackberries

1 red bell pepper, diced

1 small red onion, diced

1 jalapeño pepper, minced

½ cantaloupe, finely diced

Juice of ½ lemon

1 teaspoon chopped fresh parsley

1 tablespoon chopped fresh cilantro

Salt and pepper to taste

To make steak, place ingredients in a large zip-style plastic bag and marinate, preferably overnight or at least 8 hours. Grill over hot coals, about 6 minutes a side for medium-rare or 8 minutes a side for medium. Slice steak against the grain on the bias.

To make salsa, combine ingredients in large bowl. Refrigerate until ready to serve on the side.

Yield: 4 servings

✍ SOUTHWEST SLOW-COOKER ✍ BURRITOS

1 (2-pound) boneless chuck roast

1 jalapeño pepper, seeded and chopped

2 cloves garlic, crushed

1 teaspoon beef bouillon granules, or 1 cube beef bouillon

1 medium onion, finely chopped

½ teaspoon chili powder

½ teaspoon ground cumin

2 ½ tablespoons chopped fresh cilantro

½ teaspoon salt

8 large flour tortillas, warmed

About 2 cups refried beans

2 cups shredded cheese for topping (I use Monterey Jack)

Place ingredients—except tortillas, beans, and cheese—in slow cooker. Cook on low setting for 8 to 9 hours or until tender.

Remove meat, shred, and place in bowl. Combine meat with 1 cup of the cooking juices and toss or stir. Spread tortillas with beans, add beef, and top with cheese.

Yield: 8 servings

❧ VEAL ROAST WITH DILL ❧

2 tablespoons butter

1 (3-pound) veal shoulder roast, boned, rolled, and tied

1 (8-ounce) package sliced mushrooms

2 dozen baby carrots

2 tablespoons fresh dill, or 2 teaspoons dried dill weed

1 teaspoon salt

⅛ teaspoon freshly ground pepper

¼ cup lemon juice

½ cup dry white wine or beef broth

3 tablespoons cornstarch

⅓ cup heavy cream or fat-free half-and-half

Lemon zest

In large nonstick skillet, melt butter over medium-high heat. Add veal and sear on all sides. Place in 4-quart or larger slow cooker. Scatter mushrooms and carrots around roast and sprinkle with dill, salt, and pepper. Pour in lemon juice and wine or broth. Cover and cook at low setting until veal is very tender, around 7 to 9 hours.

About half an hour before serving, remove veal and vegetables, and cover with foil to keep warm. Mix cornstarch and cream or half-and-half, and blend liquid into cooker. Increase heat to high setting, cover, and cook, stirring 2 or 3 times, until sauce is thickened, about 15 to 18 minutes.

Remove string from veal, transfer to a platter, and slice across the grain. Arrange mushrooms and carrots around roast, pour sauce over meat, and sprinkle with lemon zest.

Yield: 6 servings

❧ JEAN'S MEAT LOAF ❧

2 slices bread

Enough milk to saturate bread

2 pounds ground chuck

2 eggs, lightly beaten

2 heaping tablespoons flour

1 medium onion, chopped

1 green bell pepper, chopped

½ teaspoon garlic powder

1 teaspoon salt

½ teaspoon pepper

1 cup ketchup

2 tablespoons water

Preheat oven to 350 degrees. In small bowl, crumble bread, add milk, and allow to saturate completely. Combine remaining ingredients, except ketchup and water, and form two loaves in large baking dish. Mix ⅓ cup ketchup with water and pour around meat loaves. Rub tops of loaves with remaining ketchup and bake, covered tightly with foil, for 50 to 60 minutes. Uncover and bake for 15 minutes.

Yield: 8 to 10 servings

∾ PARMESAN-CRUSTED ∾ CHICKEN BREASTS

6 chicken breasts, skinned, with bones

½ cup (1 stick) butter

3 sleeves buttery crackers

½ cup Parmesan cheese

Preheat oven to 350 degrees. Pat chicken dry. Place crackers in blender and blend until finer than bread crumbs. Melt butter completely (I microwave it). Dip chicken in melted butter. Coat chicken with crumbs and cheese, and place on baking sheet. Bake for 45 minutes.

Yield: 6 servings

∾ CREAMED SALMON ON TOAST ∾

I don't know about you, but I have the worst time with hard-boiled eggs. Half the time, my peeled eggs are such a mess that I end up making something else with them. This is a favorite fix for me. It's one of the first dishes I learned to make when I was very young, and it's still great comfort food.

2 tablespoons butter

2 tablespoons flour

2 cups milk

4 hard-boiled eggs, sliced

1 (14¾-ounce) can salmon, drained, cleaned, and flaked

1 (14-ounce) can tiny peas

Salt and pepper to taste

4 to 6 slices toast

In medium pan, heat butter until melted. Add flour and combine well. Cook for 1 minute and then slowly add milk. Stir constantly until white sauce is thickened. Add eggs, salmon, and peas; season with salt and pepper, and pour over toast.

Yield: 4 to 6 servings

❧ TURKEY IN THE SACK ❧

1 teaspoon pepper

1 teaspoon salt

1 teaspoon seasoned salt

3 teaspoons paprika

4 teaspoons hot water

1 cup peanut oil

1 (14- to 16-pound) turkey

1 large brown-paper sack (grocery bag)

Combine pepper, salt, seasoned salt, paprika, and water. Let stand for 15 minutes. Add oil and mix thoroughly.

Rinse and dry turkey, which must not exceed 16 pounds. Rub oil mixture inside and outside of turkey. Pour remaining oil into bag, and rub it until every pore in every inch of the bag is sealed, adding oil if needed. Place turkey in the sack, breast side up. Fold over end of sack and tie securely with string. Preheat oven to 325 degrees. Bake for 10 minutes a pound, until juices in the deepest part of thigh run clear or internal temperature reaches 165 degrees. (The sack is airtight, so the turkey will cook by steam. Be careful when opening the bag: steam is very hot.)

Yield: 14 to 16 servings

CRISPY OVEN-FRIED CHICKEN

1 (3-pound) frying chicken, cut into 8 pieces and skinned

4 cups crushed potato chips

1 tablespoon fresh oregano, or 1 teaspoon dried oregano

¼ cup finely chopped parsley

2 teaspoons seasoned salt

½ teaspoon pepper

2 eggs

3 tablespoons water

4 tablespoons (½ stick) butter or margarine, melted

Preheat oven to 375 degrees. Grease a large baking sheet. Pat chicken dry. Combine potato chip crumbs, oregano, parsley, seasoned salt, and pepper. Beat eggs with water. Dip chicken in egg mixture and roll in crumbs. Pat crumbs in place with fingers. Place chicken on baking sheet and drizzle with butter or margarine. Bake for 50 to 60 minutes, until browned and crisp.

Yield: 8 servings

Side Dishes

Side Dishes

"It's raining beans."

 Annette Ragg of Lebanon Junction, Kentucky, had been married for about five years when her mother gave her a pressure cooker. It was an hour before supper, and she had promised her husband, Frank, a big pot of beans. They were cooking in the new pressure cooker, and Annette had gone out in the yard to take the laundry off the clothesline. All of a sudden, her four-year-old son, Mark, ran out onto the porch screaming, "Mom, it's raining beans." Annette ran inside to find beans on the ceiling, on the cabinets, and all over the walls. It truly was "raining beans." As you may have guessed, Annette has never used a pressure cooker again. And as she emptied her house before moving to her new home, she found beans that had rained in places she couldn't believe.

One of the most challenging cooking tasks I face is to make side dishes exciting. I'm always looking for new ones and those that are pleasing to the eye as well as the palate. My Polenta-Stuffed Red Bell Peppers have always been a hit at my table, and Grilled Balsamic Vegetables are a great choice when I entertain outside. I've included good comfort dishes, such as Creamed Potatoes and Peas and Layered Sauerkraut and Neffles, passed down to my mom from my great-aunts (one of only a handful I've included since writing *Kentucky's Best*). As always, take advantage of the bounty of vegetables that are in season, and you can't go wrong.

↩ BRAISED CABBAGE ↩

½ cup (1 stick) butter

1 (3-pound) green cabbage, cored and coarsely chopped

1 cup dry white wine, or 1 cup chicken broth with 1
    tablespoon cider vinegar

1 teaspoon dried tarragon

1¼ teaspoons salt

¼ teaspoon freshly ground pepper

In large skillet, melt butter. Add cabbage and stir to coat with butter. Cook for about 15 minutes, until cabbage is wilted. Add remaining ingredients. Bring to a boil and reduce heat, cover, and simmer until cabbage is tender, about 10 minutes. Remove cover and let juice reduce, stirring occasionally.

Yield: 6 servings

↩ BAKED SPAGHETTI SQUASH ↩ CASSEROLE

1 spaghetti squash, halved and seeded

1 pound ground beef

½ cup diced green bell pepper

½ cup diced red bell pepper

¼ cup diced red onion

1 clove garlic, chopped

1 (14½-ounce) can Italian-style diced tomatoes, drained

½ teaspoon dried oregano

½ teaspoon dried basil

¼ teaspoon salt

¼ teaspoon pepper

2 cups shredded sharp Cheddar cheese

Preheat oven to 375 degrees. Place squash on baking sheet and bake for 40 minutes, or until tender. Cool and shred pulp with a fork.

Reduce oven to 350 degrees. Lightly grease a casserole dish. In a skillet, cook ground beef over medium heat until evenly brown. Drain and mix in green and red peppers, onion, and garlic. Continue to cook and stir until vegetables are tender. Mix shredded squash and tomatoes into the skillet, and add oregano, basil, salt, and pepper. Cook and stir until heated through. Remove skillet from heat and mix in 1¼ cups cheese until melted. Transfer to casserole dish. Bake for 25 minutes. Sprinkle with remaining cheese and bake for 5 minutes, until cheese is melted.

Yield: 6 servings

❧ ACORN SQUASH SOUP ❧ WITH CROUTONS

I've included this recipe with the side dishes because it makes a great accompaniment to a meat entrée.

Squash Soup

Vegetable or olive oil

2 small acorn squash, halved and seeded

1 onion, diced

2 parsnips, diced

2 celery stalks, diced small

2 cups clear vegetable broth

2 cups chicken broth

2 teaspoons butter

¼ teaspoon cayenne pepper

¼ teaspoon ground cinnamon

1 cup milk

2 to 3 teaspoons salt

½ to 1 teaspoon white pepper

Croutons

4 slices stale bread, cubed

4 tablespoons (½ stick) butter, melted

¼ teaspoon ground cinnamon

Pinch of salt and white pepper

Preheat oven to 350 degrees. To make soup, rub oil on inside of squash halves and lay face down on baking sheet. Bake until fork-tender and can easily be peeled, about 15 to 20 minutes. Cool and cut into 2-inch chunks. In medium saucepan, bring squash, onion, parsnips, celery, and vegetable and chicken broth to a boil. Reduce heat and simmer, covered, for 15 minutes. Strain the soup and reserve the liquid. In a food processor, puree the solids with 1 cup of the reserved liquid.

In medium saucepan, warm butter over low heat. Stir in cayenne pepper and cinnamon, and cook for 2 minutes. Stir in the puree and 1 cup of the reserved liquid. Bring to a boil, reduce heat, and simmer for 5 minutes. Stir in milk, salt, and pepper. If you prefer thinner soup, add more of the reserved liquid.

Preheat oven to 300 degrees. To make croutons, combine ingredients in a bowl and toss until butter is absorbed and spices completely coat the bread. Place on cookie sheet and bake for 25 minutes, tossing often to ensure proper browning and crispness. Serve soup topped with croutons.

Yield: 4 servings

✌ HONEY-BAKED APPLES ✌

4 cups good-quality apple cider

½ cup light brown sugar, packed

⅓ cup honey

1 teaspoon ground cinnamon

¼ teaspoon ground nutmeg

Pinch of salt

2 tablespoons butter

6 Golden Delicious or McIntosh apples, unpeeled, halved,
and cored with a melon baller

½ cup golden raisins

In medium saucepan, combine cider, sugar, honey, cinnamon, nutmeg, salt, and butter. Bring to a boil, reduce heat, and simmer for 25 minutes, until mixture is syrupy.

Preheat oven to 350 degrees. In large baking dish, place apples cut side down and pour syrup over them. Distribute raisins evenly over apples. Cover tightly with aluminum foil. Bake for 25 to 30 minutes or until apples are almost tender when pierced with the tip of a sharp knife. Remove from oven and turn apples over. Baste with syrup several times and cover with aluminum foil. Return to oven for 5 minutes, remove from oven, and allow to set, covered, for 15 minutes. Baste before serving.

Yield: 6 servings

✆ SCALLOPED CORN ✆

2 tablespoons butter

1 medium onion, chopped

½ cup chopped red bell pepper

1 (10-ounce) bag frozen corn kernels, thawed

2 eggs, lightly beaten

1 (15-ounce) can cream-style corn

¼ teaspoon salt

⅔ cup crushed buttery crackers

1 cup milk

2 ounces sharp Cheddar cheese, shredded

Preheat oven to 325 degrees. Grease 2-quart baking dish. In small pan, heat butter and sauté onion and red pepper until tender. Remove from heat and add corn kernels. In a bowl, combine eggs, cream-style corn, salt, cracker crumbs, and milk. Add to onion mixture and pour into baking dish. Sprinkle with cheese. Bake, uncovered, for 40 minutes, until golden brown.

Yield: 8 servings

ᘓ CORN QUICHE ᘓ

1 bunch green onions

2 tablespoons olive oil

1 cup fresh corn kernels (2 ears of corn)

1 tablespoon chopped fresh thyme

Coarse salt and freshly ground pepper to taste

1 9-inch pie crust, unbaked

½ cup milk

½ cup heavy cream

2 eggs

6 ounces Gruyère or Monterey Jack cheese, shredded

Freshly grated nutmeg

Cut off 1 inch of stalks of green onions and then cut into ½-inch pieces. Sauté onion in oil until translucent. Add corn and thyme, season with salt and pepper, and cook for 3 to 5 minutes. Place corn mixture in pie crust.

Preheat oven to 350 degrees. Whisk together milk, cream, and eggs. Sprinkle half the cheese over corn mixture. Pour milk mixture over corn mixture and cheese, and grate nutmeg over quiche. Top with remaining cheese. Bake for 30 to 45 minutes or until center is set.

Yield: 6 to 8 servings

✌ CREAMED POTATOES AND PEAS ✌

4 medium potatoes, peeled and cubed

1 (15-ounce) can sweet peas, very early young

1 teaspoon sugar

3 tablespoons butter

¾ cup flour

¼ teaspoon salt

¼ teaspoon pepper

1½ cups milk

In pot, cover potatoes with water and cook over medium heat until fork-tender. Simmer peas until heated thoroughly. Drain and add sugar. In saucepan, melt butter and add flour, salt, and pepper to form a paste. Gradually stir in milk and, stirring constantly, bring to a boil over medium heat. Boil for 1 minute. Drain potatoes and combine with peas in a bowl. Pour white sauce over potatoes and peas, and stir to coat. Serve immediately.

Yield: 6 to 8 servings

❧ HONEY-BAKED TOMATOES ❧

Some of the greatest side dishes are those made with garden-fresh tomatoes. This is one of my favorite summer go-to sides.

1⅓ cups fresh bread crumbs

⅓ cup olive oil

1 teaspoon coarse salt

½ teaspoon freshly ground pepper

5 tablespoons honey

Pinch of ground nutmeg

5 or 6 medium ripe heirloom tomatoes (if not available, I use ripe Better Boy variety)

Fresh parsley or basil leaves for garnish (I prefer basil)

Preheat oven to 350 degrees. Sprinkle bread crumbs in square baking dish and toss with oil. Sprinkle with salt and pepper. Bake, stirring often, until golden brown and crunchy, about 20 minutes. Remove bread crumbs from dish and set aside.

In small saucepan, warm honey over low heat and add nutmeg. Cut tops off tomatoes and set them in the baking dish. Drizzle half the honey mixture over tomatoes and gently mound bread crumbs on each one. Bake for 25 minutes, basting frequently with honey mixture. Garnish with parsley or basil.

Yield: 5 or 6 servings

❧ GREENS WITH PINTO BEANS ❧

1 pound fresh greens of choice (collard, spinach, kale, turnip),
   rinsed several times

1 tablespoon olive oil

3 gloves garlic, minced

3 green onions, finely chopped

1 cup canned pinto beans, undrained

1 teaspoon chili powder

Salt and pepper to taste

In tightly covered pot, steam greens until wilted. Drain and finely chop them. In large skillet, heat oil over medium heat. Add garlic and green onions, and cook, stirring often, until onions are soft, about 3 minutes. Stir in greens, beans, and chili powder. Cover and cook over low heat for 5 minutes or until heated through. Season with salt and pepper.

Yield: 6 servings

ᴄᴐ BAKED ACORN SQUASH ᴄᴐ

1 acorn squash, halved and seeded

2 teaspoons plus 1 tablespoon butter or margarine

1 tablespoon dark brown sugar

3 tablespoons crushed pineapple

Ground nutmeg

¼ teaspoon salt

Preheat oven to 400 degrees. Grease baking dish. Place squash in baking dish and put 1 teaspoon butter or margarine and ¼ tablespoon sugar in each half. Cover with aluminum foil and bake for 30 to 40 minutes. Carefully scoop cooked squash out of shells, reserving shells. Mash squash and combine with 1 tablespoon butter or margarine and remaining brown sugar, pineapple, nutmeg, and salt. Fill shells and serve immediately.

Yield: 2 servings

ᴄᴐ OVEN-ROASTED ᴄᴐ SWEET POTATOES

3 sweet potatoes, peeled and thinly sliced

1 clove garlic, crushed

2 tablespoons olive oil

¼ cup chopped fresh parsley

1 teaspoon chopped fresh thyme

Zest of ¼ orange, finely chopped

Salt and pepper to taste

Preheat oven to 400 degrees. In large bowl, combine sweet potatoes, garlic, and oil. Toss to coat. Spread on a nonstick baking sheet. Bake, turning potatoes as they begin to brown, for about 35 to 40 minutes.

Mix parsley, thyme, and orange zest. Sprinkle over potatoes and season with salt and pepper. Return to oven and bake for 10 to 15 minutes until potatoes are tender, turning once.

Yield: 4 servings

∾ GRILLED BALSAMIC VEGETABLES ∾

¼ cup extra-virgin olive oil

¼ cup balsamic vinegar

1 zucchini, cut into long wedges or peeled into long ribbons

1 large tomato, halved

1 red bell pepper, cut into thick strips

1 yellow or orange bell pepper, cut into thick strips

1 large portobello mushroom

1 red onion, halved

Sea salt, coarsely ground, to taste

Mix oil and vinegar, and brush onto vegetables. Sprinkle with sea salt. Grill over hot coals, turning until grill marks appear on both sides.

Yield: 2 or 3 servings

❦ POLENTA-STUFFED ❦
RED BELL PEPPERS

6 red bell peppers

1 tablespoon butter

½ cup chopped onion

1 tablespoon minced garlic

1 cup polenta or coarse cornmeal

3 ½ cups chicken broth

½ cup heavy cream

¾ cup corn kernels, fresh or frozen

4 tablespoons fresh basil (no substitutions)

¼ cup chopped fresh cilantro (no substitutions)

½ teaspoon salt

½ teaspoon freshly ground pepper

½ cup freshly grated Romano or Parmesan cheese

½ cup Fontina cheese

Grease shallow baking dish with butter. Slice the tops off red peppers and remove seeds and ribs. Flatten peppers for standing by trimming off a small amount from the bottom, making sure not to cut all the way through. Arrange peppers in baking dish.

In saucepan, melt butter over medium heat. Add onion and garlic, and cook until onion is wilted, about 3 minutes. Add polenta or cornmeal and mix well. Slowly pour in broth, stirring constantly to combine. Add cream, corn, basil, cilantro, salt, pepper, and ¼ cup Romano or Parmesan cheese. Cook, stirring constantly with a wooden spoon, until polenta becomes very thick, about 8 to 10 minutes.

Fill peppers with polenta mixture and sprinkle with remaining Romano or Parmesan and Fontina cheeses. Stand peppers upright. Preheat oven to 375 degrees. Bake for 25 minutes, until golden brown. Serve immediately.

Yield: 6 servings

❧ GLAZED FALL VEGETABLES ❧

Vegetable or olive oil

1 acorn squash, halved and seeded

2 sweet potatoes, peeled and cut into ½-inch slices

1 large white potato, peeled and cut into ½-inch slices

3 carrots, peeled and cut into ½-inch slices

1 large yellow onion, cut into ½-inch slices

½ cup dark brown sugar, packed

¼ cup maple syrup

1 teaspoon vanilla extract

1 teaspoon ground cinnamon

4 tablespoons (½ stick) butter

¼ cup water

Preheat oven to 425 degrees. Rub oil on inside of squash halves and lay face down on baking sheet. Bake until squash can easily be peeled, about 15 to 20 minutes. Cool and cut into quarters.

Place squash, sweet potatoes, white potato, carrots, and onion in a bowl. Add sugar, maple syrup, vanilla extract, and cinnamon. Toss well. Place in 9 × 13-inch glass baking dish. Cut butter into pieces and scatter over the top. Pour water into baking dish. Cover tightly with foil and bake for 45 minutes. Remove foil and stir vegetables. Bake, uncovered, for 15 to 20 minutes or until vegetables are tender and lightly browned.

Yield: 4 servings

◇ LAYERED SAUERKRAUT ◇ AND NEFFLES

My great-aunts, Matt and Frank, were as spirited as their nicknames. We looked forward to their visits because we knew that they would cook all day. Aunt Matt made the most wonderful little German dumplings that were as light as a feather—not at all like traditional egg dumplings.

2 cups flour

1 teaspoon salt

1 teaspoon baking powder

2 tablespoons oil or melted shortening

1 egg, lightly beaten

¾ cup cold water

4 strips bacon

2 large onions, thinly sliced

1 (8-ounce) bag fresh sauerkraut

Bring 2 quarts water to a boil. Combine flour, salt, and baking powder. Add oil, egg, and cold water. Mix well. Drop by the teaspoonful into boiling water. Cook, uncovered, over medium heat for about 15 minutes. Drain and set aside.

In heavy skillet, fry bacon until crisp. Remove, drain, and crumble when cool. Sauté onions in bacon fat until clear. In another saucepan, heat sauerkraut thoroughly.

In a 9 × 13-inch glass baking dish, layer half the sauerkraut, dumplings, bacon, and onions. Layer remaining half and serve immediately.

Yield: 6 to 8 servings

↔ SOUTHERN TURNIP GREENS ↔

4 to 5 pounds turnip greens

1 pound salt pork, rinsed and diced

1½ cups water

1 cup finely chopped onion

½ teaspoon pepper

1 teaspoon sugar (optional)

Dash of crushed red pepper (optional)

Salt and pepper to taste

Cider vinegar

Cut off and discard tough stems and discolored leaves from turnip greens. Wash thoroughly and drain well.

In large pot or Dutch oven, cook pork over medium heat until crisp and brown. Add turnip greens, water, onion, pepper, sugar, and red pepper, and bring to a boil. Reduce heat, cover, and simmer for 40 to 45 minutes or until greens are tender. Season with salt and pepper, and serve with vinegar.

Yield: 6 to 8 servings

❧ GARLIC MASHED POTATOES ❧

6 large Idaho potatoes, peeled and cut into small pieces

4 tablespoons (½ stick) butter

¾ cup milk or half-and-half

2 teaspoons minced garlic

Salt and pepper to taste

Boil potatoes until fork-tender. Remove from heat and drain. Melt butter and warm milk or half-and-half. Mash potatoes, with either a hand masher or a mixer, adding butter, garlic, and salt and pepper. Once potatoes are no longer lumpy, slowly add milk, mashing until desired consistency is reached. You may not need all the milk. Season with salt and pepper.

Yield: 6 servings

❧ MEXICAN CHARRO BEANS ❧

1 pound dried pinto beans

6 strips bacon, chopped

2 cloves garlic, chopped

4 medium fresh plum tomatoes, chopped

2 medium onions, chopped

1 medium green bell pepper, chopped

1 (12-ounce) can beer, or 1½ cups water

½ bunch fresh cilantro, chopped

2 jalapeño peppers, seeded and chopped

Salt and pepper to taste

Soak beans in cold water for 30 minutes. Rinse and pick over beans. In large pot, bring to a boil and cook over medium heat for 1½ to 2 hours, until tender but still firm.

Before beans are done, fry bacon in large skillet until halfway cooked. Add garlic, tomatoes, onions, and green pepper, and continue to cook until bacon is crisp. Add beer or water to bacon mixture and simmer for a few minutes, or longer if you like beans softer and less soupy. Add cilantro and jalapeños, and combine bacon mixture with beans. Season with salt and pepper.

Yield: 6 servings

✌ GREAT GARBANZOS ✌

1 medium onion, chopped

1 clove garlic, minced

2 carrots, grated

½ teaspoon grated ginger root

¼ cup vegetable broth

2 potatoes, peeled and cubed

1 fresh tomato, chopped

2 cups garbanzo beans, cooked

½ cup tomato paste

1 (15-ounce) can diced tomatoes, drained

¼ teaspoon coriander

¼ teaspoon ground cumin

¼ teaspoon ground cloves

¼ teaspoon ground cinnamon

Salt and pepper to taste

In a large stockpot, sauté onion, garlic, carrots, and ginger root in broth for 10 minutes. Add potatoes and tomato. Cook over medium heat, stirring occasionally, for 8 to 10 minutes. Add remaining ingredients and bring to a boil. Cover, reduce heat, and simmer for 30 minutes.

Yield: 6 to 8 servings

❧ NOODLE KUGEL ❧

2 cups chopped onion

2 tablespoons vegetable oil

2 (8-ounce) packages cream cheese

1 (12-ounce) package wide egg noodles, cooked until soft

¾ cup golden raisins

1 tablespoon chicken bouillon granules

1 pint small-curd cottage cheese

1 pint sour cream

6 large eggs

Salt and pepper to taste

1 tablespoon butter, cut into small pieces

Preheat oven to 375 degrees. Lightly grease a casserole dish. In medium skillet, sauté onion in oil until brown and caramelized. In large bowl, pour onion over cream cheese and allow cheese to melt. Add noodles to cream cheese mixture. Stir in raisins, bouillon, cottage cheese, and sour cream.

Beat eggs with a fork until well blended. Pour into noodle mixture and blend well. Season with salt and pepper. Put noodle mixture in casserole dish and dot the top with butter. Bake for 35 to 45 minutes.

Yield: 6 to 8 servings

❧ MARINATED TOMATOES ❧ AND ASPARAGUS

1 pound fresh asparagus, with ends trimmed and outer skin peeled from bottom of stalks

1 pound grape tomatoes, halved

4 cloves garlic, minced

⅓ cup extra-virgin olive oil

1 teaspoon salt

1 tablespoon fresh basil

2 tablespoons fresh lemon juice

In large skillet, bring a small amount of salted water to a boil. Cook asparagus for 2 minutes. Immediately put in ice water to stop cooking. Drain well. Cut into 1-inch pieces. In a large bowl, mix asparagus with remaining ingredients and toss gently. Refrigerate overnight.

Yield: 8 servings

∽ PUREED BUTTERNUT SQUASH ∽

4 tablespoons (½ stick) butter

1 small onion, sliced

1 butternut squash, peeled, seeded, and cut into chunks

1 white turnip, peeled and sliced

1 large ripe pear, peeled and cored

Salt and pepper to taste

In large, heavy pan, melt butter and sauté onion until soft. Add squash, turnip, and pear. Simmer, covered, until tender, about 15 to 20 minutes. Add a small amount of water if vegetables become dry. Remove mixture from pan and puree in a food processor until smooth. Season with salt and pepper.

Yield: 8 servings

ɛↄ CELERY BAKE ɛↄ

2 cups sliced celery

1 (8-ounce) jar water chestnuts

1 (15-ounce) can cream of mushroom soup

½ cup (1 stick) butter, melted

1 sleeve crackers, such as Ritz or Town House, finely crushed

Preheat oven to 350 degrees. Cook celery in boiling water for about 7 minutes and drain. Combine with water chestnuts, soup, and half the butter, and place in 2-quart baking dish. Mix cracker crumbs with remaining butter and sprinkle on top of mixture. Bake for 30 minutes.

Yield: 4 to 6 servings

Sandwiches
and Snacks

Sandwiches and Snacks

"I learned to cook from my grandmother."

 I learned to cook from my grandmother. As a newlywed, I was preparing my first baked ham. Recalling the hundreds of times I'd seen Nanny do it, I scrubbed the ham and then hacked away on the hock end until I had cut it off. Job completed, I baked and served my first ham. I had to brag to Nanny about my wonderful cooking expertise, so I told her step by step what I had done.

Throwing her hands into the air, she laughed, "Lord, child, the only reason I cut off that hock end was because I didn't have a pan big enough to hold the whole thing!"

Monica Pickerill, *Kentucky Living* staff

I never miss eating a full hot meal if I have a delicious sandwich. I love great burgers, such as Mushroom Stilton Burgers, Grilled Portobello Burgers, and South-of-the-Border Guacamole Burgers. Vidalia Onion Finger Sandwiches and Turkey Reuben Melts are two of my favorites in this category, and Kids' Healthy Wrap and Rolls are great lunch-box additions and a good way to introduce the little ones to cooking and making good choices.

There's no need to feel guilty about serving sandwiches when you use your imagination and make dinner an adventure.

❧ KIDS' HEALTHY WRAP ❧ AND ROLLS

1 package flour tortillas

Assorted cheese slices

Turkey slices

Thinly shredded lettuce

Finely sliced cucumbers

Assorted vegetables

Let the kids choose from healthy ingredients. When shopping, let them use their imagination when buying veggies, such as colored peppers, red cabbage, bok choy, tomatoes, and others they find appealing. Slice the vegetables and arrange them on a large platter with the other ingredients. Show the kids how to wrap and roll a variety of healthy ingredients.

Yield: 8 wraps

ഈ BLUE CHEESE AND BACON ഈ
ON RYE

A great TV snack when watching the big game!

1 (8-ounce) package cream cheese, softened

½ cup crumbled blue cheese

½ cup crumbled crisply fried bacon

¼ cup Italian dressing

8 slices rye bread

Combine cream cheese, blue cheese, bacon, and 2 tablespoons dressing. Spread cheese mixture evenly on 4 bread slices and top with remaining bread. Brush sandwiches on both sides with remaining dressing. In nonstick skillet, grill sandwiches over medium heat until golden brown on both sides and filling is melted.

Yield: 4 servings

ഈ GREEK SALAD ON PITA ഈ

1 large ripe tomato, cut into ¼-inch slices

1 small cucumber, peeled and thinly sliced

¼ pound feta cheese, crumbled

20 Greek-style black olives, pitted and halved

1 tablespoon fresh oregano

Salt and freshly ground pepper to taste

2 tablespoons olive oil

1 tablespoon balsamic vinegar

4 pita breads, halved and opened into pockets

In large bowl, layer tomato and cucumber. Add cheese, olives, and oregano, and season with salt and pepper. Sprinkle with oil and vinegar. Let stand for 30 minutes. Slip one-quarter of the tomato mixture into each pita pocket. Cut in half to serve.

Yield: 4 to 8 servings

✌ GRILLED TOMATO ✌ AND ONION SANDWICHES

⅓ cup olive oil

Salt and freshly ground pepper to taste

1 tablespoon fresh rosemary, or 1 teaspoon dried rosemary

2 large ripe tomatoes, cut into ¼-inch slices

2 onions, cut into ¼-inch slices

4 large kaiser rolls, split

1 bunch arugula

½ pound fresh mozzarella cheese, drained and thinly sliced

Preheat grill or broiler to medium heat. Combine olive oil, salt and pepper, and rosemary. Brush over each tomato slice, onion slice, and half roll. Grill or broil onion slices until tender and blackened. Briefly grill or broil tomato slices until warm. Do not overcook. Grill or broil rolls on one side until golden brown. Transfer all to a warm platter.

To assemble sandwiches, layer arugula, tomatoes, onions, and cheese on the bottom half of each roll. Cover with the top half. Cut in half to serve.

Yield: 4 servings

∾ PIMIENTO CHEESE SPREAD ∾

This makes an excellent sandwich when served on toasted slices of Cheddar Braid.

½ pound extra-sharp white Cheddar cheese

½ pound extra-sharp orange Cheddar cheese

1 (7-ounce) jar pimientos, drained and finely chopped

½ teaspoon pepper

Cayenne pepper to taste (a few dashes is plenty)

Salt to taste

⅔ cup mayonnaise

Finely grate both cheeses into a bowl. Stir in pimientos and pepper, and season with cayenne pepper and salt. Stir in mayonnaise and mash with a fork until smooth. Refrigerate to allow flavors to develop.

Yield: about 2 cups

✺ MUSHROOM STILTON BURGERS ✺

2 tablespoons olive oil

1 large green onion, finely chopped

8 portobello mushrooms, finely chopped

¾ cup coarsely chopped button mushrooms

3 cloves garlic, minced

½ cup finely shredded carrots

1 cup Italian parsley, stems removed and finely chopped

3 slices bread, finely crumbled

1 egg

1½ tablespoons balsamic vinegar

Salt and pepper to taste

4 ounces Stilton cheese, crumbled

4 sesame seed buns

Red onion, sliced, for topping

Lettuce for topping

Tomato, sliced, for topping

Heat 1 tablespoon oil and sauté green onion until soft and bulb is translucent. Add portobello and button mushrooms, garlic, and carrots, and sauté for 12 to 15 minutes, until mushroom liquid has almost evaporated. Let cool. Stir in parsley, bread, egg, and vinegar, and season with salt and pepper. The mixture should be very stiff. If not, add more bread. Shape into 4 patties.

In large ovenproof skillet, heat remaining oil over medium high heat and sear burgers until golden brown on both sides. Crumble cheese over top, place skillet in preheated 400-degree oven, and cook burgers for 15 minutes, until browned. Serve on buns, topped with red onion, lettuce, and tomato.

Yield: 4 servings

∾ TURKEY REUBEN MELTS ∾

1 cup sliced green onions

Vegetable oil

8 slices rye bread

½ cup Thousand Island dressing

8 slices turkey breast, cooked

8 slices Swiss cheese

Butter

In nonstick skillet, sauté green onions in a small amount of oil. Spread each slice of bread with a thin layer of dressing. Layer each slice with green onions, turkey, and cheese. Combine slices to make 4 sandwiches. In skillet, melt a small amount of butter and brown each sandwich on both sides. Slice and serve immediately.

Yield: 4 servings

∾ BLUE CHEESE AND ∾ GARLIC BURGERS

2 pounds ground chuck

4 ounces blue cheese

2 tablespoons garlic, minced and drizzled with olive oil

Sea salt and freshly ground pepper to taste

1 loaf good Italian bread, sliced lengthwise and then into 4 pieces

Condiments for topping

Preheat grill. Divide chuck equally into 8 balls. Press down center of 4 balls and fill each indentation with 1 ounce of cheese and 1½ teaspoons garlic mixture. Sprinkle with a small amount of sea salt and a generous twist of pepper. Flatten remaining 4 balls, place over filled balls, and seal lightly around the edges. Grill over hot coals for 4 to 5 minutes per side.

While meat is grilling, scoop out some of the bread and grill the bread until grill marks appear. To serve, place burgers in hollows of bread and top with your favorite condiments.

Yield: 4 servings

ᑲ BEST BURGERS ᑲ

Serve Best Burgers with a crusty artisan bread, a great salad, and a good red wine. The flavor doesn't get any better than this simple burger.

8 ounces ground sirloin

8 ounces ground chuck

1 teaspoon kosher salt

½ teaspoon pepper

1 teaspoon grilling seasoning (I use steak grilling powder)

Preheat grill. Combine ingredients well and divide equally into 3 patties. Grill over hot coals for 4 to 5 minutes a side for medium, flipping only once.

Yield: 3 servings

ᔆ GRILLED PORTOBELLO BURGERS ᔆ

Olive oil

6 large portobello mushrooms

Salt and pepper to taste

1 long loaf crusty French bread, sliced lengthwise and then
    into 6 pieces

1 (8-ounce) container hummus

6 ounces feta cheese

Preheat grill. Drizzle oil on both sides of mushrooms, and season with salt and pepper. Grill over hot coals for 2 to 3 minutes, turning often. Place a mushroom on the bottom half of each bread slice.

Hollow out the top half of each bread slice, drizzle oil inside bread slices, and grill over hot coals until grill marks appear. Fill hollows of bread with 1 tablespoon hummus and a chunk of cheese. Turn over and place top halves on bottom halves.

Yield: 6 servings

ᔆ SMOKED SAUSAGE WITH ᔆ PEPPERS AND ONIONS

*Sausages are great when served over rice or piled high on a
hoagie roll and enjoyed state fair style.*

1 tablespoon vegetable oil

¾ pound smoked sausage (such as kielbasa), cut into 1-inch
    slices

1 yellow bell pepper, cut into ¼-inch strips

1 red bell pepper, cut into ¼-inch strips

1 medium onion, thinly sliced

½ cup water

In large heavy skillet, heat oil over medium heat until very hot but not smoking. Brown sausage and add yellow and red peppers and onion, stirring for about 1 minute. Add water and simmer, partially covered, for 8 to 10 minutes, until vegetables are tender.

Yield: 2 servings

❧ SOUTH-OF-THE-BORDER ❧ GUACAMOLE BURGERS

1½ pounds ground chuck

2 ounces Monterey Jack cheese, quartered

4 jalapeño peppers, seeded and finely chopped

Salt and pepper to taste

4 English muffins, toasted

Guacamole for topping

1 tablespoon chopped fresh cilantro for topping

Preheat grill. Divide chuck equally into 4 balls and press down center of each ball. Fill each indentation with 1 piece of cheese and one-quarter of the jalapeños. Close meat around filling and form into 1-inch-thick patties. Season with salt and pepper.

Grill over hot coals, in oiled disposable aluminum pan, for 5 minutes a side. Serve immediately on English muffins, topped with guacamole and cilantro.

Yield: 4 servings

❦ VIDALIA ONION ❦
FINGER SANDWICHES

2 medium Vidalia onions, thinly sliced

Fresh lime juice to taste

8 slices soft wheat bread

½ cup (1 stick) butter or margarine, softened

¼ cup chopped cilantro

⅓ cup chopped tomatoes

Place onions in bowl, sprinkle with lime juice, and toss gently. Lay out bread and spread with a very thin layer of butter or margarine. (This keeps the bread from getting soggy.) Put onion on 4 bread slices and top with cilantro and tomatoes. Cover with remaining bread slices. Carefully cut off and discard crusts, and cut sandwiches diagonally. Cover loosely with plastic wrap and refrigerate.

Yield: 8 servings

✂ TURKEY QUESADILLAS ✂

6 strips bacon

Vegetable oil

1 medium onion, chopped

8 (6- or 7-inch) tortillas

2 cups chopped cooked turkey

1 cup coarsely grated Gruyère or Swiss cheese

2 tablespoons chopped fresh parsley for garnish

Fry bacon, drain, and crumble. In a small amount of oil, sauté onion until soft and translucent. Layer 4 tortillas with equal amounts of bacon, onion, turkey, and cheese. Cover with remaining tortillas.

In heavy skillet with no oil, grill until lightly browned. Carefully flip and grill on the other side until cheese is melted. Cut each tortilla into 4 wedges, garnish with parsley, and serve immediately with a mild salsa, if desired.

Yield: 4 servings

Breakfast and Brunch Dishes

Breakfast and Brunch Dishes

"Something is very wrong here."

Back in college, I lived with three other women in an off-campus apartment. In an effort to eat better meals and avoid fast food, we decided that each of us would cook well-balanced dinners for a week at a time. We each paid a flat fee per week, and the roommate whose turn it was would use the money to plan the menus and do the shopping. Two of us were from farming areas, so they learned early how to cook. Although I wasn't from a farming community, my mother had taught me a lot of the basics, so I could hold my own in the kitchen. The fourth roommate, Cheryl, was from the city and had not learned to cook. We didn't know this.

One time, during Cheryl's week to cook, she found a recipe for beef stew and was very excited about making it. She'd talked about it for days, and it was to be our Saturday-night dinner. When we all sat down to eat, we took one bite and looked at one another, as if to say, "Something is very wrong here." It seems that Cheryl had misinterpreted the recipe. When it called for a cup of bouillon, she had used a cup of bouillon cubes!

We ordered pizza that night.

Lynne Christenson, *Kentucky Living* staff

I have always loved breakfast and the idea of making brunch for friends and family. Lately, I have been on a crepe kick. I daydream about savory and sweet crepes and ways to present them. Mastering crepe making was a bit of a trick, but I have it down now. I can flip with the best of them.

Lots of great choices are available in this chapter. I get just as excited about cooking my mom's Fried Cornmeal Mush as I do about making Gingerbread Waffles to serve with fresh sausage, such as Olde Delaney's. Meals made early in the day take on new life when you pass on the ordinary and choose a Banana and Pineapple Fritter instead. See how Blueberry Curd will turn an ordinary piece of toast into a reason to linger over a second cup of tea. Put your family to the test and jazz up your morning meals with dishes that will make you eager to start the day despite the weather.

✑ FRENCH CREPES ✑

Crepes are thin French pancakes that are versatile not only for delicious desserts but also for brunches or even entrées when filled with meats, vegetables, and egg dishes. They originated in Brittany, a region in the northwest of France. If you haven't tried crepes, don't be intimidated. Get out the pan, make a simple batter, and you'll be flipping before you know it.

1 cup cold water

1 cup cold milk

4 eggs

½ teaspoon salt

2 cups sifted flour

4 tablespoons (½ stick) butter, melted

In a deep bowl, combine ingredients and whisk until very smooth, or use an immersion blender to blend well. Cover and refrigerate for several hours. Lightly butter inversion pan or spray it with nonstick cooking spray. Spoon ½ cup batter into pan for each crepe. Cook until light brown on both sides.

Yield: 12 crepes

SPINACH, CHEESE, AND MUSHROOM CREPES

French Crepes

6 strips bacon

4 tablespoons (½ stick) butter

½ pound mushrooms, sliced

¼ cup flour

1 cup milk

1 (10-ounce) package frozen chopped spinach, thawed and drained

1 tablespoon chopped fresh parsley

2 tablespoons grated Parmesan cheese

Salt and pepper to taste

⅔ cup chicken broth

2 eggs

¼ cup lemon juice

Prepare French Crepes according to recipe on page 139. Separate with waxed paper and keep warm until ready to serve.

In large, deep skillet, fry bacon over medium-high heat until evenly brown. Drain, reserving about 1 tablespoon drippings; crumble and set aside. To drippings, add 1 tablespoon butter and sauté mushrooms. In another saucepan, melt 3 tablespoons butter over medium heat. Whisk in flour, stirring constantly until a smooth sauce is formed. Gradually stir in milk, stirring constantly until smooth thick gravy is formed. Add bacon, mushrooms, spinach, parsley, and cheese, and season with salt and pepper. Cook until somewhat thick, about 10 minutes.

In saucepan, bring broth to a boil. In small bowl, whisk together eggs and lemon juice. Temper eggs by adding slowly to broth, whisking constantly to cook but not scramble the eggs. Season with salt and pepper. Spoon spinach and mushroom filling down middle of each crepe, fold over to form a semicircle, and top with warm egg sauce.

Yield: 4 to 6 servings

✌ JALAPEÑO PEPPER, CHICKEN, ✌ AND MUSHROOM CREPES

French Crepes

2 tablespoons butter

2 jalapeño peppers, seeded and diced

2 cups button mushrooms, sliced

½ cup chicken broth

1 clove garlic

1 cup shredded Monterey Jack cheese

½ cup sour cream

1 teaspoon salt

½ teaspoon pepper

3 cups shredded cooked chicken

Prepare French Crepes according to recipe on page 139. Separate with waxed paper and keep warm until ready to serve.

In large saucepan, melt butter and sauté jalapeño peppers and mushrooms. Add broth, garlic, and cheese, and simmer until cheese melts. Fold in sour cream, and add salt and pepper. Spoon ½ cup chicken down middle of each crepe, fold over to form a semicircle, and top with warm cheese sauce.

Yield: 6 servings

෫ BLUEBERRY CURD ෫

This is a favorite in my home for spreading on toast, hot biscuits, and English muffins!

8 ounces blueberries

1 tablespoon water

4 tablespoons (½ stick) butter, diced

1¼ cups superfine sugar

3 large eggs, lightly beaten

In covered saucepan, gently cook blueberries in water, shaking pan occasionally, until very soft, about 10 minutes. Press through a fine sieve into a heat-proof bowl or the top of a double boiler. Stir in butter and sugar, and put the bowl over a saucepan of gently simmering water; do not allow the bottom of the bowl to sit in the water. Heat gently, stirring, until sugar dissolves and butter melts.

Whisk in eggs and continue to stir over gently simmering water until the curd thickens enough to coat the back of a spoon, 30 to 40 minutes. Stir only occasionally at first, more frequently as the cooking progresses, and then constantly toward the end, so the curd cooks evenly and does not curdle. The water must not boil. Strain the curd into a container. Refrigerate after opening, and use within a week.

Yield: 1½ cups

❧ APPLE BUTTER ❧

Slow cookers make great apple butter.

8 cups unsweetened applesauce

4 cups sugar

4 teaspoons ground cinnamon

2 teaspoons ground allspice

2 teaspoons ground nutmeg

2 teaspoons ground cloves

Place ingredients in slow cooker and stir. Cook, uncovered, on high setting for 6 to 7 hours. Cool and pour into 4 pint jars. Process for 10 minutes in a hot-water bath, until jars are sealed according to directions on lids or rings, or freeze in freezer-safe containers.

Yield: 4 pints

ᔓ BACON, CHEDDAR, ᔓ
AND APPLE BAKE

This is a great side dish for a Sunday or holiday brunch.

3 medium apples, peeled and sliced

2 tablespoons sugar

2 cups shredded sharp Cheddar cheese

1 pound bacon, crisply fried and crumbled

2 cups flour

3 tablespoons baking powder

½ teaspoon salt

2 cups milk

5 eggs

Maple syrup for topping

Powdered sugar for topping

Preheat oven to 375 degrees. Mix apples and sugar. Arrange in rows on an ungreased 9 × 13-inch baking pan. Cover apples with cheese and sprinkle with bacon. Mix remaining ingredients and pour over apples. Bake uncovered for 30 minutes. Serve immediately with maple syrup and powdered sugar for topping.

Yield: 8 servings

CRAB AND CREAM CHEESE DILL BAKED EGGS

4 tablespoons (½ stick) butter, melted

9 eggs

½ cup milk

1 (8-ounce) package cream cheese, cubed

6 ounces lump crabmeat, cartilage removed and picked clean for shells

Salt and freshly ground pepper to taste

1 tablespoon chopped fresh dill

4 slices toast, cut diagonally

Preheat oven to 350 degrees. Grease a 7 × 12-inch casserole dish with melted butter. In large bowl, beat eggs and milk until light and fluffy. Fold in cream cheese and crabmeat, and season with salt and pepper. Pour egg mixture into casserole and sprinkle with dill. Bake for 30 minutes. Serve immediately on toast slices.

Yield: 4 servings

❧ GINGERBREAD WAFFLES ❧

2 ½ cups flour

¼ cup dark or light brown sugar, packed

4 teaspoons baking powder

1 teaspoon baking soda

1 tablespoon ground ginger

1 teaspoon ground cinnamon

1 teaspoon ground allspice

2 egg whites, whipped until stiff peaks form

1½ cups buttermilk

¼ cup molasses

6 tablespoons sour cream

¾ cup raisins

Sweetened whipped cream for topping

Ground cinnamon

Prepare waffle iron according to the manufacturer's instructions. In mixing bowl, combine flour, sugar, baking powder, baking soda, ginger, cinnamon, and allspice. In another mixing bowl, combine remaining ingredients, except toppings. Fold dry ingredients into wet ingredients until just moistened. Pour enough batter into waffle iron to fill two-thirds of the iron. Cook until golden brown and set aside. Repeat with remaining batter. Top with whipped cream and sprinkle with cinnamon.

Yield: 8 waffles

❧ MAPLE-SUGARED BACON ❧

This is one of my favorite brunch items, and it is simply addictive. Maple sugar can be found at many stores in the baking or breakfast section, but brown sugar can be substituted.

8 strips bacon

3 tablespoons and 2 teaspoons maple sugar

Preheat oven to 350 degrees. Line a baking sheet with heavy-duty aluminum foil. Arrange bacon on baking sheet and cook for 10 minutes. Transfer bacon to a dish and drain off the fat. Dust bacon with maple sugar (or, if preparing a large amount of bacon, roll bacon in a pie plate filled with maple sugar). Return to baking sheet and cook until crisp and browned, about 10 minutes. Cool on a wire rack for about 5 minutes. Serve immediately.

Yield: 4 servings

໑ ON-THE-FARM ໑ BLUEBERRY-TOPPED PANCAKES

2 cups pancake mix

1⅓ cups milk

¼ cup vegetable oil

2 eggs, lightly beaten

2 cups blueberries

Blueberry syrup for topping

Whipped cream for topping

In bowl, mix pancake mix, milk, oil, and eggs. Pour batter onto hot griddle. When pancakes are set (they will bubble on top), flip and cook on other side. Place in stacks, and evenly divide blueberries among servings. Top with syrup and dollops of whipped cream. Serve with sausage on the side.

Yield: 6 to 8 generous stacks

❧ BANANA AND PINEAPPLE ❧
FRITTERS

2 eggs

¼ teaspoon ground cinnamon

⅛ teaspoon ground nutmeg

2 cups bread crumbs (preferably brioche or French bread)

2 bananas, cut into 1-inch slices

1 (15-ounce) can pineapple rings, drained and halved

Vegetable oil

Honey

In shallow bowl, whisk eggs with cinnamon and nutmeg. Place bread crumbs in a pan. Dip bananas and pineapple in egg mixture and coat with crumbs. Drop into oil, heated to 375 degrees, and cook until brown on all sides. Drain well and drizzle with honey.

Yield: 8 to 10 fritters

❧ SAUSAGE QUICHE ❧

1 cup crumbled fresh sausage, such as Olde Delaney's

1 cup shredded Cheddar cheese

¼ cup chopped green onion

1 9-inch pie crust, unbaked

3 eggs

1½ cups half-and-half

½ teaspoon salt

¼ teaspoon cayenne pepper

Brown sausage and drain. Preheat oven to 400 degrees. Sprinkle sausage, cheese, and green onion in pie crust. Beat eggs lightly with half-and-half, salt, and cayenne pepper. Pour egg mixture over sausage mixture. Bake for 35 to 40 minutes or until a knife inserted into the center comes out clean. Let stand for 10 minutes. Serve with sliced tomatoes or fresh fruit on the side.

Yield: 6 servings

Note: Olde Delaney's sausage can be found at Olde Delaney's Grocery in Bardstown, Kentucky.

∾ APPLE PECAN PANCAKE ∾

3 tablespoons butter

½ cup pecan pieces

2 large apples, peeled and coarsely chopped

⅓ cup dark brown sugar, packed

1 teaspoon ground cinnamon

3 large eggs, beaten

1¼ cups milk

1 teaspoon baking powder

1 cup flour

Powdered sugar

Preheat oven to 400 degrees. In an iron or a very heavy skillet, melt 2 tablespoons butter and toast pecans until brown. Remove from pan. In the same pan, sauté apples, sugar, and cinnamon over medium-low heat until apples are very tender, about 6 to 8 minutes. Add pecans and continue to cook, stirring constantly, for 2 minutes. Add 1 tablespoon butter, stir, and remove from heat.

Combine eggs, milk, baking powder, and flour, and stir or whisk until just blended. Pour batter over apples, and bake until golden brown and puffy, about 20 minutes. Dust with powdered sugar and serve warm.

Yield: 4 servings

❧ RANCHER'S STYLE ❧ EGG SCRAMBLE

2 cups chopped tomatoes

2 teaspoons mashed garlic

1 small dried arbol chili

6 tablespoons olive oil

2 large potatoes, peeled, shredded, and drained well on paper towels

½ onion, sliced

½ teaspoon salt

½ teaspoon dried oregano, crushed

6 small corn tortillas

Butter

6 eggs

In blender, puree tomatoes, garlic, and arbol chili until smooth. In medium saucepan, heat 2 tablespoons oil and brown potatoes until crisp. Remove from pan. In same pan, sauté onion for 2 minutes. To onion, add tomato sauce, salt, and oregano. Cook over medium heat for 3 to 4 minutes. Reduce heat to lowest simmer.

Fry tortillas in 4 tablespoons oil and drain. Evenly divide potatoes among tortillas. In butter, fry eggs over easy and place 1 on each tortilla. Top with tomato sauce.

Yield: 6 servings

❧ CECILIA SECORD'S ❧
CREAM PUFFS SUPREME
WITH BLUEBERRIES

Dough

1 cup water

½ cup (1 stick) butter or margarine

1 cup flour

4 eggs

Filling

½ cup sugar

¼ cup plus 1 tablespoon flour

2 cups milk

2 egg yolks, lightly beaten

1 teaspoon vanilla extract

2 cups blueberries

Powdered sugar

Preheat oven to 400 degrees. To make dough, in small saucepan, bring water and butter to a rolling boil, about 1 minute. Remove from heat. Stir in flour and beat in eggs. Transfer to large mixing bowl and continue to beat dough until smooth. Drop by scant ¼ cupfuls onto ungreased baking sheet, 3 inches apart. Bake for 35 to 40 minutes or until puffed and golden. Allow to cool away from drafts.

To make filling, mix sugar and flour, and add milk and egg yolks. In double boiler, cook until smooth and thick, stirring constantly, about 10 minutes. Cool. Add vanilla extract.

To assemble cream puffs, cut off tops with sharp knife. Spoon in filling and blueberries. Place tops over filling and dust with powdered sugar.

Yield: 18 cream puffs

∾ FRIED CORNMEAL MUSH ∾

1 teaspoon salt

3 cups water

⅔ cup white cornmeal

Flour

Vegetable oil

Melted butter for topping

Maple syrup for topping

Grease a loaf pan. In heavy saucepan, add salt to water and bring to a boil over medium heat. Sprinkle in cornmeal, stirring occasionally. When cornmeal becomes thick, reduce heat and cook for 30 to 40 minutes, stirring occasionally. Remove from heat, pour into loaf pan, and smooth the surface with spatula. After mixture cools, cover with plastic wrap and refrigerate for several hours or overnight until very firm.

When ready to serve, cut dough into ¾-inch slices and dredge in flour. In skillet, brown in oil. Top with melted butter and maple syrup.

Yield: 6 servings

❧ APPLE BROWN BETTY ❧

4 cups bread crumbs

½ cup (1 stick) butter, melted

4 medium Granny Smith apples, peeled and thinly sliced

⅓ cup light brown sugar, firmly packed

1 tablespoon fresh lemon juice

1 teaspoon ground cinnamon

½ teaspoon ground ginger

Whipped cream

Preheat oven to 375 degrees. Lightly grease a 2-quart casserole with butter. Stir together bread crumbs and butter, and set aside. Combine remaining ingredients, except whipped cream, and mix until well blended. Spread half the bread crumbs on bottom of casserole and cover with half the apple mixture. Layer the remaining crumbs and apples. Cover with aluminum foil and bake for 30 minutes. Remove foil and bake for 30 minutes. Top with whipped cream.

Yield: 6 servings

↷ SAUSAGE SOUTHWESTERN CREPES ↷ WITH HOLLANDAISE SAUCE

This one takes some time, but it's certainly worth it!

Filling

1 pound ground sweet sausage

1 small onion, diced

1 red bell pepper, seeded and diced

2 cups shiitake mushrooms, sliced

⅓ cup finely chopped cilantro

5 eggs

6 egg whites

¼ cup milk

1 cup shredded Cheddar cheese

Salt and pepper to taste

Hollandaise Sauce

6 egg yolks

¾ cup (1½ sticks) butter

Juice of 2 lemons

Crepes

1 cup flour

1 egg

2 cups milk

1 pinch paprika

1 (16-ounce) jar salsa

To make filling, cook sausage over medium heat in large skillet. When sausage is half cooked through, drain off most of the fat. Add onion, red pepper, mushrooms, and cilantro. Cook until vegetables are tender and sausage is browned. Remove sausage and vegetables from pan, leaving a slight coating of oil.

Whisk together eggs, egg whites, milk, and cheese, and season with salt and pepper. Pour into skillet in which sausage was browned and cook over medium-high heat, stirring occasionally, until eggs are set. Remove from heat but keep warm.

To make Hollandaise sauce, combine egg yolks, butter, and lemon juice in double boiler over medium heat. Whisk continuously and watch the heat so eggs will not curdle. Remove from burner when butter has completely melted.

To make crepes, whisk together flour, egg, and milk in mixing bowl. Pour mixture through a fine sieve to eliminate lumps. Heat a nonstick crepe pan on medium-high heat. Spray with nonstick cooking spray and pour about ⅓ cup batter into the pan. Rotate to spread a paper-thin amount of batter around the pan. Flip when crepe starts to bubble and cook until golden on both sides. Repeat until all batter is used.

To assemble crepes, spoon egg and sausage filling down middle of each crepe, fold over to form a semicircle, top with Hollandaise sauce, and sprinkle with paprika. Serve with salsa on the side.

Yield: 6 to 8 servings

❧ CARAMEL APPLE–FILLED CREPES ❧

Filling

2 large apples, peeled and thinly sliced

¼ cup sugar

2 tablespoons butter

Few drops vanilla extract

Crepes

4 eggs

2½ cups milk

2 cups flour

2 tablespoons sugar

Pinch of salt

Vegetable oil (for pan)

Topping

Caramel syrup

Powdered sugar

Sweetened whipped cream

Caramel sprinkles

To make filling, toss apples with sugar. In nonstick pan, melt butter, add apples, and sauté until soft. Add vanilla extract. Set aside.

To make crepes, beat eggs with milk, and add flour, sugar, and salt. Give the batter a few swift strokes to avoid lumping. Heat a 6-inch nonstick pan almost to the smoking point, add a few drops of oil, and pour in just enough batter to coat the bottom of the pan. Allow the crepe to brown, then flip. Repeat until all batter is used.

To assemble crepes, lay them out on a work surface, place some apple filling in the middle of each, and roll. Reheat in oven or serve immediately. Drizzle with caramel syrup and dust with powdered sugar. Garnish with whipped cream and caramel sprinkles, if desired.

Yield: 10 crepes

∾ BREAKFAST IN A BLENDER ∾

1 ripe peach or banana

½ cup milk

½ cup regular or light yogurt

1 teaspoon honey or maple syrup

1 tablespoon bran cereal or wheat germ

In blender or food processor, combine ingredients and blend until smooth. Pour into a tall glass and serve immediately.

Yield: 1 serving

∾ BREAKFAST TORTILLA ROLL UPS ∾

6 slices Canadian bacon or thinly sliced ham, cut into thin strips

2 cups hash brown potatoes

2 cups Egg Beaters

6 tablespoons salsa

6 large flour tortillas, warmed

In skillet coated with cooking spray, brown Canadian bacon or ham and hash browns. In bowl, combine Egg Beaters and salsa, and pour into skillet. Stir until thoroughly cooked. Spoon filling down middle of each tortilla and roll up.

Yield: 6 servings

Sweets

Sweets

A cup of coffee, anyone?

 My daughter-in-law, Andrea Lewis, decided shortly after marrying my son, Christian, that she would fix him baked beans using a relative's special recipe with a secret ingredient. She set out to make her special beans and saw that the recipe called for three-quarters of a cup of coffee. She was not an experienced cook and certainly wasn't a coffee drinker, so she thought nothing of adding three-quarters of a cup of coffee grounds as the special ingredient. Like any young newlywed, my son ate the beans and crunched away. I wonder how long it took to get all the grounds out of his teeth.

The end of a meal is your chance to shine. Take advantage of some great ideas from this list of favorite sweet comfort foods, big-fuss items, and even healthy treats, such as Grilled Pineapple Slices, that will make kids of all ages think they are indulging to the max. Jeanne Kemper and Brenda White are two of our Kentucky State Fair winners who offer us Jam Cake and Angel Food Cake, respectively. They are part of Kentucky's "family of finalists" who took the 2007 state fair by storm. Jeanne has won the Spam, Refrigerated Pie Crust, and Archway Cookie contests and last year took the grand prize for the favorite cake class with her heart-shaped Sweetheart Chocolate Cake with Raspberry and Lemon Fillings. You'll find it here.

Who doesn't get a rush at the thought of Cannoli Cookies or Blueberry Pandowdy? And if you really want to dazzle guests, try the elegant Coeur à la Crème or end a barbeque with Tropical Rum-Flavored Bananas.

I've loved working my way through this category, and if I live to be a hundred I will never taste a cobbler with a topping as buttery and great as that for Quick-and-Easy Blackberry Cobbler. It's amazing how something so *quick and easy* can be so good. So grab a latte, loosen your belt, and enjoy!

✥ QUICK-AND-EASY ✥ BLACKBERRY COBBLER

This cobbler has absolutely the best topping I have ever tried.

1 cup flour

1½ cups sugar

1 teaspoon baking powder

½ teaspoon salt

6 tablespoons (¾ stick) cold butter

¼ cup boiling water

2 tablespoons cornstarch

¼ cup cold water

1 cup sugar

1 tablespoon lemon juice

4 cups blackberries

Preheat oven to 400 degrees. Line a baking sheet with aluminum foil. In large bowl, mix flour, ½ cup sugar, baking powder, and salt. Cut in butter until the mixture resembles coarse crumbs. Stir in boiling water just until mixture is evenly moist.

In separate bowl, dissolve cornstarch in cold water. Mix in 1 cup sugar, lemon juice, and blackberries. Transfer to a cast-iron skillet and bring to a boil, stirring frequently. Drop dough by the spoonful into the skillet. Place skillet on baking sheet. Bake for 25 minutes, until dough is golden brown.

Yield: 6 to 8 servings

✑ RASPBERRY PUDDING ✑

3 cups raspberries, fresh or frozen

¼ cup sugar

1 tablespoon unflavored gelatin

2 teaspoons lemon juice

4 cups whipped cream, whipped until soft peaks form and
   then refrigerated

Fresh mint for garnish

In saucepan, combine raspberries and sugar. Cook over medium heat, stirring, until mixture turns to liquid. Remove from heat and stir in gelatin. Scrape into a large bowl. Cool for 10 minutes. Remove whipped cream from refrigerator and mix 1 cup with raspberry mixture until combined. Fold in remaining whipped cream and chill. Serve in pretty, tall glasses and garnish with fresh mint.

Yield: 4 servings

✥ RASPBERRY AND WHITE ✥ CHOCOLATE PARFAITS

12 ounces cream cheese, softened

1 cup heavy cream

6 ounces white chocolate, coarsely chopped

3 cups raspberries

20 gingersnaps, coarsely crushed

Raspberries for garnish

Fresh mint for garnish

With an electric mixer on medium speed, beat together cream cheese and cream until smooth, about 15 seconds. In double boiler, melt half of the white chocolate pieces, reserving the rest. Add melted chocolate to cream cheese mixture and stir until blended.

In 6 tall glasses, layer 2 tablespoons raspberries, 2 tablespoons cream cheese mixture, one-third of remaining chocolate pieces, and 1 tablespoon crushed cookies. Repeat layering twice, ending with cream cheese mixture. Garnish with a few raspberries and mint sprigs, and refrigerate for 2 hours.

Yield: 6 servings

❧ DELUXE BANANA ICE CREAM ❧

6 egg yolks

2 cups milk

2 cups heavy cream

½ cup plus 2 tablespoons sugar

½ teaspoon ground nutmeg

2 large ripe bananas, mashed

1 teaspoon vanilla extract

¼ teaspoon salt

Beat egg yolks with a whisk until well blended. In saucepan, combine milk, cream, sugar, and nutmeg. Cook over medium heat, stirring constantly, until sugar is dissolved and small bubbles form along sides of pan. Stir in bananas. Add a little of the milk mixture to the egg yolks, whisking constantly, to bring the temperature of the eggs up gradually and prevent curdling. Whisk in a little more of the milk mixture and finish by adding the egg mixture to the remaining milk mixture, whisking constantly. Cook over medium heat, stirring constantly, until the custard coats the back of a spoon, 3 to 5 minutes. Remove pan from heat and set in an ice bath. Add vanilla extract and salt. When cool, remove pan from the ice bath and refrigerate for several hours, to allow flavors to blend. Pour custard into an ice cream maker and process according to the manufacturer's instructions. Transfer to a plastic container after ice cream is processed.

Yield: 6 servings
Note: The custard may be made and refrigerated
the night before it is made into ice cream.

✌ FROZEN CHOCOLATE BANANAS ✌

8 bananas

16 ounces semisweet chocolate chips

4 tablespoons (½ stick) butter

8 wooden sticks

Peanuts or cashews, crushed, or sprinkles

Line a cookie sheet with waxed paper. Cut off one end of each banana and insert a wooden stick into the banana, until half the stick remains outside. Place bananas on cookie sheet and freeze for 1 hour.

In a double boiler, melt chocolate and butter over simmering water until melted. Dip bananas, one at a time, in chocolate and turn to coat completely. Roll each banana in crushed nuts or sprinkles. Place bananas on cookie sheet and freeze until chocolate hardens.

Yield: 8 pops

⚘ TROPICAL RUM-FLAVORED ⚘ BANANAS

This is also a great dish cooked on the grill if you have one that lets you control temperature. A great ending to an outdoor meal.

4 ripe bananas

¼ cup light brown sugar

5 teaspoons butter, cut into pieces

1¼ cups orange juice

2 to 3 teaspoons rum flavoring

Vanilla ice cream

Maraschino cherries for garnish

Preheat oven to 350 degrees. Grease baking dish. Place bananas in baking dish. Sprinkle with sugar and dot with butter. Mix orange juice with rum flavoring and pour around bananas. Bake for 20 minutes. Serve with ice cream topped with cherries.

Yield: 4 servings

⚘ GRILLED PINEAPPLE SLICES ⚘

1 fresh pineapple, or 8 slices canned pineapple

½ cup light brown sugar

¼ cup lime juice

¼ cup honey

1 (8-ounce) container whipped cream cheese

If using a whole pineapple, remove skin, core, and slice. In saucepan, heat sugar, lime juice, and honey over medium heat until sugar dissolves. Place pineapple slices over hot coals and grill for 2 to 4 minutes on each side, basting several times with honey-lime mixture. Remove from heat onto platter. Drizzle remaining honey-lime mixture over pineapple and top each slice with a spoonful of cream cheese.

Yield: 8 servings

↬ CREAM CHEESE POUND CAKE ↬

¾ cup (1½ sticks) butter

1 (8-ounce) package cream cheese

1½ cups sugar

4 eggs

1½ teaspoons vanilla extract

2 cups flour

1½ teaspoons baking powder

Fresh fruit for topping

Preheat oven to 350 degrees. Grease and flour a large tube or Bundt pan. In a mixing bowl, cream butter, cream cheese, and sugar together until light in color and very fluffy. Add remaining ingredients and beat until smooth.

If using small pans, divide batter evenly between prepared pans. Bake for 1 hour or until a toothpick inserted into the center comes out clean. The top of cake should be golden brown and will crack. Cool for 10 minutes in pan and turn out onto cake rack. Cool completely before slicing. Top slices with fresh fruit.

Yield: 10 to 12 servings

❧ BLACKBERRY TRIFLE ❧

1 (11-ounce) frozen pound cake

⅔ cup blackberry jam or preserves

3 cups blackberries

3 kiwifruits, peeled and cut into chunks

2 peaches, peeled and cut into chunks

2 cups milk

8 egg yolks

¾ cup sugar

1 teaspoon vanilla extract

1 cup heavy cream

2 tablespoons powdered sugar

Blackberries for garnish

Cut pound cake to cover bottom of trifle bowl. Spread cake with jam (heating jam briefly will make it easier to spread). Place blackberries, kiwis, and peaches on top of cake.

In double boiler, heat milk over medium-low heat until film forms. Beat egg yolks with sugar and vanilla extract until mixture forms a ribbon. Slowly pour hot milk into egg mixture, beating constantly. In heavy saucepan, cook mixture over low heat, stirring, until the custard coats the back of a spoon. Don't let it boil. Strain through a fine sieve and cool in a bowl set in ice water. Pour cooled custard over the fruit-topped cake and refrigerate, covered, for 4 hours.

Whip cream until soft peaks form and beat in powdered sugar. Continue to beat until stiff. Spread over the trifle and garnish with blackberries.

Yield: 6 to 8 servings

❧ CHOCOLATE CINNAMON ❧ PUDDING

1 cup heavy cream

8 ounces dark chocolate, grated or finely crushed

¾ teaspoon ground cinnamon

1 tablespoon unsweetened cocoa powder

In small saucepan, heat ⅓ cup cream over low heat until it is just about to boil. Mix chocolate and cinnamon, pour cream over chocolate mixture, and stir gently until chocolate melts. Set aside.

With electric mixer, beat remaining cream until stiff peaks form. Using a wooden spoon, blend chocolate with cocoa very gently into whipped cream. Refrigerate for several hours before serving.

Yield: 4 servings

❧ ORANGE-SLICE CAKE ❧

Cake

½ cup vegetable shortening

½ cup (1 stick) margarine

2 cups sugar

4 eggs

2 teaspoons vanilla extract

3 ¼ cups plus 1 tablespoon flour

1 teaspoon baking soda

1 cup buttermilk

2 cups chopped pecans

1 (16-ounce) package candied orange slices, chopped

Glaze

½ cup orange juice

1 cup light brown sugar

Preheat oven to 300 degrees. Grease and flour a tube pan. Cream together shortening, margarine, and sugar. Beat until light and fluffy. Add eggs, one at a time, beating well after each addition. Add vanilla. Sift together 3 ¼ cups flour and baking soda. Alternately, add buttermilk and flour mixture to egg mixture and mix well. Toss pecans and orange pieces in 1 tablespoon flour (to prevent settling to the bottom of cake), and fold into batter. Bake for 1½ hours or until well done. Let sit for 30 minutes or until pan is lukewarm.

To make glaze, heat orange juice and sugar in small saucepan until sugar is dissolved. Drizzle over top of cake.

Yield: 16 servings

✎ HOLIDAY GINGERBREAD ✎

½ cup crystallized ginger

2 ¼ cups unbleached flour

½ teaspoon baking soda

¼ teaspoon salt

¼ teaspoon pepper

1 teaspoon ground ginger

1 teaspoon ground cinnamon

¼ teaspoon ground nutmeg

¼ teaspoon ground cloves

6 tablespoons (¾ stick) butter

½ cup dark brown sugar, firmly packed

½ cup molasses

¼ cup water

¼ cup coffee, strongly brewed

2 eggs, lightly beaten

Powdered sugar for garnish

Caramel syrup for garnish

Grease an 8-inch-square cake pan. In food processor, process crystallized ginger until pureed or chop ginger very fine with a knife. In a bowl, sift together flour, baking soda, salt, pepper, ground ginger, cinnamon, nutmeg, and cloves. Set aside.

Melt the butter over low heat and stir in sugar, molasses, water, and coffee. Transfer to a large bowl and beat in ginger puree and eggs. Add flour mixture and stir only until thoroughly moistened and evenly colored.

Preheat oven to 350 degrees. Bake for 45 to 50 minutes or until a toothpick inserted into the center comes out clean. Let cool until warm or room temperature. When ready to serve, cut into squares, sprinkle with powdered sugar, and drizzle caramel syrup around gingerbread squares.

Yield: 9 squares

↬ SWEETHEART CHOCOLATE CAKE ↬ WITH RASPBERRY AND LEMON FILLINGS

Jeanne Kemper sums up her culinary experience for us:
"Entering contests is a constant learning process, as I'm always
trying new recipes and techniques from year to year. I begin
planning for the following year immediately after each fair. I'm
always on the lookout for something new and different as well
as sticking to the tried-and-true favorites."

Cake

2 ½ cups sifted flour

1 teaspoon baking powder

2 teaspoons baking soda

⅔ cup cocoa powder

¼ teaspoon salt

1 cup vegetable oil

1 cup sour cream

1½ teaspoons vanilla extract

2 cups sugar

2 eggs

1 cup milk

Raspberry Filling

1 (10-ounce) package frozen raspberries

¼ cup water

3 tablespoons flour

½ cup sugar

1 tablespoon butter

Lemon Filling

⅔ cup sugar

¼ cup flour

¾ cup water

2 egg yolks, lightly beaten

1 teaspoon grated lemon zest

3 tablespoons lemon juice

1 tablespoon butter

Icing

4 ounces unsweetened chocolate squares

6 tablespoons (¾ stick) butter

1 pound powdered sugar, sifted

1½ teaspoons vanilla extract

⅓ cup milk

Preheat oven to 350 degrees. Grease and flour 2 9-inch cake pans (I used heart-shaped pans rather than round).

Sift together flour, baking powder, baking soda, cocoa powder, and salt. Add oil, sour cream, vanilla extract, sugar, and eggs. Beat, starting slowly, then with more vigor, until blended. Add milk and continue to beat until batter is smooth and well blended. Divide between the pans and bake for 25 to 30 minutes, until a toothpick inserted into the center comes out clean. Cool and remove from pans.

To make raspberry filling, combine ingredients in saucepan and cook over medium heat, stirring constantly, until thickened. Set aside to cool.

To make lemon filling, combine sugar and flour in saucepan, and add water. Stir in egg yolks, lemon zest, and lemon juice. Cook over medium heat, stirring constantly, until thickened and bubbly. Add butter and set aside to cool, without stirring.

To make icing, in saucepan, melt chocolate and butter over low heat, stirring. Remove from heat. In bowl, combine remaining ingredients and stir until blended. Beat in chocolate mixture until blended to spreading consistency. If too thick to spread, add milk; if too thin, add more sugar, beaten in a little at a time.

To assemble cake, carefully cut cake layers to make 4 thin layers. Put 1 layer on a serving plate. Spread with half the raspberry filling, to about ½ inch from the edge. Top with second layer and spread with lemon filling. (You will not need it all and can save the rest for another dessert.) Top with third layer and spread with the remaining raspberry filling. Top with fourth layer and frost top and sides of cake with icing. Decorate as you wish.

Yield: 10 to 12 servings

❧ RED VELVET CAKE ❧

This is a favorite at my house and one I traditionally bake for Valentine's Day. Also, this is my favorite frosting. My daughter, Noélle, prefers this recipe made into cupcakes.

Cake

2 ½ cups flour

2 tablespoons plus 1 teaspoon unsweetened cocoa powder

1 teaspoon baking soda

½ teaspoon salt

1 cup buttermilk

1 tablespoon red food coloring

1 cup (2 sticks) butter

1½ cups sugar

3 large eggs

1½ teaspoons vanilla extract

1 tablespoon white vinegar

Icing

¼ cup plus 2 tablespoons flour

1 cup water

1 cup (2 sticks) butter

1 cup sugar

1 teaspoon vanilla extract

Preheat oven to 350 degrees. Grease and flour 2 9-inch cake pans.

Sift together flour, cocoa, baking soda, and salt. In separate bowl, combine buttermilk and food coloring. In another bowl, cream together butter and sugar. Add eggs, one at a time, and beat thoroughly. To egg mixture, alternate adding flour mixture and buttermilk mixture, a little at a time, until incorporated. Add vanilla extract and vinegar, and beat until batter is smooth and evenly colored.

Bake for 30 minutes or until a toothpick inserted into the center comes out clean. Cool in pans for 10 minutes. Turn out onto cake racks and cool completely before frosting.

To make icing, cook flour and water until slightly clear. Cool completely. Cream remaining ingredients and add to flour mixture. With electric mixer, beat until light and fluffy. Frost bottom layer, top, and sides of cake with icing.

Yield: 12 to 16 servings

❧ ALMOND MACAROONS ❧

2 egg whites

¾ cup sugar

1 cup ground almonds

1½ tablespoons cocoa powder

2 teaspoons grated lemon zest

¾ teaspoon vanilla extract

Pinch of salt

Preheat oven to 300 degrees. Grease a cookie sheet.

Beat egg whites until stiff. Add sugar and continue to beat until stiff peaks form. Gently fold in remaining ingredients. Drop by teaspoonfuls onto cookie sheet, 1 inch apart. Let stand for 30 minutes. Bake for 30 minutes. Be very careful when transferring macaroons to a cooling tray, so they will not fall apart. Cool completely and store in airtight tin.

Yield: about 24 macaroons

❧ RICE PUDDING SOUTHERN STYLE ❧

2 ½ cups water

½ cup uncooked long-grain rice

1 cinnamon stick

1 teaspoon grated lemon zest

Dash of salt

1 (14-ounce) can sweetened condensed milk

Dash of ground cinnamon for garnish

In medium saucepan, combine water, rice, cinnamon stick, lemon zest, and salt. Let stand for 30 minutes. Bring mixture to a boil over medium heat, stirring constantly. Add condensed milk and return to a boil, stirring constantly. Reduce heat and cook uncovered, stirring frequently, for about 20 minutes or until liquid is absorbed. Remove from heat and allow to cool completely. Pudding will thicken as it cools. Remove cinnamon stick. When ready to serve, at either room temperature or chilled, sprinkle with ground cinnamon.

Yield: 6 to 8 servings

ꙮ MERRY CHRISTMAS CAKE ꙮ

Cake

3 cups flour

1½ cups sugar

1 cup mayonnaise

1 (16-ounce) can whole-berry cranberry sauce

⅓ cup orange juice

1 tablespoon grated orange peel

1 teaspoon baking soda

1 teaspoon salt

1 cup chopped walnuts

Glaze

2 tablespoons orange juice

1½ cups powdered sugar

Preheat oven to 350 degrees. Grease and flour a 10-inch tube pan. In bowl, combine ingredients, except walnuts, and mix well. Fold in walnuts. Bake for 60 to 65 minutes or until a toothpick inserted into the center comes out clean. Cool in pan for 12 minutes before turning out onto a wire rack.

To make glaze, combine orange juice and powdered sugar, and drizzle over warm cake.

Yield: 12 to 16 servings

ᏍᎧ AFTER-DINNER ᏍᎧ
CAPPUCCINO DESSERT

4 teaspoons instant-coffee granules

¼ cup hazelnut or caramel syrup

1 teaspoon vanilla extract

2 scoops vanilla ice cream for topping

Chocolate shavings for garnish

Bring 2 cups water to a boil. Pour coffee granules into water and add syrup and vanilla extract. Divide between two mugs. Top each mug with a scoop of ice cream, garnish with chocolate shavings, and serve immediately.

Yield: 2 servings

ᏍᎧ BRENDA WHITE'S ᏍᎧ
ANGEL FOOD CAKE

Brenda White is one of the state fair winners. This great Kentucky cook writes, "I love all the holidays, but my favorite is Christmas. We all get together and have a wonderful time. We have lots of gifts and lots of good food. The kids love my chocolate chip cookies. They call me Aunt B. This makes me very happy!"

1½ cups powdered sugar

1 cup flour

1½ cups egg whites (10–12 large eggs), at room temperature

1½ teaspoons cream of tartar

1 teaspoon vanilla extract

1 cup sugar

Preheat oven to 350 degrees, with rack at lowest position.

Sift together powdered sugar and flour, 3 times. In large bowl, with an electric mixer on medium speed, beat egg whites, cream of tartar, and vanilla extract until soft peaks form. Gradually add sugar, about 2 tablespoons at a time, beating until stiff peaks form. Sift about one-quarter of the flour mixture over egg white mixture and fold in gently. Repeat folding in remaining flour mixture by quarters. Bake in an ungreased 10-inch tube pan for 40 minutes. Leaving cake in pan, immediately invert and cool completely.

Yield: 10 to 12 servings

BANANA POPS

National Honey Board

1⅓ cups topping (toasted and ground almonds, toasted coconut, sprinkles, or graham cracker crumbs)

4 just-ripe bananas, halved crosswise

½ cup honey

8 wooden sticks

Line a cookie sheet with waxed paper. Spread toppings of your choice on a plate or plates. Insert a wooden stick into the cut end of each banana, until half the stick remains outside. Holding each banana over plate or waxed paper to catch drips, spoon about 1 tablespoon honey over banana, rotating and smoothing honey with back of spoon to coat. Roll banana in topping until coated, pressing with fingertips to help topping adhere. Place finished pops on cookie sheet. Serve immediately.

Yield: 8 pops

❧ APPLE CUSTARD ❧

6 small apples, thinly sliced

2 large eggs

½ cup 1 percent milk

½ cup plus 1 tablespoon sugar

¼ cup reduced-fat sour cream

3 tablespoons flour

½ teaspoon vanilla extract

½ teaspoon almond extract

Pinch of salt

1 tablespoon sliced almonds

Preheat oven to 350 degrees. Coat a 10-inch glass pie plate with nonstick cooking spray. Arrange apples in pie plate. With an electric mixer on medium speed, beat eggs until frothy. Add milk, ½ cup sugar, sour cream, flour, vanilla and almond extracts, and salt. Continue to beat until well blended, about 2 minutes. Pour over apples and sprinkle with 1 tablespoon sugar and almonds. Bake until puffed and lightly browned, about 45 minutes. Cut into wedges and serve warm.

Yield: 8 servings

❧ STRAWBERRY GELATO ❧

2 cups milk

2 cups heavy cream

6 egg yolks

1 cup sugar

1 pint strawberries, pureed

4 strawberries, cut into small pieces

In medium saucepan, heat milk and cream until scalded. Remove from heat. In small bowl, whisk egg yolks and sugar. Temper egg yolks by adding slowly to cream mixture, whisking constantly to prevent curdling. Return to medium heat and cook, stirring constantly, until mixture reaches 160 degrees and is thick and creamy. Remove from heat and add strawberry puree and pieces. Refrigerate for several hours before pouring into an ice cream maker and processing according to the manufacturer's instructions. Transfer to a plastic container after ice cream is processed.

Yield: 4 to 6 servings

↔ COCONUT PINEAPPLE ICE CREAM ↔

½ cup heavy cream

1½ cups unsweetened coconut milk

1 cup milk

½ cup sugar

6 large egg yolks

½ cup crushed pineapple, undrained

½ cup grated unsweetened coconut, toasted

In large saucepan, combine cream, coconut milk, milk, and sugar. Bring to a simmer over medium heat, stirring constantly to dissolve sugar. Remove from heat. Beat egg yolks until pale yellow and frothy. Add ½ cup coconut milk mixture to eggs and whisk to combine. Add egg mixture to remaining coconut mixture in saucepan and whisk vigorously. Return to heat and simmer, stirring constantly, until mixture coats the back of a spoon. Strain through a fine sieve and refrigerate until well chilled. Pour into an ice cream maker, add pineapple and coconut, and process according to the manufacturer's instructions. Transfer to a plastic container after ice cream is processed.

Yield: 4 servings

❧ BETTY RUSSELL'S ❧ BUTTERSCOTCH PIE

Betty Russell gives us this fifty-year-old recipe, a delicious comfort dish for cold winter days.

Filling

2 cups light brown sugar

½ cup (1 stick) margarine

2 ½ cups milk

3 egg yolks

3 tablespoons flour

½ teaspoon salt

1 9-inch pie crust, baked

Meringue

3 egg whites

½ teaspoon cream of tartar

3 tablespoons sugar

1 teaspoon vanilla extract

Preheat oven to 400 degrees. In a microwave-safe glass bowl, combine sugar, margarine, and ½ cup milk. Cook for 5 minutes on high setting, stir, and cook for 5 minutes more. Mix egg yolks, flour, 2 cups milk, and salt. Gradually stir into brown sugar mixture. Microwave for a few minutes, until thick, stirring every 60 seconds. Pour into pie crust.

To make meringue, beat egg whites with cream of tartar until peaks form. Add sugar and vanilla extract, and continue to beat until blended, maintaining peaks. Spoon onto pie and brown the meringue in oven.

Yield: 8 servings

✂ YUMMY MICROWAVE ✂
CARAMEL CORN

1 cup light brown sugar

½ cup (1 stick) butter or margarine

½ cup corn syrup

½ teaspoon salt

½ teaspoon baking soda

4 quarts cooked popcorn

In 2-quart microwave-safe dish, combine sugar, butter or margarine, corn syrup, and salt. Microwave on high setting until mixture begins to boil. Continue to cook on high for 2 minutes. Remove from microwave and stir in baking soda. Mix well.

Pour popcorn into heavy brown bag. Pour hot syrup over popcorn and close bag. Shake well to coat popcorn. Make sure top is securely folded down. Microwave on high setting for 90 seconds and remove. Shake again and return to microwave. Cook 90 seconds more on high and remove. Pour into shallow buttered pan. Cool and break apart in clusters.

Yield: 8 servings

❧ VANILLA COCONUT POPS ❧

1 cup vanilla low-fat yogurt

½ cup fat-free milk

2 tablespoons unsweetened coconut, toasted

½ teaspoon vanilla extract

4 (3-ounce) paper cups

4 wooden sticks

In small bowl, combine ingredients and stir well. Pour into paper cups, cover with aluminum foil, and insert a stick through foil in center of each cup. Freeze until firm. When ready to serve, remove foil and peel paper cups away from pops.

Yield: 4 pops

❧ ZUCCHINI OATMEAL BARS ❧

This is a great healthy snack for kids' lunches.

½ cup raisins

1 cup boiling water

5 ⅓ tablespoons margarine, softened

½ cup light brown sugar

1 egg

1¼ cups grated zucchini

1 teaspoon ground cinnamon

¼ teaspoon ground nutmeg

½ teaspoon freshly grated lemon peel

1 cup whole-wheat flour

½ cup quick-cooking oats

1 teaspoon baking powder

1 teaspoon vanilla extract

1 tablespoon powdered sugar

Preheat oven to 350 degrees. Grease a 9 × 13-inch baking pan. In small bowl, cover raisins with boiling water. Soak for 15 minutes and drain.

In large bowl, cream margarine and sugar until light and fluffy. Beat in egg and stir in zucchini. Add cinnamon, nutmeg, and lemon peel, and mix well. Combine flour, oats, and baking powder, and add to zucchini mixture. Beat well until blended. Add vanilla extract and mix well. Stir in raisins.

Spread in baking pan. Bake for 20 to 25 minutes or until browned. Cool completely, sprinkle with powdered sugar, and cut into bars.

Yield: 24 bars

✍ CEREAL SNACK MERINGUES ✍

Another great healthy kids' snack.

3 egg whites

⅔ cup sugar

4 cups healthy cereal (I use Total)

½ cup semisweet chocolate chips (optional)

Preheat oven to 325 degrees. Coat cookie sheet with nonstick cooking spray. In medium cold bowl, beat egg whites and sugar until glossy. Fold in cereal and chocolate chips. Drop by tablespoonfuls onto cookie sheet, 2 inches apart. Bake for about 15 minutes or until golden brown. Cool completely. Store in airtight container.

Yield: 12 to 15 meringues

✌ FANCY FRUIT PIZZA WITH ✌ THREE-CHOCOLATE SAUCE

Three varieties of chocolate adorn this old favorite.

1 roll refrigerated sugar-cookie dough

1 (8-ounce) package cream cheese, softened

¼ cup powdered sugar

2 tablespoons orange juice

2 kiwifruits, peeled and sliced

1 pint strawberries, sliced lengthwise

1 cup canned peaches, well drained and thinly sliced

½ cup purple or red seedless grapes, halved

½ cup white chocolate chips, melted until smooth

½ cup semisweet chocolate chips, melted until smooth

½ cup milk chocolate chips, melted until smooth

Fresh mint for garnish

In large greased baking pan, roll out cookie dough in a 12-inch circle. Mix cream cheese, sugar, and orange juice until creamy. Spread over cookie dough and top with kiwis, strawberries, peaches, and grapes.

Melt chocolate chips separately in double boiler or in microwave in 30-second intervals. Drizzle over pizza. After chocolate cools, cut into pie slices or small appetizer pieces.

Yield: 12 servings

✑ CHOCOLATE HONEY BRULÉES ✑

*I received lots of mail when this recipe ran. The National
Honey Board always comes up with great ideas!*

1 (12-ounce) can evaporated milk

1 cup milk

2 eggs

½ cup honey

1 tablespoon cocoa powder

2 teaspoons grated orange peel

1 teaspoon vanilla extract

3 tablespoons sugar

Preheat oven to 325 degrees. In medium bowl, whisk together
evaporated milk, milk, and eggs until well blended. Mix in honey,
cocoa powder, orange peel, and vanilla. Divide mixture evenly into
4 ¾- to 1-cup ramekins. Place ramekins in baking pan and fill pan
with boiling water until halfway up the side of the ramekins. Bake
for 1 hour or until a knife inserted into the center comes out clean.
Remove ramekins from baking pan, cool, cover, and refrigerate for 4
hours or overnight. When ready to serve, sprinkle sugar evenly over
tops of custard and broil until sugar melts and caramelizes.

Yield: 4 servings

❧ QUICK CHEESECAKE BONBONS ❧

These make great little lollipops, too, when served as a sweet hors d'oeuvre.

1 large frozen cheesecake
16 ounces semisweet chocolate chips

Line cookie sheet with waxed paper. With a small melon baller, scoop out cheesecake. Place balls on cookie sheet and put in freezer.

In double boiler, melt chocolate chips and stir until smooth and glossy. Using a thin wooden skewer, dip cheesecake balls into melted chocolate, coating completely. Return bonbons to freezer for 20 minutes.

Yield: 30 bonbons

Note: If using assorted cheesecake flavors, drizzle white or tinted chocolate over the top, so guests know what flavors to choose.

❧ CHOCOLATE HAZELNUT ❧ ICE CREAM SAUCE

⅓ cup hazelnuts, toasted
1 cup heavy cream
1½ tablespoons orange liqueur
8 ounces semisweet chocolate chips
1 quart ice cream

In food processor, pulse hazelnuts until finely ground. In medium saucepan, heat cream and orange liqueur to a gentle boil. Remove from heat and add chocolate chips and hazelnuts. Whisk until chocolate melts. Cover to keep warm. When ready to serve, spoon over scoops of your favorite ice cream.

Yield: 1½ cups

❧ CHOCOLATE TRUFFLES ❧

A must-have recipe for holiday candy making.

8 ounces bittersweet chocolate, finely chopped

8 ounces semisweet chocolate, finely chopped

1 cup heavy cream

2 tablespoons coffee, brewed

1 tablespoon Grand Marnier or other flavoring (optional)

½ teaspoon vanilla extract

Powdered sugar

Cocoa powder

Line cookie sheet with waxed paper. Put chocolate in heat-proof mixing bowl. Heat cream until it begins to boil and pour over chocolate. Whisk slowly until chocolate melts. Whisk in coffee, Grand Marnier or other flavoring, and vanilla extract. Allow to sit at room temperature for 1 hour.

Spoon about 50 balls of the chocolate mixture onto cookie sheet. Refrigerate for about 1 hour. With hands, roll each spoonful of chocolate until round and cover in powdered sugar or cocoa powder. Store in refrigerator for up to 2 weeks.

Yield: about 50 truffles

❧ JEANNE KEMPER'S JAM CAKE ❧

*Christmas sounds great at Jeanne's house: "It's a family
tradition to have Christmas holidays at my house, and I love to
decorate the whole house for the occasion and bake jam cakes,
fruitcakes and cookies, and to make bourbon balls, fudge,
peanut brittle, or whatever else anyone desires. My family
consists of many wonderful cooks, so we always have a festive
feast and so much to be thankful for, especially me for my mom
starting me out making biscuits for the county fair so many
years ago."*

Cake

1 cup (2 sticks) butter

2 cups sugar

5 eggs, lightly beaten

3 cups flour, sifted

2 teaspoons ground cinnamon

½ teaspoon ground cloves

½ teaspoon ground allspice

¼ teaspoon ground nutmeg

¼ teaspoon salt

1 teaspoon baking soda

1 cup buttermilk

1 cup raisins

1 cup chopped walnuts

1½ cups seedless blackberry jam

Icing

1½ cups (3 sticks) butter or margarine

1½ cups light brown sugar, firmly packed

¼ cup milk

1½ teaspoons vanilla extract

3 cups powdered sugar

Preheat oven to 325 degrees. Grease and flour 3 9-inch cake pans.

Cream butter, gradually adding sugar, until light and fluffy. Add eggs. To sifted flour, add cinnamon, cloves, allspice, nutmeg, and salt. Dissolve baking soda in buttermilk and add to flour mixture. To butter mixture, add flour mixture, raisins, walnuts, and jam. Bake for 25 minutes. Cool and remove from pans.

To make icing, melt butter in saucepan over low heat. Stir in brown sugar and bring to a boil over medium heat, stirring constantly for 2 minutes. Remove from heat. Stir in milk and return to heat, just until mixture comes to a full boil. Allow to cool until lukewarm. Add vanilla extract and beat in powdered sugar until smooth. Add a little milk or powdered sugar to icing until it reaches spreading consistency. Frost bottom and middle layers, top, and sides of cake.

Yield: 12 to 15 servings

❦ HOT APPLE CAKE ❦

1 cup (2 sticks) butter, softened

1 cup sugar

2 eggs, lightly beaten

1½ cups flour

½ teaspoon freshly grated nutmeg

1 teaspoon ground cinnamon

1 teaspoon baking soda

½ teaspoon salt

3 medium tart apples, chopped

¾ cup chopped walnuts

1 teaspoon vanilla extract

Vanilla ice cream for topping

Preheat oven to 350 degrees. Grease a 10-inch pie plate. With an electric mixer, cream butter and sugar together. Add eggs and beat well. In a separate bowl, sift together flour, nutmeg, cinnamon, baking soda, and salt. Blend into butter mixture. Add apples, walnuts, and vanilla, and mix well. Pour into pie plate and bake until lightly browned, about 45 minutes. Serve warm, topped with ice cream.

Yield: 6 to 8 servings

❦ BLUEBERRY PANDOWDY ❦

1½ cups heavy cream or half-and-half

2 cups flour

1½ tablespoons baking powder

2 teaspoons salt

4 pints blueberries

¼ cup sugar

1 teaspoon ground cinnamon

½ teaspoon ground nutmeg

1 cup light molasses

4 tablespoons (½ stick) butter, cut into pieces

Whipped cream for topping

Preheat oven to 375 degrees. Whip cream or half-and-half until soft peaks form. In bowl, mix flour, baking powder, and salt. Fold whipped cream into flour mixture just until combined. Roll out dough on lightly floured surface to ½-inch thickness. Set aside.

Toss blueberries with sugar, cinnamon, and nutmeg. Pour into 9-inch baking dish, drizzle with molasses, and dot with butter. Carefully cover with dough and tuck dough into edges of mixture. Cut slits in dough to vent. Bake for 30 to 40 minutes or until golden brown. Serve warm, topped with whipped cream sweetened with molasses, if desired.

Yield: 6 to 8 servings

❧ MEXICAN FLAN ❧

*This is a Linda all-time favorite. I think that during my years
as a restaurant critic, I dreamed about great Mexican Flan
on a weekly basis. I love to try differently flavored flans—
especially pumpkin!*

1¼ cups sugar

2 tablespoons water

½ teaspoon fresh lemon juice

1 quart milk

6 large eggs

2 teaspoons vanilla extract

Preheat oven to 350 degrees, with rack in middle. Set an 8 × 8
× 2-inch glass baking dish next to the stove.

In small saucepan, combine ¾ cup sugar, water, and lemon
juice. Bring to a boil over medium-high heat and cook, swirling the
pan but not stirring, until sugar is amber-colored caramel. Remove
from heat and pour caramel into baking dish. Working quickly so
caramel does not harden, tilt and rotate the dish to coat the bottom
and sides. Set aside.

In medium saucepan, bring milk to a simmer over medium
heat, stirring occasionally. Whisk eggs with ½ cup sugar. Temper egg
mixture by adding hot milk to eggs a small amount at a time to prevent curdling. Whisk vigorously and add vanilla extract. Do not beat
mixture too much, or flan will have air bubbles. Pour egg mixture into
caramel-lined dish. Skim foam or bubbles from the surface.

Put a roasting pan in the oven and set flan in the center. Pour
enough hot water into the pan to reach halfway up the sides of the
baking dish, and tent loosely with aluminum foil. Bake for about
1 hour and 10 minutes, until flan is set around the edges but still
wobbles a bit in the center when the dish is shaken gently. On a rack,
cool flan in the water bath until the water reaches room temperature.
Remove flan from water and cool. Stretch and seal plastic wrap across

the top of the dish but not on the surface of the flan. Refrigerate for at least 4 hours and up to 2 days.

When ready to serve, gently pull edges of the flan away from the dish with fingertips. Invert a large, deep serving platter over the baking dish and flip. The flan should fall gently onto the platter, and caramel will flow over it. Cut into squares and serve with a spoonful of caramel drizzled around each piece.

Yield: 6 to 8 servings

✄ LIME MASCARPONE TRIFLE ✄

When I'm lucky enough to be cooking with lime and mascarpone cheese, it must be my birthday or Christmas or a day that is going to taste wonderful. Definitely two of my favorite ingredients!

1¾ cups sugar

2 tablespoons cornstarch

2 teaspoons lemon peel, either zest or finely shredded (not white part)

¼ cup lemon juice

1 teaspoon lime peel, either zest or finely shredded (not white part)

2 tablespoons lime juice

⅔ cup water

4 egg yolks, lightly beaten

4 tablespoons (½ stick) butter, cut into pieces

2 (8-ounce) packages mascarpone or cream cheese, softened

½ cup milk

1 (11-ounce) frozen pound cake, thawed and cubed

½ cup orange, pear, or peach juice

In medium saucepan, stir together 1 cup sugar, cornstarch, lemon peel, lemon juice, lime peel, lime juice, and water. Cook over medium heat, stirring, until thickened slightly and bubbly. Temper egg yolks by adding slowly to juice mixture to prevent curdling. Cook over medium heat until mixture comes to a gentle boil. Cook for 2 minutes and remove from heat. Add butter. Whisk until blended and cover curd with plastic wrap. Refrigerate for 2 hours.

With wooden spoon, beat together cheese, ¾ cup sugar, and milk until smooth. In trifle bowl or deep glass bowl, layer pound cake; orange, pear, or peach juice; cheese mixture; and curd. Repeat layers and refrigerate until ready to serve.

Yield: 8 servings

๛ CANNOLI COOKIES ๛

Filling

4 ½ cups ricotta cheese

1 cup sugar

1 tablespoon vanilla extract

¼ cup semisweet chocolate chips, coarsely chopped

Pastry Tubes

2 ½ cups flour

¼ cup sugar

1 teaspoon ground cinnamon

¼ teaspoon salt

¼ cup shortening

2 eggs, beaten

¼ cup cold water

2 tablespoons cider vinegar

1 egg white, lightly beaten

Vegetable oil

Powdered sugar

To make filling, combine cheese, sugar, and vanilla extract. Beat until smooth and fold in chocolate chips. Cover and refrigerate.

To make pastry tubes, combine flour, sugar, cinnamon, and salt. Cut in shortening until mixture is crumbly, the size of peas. Combine eggs, water, and vinegar. Add to flour mixture and stir until dough forms a ball. Divide in half and roll each half on a lightly floured surface to ⅛-inch thickness. Cut dough into 6 × 4-inch ovals. Do not try to roll leftover trimmings.

Starting with a long side, roll dough loosely on metal cannoli tubes. Moisten overlapping dough with egg white and press gently to seal. Fry in oil heated to 375 degrees for 1 to 2 minutes. Drain on paper towels. When cool, remove cannoli from tubes and continue to cool. One hour before serving, fill cannoli using a decorator's bag (or plastic bag with corner cut off) to squeeze cheese mixture into tubes. Sprinkle with powdered sugar.

Yield: 20 cookies

ᴄᴏ SPRINGERLE ᴄᴏ

These cookies were such a hit in our family bakeries when I was young. The taste is unmistakable and a favorite at holiday time. Recipes for springerle call for molds, but you can cut yours into squares and enjoy the same great cookie.

4 eggs

2 cups sugar

2 tablespoons butter

2 teaspoons baking powder

¼ teaspoon salt

4 cups flour

¼ cup aniseed

In large mixing bowl, beat eggs until very light. Add sugar and butter, and cream until light and fluffy. In another bowl, mix or sift together baking powder, salt, and flour. Combine with egg mixture. Knead dough until smooth, adding more flour if necessary. Cover and refrigerate for 2 hours.

Roll out dough on lightly floured surface to ⅓-inch thickness. Cut into 1½-inch squares. If you have a springerle mold, roll out a second time with mold and trim cookie around mold, removing cookie carefully. Sprinkle aniseed on clean, dry dish towel and place cookies on the seeds. Allow to stand overnight to dry, but do not cover.

Preheat oven to 325 degrees. Line a large cookie sheet with parchment paper. Carefully move cookies to cookie sheet and bake for 12 to 15 minutes. Cool completely and store in airtight tins. The anise flavor intensifies the longer the cookies are stored.

Yield: number of cookies varies, depending on size of molds

✍ BAKED FUDGE PUDDING ✍

This is one of the few recipes from Kentucky's Best *that I decided to include here. Many people have told me that it's a standby in their kitchens.*

2 eggs

1 cup sugar

2 tablespoons flour

2 tablespoons cocoa powder

½ cup (1 stick) butter, melted

½ cup chopped pecans

1 teaspoon vanilla extract

Dash of salt

Whipped cream for topping

Preheat oven to 300 degrees. In large bowl, beat eggs with sugar, flour, and cocoa powder. Mix well. Add butter, pecans, vanilla extract, and salt. Pour into 6 ramekins or a large baking dish, such as a 9 × 9-inch baking pan. Place ramekins or baking dish in a larger pan and fill pan with hot water until halfway up the side of the ramekins. Bake for 50 minutes. Refrigerate for several hours. When ready to serve, top with whipped cream.

Yield: 6 servings

ఴ BANANA CREAM PIE ఴ

As long as I can remember, this has been my mom's favorite dessert. Although different from her version, this one is quite good.

Crust

2 ½ cups graham cracker crumbs

⅓ cup sugar

¼ cup mashed banana

4 tablespoons (½ stick) butter, melted

Filling

½ cup sugar

⅓ cup cornstarch

¼ teaspoon salt

1½ cups heavy cream

1½ cups milk

3 large egg yolks, lightly beaten

½ vanilla bean, split lengthwise

2 tablespoons butter

1 teaspoon vanilla extract

5 ripe bananas, cut crosswise into ¼-inch slices

To make crust, stir graham cracker crumbs, sugar, and banana in large bowl to blend. Add butter and stir to moisten evenly. Press onto bottom and sides of a 10-inch glass pie dish. Refrigerate until firm, about 30 minutes. Preheat oven to 350 degrees. Bake crust until set and golden pale, about 15 minutes. Cool completely.

To make filling, whisk sugar, cornstarch, and salt in heavy, medium saucepan to blend. Gradually whisk in cream and milk, and then egg yolks. Scrape in seeds from vanilla bean and add vanilla bean. Cook over medium-high heat, whisking, until custard thickens and boils, about 6 minutes. Remove from heat. Whisk in butter and vanilla extract. Discard vanilla bean. Transfer custard to large bowl and cool completely, whisking occasionally, about 1 hour.

Spread 1 cup custard over bottom of crust. Top with half the banana slices and then 1 cup custard, covering bananas completely. Repeat layering with remaining custard and bananas. Refrigerate until filling is set and crust softens slightly, at least 8 hours and up to 1 day.

Yield: 8 servings

⌒ BLACK FOREST FUDGE TRIFLE ⌒

Have you ever made brownies that weren't quite done in the center or too done around the edges? This solution for fixing flops works wonderfully. Be creative with your choice of pie fillings and chips.

1 8 × 8-inch pan failed brownies, broken into pieces

1 can cherry pie filling

½ cup semisweet chocolate chips

1 (12-ounce) container whipped topping

In 6 to 8 tall glasses or a trifle bowl, layer brownie pieces, pie filling, a few chocolate chips, and whipped topping. Repeat layers, sprinkling a few chips over last layer of whipped topping.

Yield: 6 to 8 servings

✂ COEUR À LA CRÈME ✂

This beauty is time consuming but certainly worth the effort!
Make sure that all the ingredients are at room temperature.

2 cups cottage cheese

2 (8-ounce) packages cream cheese

1 cup sour cream

1 cup heavy cream

1 cup and 1 tablespoon sugar

Raspberries, strawberries, or sliced peaches (optional)

Line a Coeur à la Crème heart mold (or a disposable foil heart-shaped cake pan, with holes punched in it ¾ inch apart) with a double layer of cheesecloth that overhangs on the sides. Place the mold on a large plate.

In a food processor, process ingredients, except fruit, until mixture is smooth. Pour the mixture into the mold and, using a rubber spatula, smooth the top. Fold excess cheesecloth over the top and refrigerate for 24 hours. Place the mold over a bowl to catch the clear liquid or whey.

When ready to serve, unfold the cheesecloth and invert a serving plate over the mold. Flip the Coeur à la Crème onto the plate. Gently remove the mold and cheesecloth. Cut into squares and, if desired, serve with raspberries, strawberries, or sliced peaches.

Yield: 8 servings

Note: Coeur à la Crème ceramic molds are available
at gourmet food shops, but a disposable foil heart-shaped
cake pan works just as well.

Drinks

Drinks

"And the flames were this high!"

Same apartment . . . same roommates!

Although I could cook, I wasn't very good at deep frying. One time when it was my week to prepare the meals, I decided to fry Tater Tots on the stove in a skillet. It wasn't long before the oil caught fire, and the flames were about two feet above the stove. I grabbed the fire extinguisher, aimed it at the fire, and pulled the trigger. The hot oil shot everywhere! (No one had told me that there's a better way to put out a grease fire.)

Several months later, I was at an auction with a friend when a fire extinguisher was put up for sale. It reminded me of the incident with the Tater Tots, and I quietly told my friend the story of the grease fire, gesturing with my arm as I said, " . . . And the flames were this high!"

"SOLD!" said the auctioneer, who saw my arm up in the air to show the height of the flames.

Lynne Christenson, *Kentucky Living* staff

When serving food or entertaining, it can be very tempting to offer guests a soda or tea and coffee. Let the beverage choices fit the occasion or the season. And always think about serving a punch at a kids' party. There is just something they love about a big bowl, a ladle too big for their little hands, and getting to serve their own drink.

❧ WEDDING SHOWER ❧
PINK PUNCH

2 (46-ounce) bottles cran-raspberry juice

1 (32-ounce) box piña colada mix

1 (2-liter) bottle raspberry ginger ale, chilled

12 ounces raspberries, fresh or frozen

In large freezer-safe container, mix cran-raspberry juice and piña colada mix. Freeze overnight or up to 3 weeks. Remove from freezer half an hour before serving. Place frozen mixture in large punch bowl and add ginger ale and raspberries.

Yield: 20 servings

❧ MULLED-CIDER PUNCH ❧

2 small apples, peeled chopped

6 whole cloves

1 (4-inch) cinnamon stick

2 teaspoons ground ginger

2 tablespoons light brown sugar

¼ cup water

Juice of 1 small orange

1½ gallons good-quality apple cider

In large pot, combine ingredients and simmer for about 15 minutes. Remove cloves and cinnamon stick, and serve warm.

Yield: 12 to 16 servings

❧ MINT PUNCH ❧

1 cup water

1 cup sugar

Bunch of fresh mint

1 cup orange juice

3 (2-liter) bottles Sprite, chilled

Fresh mint for garnish

In pot, bring water and sugar to a boil. Cook until sugar is completely dissolved. Place mint in cheesecloth and pour sugar mixture over mint into 2-gallon container. Add orange juice. Let steep in refrigerator for at least 2 hours. The longer punch steeps, the stronger the mint flavor. When ready to serve, remove cheesecloth from punch and add Sprite. Pour over ice and garnish with fresh mint sprigs.

Yield: 2 gallons

❧ HARVEST PUNCH FOR A CROWD ❧

Goes great with pumpkin pie!

1 gallon apple cider

1 quart orange juice

1 cup lemon juice

1 quart pineapple juice

24 whole cloves

4 cinnamon sticks

1 cup sugar

In pot, mix ingredients and simmer for about 10 minutes. Remove cloves and cinnamon. May be reheated in mugs in the microwave.

Yield: 1½ gallons

❧ WHITE HOT CHOCOLATE ❧

1½ teaspoons vanilla powder

1 teaspoon dried orange peel

½ cup grated white chocolate

1½ cups milk

In small bowl, combine and blend ingredients. Store in an airtight container.

When ready to use, heat milk in small saucepan until bubbles form around the edge. Add white chocolate mix and whisk until chocolate melts. Continue to whisk until mixture is hot.

Yield: 2 servings

Note: Vanilla powder can be found in food specialty or cake-decorating stores or ordered online.

❧ STRAWBERRY COOLER ❧

2½ cups strawberries, sliced

1½ cups water

⅓ cup sugar

1 teaspoon grated lemon zest

3 tablespoons lemon juice

½ cup ginger ale

Fresh whole strawberries with stems for garnish

In blender, process strawberries for about 30 seconds. Add water, sugar, lemon zest, and lemon juice, and continue to blend until smooth. Pour mixture into small pitcher and add ginger ale. Stir until blended. Serve over crushed ice and garnish with strawberries.

Yield: 4 servings

✌ PEPPERMINT PUNCH ✌

When my daughter, Noélle, was planning a wedding that would take place during the holidays, we tried this recipe and found it to be one of our favorites. Kids will also love the crushed peppermint candy and the fresh, cool taste.

1 quart peppermint ice cream

1 jar strawberry preserves

1 (2-liter) bottle of Sprite, chilled

½ cup finely crushed peppermint candy for garnish

4 to 6 candy canes for garnish

Place ice cream in punch bowl and let soften. Swirl preserves through ice cream. When ready to serve, add Sprite. Sprinkle peppermint candy and float candy canes on top of punch.

Yield: 24 servings

∾ OLD PLANTATION ∾ WEDDING PUNCH

This is an old southern favorite.

1 quart brewed tea, chilled

1 quart apple juice, chilled

2 cups unsweetened pineapple juice, chilled

2 quarts club soda

Orange and lemon slices for garnish

Fresh mint for garnish

In punch bowl, combine tea, apple juice, and pineapple juice, and refrigerate. When ready to serve, add club soda and garnish with fruit slices and mint. Serve over ice.

Yield: 24 to 36 servings

Index

ly engaged in the act of throwing, the whole body is involved in the performance, and it is important that the whole body be properly conditioned. Experienced athletes in throwing events know that the legs are just as important as the upper body in successfully performing the event. Weight-training for throwers is a great means of improving their performance by strengthening the upper arm muscles. It also aids in protecting against muscle pulls and separations at the shoulder.

The athlete should never attempt an all-out throwing effort until she has gone through the throwing movements many times and has her timing down perfectly. A gradual approach is always best. In cold weather she should always give herself additional time, and perhaps stay in sweat clothes until it is time to compete.

Safety procedures in throwing events may seem rather obvious, but they are very important. The athlete should know what direction she is throwing in and not throw unless she is sure she knows the placement of everyone in the throwing area and they are aware of her impending throw.

The discus poses a further problem of slipping out of the thrower's hand before the completion of her spin. Many bystanders have been seriously injured by being too close or to the side or to the back of a discus thrower during practice. In most competitions, the thrower is within a netted area, but this is not always true on a practice field, and it is here that a misthrow could cause a serious injury.

The javelin, of course, could impale an individual who accidentally walked into the path of the throw. Softball throws are less likely to cause severe injuries, but they could cause contusions, or even concussions, if the throw were hard enough.

Gymnastics: Among the more important aspects of gymnastics as a whole is that the athlete know what her capabilities are and where the risk lies in every event. If she has any doubt of missing the move, she must use a spotter or safety device. Doing difficult tricks without taking the proper precautions causes most gymnastic accidents.

Some pieces of apparatus are more dangerous than others, and the trampoline probably heads the list. This should always be locked up when not in use. In use, at least four spotters should protect the performer from landing outside the bed of the device.

No apparatus should be used unless the performer has had instruction in its use. Careless use of gymnastic equipment has produced some expensive lawsuits.

Weight-training is a necessary tool in gymnastics. Many girls are still under the impression that weight-training produces bulky muscles, but we know this isn't true. The use of weights strengthens those muscles in the upper arms that are particularly required for performances on parallel bars and over the horse in gymnastics. Muscles that are strengthened are usually more attractive in a healthy-looking body.

Tennis: Although a warm-up procedure for tennis is not as necessary as for most other individual sports, it is still very important. The arm and hand that hold the racquet should go through a whole range of motion before striking the ball. Some stretching exercises are usually advised before any strokes are done. These should be followed by a slow warm-up volley; the colder the weather, the longer the warm-up.

Tennis elbow is a term associated with soreness developed from a strain in the attachment of the arm muscles on either side of the elbow joint. Ligamental strain may also be involved. The best way to head off permanent injury is to recognize the injury in its early stages. The use of a band on the forearm muscles helps prevent the transmission of the force of the blow of the tennis racquet on the ball from the attachment of the muscles to the elbow area, and may help prevent further tennis elbow.

Probably the most important factor in prevention of tennis elbow is to make sure the right tennis strokes are being used. In particular, an improper backhand may lead to tennis elbow. A good tennis coach may obviate the problem.

It is also important that the tennis player who wears glasses use safety glass. If she has plastic lenses, it might be wise to consider the use of an eyeguard device. There have been serious injuries in racquetball and tennis players caused by the ball striking the eye.

Skiing: Downhill skiing can produce many injuries, most of them attributed to carelessness, overaggressive skiing, recklessness, or in particular, poor training and conditioning.

The athlete does not have to be a competitive skier to suffer an injury. As a matter of fact, the professional usually has fewer injuries than the amateur who tries to exceed her skill. Some type of conditioning routine, with stretching, is important before the skiing season begins. Jogging is a good way to get into shape. A skier whose reflexes are up to par is more able to avoid a sudden obstruction in her path.

Competitive skiing involves increased risk, and therefore calls for preplanning and knowing how to minimize the risk. It is important for every skier to know how to fall and to have proper skis and proper binding; then, when she does fall, the ski will separate properly from the shoes and not become part of the fall. It is also probably not advisable to use straps that go over the thumb area to hold the ski poles. Injuries to the base of the thumb have occurred from the ski strap catching on it when the skier falls. It is better to lose or drop a ski pole than to have it cause injury.

Proper care of the equipment, particularly the skis, is important. Skis should be smooth and free of any foreign objects; they should always be checked before use. Also, the condition of the ski-run itself should be known, and the skier should be aware of any possible obstacles in the path she is using to go down.

The cross-country skier should not go out alone. She may be in a wilderness area, off the beaten track; if she slips and sustains an injury, she could freeze to death. If the skier must go out alone, someone should know her route and what time to expect her back.

Remember that, as in jogging, it is important that the athlete do a conditioning exercise routine prior to cross-country skiing; she should start gradually and build up distance as her technique improves. She should set some specific distance as a goal before trying to increase her speed. Once she knows she has the stamina to ski that distance, she can work on increasing her time.

Properly fitting skis and light, warm ski clothing are a must for safety as well as performance. Basically, the athlete is a cross-country runner with skis on; the lighter her clothing, without sacrificing warmth, the better off she will be.

Golf: A correct set of golf clubs is the obvious place to start for a golfer, yet this is often an overlooked area. She should have a golf pro or someone with similar experience suggest the correct weight and length of the woods and irons.

Taking care of the equipment is also important. Clubs should be cleaned after each day's play, and the grooves of the head should be free of embedded dirt.

Although very few injuries occur in golf, a short warm-up period of stretching, particularly in the upper arms, to a full range of motion is a must. Hitting some practice balls, if time permits, is also valuable, so that when the golfer strains during her first tee-shot, she won't pull a muscle.

One must always make sure, when hitting a long drive, that there is no one who might possibly be struck by the ball.

Bicycling: Bicycling is a very good all-round sport, primarily for the legs, but will also, to some extent, build the upper part of the body. A total body conditioning routine should be used before beginning. If the athlete has never ridden a bicycle before, it is important for her to learn from somebody who knows proper techniques and to observe all safety rules.

Clothing, again, should be comfortable and light, and in particular, long pants must either be skintight, or the biker must use a safety clip so that pants won't catch in the bicycle chain.

For cycling in the evening the bike must be well marked with lights. Using the bike on the sidewalk is safer; if this is impossible, the rider should go against traffic (if she is on a country road). In the city, where she must observe traffic regulations, the cyclist should ride on streets with light traffic.

A good way to prepare for bicycling is to jog first. This builds up the legs and permits bicycling without straining the muscles.

Team sports

Softball: The amount of exercise achieved in playing softball depends on the position the athlete plays. The catcher and pitcher get more exercise than the fielders. Nevertheless, the entire team should go through a warm-up routine prior to play. It is also advisable for the athlete to run a few wind sprints around the field to loosen up the legs for baserunning.

Proper sliding technique is important, and the catcher should be taught how to avoid being hit by the runner at homeplate. Interference with runners coming into the bases should be avoided. Care must be taken that players are not spiked.

It is advisable that women wear long pants rather than shorts, particularly if they intend to slide into bases. Severe abrasions to the thighs can occur when a player is wearing shorts.

Basketball: Although it is not supposed to be a collision sport, collisions do occur frequently in basketball. Padding of the elbows and knees has gone out of vogue. However, a player with knee problems should wear padded knee supports.

Proper shoes are a must in basketball, but until recently, it was difficult to get shoes that were made on a woman's last. As a result, there was frequently too much room inside the shoe, and it was necessary to either pad the tongue or wear heavy socks to keep the foot from sliding forward and causing the large toe to be contused—the so-called black toe. An aid to blister prevention is plenty of powder in the socks.

If a player requires taping, she should wear the tape throughout the season.

Other team sports: Soccer has recently become popular with women; the precautions are similar to those taken in basketball. Sports such as squash and lacrosse require similar precautions. Head and eye protection in the latter two sports is very important, as the player may easily be struck by a ball or racquet. Players who need glasses should have safety-glass lenses, and all players should wear helmets and masks.

Areas of controversy

Football: Should the female be allowed to play contact football? There have been a number of women's professional teams in the Midwest, and judging by their experience, there seems to be no real objection to women playing against women. However, a women's team should not play a men's team, and we don't think a woman should play on a men's team.

Tackle football was designed by men, for men, to play in a violent manner. Regardless of how you change the rules, blocking, running, and tackling demand a collision of bodies. While the female body may be able to sustain such collisions with a woman of about the same weight and height, a woman colliding with a man who outweighs her by 15 or more pounds could sustain a serious injury. We do not advocate such play.

Women in this sport have had difficulty finding comfortable equipment. Most hip and shoulder pads are too large and not properly contoured for the female body.

Not many females want to play contact football, so this doesn't represent a significant problem. Most women feel that football is beyond their physical capabilities, and many express fear of injuries they see in males who play tackle football. There are much better sports for women than football.

Hockey: Girls have been playing field hockey for many years. Therefore, making the transition to ice hockey is not difficult for women. There is no doubt that ice hockey, as it is played by men, is a collision sport. However, if ice hockey is played properly, by the rules, there is no reason women cannot play.

It is important that proper equipment be used. Equipment for ice hockey is essentially the same for women as for men, and most of the girls appear to be able to use available equipment. Should the sport become more popular with adult females, some modifications of equipment might be indicated.

Both skates and hockey sticks can cause lacerations of the face or other exposed portions of the body and all recommended equipment should be worn by all players.

Boxing: This is a questionable sport for males and females because points are scored by blows to the head. There are very few educational institutions that currently include boxing in their physical-education curricula.

Most physicians, especially neurosurgeons, are totally opposed to boxing because of the potential for brain damage and death. We therefore conclude that boxing is not for females any more than it is for males.

However, should a woman wish to box with another woman, her risk of injury from body blows is no greater than a man's.

Auto racing and horse racing: Women have already participated, with moderate success, as jockeys and racing car drivers. There is no more risk to women than there is to men in these events. The skills that are required for both of these sports are totally within the capability of the female. In fact, the female, because of her lighter weight, may have an advantage over the male jockey. On the other hand, if she is a very small woman, she is under some disadvantage in handling a heavy automobile, but this should certainly not be taken to be a barrier to participation. A woman entering into either of these sports must accept the danger of severe injury and death.

Wrestling: There is no reason that women cannot wrestle on a women's team. There seems to be little interest in wrestling as a female sport, but there is no reason not to participate. The risks to women are no greater than the risks to men. The uniforms worn are similar—a gymnastic uniform with tights; women use leotards to cover the upper torso. Long hair would be a problem, but it can be tied, braided, or concealed under the ear protector straps to keep it out of the way.

Although co-ed wrestling is a future possibility, it would be frowned upon now. Strength would also be a problem because, when individuals wrestle, even according to weight, the men would probably be stronger than the women. Rule changes would have to be made to accommodate sex differences and to make some holds illegal.

Sex changes: Should persons who undergo sex change be allowed to compete against members of their new gender? We are speaking primarily about males who become females and continue to have the strength they had when male.

Many females feel that they are or can be physically equal to men, and therefore can compete with them at various levels of athletics. If we adopt this philosophy, we cannot object or bar the participation of a female who has previously been a male. Conflict, however, does occur in the area of professional individual athletics when money is involved.

If the female athlete is beaten by a former male, she will inevitably blame her loss on this fact. The cry of unfair match-up will be raised. A former male could very well be much stronger and faster than the average female and thus have a decided advantage in competing with females.

Suppose that one of our leading golfers, for example, were to change from a male to a female without losing any of his golfing ability. Would he not outpower and consistently defeat the best women professional golfers? If we extend that line of reasoning further, it's quite possible the top 30 to 50 professional male golfers would consistently defeat the top five women golfers. We might argue that finesse on the part of a woman could compensate for some of the ability of a man to power a ball in a long drive, but we feel that the basic strength of the male would probably enable him to outpower the female.

There has been much discussion of this by the Olympic Committee, and athletes have been barred from Olympic participation on the basis of sex testing. Obviously, conditions and rules should be set up by all athletic governing bodies. It will take a combination of scientific facts and surveys of athletes to make a sound judgment on the matter.

WOMEN, SPORTS, AND THE LAW

Leslie M. Bodnar, M.D., and
Thomas L. Bodnar, J.D.

CHAPTER

31

T he rules by which we regulate our lives are the product of religion, custom, socialization, and usage. Sports are subject to the same controls, particularly today. Therefore, in relating women, sports, and the law, one should understand the bias that has ruled women's lives.

The beginning

In the beginning, the roles of man and woman must have been equal. Undoubtedly, both foraged, hunted, fished, fought, wrestled, climbed, jumped, vaulted, hurdled, and swam. They survived; and although the burden of pregnancy may have slowed women for periods of time, and although they may have been relegated for periods of time to child-rearing, women had to be of hardy stock or perish.

It has been presumed that women in ancient cultures performed certain rites as part of agricultural and fertility rituals, and that these were slowly transformed into sports and games. During the Bronze Age on Crete (about 2000 B.C.), women participated in hunting, fishing, dancing, and a type of bullfighting.[1] The literature of ancient India describes the value of daily exercise, but relates nothing of sports. Artifacts from ancient Mesopotamia indicate that women participated in dancing and games as part of their socially approved activities.

The women of Athens were brought up in seclusion and forced inactivity. The girls of Sparta took part in exercises with boys. The maids of Cyrene ran footraces with the boys. The Chian maidens wrestled and ran races with boys.[2] Therefore, even in those days, traditional cultural differences determined whether or not such activities were acceptable for women.

In the early Roman period, women did not participate in sports. As social institutions were humanized, women became freer to participate in such activities. During the early Republic, a woman had no voice in the choice of a husband. But by the first century B.C., marriage was a contract that required consent of both parties. It was then that women began to be seen at the baths, playing ball, involved in running and throwing events; some participated in gladiatorial combat against other women.[3]

During the colonial period in the United States, women were very restricted in their sports and games; the model was women in Europe and the British Isles. After the time of George Washington, sports developed for men and gradually some room was made for women—at least in the more genteel sports.[4] With the Civil War and the Industrial Revolution, women gained new respect and status. The bicycle craze of 1896 allowed for looser clothing and this, in turn, led to the entry of women into swimming and boating.[5] Women's basketball was taken up by girls soon after Dr. James Naismith originated the game. It was played at Smith College as early as 1892; the first women's college game was held in 1893.[6] In the early 1900s, high school girls and college women were allowed to participate in sports on an intramural basis.[4]

After World War I, women's athletics and games evolved with women's rules. There was emphasis on intramural games in the colleges, but objection to their participation in international and Olympic games delayed the development of competitive female athletics.[7] The rowdyism of the late '20s caused varsity-type competition to become limited, and by the 1930s it was virtually eliminated. The Women's Committee and later the Section on Women's Athletics of the American Physical Education Association and the Women's Division of the National Amateur Athletic Federation exercised rigid control of women's college-sports programs. They resolved that sports should be for everyone. Enjoyment was stressed at the expense of winning.[8]

Women in the Olympics

Early in the history of the Olympics, women were excluded because of religious taboo. So strict was this taboo that the penalty for attendance was death. Women conducted their own festival at Olympia, the Heraea, and races were held there for maidens of various ages.[9]

The fondness of the Greeks for sports and games existed at least 500 to 1,000 years before the first Olympics, which were held in 776 B.C. For the Greeks and Romans, nonwarlike sports were essentially the privilege of the leisure class. Horse racing, chariot racing, boxing, wrestling, races in armor, armed combat, and in medieval times, the jousting of knights in armor all related to warlike preparation that excluded women.

The Olympic games were dissolved by Emperor Theodosius I in 394 A.D. because he considered them barbaric and un-Christian. They were restored in 1876 through the efforts of the Baron Pierre de Coubertin.[10]

Women first competed in Olympic golf and tennis in Paris in 1900. These same competitions were not open to women in 1904 because the chairman of the Organizing Committee, James E. Sullivan of the United States, was opposed to their entry. Until 1914, when he died, he effectively barred women from the A.A.U., and therefore, American women could not compete in the Olympic swimming competition in 1912. At the Congress of Paris in 1914, the matter of women in the Olympic games was brought to a vote. The vote was never made public, but approval was denied. After World War I came the feminist movement. With the Women's Suffrage Movement, there also developed strong pleas from women in the sporting world. Admission to the Olympic games came slowly as a result of continuous struggle against the views of the sports establishment.[4]

Margaret Abbott achieved Olympic victory for America in the women's singles golf event in 1900. Although women's archery was an exhibition sport at St. Louis, women did not formally compete in the Olympics again until 1920.[11] In the 1920s, increased attention was given to women's sports, as evidenced by the *New York Times*'s increased news coverage of women's events. This also heralded increased feminist activities.[4]

The feminist movement

With the liberation of women came the entry of women into sport. Not all women who participated considered themselves "liberated women." It was simply that the movement made it easier for women to pursue sport and other endeavors.

The feminist movement of the late 1960s, in tune with the newly emerging protest movements, was not intended to eliminate the differences between the sexes or simply to achieve equal opportunity; rather, it emphasized the individual's right to determine his or her own being and to strive to become that person.

Many women had abandoned the leftist organizations of the 1960s because of the supremacy of males in those organizations and their refusal to treat women's complaints seriously. The media, too, were critical and cynical but the adverse publicity may have had some beneficial effect on the movement by bringing it to the public's attention. As women and their organizations worked for equality, they developed the aspiration to be permanently rid of the oppression of women—to eliminate their second-class citizenship status. Among other things, the movement worked for passage of the Equal Rights Amendment.[12, 13]

This demand for equality found the field of sport to be fertile ground. The old arguments that athletics were bad for the health of women and their femininity and that women were not skillful enough or interested in playing games and sports were based on easily disproven presumptions.[14]

The New York State Department of Education reported a 1972 experiment in which girls were permitted on previously all-male interscholastic teams; 100 high schools and 10 noncontact sports were involved. It was proved that there was no physical or psychological harm in allowing females to compete against males. Actually, very few girls made the teams, and their success in competition was infrequent.[15]

On the physical side, studies indicate little physiologic difference that is not the result of cultural and social custom. In fact, up to the age of nine, boys and girls are evenly developed and physically equal. Then for the next few years, girls may become more competent. However, at 15 or 16, the boy continues to develop, becoming heavier, larger, and more rugged—particularly in the upper body.

Therefore, boys and girls past the age of 11 or 12 are different, and the differences establish limits to their athletic performances.[16, 17]

As liberation proceeds, women's sports have evolved from the very feminine sports of yesteryear to more masculine sports. Women have relinquished "playing like little girls." They want to play by the rules of men's competition, which is still considered to be of higher caliber. Furthermore, although female sports have grown at a tremendous rate in the last few years, the liberation movement does not choose to wait.[18] Women are anxious to make up for lost time; and whether or not the Equal Rights Amendment is passed, they are about to have their day, as required by Title IX of the Education Acts of 1972, as amended, and according to the guidelines issued by the Department of Health, Education, and Welfare.

Legal advances in women's rights

Before women could be completely liberated to pursue sport, it was necessary to remove legal obstructions and affirm women's rights. Article IV, Section 2, of the Constitution states that citizens of each state shall be entitled to all privileges and immunities of citizens of the several states. The Fifth and Fourteenth Amendments to the Constitution, as interpreted by the courts, guarantee to all persons due process and equal protection of the law without arbitrary discrimination. This includes the principle of equality of rights of males and females. Legal decisions have held that women are "persons" and entitled to equal protection under the Fourteenth and Fifteenth Amendments.[19-22]

The Equal Pay Act, under the Fair Labor Standards Act, was amended in 1963, and Title VII of the Civil Rights Act of 1964 was amended by debate in the House of Representatives to include sex as a prohibitive ground for discrimination in employment and "guaranteed for equal work on jobs—equal pay, within certain limits." Women have not always fared so well in the courts.

The decision in *Minor* v. *Happersett* (1875) in Missouri, delivered for the Supreme Court by Chief Justice Waite, denied suffrage to Virginia Minor by denying registration as a lawful voter.[19]

In *Lochner* v. *New York* in 1905, the Supreme Court struck down a statute limiting the number of hours which could be worked by male employees in bakeries on the basis that it arbitrarily interfered with the liberty of the individual and was in conflict with the Fourteenth Amendment. But in *Muller* v. *Oregon* (1908) the court upheld an Oregon statute that limited a female worker to 10 hours a day, based on the differences in the sexes. Justice Brewer stated: "Woman has always been dependent upon man—she has been looked upon in the courts as needing especial care—she is so constituted that she will rest upon and look to him [man] for protection." From this decision was extracted the principle that sex is a valid basis for classification.[19]

However, changes in attitudes gradually developed. Women were accorded the right to vote in 1920 when the Nineteenth Amendment removed all barriers to female suffrage.

Opportunities for employment changed. In *Goesaert* v. *Cleary* (1948) Justice Frankfurter delivered the opinion of the court that "Michigan cannot forbid females generally from being barmaids." Thus, under the Fourteenth Amendment, women were granted the "equal protection" of the opportunity for bartending. Although three justices dissented, the opinion of the Supreme Court affirmed the opinion that "women may now have achieved the virtues that men have long claimed as their prerogatives and now indulge in vices that men have long practiced." In a decision involving a Paterson tavern, the Supreme Court of New Jersey in 1970 reversed a decision that prohibited the employment of female bartenders because it was an exclusion grounded solely on sex.[19]

Eleanor Roosevelt, who in 1961 headed the President's Commission on the Status of Women, recommended developing a comprehensive, national employment policy favoring the position of women. Under President Kennedy in 1963, the United States Civil Service Commission developed a policy of nondiscrimination.[20] There were other equalizing legalities, not all of benefit to women. In 1960 the Supreme Court of Pennsylvania, in *Commonwealth* v. *Daniel*, denied differentiation between men and women in sentences imposed for commission of the same crime.[19]

A Federal Court ruled that the Fourteenth Amendment prohibited sex discrimination in jury service (*White* v. *Cook*, 1966). In *Kirstein* v. *the Rector and Visitors of the University of Virginia* in 1970, it was held that the exclusion of women from the University of Virginia at Charlottesville was a violation of their constitutional rights under the Fourteenth Amendment.[20, 23] In 1979, the Supreme Court ruled women liable for payment of alimony under certain conditions.

Association of Intercollegiate Athletics for Women

The development of an organization to promote women in sports was long delayed, as were the role of women in education and attention to their needs in physical and mental health. Judith Sargent Murray, in 1790, deplored the limited education, employment, and recreation permitted women. Charles Brockton Brown, in 1798, noted the lack of perception in those who felt that one sex would find vigorous health and suppleness more valuable than would the other sex. From the early 1800s onward, women were gradually accorded rights similar to, if not identical with, those of men. Emma Willard, in 1819, in promoting education, also noted the lack of attention to the physical welfare of schoolgirls.[24]

After World War I, when women's equality was becoming recognized, women began to participate in various sports. The Women's Division of the National Amateur Athletic Federation, composed mainly of physical educators and women involved in community sports, evolved women's rules for games and worked for strong intramural games. In general, they objected to fierce competitive contests, which they felt encouraged spectatorism rather than the ideal of universal participation for physical recreation. Under this philosophy, women were not encouraged to compete. It would seem that this acceptance of a diminished role delayed the coming of age of women's sports.[7, 8, 14, 25]

Because sex involves inherent physiological differences, it is necessary to maintain separate teams for men and women to ensure equal opportunities for participation to members of both sexes. It was from this effort to promote separate teams for women, and to separate them from competition with males to ensure their opportunity for participation, that the Association of Intercollegiate Athletics for Women evolved.[18]

Differences in rules and regulations between the A.I.A.W. and the National Collegiate Athletic Association are such that in its earlier years the A.I.A.W. allowed only tuition and fees to athletes, rather than full scholarships. But in 1977, it accepted the philosophy of full scholarship-type grants-in-aid. However, women transferring from one college to another are not allowed financial aid during the semester in which they transfer. Recruiting has been done on a very minimal basis, but as of 1979, universities are permitted to use their money to "assess talent."

The A.I.A.W. was formally organized in 1971-72 and is composed of more than 900 member colleges and universities. It evolved from the Division of Girls' and Women's Sports. It has an established relationship with the National Federation of State High School Associations, the American Basketball Association of the U.S.A., the United States Olympic Committee and the United States Collegiate Sports Committee. The earlier organization held to a philosophy of "sport for all," exercising control over collegiate women's sports programs. Today, the A.I.A.W. governs women's college athletics, conducts competitive contests for national championships, and standardizes policies and codes of ethics for its athletes and those concerned with these programs.

The A.I.A.W., the National Organization for Women, Title IX, and the E.R.A. are in agreement that equality should not be denied on account of sex.

The E.R.A.

In 1972, the Equal Rights Amendment was submitted to the states for ratification. This Amendment provides that equality of rights under the law is not to be denied or abridged by the United States, or by any state, on account of sex. The purpose of the Equal Rights Amendment is to require that laws deal with the individual attributes of the particular person, not with the overclassification based on the irrelevant factor of sex.[15, 19, 22, 26] This absolutely prohibits sex discrimination.

It also addresses the problems of female athletes, providing an ultimate guarantee of equality for both sexes in athletics.

The "Hayden Rider," added as an amendment, provides that it "shall not be construed to impair any rights, benefits, or exemptions, now or hereafter, conferred by law upon persons of female sex." The effect of the Hayden Rider is to grant certain special legal privileges to women, which disturbs the sense of equality in this Amendment.[27]

Women's rights in sports

Even before ratification of the E.R.A., the courts have been a busy battleground for the advancement of women's equality in sports. Most cases so far deal with sports at the high school or junior high school level.

In *Bucha* v. *Illinois High School Association* (1972), the District Court ruled that physical and psychological differences between male and female athletes were a constitutionally sufficient reason for prohibiting athletic interscholastic competition between the sexes. The female plaintiffs sought positions on the boys' varsity swimming team. The court noted that there was a girls' interscholastic team on which they could participate.[28]

However, in *Haas* v. *South Bend Community School Corporation*, 1972, the plaintiff succeeded in gaining admission to the boys' golf team. The suit argued that a female was denied equal protection under the Fourteenth Amendment because boys and girls are not permitted to participate in interschool athletic games as mixed teams under the Indiana High School Athletic Association rules. In the Haas decision, the Indiana court commented that: "Until girls' programs comparable to those maintained for boys exist, the difference in athletic ability alone is not justification for the rule denying mixed participation in non-contact sports."[28, 29] *Reed* v. *Nebraska School Activities Association*, 1972, also upheld, on equal-protection grounds, the right of a female to try out for the golf team,[30] and in *Gilpin* v. *Kansas State High School Activities Association*, 1973, the District Court ruled for the plaintiff, stating that the female high school student had been prevented from participating on the boys' cross-country team, and therefore in cross-country competition, solely on the basis of her sex.[31]

In *Brenden* v. *Independent School District*, 1972, the court held that the Minnesota High School League failed to demonstrate that a sex-based classification fairly and substantially promoted the stated purpose of assuring that persons of similar qualifications compete among themselves, as the school provided no teams for females who desired to participate in interscholastic tennis, cross-country skiing, and running. The practice of barring females from participating with males in athletics under these circumstances was declared unconstitutional.[32]

Numerous cases involved Little League teams. In one of these, *Magill* v. *Avonworth Baseball Conference*, 1975, the Pennsylvania Court found for the defendant, holding that the situation could not be treated as a state action; and, therefore, the ruling of admission of a female to this baseball conference could not be applied to Little League Baseball.[33] However, in *N.O.W.* v. *Little League Baseball*, 1974, the Supreme Court of New Jersey declared that Little League Baseball, chartered by Congress, was not intended to be limited to boys and ordered that girls be permitted to participate.[34] The same result was reached in *Blank* v. *Little League*, 1975, a United States Court of Appeals case.[35]

Most of the litigation has been by female students attempting to perform on male teams in noncontact sports; however, women have also made some inroads in contact sports. In addition, they have been permitted to participate as jockeys; progress has been made in wrestling, bowling, and baseball. Again, the cases hold that to prohibit girls from participating on or against male teams constitutes a denial of equal protection and due process under the Fourteenth Amendment.[36]

In *Yellow Springs* v. *Ohio High School Athletic Association* in 1970, two female high school students competed for and were awarded positions on the high school's interscholastic basketball team, although this was contrary to regulations of the State Association. The court found that girls who desire to play must be given the opportunity to compete with boys in interscholastic contact sports and that it is unconstitutional to deny girls this right.[37]

In Pennsylvania, in 1973, a girl was dropped from the rifle team, which had been co-ed for 30 years. This was done to maintain a rule adopted in 1970 prohibiting girls from playing or practicing with boys. Other inequities brought out by subsequent events were the facts that the Pennsylvania Interscholastic Athletic Association consisted of an all-male board and that there were inequalities in the number of games played by the male and female teams, payment to male and female officials and coaches, uniforms (women's required "ladylike" qualities), character of laundry services, use of cheerleaders, budget allowances, and so forth; all favored the male teams. In the course of events, the courts pointed out that sex was not a factor on which discrimination could be based because, in spite of physical differences and characteristics, the factors of mind, body, coordination, mental determination, sensory perception, courage and intelligence, willingness to practice, and experience were also necessary for success in athletics.[38] Thus, in *Commonwealth* v. *Pennsylvania Interscholastic Athletic Association*, 1975, it was declared unconstitutional to prohibit females from competing and practicing against males in high school athletic contests, including football.

The Supreme Court of the State of Washington in *Darrin* v. *Gould*, 1975, held that it was unconstitutional to forbid qualified females from playing on high school football teams in interscholastic competition. This was the first case that dealt with the question of sex discrimination in contact sports.[29]

Title IX

Congress passed Title IX of the Education Amendments Act of 1972 in an attempt to resolve the sex-discrimination problem. It is patterned after Title VII of the Civil Rights Act of 1964. That act prohibits Federal agencies from granting financial assistance to those who discriminate on the basis of race, color, or national origin. Section 1681 of Title IX states: "No person in the United States shall, on the basis of sex, be excluded from participation in, be denied the benefits of, or be subjected to discrimination under any education program or activity [that is] receiving federal financial assistance."

The express purpose of Title IX was to protect women from biased educational policies. The courts have consistently considered athletics sponsored by educational institutions to be an integral part of the educational program and consequently covered by Title VII and now by Title IX. Congress, in 1974, directed the implementation of Title IX by directing the Department of Health, Education, and Welfare to provide regulations for equal opportunity in athletics for women.

The regulations require the existence of equal opportunity for both sexes in athletics. Flexibility is allowed to schools and colleges in determining how best to provide such opportunity. Opportunities for participation and awards, scholarships, financing, publicity, coaching, salary structures, levels of competition, scheduling, practices, travel, per diem allowance, facilities, services including medical and training-room facilities, and other matters pertaining to sports must be equalized for members of each sex in proportion to the number of students of each sex participating in interscholastic or intercollegiate athletics.[40]

The regulations of Title IX do not require coeducational physical education in classes. Groupings may be made totally on the basis of ability, without regard to sex. If separate physical instruction is justified by standards developed without regard to sex, such separation is justifiable. If only one team is maintained in a sport, individuals of a sex usually excluded from that team must be given an opportunity to compete for a position on that team, except in contact sports. Thus, although segregated teams are allowed, the exceptional female athlete is nevertheless not precluded from an appropriate level of competition.[21]

Expenditures on men's and women's athletics is to be substantially equal on a per capita basis. An exception includes the differences based on nondiscriminatory factors such as the cost of a particular sport, or the scope of competition. This includes athletic scholarships, recruitment, and other readily measurable financial benefits, such as equipment and supplies, travel, and publicity. There must be comparability of opportunities to compete, in practice, coaching, academic tutoring, locker room facilities, medical services, and housing facilities.[41]

Separate teams may be offered for those chosen by competition or if the sport is a contact sport. Contact sports are defined as football, basketball, boxing, wrestling, rugby, ice hockey, and any other sport, the purpose or major activity of which involves bodily contact. The school may thus limit the contact sport to one sex or the other. If there is enough interest by the other sex to compete in that sport, a team of that sex must be provided as well.[16, 21, 41]

In December 1978, H.E.W. issued uniform enforcement procedural rules to be applied to civil-rights programs administered by that department. The enforcement provisions include termination of funds to particular programs in which noncompliance occurs.[41]

H.E.W. has not yet penalized any college for failure to comply with Title IX. However, the law requires that as of September 1979 the regulations and penalties be applied.[40, 41] The consternation of the colleges and the N.C.A.A. over the financial impact of this act has been considerable.[42]

An early attempt to invoke H.E.W. and Title IX failed when Vanessa Calabrese settled her suit against the University of Illinois out of court; she attempted to force the university to elevate women's sports to the level of men's minor sports; her grounds were sexual discrimination.[43] There is no doubt that there will be many such court actions involved in the procedure of establishing equality for women in sports.

Professionalism

Women have entered such violent professional sports as wrestling, boxing, and demolition derbies. Some of the attraction to the public is probably the desire to see women lower themselves into "unladylike" situations. Nevertheless, women have earned the right to participate. Most of the sports in which women have become involved are the ladylike sports of tennis and golf. Basically, these are individual sports rather than team sports.[44] Women have become involved in competition with men and finally they are developing a following and financial support approaching what men receive.

Professional baseball began for women at the time of World War II. Professional women in golf and tennis now have six-figure incomes. In 1979, for the first time, women and men competed against each other in the $100,000 Spalding Invitational Pro-Am Golf Tournament on the Monterey Peninsula. Women professionals are also making their mark in basketball, auto racing, ice skating, and as jockeys. There are many who feel that in time women's teams will be financially attractive in contact sports such as basketball and football.[16]

Although Title IX does not apply to professional athletics, litigation has forced professional sports to grant greater equality of opportunity to women. In *State* v. *Hunter*, 1956, the court noted that a statute forbidding the licensing of women as professional wrestlers had the purpose of monopolizing the calling in favor of men.[36, 38]

In *New York State Division of Human Rights* v. *New York-Pennsylvania Professional Baseball League*, 1972, a woman was successful in her effort to qualify as a professional umpire, despite the fact that she lacked the minimal physical requirements that were established by the defendant, when the court decided that the physical requisites did not bear a reasonable relationship to the requirements of the job and that they were, therefore, inherently discriminatory.

As in the cases involving high schools, these decisions were based upon the Fourteenth Amendment. Certain principles of law may be deduced from the cases discussed. [22, 27, 29, 39, 45-48] First, it may be permissible to make a distinction based upon sex when it is based upon the physiological differences between the sexes. However, not all sex distinctions are valid, because there may not be a rational basis for differentiating between the sexes on that physiological basis. In noncontact sports, equal opportunity must exist. In contact sports, there may be a rational basis for denial of opportunity to participate in a sport based on physiological differences. But even in the case of contact sports, it may be necessary to allow at least the opportunity to participate, depending upon the individual's ability. It should be noted that applications of constitutional rights are dependent upon state action and do not apply in private matters in which discrimination may not be unconstitutional.

Civil actions

Civil actions in the courts have touched on a wide range of subjects related to sports and their conduct. The causes and results of such actions apply no less to girls and women than to others.

Litigation has been invoked as a means of redress for all types of injury. Society and its attitudes and philosophies change with time. Such changes in attitude toward the rights of women have been recognized by our courts. Similarly, attitudes toward litigation have changed and the courts are more and more called upon to make judgments and, in cases of injury, to award damages.

The conduct of physical education, athletics, and sports involves not only the athlete or the student, but teachers, physical educators, coaches, school officials and administrators, units of government, managers and owners of teams, those who rule league activities, the manufacturers of equipment involved in sports, sports trainers, therapists, physicians, and many others.

Much of the litigation involving schools is related to accidents.[49, 50] Many of these accidents are preventable with proper supervision and by maintaining equipment in good condition. Those supervising these activities must take preventive measures and remain closely available to properly instruct students and oversee their activities. They have an obligation to warn students of inherent dangers in activities and facilities, and to make such available only with proper supervision. Teachers and coaches involved in activities in which an injury occurs must be capable of immediate emergency care, but are warned not to attempt treatment. They must heed the advice of physicians about the advisability of returning players to athletics following injuries.[49]

An area of significant litigation in recent years has involved the use of equipment that is dangerous or defective. This has involved the manufacturers of athletic equipment and those who supply and maintain it. Such equipment must be reasonably safe for use. In cases of inherent dangers, such as in the use of trampolines, special precautions must be taken to ensure their use only under proper instruction and supervision. In the manufacture of equipment, it is required that certain bodies establish standards, and that these standards be met. Faulty design and manufacture have led to some injuries, exposing the manufacturers of such athletic equipment to serious litigation.[50]

Players injured in the conduct of sport have probably suffered such injury only as a result of the manner in which such sports are performed. The player assumes a certain risk when he participates in a game. He manifests a willingness to submit to body contact in certain sports. He also recognizes restriction of certain of his activities by the rules and usages of the game. Some sports are more violent than others. Players have accepted a certain amount of roughness and physical interaction, but intentional injury to another is not acceptable. It is understood that a participant assumes all the usually anticipated risk incidental to the sport. But a player does not assume the risk of injury from fellow players who act in an unexpected, unsportsmanlike, and reckless manner. Liability does not, however, arise from the mere fact that an injury occurred.[50]

Certain rules and usages of sports and games are designed to protect the participants as well as to outline the manner in which the game is to be played. It is the legal duty of each player to follow the rules, to protect other players from serious injury. If a player, in a deliberate and willful manner, demonstrates reckless disregard for the safety of the other player, he is liable for that injury. There is a similar assumption of risk in sports that do not involve teams or contests. Participation in any sport and in any capacity, even as a spectator, implies that one is willing to assume certain risks at sports events.

In professional sports, the demands of the public further affect the assumption of risk. The fans, who pay the price of admission, demand a good show, and for many of them this includes the fights, violence, and brutality that characterize a game conducted in semirage. In spite of recent attempts to better control this factor in contact sports, the acceptance of some degree of violence has become commonplace in these sports, and this serves to increase the risks to the participants. This usage enters into the degree of "assumed risk" to which the participant elects to be exposed. As a result, even certain degrees of reckless behavior performed willfully and intentionally have been accepted as being unpremeditated and unavoidable in an emotionally charged athletic contest.[50]

Supervisors, coaches, officials, and volunteers involved in activities assume the risk of liability when negligence is implicated.[50] Negligence implies failure to perform as a reasonable person would under the same circumstances. Negligence, therefore, implies that a standard has been established for the protection of others against unreasonable risk of harm. One must, therefore, refrain from creating situations in which there is such unreasonable risk of injury to others.[51] There is also the responsibility of the injured; if the conduct of an injured party falls below what a reasonable person would do for self-protection, the action may be considered contributory to the injury and prevent recovery of damages. The accusation of negligence has been brought against those involved in the medical management of athletes. Such suits have involved the administrators of such programs, supervisors, trainers, therapists, and physicians.[52]

Medical care must be delivered at the level of reasonable skill and knowledge for members of the medical profession in good standing. Such liability may not be altered by the fact that the physician or others may be acting charitably. Physicians accepting an athlete for treatment are obligated to treat the athlete in accordance with the usual standards of care. One who specializes in a certain practice would be expected to meet the standards of that specialty. The examination of athletes must be conducted with skill and knowledge normally utilized by other members of the profession in similar examinations.

The use of drugs and medications may lead to legal action if the prescription causes an injury or worsens an existing injury. Drugs to improve performance or delay the need for corrective surgery or treatment or given an athlete to enable him or her to return to play, if used at all, should be used only with the informed consent of the athlete. Consent for treatment must be informed and requires that the patient receive information relative to the treatment, risks, and alternatives, enabling an intelligent choice. Consent is ideally obtained in writing and in clear terms.[52] Consent for treatment of minors must be obtained from a parent or guardian, except when an emergency exists and a parent or guardian is not available.

Schools and administrators become liable if they do not provide reasonable medical care for those injured in the course of their athletic programs. It may be judged that care is deficient when given by persons who are not adequately trained for the responsibility they assume.[52]

Certain laws of privileged communication preclude the disclosure of information about injuries sustained by athletes. Disclosure of such information relating to the physical condition of an athlete becomes a problem if there is some public interest to be considered. In general, only the general nature of an injury and its treatment can be divulged.

There are other rights to which athletes and sports programs are entitled. The courts have maintained that institutions have the right to set reasonable rules to govern their campuses, and students have a responsibility to observe the rules. The courts support policies that are fair, reasonable, and understandable, but not those that are too vague or broad or that are run arbitrarily or are applied unequally.

When training rules are broken, due process involves a hearing with the athlete. Serious action may not be taken in the absence of published rules. Coaches are not the sole executioners of justice. The Fifth Amendment provides due process of law. The Fourteenth Amendment extends to the operations of state governments. When due process is involved, an individual must have proper notice and be given the opportunity to be heard and be afforded a fair trial and hearing. In private educational institutions, students do not have as much constitutional protection under the Fourteenth Amendment. However, the decision in *Dixon v. Alabama State Board of Education* protects the rights of private school students so that an institution will not act in an arbitrary manner.[49]

The Amateur Sports Act

The 97th Congress, in 1978, passed the Amateur Sports Act. The United States Olympic Committee and many others worked for this legislation to strengthen amateur sports in the United States. Funds have been made available for the construction, improvement, and maintenance of facilities and to defray operating costs for programs in amateur athletics. The importance of various national sports organizations is recognized. This act guarantees the rights of athletes to participate freely in tests and competitions. It establishes procedures to resolve disputes between athletes and sports bodies and accepts the authority for a national sports body to govern international competition. It recognizes the United States Olympic Committee as the coordinating agency for all organizations that may be concerned with the Pan-American and Olympic games.[53]

The power of the above legislation will, no doubt, be tested by the legal action that is imminent as confrontation looms between the N.C.A.A. and the A.I.A.W. The N.C.A.A. decided in January 1980 to conduct championship competition in five women's sports for Division II and Division III colleges, leaving it to the A.I.A.W. to continue to conduct the events for Division I schools. The A.I.A.W., however, wants to maintain autonomy over women's sports and has vigorously protested the N.C.A.A. decision.[54]

References

1. Howell R and Howell ML: Women and sport in Minoan civilization. In *Proceedings of the North American Society for Sport History,* University of Oregon, Eugene, June 16-19, 1976, pp 9-10

2. Gardiner EN: *Athletics of the Ancient World*: Oxford: At the Clarendon Press, 1930

3. Bazzano C: Women and sport in ancient Rome. In *Proceedings of the North American Society for Sport History,* University of Windsor, Ontario, May 17-21, 1977, p 6

4. Evans V: Women's sports in the 1920 era. In *Proceedings of the North American Society for Sport History,* Ohio State University, Columbus, May 24-26, 1973, pp 28-29

5. Storstad LD: The development of the American woman kayaker. In *Proceedings of the North American Society for Sport History,* University of Oregon, Eugene, June 16-19, 1976, p 14

6. Dewar J: The beginnings and directions of Ms. Basketball in North America. In *Proceedings of the North American Society for Sport History,* Boston, April 16-19, 1975, pp 33-34

7. Theirot NM: Towards a new sporting ideal: The Women's Division of the National Amateur Athletic Federation. In *Proceedings of the North American Society for Sport History,* University of Oregon, Eugene, June 16-19, 1976, p15

8. Gerber EW: The controlled development of collegiate sport for women, 1923-1936. In *Proceedings of the North American Society for Sport History,* Ohio State University, Columbus, May 24-26, 1973, pp 27-28

9. Gardiner EN: *Greek Athletic Sports and Festivals.* London: Macmillan, 1910

10. Leigh M: Women's entry into the Olympic games in the 20th century. In *Proceedings of the North American Society for Sport History,* University of Oregon, Eugene, June 16-19, 1976, p 17

11. Welch P: American women: Early pursuit of Olympic laurels. In *Proceedings of the North American Society for Sport History,* Boston, April 16-19, 1975, pp 34-35

12. Hogan CL: Football must not be a sacred cow. *Chicago Tribune,* sec 4, p 9, Jan 28, 1979

13. Carden ML: The New Feminist Movement. New York: Russell Sage Foundation, 1974

14. Gilbert B and Williamson N: Sport is unfair to women. *Sports Illustrated*, pp 88-98, May 28, 1978

15. *Wiesenfeld v. Secretary of Health, Education, and Welfare*, 367 Federal Supplement, 981

16. Gilbert B and Williamson N: Women in sport: A progress report. *Sports Illustrated,* pp 26-31, July 29, 1974

17. Wilmore JH: Inferiority of the female athlete: Myth or reality? *J Sports Med* p 1, Jan-Feb 1975

18. Oglesby CA: Women sport: From myth to reality. Bruder-Immaculata Papers, Immaculata College, 1975

19. Kanowitz L: *Sex Roles in Law and Society.* Albuquerque, NM: University of New Mexico Press, 1973

20. Murray P: The rights of women. In *The Rights of Americans* (Dorsen N, ed) New York: Random House, 1970

21. Oliphant JL: Title IX's promise of equality of opportunity in athletics. 64 *Kentucky Law Journal* 442 (1975-76)
22. Note: Sex discrimination and intercollegiate athletics. 61 Iowa L. Rev. 420 (1975)

23. 184 Fed. Supp. 309 (E.D. Va. 1970)

24. Park RJ: Our bodies—ourselves: The rise of concern for the physical education of women, 1776-1865. In *Proceedings of the North American Society for Sport History,* University of Windsor, Ontario, May 17-21, 1977, pp 18-19

25. Fields CM: Women's athletics: Struggling with success. *Chronicle of Higher Education,* May 22, 1978

26. Brown BA, Emerson TI, Falk G, and Freedman AE: The equal rights amendment: A constitutional basis for equal rights for women. 80 Yale Law Journal 871 (1971)

27. Kanowitz L: *Women and the Law: The Unfinished Revolution.* Albuquerque, NM: University of New Mexico Press, 1969

28. Davidson KM, Ginsburg RB, and Kay HH: *Sex-Based Discrimination*. St. Paul, Minn: West Publishing, 1974

29. Note: Sex discrimination in high school athletics. 57 Minn. L. Rev. 339 (1972)

30. Commentary: Constitutional law—equal protection—sex discrimination in high school athletics unreasonable. 19 N.Y. Law Forum: 166 (1973)

31. *Gilpin* v. *Kansas State High School Activities Association, Inc.,* 377 Fed. Supp. 1233 (1974)

32. *Brenden* v. *Independent School District,* 477 F. 2d 1292 (1973)

33. *Magill* v. *Avonworth Baseball Conference,* 516 F. 2nd 1328 (1975)

34. *NOW* v. *Little League Baseball, Inc.,* 318 Atlantic Reporter 33 (1974)

35. *Fortin* v. *Darlington Little League, Inc.,* 514 F. 2nd 344 (1975)

36. Wein S: The case for equality in athletics. 22 Cleveland State L. Rev. 570 (1973)

37. *Yellow Springs* v. *Ohio High School Athletic Association,* 47 University of Missouri at Kansas City L. Rev. 109 (1970)

38. Commentary: Sex discrimination and equal protection: Do we need a constitutional amendment? 84 Harvard L. Rev. 1499

39. Commentary: Sex discrimination in athletics: Conflicting legislative and judicial approaches. 29 Alabama L. Rev. 390 (1978)

40. Lockhart B: Implications of Title IX. Bruder-Immaculata Papers, Immaculata College, 1975

41. HEW memorandum, December 1978

42. Underwood J: An odd way to even things up. *Sports Illustrated*, pp 18-19, Feb 5, 1979

43. Condon D: Court settlement hollow victory. *Chicago Tribune*, sec 4, p 2, Sept 14, 1978

44. Zoble JE: Femininity and achievement in sports. In *Women and Sport,* Penn State HPER Series No. 2 (Harris D, ed), pp 203-204

45. Jacklin PL: Sexual equality in high school athletics: The approach of *Darrin* v. *Gould.* 12 Gonzaga L. Rev. 691 (1977)

46. Rusch C: Equality in athletics: The cheerleader v. the athlete. 19 S.D. L. Rev. 428 (1974)

47. DeWolf R: The battle for coed teams. In *Sex Equality* (English J, ed) Englewood Cliffs, NJ: Prentice-Hall, 1977

48. Hayes M: The Sexual Barrier. Ann Arbor, Mich: Edwards Bros, 1977

49. Appenzeller H: *Athletics and the Law*. Charlottesville, Va: Michie Co, 1975

50. Scalf RA and Robinson RE: Injuries arising out of amateur and professional sports. Defense Law Journal 419

51. Annot., 77 A.L.R. 3d 1300 (1977)

52. Lowell CH: Legal responsibilities and sportsmedicine. *Phys Sportsmed* 5(7):60, 1977

53. Miller FD: The Amateur Sports Act of 1978. *The Olympian*, 1978

54. Associated Press: NCAA acts to sponsor the women. *South Bend Tribune,* p 48, Jan 9, 1980

THE FUTURE OF WOMEN AND SPORTS

Meredith Melvin, M.Ed., A.T.C.

CHAPTER

32

Although the future often turns into a reprise of past history, I see the future of women in sport speeding on a new course. Games and events that traditionally were male-dominated and oriented for winner-loser spectator appeal are becoming vehicles for health and fitness. Former concepts are being forced to expand to accommodate the masses seeking exercise's health benefits. Women, as part of this health movement, have a great deal to contribute in finding balance between participation and spectatorship and, we can hope, in changing the definition of sport. Women's participation may even prompt the creation of new sports events.

It used to be that the all-American boy had to play football. If he wasn't big enough, he was forced into the role of the 98-pound weakling, vulnerable to Big Moose kicking sand in his face. However, as options for boys grew, body types were taken into account, and young men were able to become involved in sports that reflected their natural attributes and capabilities. Basketball, soccer, and track and field emerged as alternatives to football. Only now are women's options beginning to open up, and sports suited to developing their specific physical attributes are likely to evolve in the near future.

For a long time, women were not allowed to engage in physical activities beyond those of their workaday lives. Eventually, they were permitted to show their strengths in such "feminine" events as figure-skating, ballet, and gymnastics. But a woman who did not have the lithe, graceful body type for these sports was considered unsuitable for athletics. All too often the chunky tomboy was forced to abandon her enthusiasm for physical activity.

Not until the recent liberation movement did women assert their desire to participate in sports previously reserved for men. The early '70s saw women demanding equal access to playing fields and locker rooms. Little League coaches had to reassure their boys that they would someday grow to be as good as the girls on the team. Women were playing baseball, hockey, and lacrosse and pressing for participation in boxing, football, and shot-put.

For a time it seemed to me that women were intent only on proving that they could perform well in men's sports. They focused their efforts on minimizing the differences between the sexes because they felt it was the only way to gain equality in facilities, training, and opportunity. I believe their efforts were misdirected. Women's physical and psychological characteristics have a place in sports as well, and men's sports do not fully make use of them. One day, women will be able to call upon *all* their qualities to excel in sports and will be fully appreciated for their differences.

Women have demonstrated their agility and balance, but are just now beginning to exhibit their natural endurance capabilities. The best example of this is that the world's long-distance swimming marks are all held by women. Women are developing their potential for endurance events, taking part in such sports as mountaineering, ultramarathoning, distance cycling, swimming, and Nordic skiing.

This attribute of endurance has become the subject of fascination for the modern physiologist, who is examining the possible mechanisms responsible for women's successes in these areas. Just as studies of men's explosive strength and speed provided new insight into the workings of the body, understanding women's endurance adaptations will expand our knowledge of exercise physiology. As this knowledge increases, there should be a parallel increase in the number of sports with the addition of those that take advantage of women's capabilities.

New sports events that show off the attributes of women are bound to develop. Endurance is just one performance factor that might characterize a women's sport specialty. Their different body type, strength, degree of flexibility, and ability to balance are other variables that can enhance our appreciation of athletic performance. And just as various combinations of men's performance variables distinguish their sports, different combinations of women's variables will lead to new sports that will be specifically for women.

I can imagine a biathlon involving long-distance swimming and a balancing event; flexibility feats performed as a team effort; and teams with a two- or three-generation span, with members playing positions determined by age attributes. The emphasis will not be on the end result, as it is in men's sports, but on enjoying participation in the activities.

As the emphasis in sport changes to fitness, performance factors will be joined by fitness factors, and all will be seen as components of health. Fitness factors, unlike performance factors, are not limited to "prime ages." Accordingly, sports activities will develop that promote fitness for people of all age groups and make the most of an individual's abilities at whatever age. No age will be seen as "prime," because fitness for health's sake is not limited to a particular time of life.

Perhaps the A.A.U. will encourage teams with the broadest span of ages to enter events. Masters' events will become as popular as the men's open divisions, women's events will become as popular as men's events, and spectators will be able to appreciate each group's performance without endlessly comparing it with that of a male in his "prime." The future will bring games that call for a wide variety of skills, so that people of all ages and both sexes can participate in a single event. In this way, none of us will have to switch from participant to spectator because of age—we can all become lifetime participants.

Women's sports of the future, by relaxing the rigid rules and games of male-dominated sports, have the potential to encourage participation. By reversing the overemphasis on competitiveness that has excluded so many because of age and lack of professional-level skills, they will further the trend toward mass participation. Sports will finally become a complete vehicle for the pursuit of fitness and health, ensuring a physically sound society.

Kate Puleo

STEPHEN PULEO is a historian, college teacher, public speaker, and the author of six books, including *Dark Tide: The Great Boston Molasses Flood of 1919* and *The Caning: The Assault That Drove America to Civil War*. A former award-winning newspaper reporter and contributor to *American History* magazine, the *Boston Globe*, and other publications, he holds a master's degree in history, has taught at Suffolk University in Boston, and has made more than five hundred appearances as an author. He and his wife, Kate, reside in the Boston area.

Additional Praise for *American Treasures*

"Stephen Puleo once again educates, enlightens, and entertains us, this time through the history of the most important documents of our democracy. A tour de force based on exhaustive research into both primary and secondary sources, he tells the miraculous stories of the survival of the most precious evidence of our freedom thanks to, until now, the unsung heroes and heroines of our past."

—David S. Ferriero, archivist of the United States

"An extraordinary and truly innovative book."

—Richard R. Beeman, author of *Plain, Honest Men:*
The Making of the American Constitution

"A rich and resonant narrative history, surging with character and in-cident, the kind of book that you will devour for the depth and breadth of its erudition and, more simply, because it's a terrific tale, told by a fine historian who also happens to write like a seasoned novelist."

—William Martin, *New York Times* bestselling author of
The Lost Constitution and *The Lincoln Letter*

"An incredible journey filled with mystery and surprise. *American Trea-sures* is an American treasure."

—Doug Most, author of *The Race Underground:*
Boston, New York, and the Incredible Rivalry
That Built America's First Subway

"Weaving together a riveting narrative of the effort to keep America's founding documents safe from harm during World War II with a stir-ring recap of the origins of the Declaration, Constitution, and other precious American treasures, this is a wonderful tale. Not only does Stephen Puleo recount the little-known heroics of Archibald Mac-Leish, the Librarian of Congress, in a post–Pearl Harbor climate of fear, he also reminds us of how these 'Charters of Freedom' are what truly make America exceptional."

—Kenneth C. Davis, author of *Don't Know Much About History* and *America's Hidden History*

"A novel perspective on American history that focuses on the story of the country's founding documents and the Americans who composed, safeguarded, and preserved them for the benefit of future generations. A fast-moving presentation and solid retelling of an inspiring story." —*Kirkus Reviews*

"His vivid and detailed descriptions of characters and events will make readers feel like they are in the room with historic figures."

—*The Patriot Ledger*

"An engrossing account of the creation, consecration, and conservation of the documents that defined American democracy."

—*Library Journal*

"Narrative nonfiction at its best: thorough research underpins an engaging—even gripping—story that captures the reader, who races along to discover what happens next." —*Historical Novels Review*

"Puleo never loses track of the documents' dual nature as both artifacts and symbols. He describes their drafting and publication, as well as the political debates that surrounded their creation, bringing new life to familiar stories in the process. . . . Ultimately, *American Treasures* is an engaging exploration of Archibald MacLeish's assessment that 'they are not important as manuscripts, they are important as themselves.'" —*Shelf Awareness*

"*American Treasures* is a nonfiction book that feels like a combination of a spy novel, Jason Bourne, and James Bond."

—Congressman Mike Rogers, WJR Radio (Detroit)

AMERICAN
TREASURES

★

The SECRET EFFORTS *to* SAVE

the DECLARATION *of* INDEPENDENCE,

the CONSTITUTION,

and the GETTYSBURG ADDRESS

★

STEPHEN PULEO

Picador   St. Martin's Press   New York

To Kate

The quiet of your love — priceless

★

AMERICAN TREASURES. Copyright © 2016 by Stephen Puleo. All rights reserved.
Printed in the United States of America. For information, address Picador,
175 Fifth Avenue, New York, N.Y. 10010.

picadorusa.com • picadorbookroom.tumblr.com
twitter.com/picadorusa • facebook.com/picadorusa

Picador® is a U.S. registered trademark and is used by Macmillan
Publishing Group, LLC, under license from Pan Books Limited.

For book club information, please visit facebook.com/picadorbookclub or
email marketing@picadorusa.com.

Designed by Donna Sinisgalli Noetzel

The Library of Congress has cataloged the St. Martin's Press edition as follows:

Names: Puleo, Stephen, author.
Title: American treasures : the secret efforts to save the Declaration of Independence,
   the Constitution, and the Gettysburg Address / Stephen Puleo.
Description: First edition. | New York : St. Martin's Press, 2016. | Includes
   bibliographical references and index.
Identifiers: LCCN 2016003702 | ISBN 9781250065742 (hardcover) |
   ISBN 9781466872745 (ebook)
Subjects: LCSH: United States—History—Sources. | United States—Politics and
   government—Sources. | United States. Declaration of Independence. | United States.
   Constitution. | Lincoln, Abraham, 1809–1865. Gettysburg address. | United States—
   Antiquities—Collection and preservation—History. | Manuscripts—Collection and
   preservation—United States—History. | Hiding places—United States—History. |
   Historic preservation—Political aspects—United States—History. | Democracy—United
   States—History. | BISAC: HISTORY / United States / General. | HISTORY / United
   States / Revolutionary Period (1775–1800).
Classification: LCC E173.P96 2016 | DDC 973—dc23
LC record available at https://lccn.loc.gov/2016003702

Picador Paperback ISBN 978-1-250-12633-7

Our books may be purchased in bulk for promotional, educational, or business use. Please
contact your local bookseller or the Macmillan Corporate and Premium Sales Department at
1-800-221-7945, extension 5442, or by email at MacmillanSpecialMarkets@macmillan.com.

First published by St. Martin's Press

First Picador Edition: September 2017

10 9 8 7 6 5 4 3 2 1

Contents

Contents

＊ 1952 ＊

Author's Note

In 2014, my family sold the home in which my parents had raised my siblings and me. My dad had passed away several years earlier and, after managing the house by herself for a time, Mom had moved into a more carefree and far less lonely independent living arrangement. My brother, my sister, and I went through the long process that millions of children endure as they prepare the family homestead for sale—reliving memories, organizing and cleaning, deciding what stays and what goes.

As we reached the completion of our melancholy task, I wandered through the near-empty house and made my way downstairs to our basement playroom for one final check. There I noticed—taped high on the wall, where it had hung for nearly forty years—the facsimile of the Declaration of Independence that my parents had purchased during the American Bicentennial in 1976. It was the "engrossed" copy that most Americans are familiar with—inked in calligraphy style with a fine hand, the bold and oversized "In Congress, July 4, 1776" at the top, followed by "The Unanimous Declaration of the thirteen united States of America." The word "united" was deliberately lowercase, merely a descriptive adjective at the time, not the first word in the name of a new country; the word "States" was far more important and capitalized for emphasis. Beneath the body text were the signatures of the founders, a who's who of American history—John Adams, Thomas

Jefferson, Benjamin Franklin among them, with Continental Congress president John Hancock's sweeping signature dominating the bottom third of the parchment, oversized, centered, brazen, and unapologetic.

Below the signatures was a message from the "sponsors" that had printed this replica: "The principles of the Declaration of Independence are as meaningful today as they were two hundred years ago. It is our hope that having this authentic copy will serve as a constant reminder of the foundations upon which the United States of America stands."

I had almost missed the worn, somewhat tattered copy hanging on the wall, but was thrilled when I spotted it. I was well into the research and writing of *American Treasures*, and viewed my late discovery as a fortunate sign. At the very least, it inspired me—throughout the writing, the copy of the Declaration remained on my desk and I referred to it often.

It is easy to get lost in the document and all it represents—the text, the marvelous variation of signature styles, the care and flair employed by the engrosser. My parents and millions of Americans everywhere had always recognized the Declaration's value, perhaps without knowing all the reasons why.

"AMERICA HAS NO CROWN jewels," a perceptive editor said to me at the outset of my work on this book, "but if she did, it would be these documents. Readers are going to be thrilled to hear about their journey over the last couple of hundred years—what people went through to create them, protect them, and preserve them."

He had offered a succinct synopsis of *American Treasures*, a story that describes how the Declaration of Independence, the Constitution, the Gettysburg Address, and many other critical documents were created, how they have defined a nation and its people throughout our history, and, for the first time, how Americans have made decisions and taken risks to protect them and ensure their preservation for future generations.

The United States was founded, and has evolved and prospered,

with these documents as its foundation. Ours is the world's first republic that can be traced back to its original founding document—the
Declaration—and the world's first country that was founded on the
principle, if not the full-fledged reality, that all men are created equal;
and just as fundamental, that government's power is derived from the
governed and not the other way around. Such principles were uniquely
American in 1776, and have guided our culture, politics, and policies
for 240 years.

As so many other nations and peoples have struggled and often
failed to advance under monarchies, theocracies, caste systems, oligar-
chies, anarchies, and dictatorships, America's prosperous and inclu-
sive democracy—its "small *r*" republicanism—remains based on and
defined by its founding documents.

THE GENESIS OF *American Treasures* came when I read a small item
about the Library of Congress's World War II decision to secretly relocate the Declaration of Independence, the Constitution, the Gettysburg
Address, and other important documents to an undisclosed and heavily
fortified location for safekeeping in the aftermath of the attack on
Pearl Harbor. The Library of Congress also transferred 5,000 additional boxes of critical documents to inland university repositories,
away from the path of potential enemy bombers; among them were the
papers of George Washington and other presidents, the text of Samuel
Morse's first telegraph message, and James Madison's detailed account
of the 1787 Constitutional Convention. I had never heard of this massive and risky relocation effort and was anxious to learn more. Because
the National Archives and Records Administration (NARA) now holds
and displays the Declaration, the Constitution, and the Bill of Rights—
collectively called the Charters of Freedom—I met with David
Ferriero, Archivist of the United States, and Jessie Kratz, historian for
the National Archives, to outline my idea. Their encouragement, enthusiasm, and ongoing cooperation inspired me and convinced me that this
was a story worth pursuing.

It quickly became apparent, however, that the saga entailed more than the Library of Congress relocation activities in the 1940s. To fully understand what was at stake when the country undertook the Herculean task of protecting those parchments from potential enemy attack, I had to go back to their creation; this would help me tell the story of the full depth of their meaning and importance, as well as the motivations and aspirations of the people who created them. The struggle to save our priceless documents included not only their physical protection but the preservation of the ideas and ideals upon which they were based—during their creation and in the years since.

What follows will tell the story of the journey of these documents—both literal and figurative—over the last two centuries. It's a saga that covers the sweep of American history—from the spring of 1776 when the Continental Congress debated whether a group of colonies should declare their independence from the mother country with whom they were at war, all the way to the present day, in which highly sophisticated preservation techniques are employed to protect and preserve the documents.

Along the way, Americans in every era took great risks and great care first to produce, and then to protect and preserve, their cherished documents. Virtually every major American historical figure and event somehow touches at least one of the documents in some way—among them the adoption of the Declaration of Independence in Philadelphia in 1776 and then the Constitutional Convention in the same city in 1787; the dramatic rescue of the Declaration of Independence and the Constitution just ahead of the British burning of Washington, D.C., in 1814; the deaths of both John Adams and Thomas Jefferson on July 4, 1826, the fiftieth anniversary of the adoption of the Declaration they helped draft, an against-all-odds moment that forevermore lent a touch of divine inspiration to America's birthday; Lincoln's majestic prose at Gettysburg that redefined the nation's dedication to freedom by including people of all races; and the palpable fear of attack on or sabotage of the United States after Pearl Harbor that prompted the stealthy relocation of irreplaceable documents to safe havens.

It is a remarkable 240-year journey that covers a spectrum of emotions, a plethora of pitfalls and celebrations: a journey fraught with peril and danger, laced with misgivings and uncertainty, infused with heroism and courage.

While of course many of the individual parts of this story have been told before, it's my hope that telling their story in this way will provide modern readers with a new appreciation of what we've been defending all of these years. The historic parchments and manuscripts provide a powerful window through which Americans view their history, understand the roots of their patriotism, and reaffirm their commitments to liberty and equality that are so deeply embedded in their national and civic DNA.

AMERICAN TREASURES IS A work of narrative history that rests on a sturdy foundation of primary and secondary sources: in other words, layers of scholarship and research. Everything that appears between quote marks is contained in a diary, a letter, a speech, a government document, a court transcript, a piece of congressional testimony, a newspaper, a magazine article, a journal, a pamphlet, or a book. My narrative and conclusions are based on an examination and interpretation of the sources (which are explained in full in my bibliographic essay) and my knowledge of the characters and events; these also provide the underpinnings for any conjecture that I engage in.

The story of the nation's priceless documents—the Declaration of Independence, the Constitution of the United States, the Gettysburg Address—and the events leading up to their creation and subsequent protection and preservation, are filled with larger-than-life personalities, dramatic episodes, and compelling moments and have sweeping, far-reaching implications for America.

I have tried to tell this rich story with as much accuracy and narrative drama as the historical record allows.

Prologue

★

December 26, 1941, Washington, D.C., Early Evening

Secret Service agent Harry E. Neal stood alone on the platform at Union Station and watched the train disappear into the darkness. It was 6:50 p.m. and the temperature had slipped into the thirties. For the first time in two days, he breathed a little easier. He wouldn't relax fully until the Baltimore & Ohio National Limited reached its final destination the following morning, but the fact that the train was leaving Washington, D.C., carrying its cargo, accompanied by two of his finest agents, was a promising milestone in this mission.

Japan had bombed Pearl Harbor three weeks earlier, and since then, fears of a German or Japanese attack on Washington, D.C., had sent American officials scrambling in all directions to prevent the potential destruction of their capital city and everything located within its borders. The Germans had overrun continental Europe, trained their sights on England, and, after Pearl Harbor, declared war on the United States. The Japanese had ravaged China and Southeast Asia, attacked the Philippines, and only days later decimated the U.S. Pacific fleet at Hawaii. And just hours ago, as if to remind Americans that nothing was the same, Britain's prime minister, Winston Churchill, had addressed a joint session of the U.S. Congress, historic both because it was unprecedented and for the magnitude of his message. "Twice in a single generation," Churchill had reminded Congress, "the catastrophe of world war has fallen upon us. . . . Do we not owe it to ourselves, to our children, to mankind tormented, to make sure that these catastrophes shall not engulf us for the third time?"

Harry Neal and his colleagues had rested little since Pearl Harbor. They had collaborated with military and civilian agencies to implement new protocols and procedures to protect the president, safeguard the White House, and defend Washington. Neal had been involved in most of these discussions, including this latest plan orchestrated by the Library of Congress, the logistics of which had only been solidified the day before, on Christmas afternoon. As the public spectacle of Churchill on Capitol Hill consumed Washington's attention, Neal had begun his day with a confidential meeting at the Library of Congress with the librarian, Archibald MacLeish, and his assistant librarian, Verner W. Clapp, to review the plan to relocate the Library's most precious possessions to a secure, inland, bombproof facility.

After the meeting, Neal, a perfectionist, double-checked everything: driving three different routes between the Library of Congress and Union Station to determine the safest for the conveyance of the packages to the train depot; ensuring that the armored truck that carried the material from the Library of Congress to Union Station was properly guarded and escorted; designating a contingent of armed agents to accompany the baggage cart from the Union Station storage room directly to the train; and confirming that a second cadre of armed agents would meet the train upon its arrival to take custody of the cargo and transfer it to its final secure destination.

After blocking the public's access to this track, Neal had insisted on accompanying the four plain-wrapped cases onto the train, supervising their placement into Compartment B in Car A-1, and reviewing the upcoming elements of the plan with his agents and with Clapp, who would travel with the Library of Congress packages. Somehow, it had all proceeded without apparently attracting the attention of the uneasy throngs that flooded the rest of Union Station on this day after "Pearl

Harbor Christmas." If it had been up to Neal, he would have accompanied the documents on their overnight rail journey, but his Secret
Service chief ordered him to remain in Washington, where he could
be more valuable should other crises arise.

With the train en route, Harry Neal left Union Station and returned
to his office in the Treasury Building to provide a telephone update to
Archibald MacLeish, who had insisted on a report as soon as the train
had departed Washington. Neal spotted the envelope that had been
delivered earlier by messenger, and, before he called MacLeish, he
read the brief, one-page memo from Clapp, dated December 26,
1941, on Library of Congress letterhead. "The following is an itemiza-
tion of the materials," the memo began.

Later in his life, following a long and storied career with the
Secret Service, Harry Neal would describe Clapp's memo as one of
his prized possessions. On this evening, December 26, 1941, with
the special packages on their way out of Washington, Clapp's itemized
list took his breath away.

★ ★ ★

EARLY 1941

★ ★ ★

1

★

"It Is Natural That
Men Should Value
the Original Documents"

★

Washington, D.C., February 1941

Earlier that year, Librarian of Congress Archibald MacLeish, who had not slept well for nearly eighteen months, sifted through voluminous reports from his key staff members. The reports, which detailed the library's most precious collections, were the source of his insomnia.

Two years earlier he'd resigned his position at a Boston law firm to write poetry full-time, basking in the boldness of his decision and contemplating the full potential of his art. President Roosevelt had changed all that when he had convinced MacLeish to take on his current position.

Now, sitting alone in his office, MacLeish felt the crushing weight of a burden he had not asked for, but for which he would assume full responsibility.

The past six months had been almost surreal at the normally staid Library of Congress. The repeated and devastating Nazi bombings of London and its institutions during the blitz this past fall, including the bombing of Buckingham Palace and Downing Street in September 1940, and the German attacks on libraries and museums taking place throughout Europe, had raised alarms in Washington. It shocked Mac-Leish to read newspaper accounts describing the forced retreat of King George and Queen Elizabeth to an underground shelter as London rocked "in an inferno of exploding bombs and fierce anti-aircraft fire."

During that period, he'd experienced deep distress about the destructive power of incendiary bombs on his library's priceless collections. He also worried each day about the potential damage to irreplaceable documents—from water, humidity, mold, vermin, accidents, and incompetence—if he were forced to relocate them for safekeeping. The original Declaration of Independence was already in fragile condition; would removing it from the Library of Congress expose it to further deterioration?

The United States had not entered this war, and there was fierce resistance across the country to do so. Still, to MacLeish's way of thinking, the possibility of Axis bombing attacks or sabotage on Washington, and the potential destruction of the nation's most important records, no longer seemed as remote as it had one year earlier.

There were sober lessons to be learned from overseas.

IN 1938, A FULL year before Hitler's invasion of Poland, the British Museum had selected a disused mine in a remote corner of the United Kingdom to store its treasures, as well as valuables from other institutions, including the National Gallery and the Victoria and Albert Museum. Manuscripts, books, historic records, and perishable relics of Britain's past were collected in this underground repository. Shelves were hollowed out of solid rock, and steel racks were constructed for manuscript boxes and other containers. Atmospheric conditions—heat, air-conditioning, humidity—were so well controlled by a self-sufficient system that ordinary folding cardboard boxes sufficed to hold England's documents.

Still, it wasn't enough. In more than a dozen cases, British libraries that hadn't been prioritized had been hit by German incendiary bombs designed to set buildings ablaze with their intense heat rather than their explosive power; the white-hot flames they created were devastating to paper documents and books. Just two months ago, on Christmas Eve in 1940, the extensive library of the Manchester Literary and Philosophical Society, England's oldest scientific society, had been destroyed by enemy attack. The collections of several eminent scientists were lost forever, including those of renowned meteorologist John Dalton. Three months earlier, an incendiary bomb fell on the east wing of the British Museum, damaging the King's Library Gallery and destroying many of the books collected by King George III. Some 1,500 rare volumes were severely damaged. Before war's end, England alone would see more than 1 million volumes destroyed in bombed-out libraries.

Other European countries took precautions, too. In the spring of 1939, intense saber-rattling from Germany convinced France to transfer many records of the French Foreign Office from Paris to a safer location. Thousands of masterpieces were moved from the Louvre to the French countryside, including Leonardo da Vinci's priceless *Mona Lisa*, swathed in layers of waterproof paper. In Budapest, areas within the Hungarian National Archives building were set aside for the preservation of valuable medieval documents and were protected by sandbags banked in the passages and against the windows. Yet even with these precautions, once fighting broke out, thousands of documents were lost or destroyed across Europe.

Fearful of war reaching North America's shores, MacLeish and others began questioning the best course of action to protect their collections. Harry McBride, administrator of the National Gallery of Art, wrote to librarians and museum executives urging that "common plans for protection" be undertaken by the National Archives, the National Museum, the Library of Congress, his own institution, and other federal repositories. He suggested that a "large subterranean shelter" be constructed, "to which the most precious part of the collections, at least, of these institutions might be conveyed in case of danger."

David C. Mearns, superintendent of the Library of Congress reading room, agreed that it would be "highly desirable" to have an underground bomb shelter but pointed out the time and expense of building something new. "Would it not be judicious for the Library to consider readapting (structurally) some of its present subterranean spaces for the purpose of safe-guarding its own rarities?" Mearns noted that currently the library's underground spaces would not be structurally strong enough to withstand direct bombing.

MacLeish had commissioned a report in November 1940 on the practicalities of the Library of Congress following the British relocation model. In reply, Lawrence Martin, the chief of the Division of Maps, addressed the possibility of storing documents in caves, mines, and the mile-long Southern Railway tunnel that began beneath Union Station, traversed under First Street right in front of the Library of Congress, and emerged at New Jersey Avenue between D and E streets SE.

Martin dismissed the possibility of using caves, since they were "generally damp, frequently wet, and often dripping." He had gone so far as to visit potential caves in New York, Wisconsin, and even central Mexico and found none suitable for storage. In addition, he pointed out that caves often have multiple entrances, "and we never dare say we know all the ways to get in from the back." Mines would be better than caves, but also presented problems with dampness, dust, rodents, insects, and access. Martin suggested that finding and modifying a natural habitat might be both financially and politically palatable. "On the side of a Kentucky gorge, for example, we could build a bomb-proof chamber," he wrote to MacLeish. To hide it from view, from the ground or the air, workers could "reinforce its concrete roof with much dirt, camouflage its new side, its ends, and its top, and have a safe place" to store documents. Such an arrangement had an added benefit: it "would not open us up to the possible ridicule that might arise over placing books in caves."

While mines and gorges were possibilities, there were two superior alternatives, Martin suggested. One was the Southern Railway tunnel, which could provide temporary shelter for the treasures of the Library of Congress and the National Archives. "They could be housed in water-proofed box cars," Martin wrote. "All passenger trains could be routed around the city on the freight line."

In his opinion, however, the safest and best location for the Library of Congress's most precious artifacts and documents was an impenetrable fortress far from Washington, D.C.

IN DECEMBER 1940, AFTER reading Martin's report, MacLeish spun into action.

He directed the chiefs of major Library of Congress divisions to prepare, "at the very earliest possible moment," detailed lists of documents and materials "which would be utterly irreplaceable" if they were destroyed, along with an estimate of how many cubic feet would be required to house them if the United States entered the war. They should select material "on the basis of irreplaceability and uniqueness" and give primary attention to those considered "most important for the history of democracy." They should divide the records into six groupings based on their intrinsic historical value, with the first including the Declaration of Independence, the United States Constitution, the Gettysburg Address, Lincoln's second inaugural, and the papers of Washington, Madison, Hamilton, and other founders.

"The fate of great libraries abroad, several of which have been completely and others partially destroyed in air raids, emphasize the importance of careful planning to meet any contingency which might arise," MacLeish stressed to his staff.

As he read those assessments now, MacLeish reflected on the breathtaking aggregate collection under his purview and for which he was responsible. In addition to the nation's preeminent founding documents, the Library of Congress also possessed a priceless Gutenberg Bible, and one of the original copies of the Magna Carta, the thirteenth-century document that first established the principal that kings must rule according to law and not mere monarchical mandate, and that citizens were guaranteed certain rights, including a fair trial.

In addition, the library held thousands of other critical documents: from the Division of Maps, there was Pierre Charles L'Enfant's original hand-drawn plan for the layout of Washington, D.C., complete with fading editorial annotations from Thomas Jefferson; from Rare Books, a richly illustrated 1340 edition of the Latin Bible, printed on vellum; and of course, from the Manuscript Division, a treasure trove of American history. Among these were the *Journals of the Continental Congress* from 1774 to 1776; George Washington's diaries, including the entries recording the British surrender at Yorktown; the works Dolley Madison had rescued from destruction when the British burned Washington in 1814, documents she later labored to publish—James Madison's *Notes on Debates* (two volumes) and *Records and Essential Papers* (two booklike boxes and one large portfolio volume) of the Constitutional Convention of 1787; and Abraham Lincoln's papers.

The Library of Congress also held Samuel Morse's first-ever telegraphic message from 1844—"What Hath God Wrought?"—that marked history's transformation in communications. And from the Mary Todd Lincoln collection was the April 29, 1865, letter of condolence from Queen Victoria after learning of the assassination of President Abraham Lincoln. Victoria, still grieving and "utterly broken-hearted" following the death four years earlier of her beloved husband, Prince Albert, told Lincoln's widow that she could not "remain silent when so terrible a calamity has fallen upon you & your country."

And on it went as MacLeish studied the reports filtering in from all sections: there were the original books donated by Thomas Jefferson to create the Library of Congress, original Stradivarius violins, aviation pioneer Octave Chanute's correspondence with Wilbur Wright, Mary Todd Lincoln's pearls, and thousands of other irreplaceable items.

MacLeish's staff had heeded his directive to be as thorough as possible.

While MacLeish had initially focused on Library of Congress records, President Roosevelt asked him to survey other agencies as well. He had heard back from several: the United States Patent Office, the Smithsonian Institution, the National Gallery of Art, and others, seeking more than 600,000 cubic feet of storage space for their documents and artifacts. Roosevelt then asked his National Resources Planning Board to assemble a Committee on Conservation of Cultural Resources to study the problem in a coordinated way. One day MacLeish would serve as a key member of the CCCR, which was made up of representatives of museums, archives, and historic sites, but for now he focused on the Library of Congress collection alone.

In early 1941, Archibald MacLeish was not sure the Library of Congress documents would ever have to be relocated for safekeeping, but he actually hoped they would. He believed America's entry into the war was the only way to halt rampaging totalitarianism in Europe.

WHILE FERVENT ISOLATIONISM WAS the majority feeling across the country in the late 1930s and into 1940, MacLeish had earned the scorn of his liberal friends and fellow intellectuals by vigorously advocating for U.S. military intervention against the scourge of fascism in Europe.

The country's indelible memory of the ghastly Great War a quarter century earlier, combined with the recent rawness of its decade-long Depression fatigue, had created in Americans an aversion to any cause beyond their own borders. Insularity became the nation's balm. Although Hitler's vow to conquer Europe had materialized with brutal swiftness, the overwhelming sentiment in the United States was to reinvigorate an ailing nation before getting involved elsewhere.

Even now, in the wake of Hitler's brutal invasions of Poland and the Low Countries, his shockingly swift conquest of France, and his relentless bombardment of England, there were protests coast to coast from political opponents and wary citizens alike over President Roosevelt's proposed Lend-Lease bill to supply the British with supplies and weapons in exchange for later payment. The House had numbered the bill HR 1776 to appeal to the nation's patriotism, but angry mothers across the country, sensing that it was only the first step in an interventionist strategy, rallied holding signs that said, KILL BILL 1776, NOT OUR SONS. Roosevelt expended enormous political capital on the lend-lease bill, which ultimately passed in March 1941, but even the president's staunchest supporters in Congress warned that they would venture no closer to the interventionist line. The United States was simply not interested in becoming involved in Europe's affairs.

MacLeish, in a series of speeches and columns, had tried to convince people that the European cause was also the American cause, especially after the fall of France in June 1940. Before the Battle of France, "we had thought ourselves spectators of a war in Europe," he told a crowd during a speech at Faneuil Hall in Boston in November 1940. "After it, we knew the war was not in Europe but nearer—in the darker and more vulnerable countries of men's hearts." He told the crowd: "Democracy in action is a cause for which the stones themselves will fight."

Time and again, in speeches and letters, MacLeish invoked the spirit of American liberty as envisioned by the founders, a spirit that required sacrifice and resoluteness to ensure the country's enduring success and ongoing freedom. No American could look at the dire situation in Europe, MacLeish said, "without asking himself with a new intensity, a new determination to be answered, how our own democracy can be preserved." MacLeish also began speaking and writing on the role of librarians in the face of the fascist threat. Describing the librarian's profession in 1940, he wrote: "In such a time as ours, when wars are made against the spirit and its works, the keeping of these records is itself a kind of warfare. The keepers, whether they so wish or not, cannot be neutral."

If armed conflict against Hitler meant war would come to the nation's shores—to Washington—MacLeish would be ready to do his part, just as so many Americans had done before him. With each day that passed, with each new assault of Nazi bombs on London, MacLeish thought it likely that he would find himself tasked with protecting America's critical documents, perhaps on a grander scale than his forebears could imagine.

ARCHIBALD MACLEISH RESPECTED, AND in many ways, loved the documents that fell under his stewardship. He knew their history, he knew of the risks taken and the bravery demonstrated by the men and women who had created and safeguarded them, and he knew the revered place they held in the hearts and spirits of Americans.

He had expressed his first public insights about the importance of cherished American documents when the Library of Congress took custody of the British Magna Carta during a moving ceremony on November 28, 1939, fewer than three months after Germany had invaded Poland to begin World War II. The so-called Lincoln Cathedral copy, from 1215, had been on display at the New York World's Fair, and, with war under way in Europe, the British ambassador had asked the United States to hold onto the document for safekeeping.

A thrill had jolted MacLeish when he had taken custody of the Magna Carta, when he held its worn parchment and contemplated its centuries-old text. There was no mistaking the power and the gravitas of the original manuscript. "It is natural that men should value the original documents which guarantee their rights," he said to mark the day. "The great constitutions and charters are not mere records of something already accomplished. They are *themselves* its accomplishment."

MacLeish immediately displayed the Magna Carta opposite the Declaration of Independence and the Constitution. He believed firmly that Thomas Jefferson, essentially the founder of the Library of Congress and the "true author of the noblest of our charters," would have relished the ironic placement of "the Great Charter of the English across the gallery from the two great charters of American Freedom." To Jefferson, the colocation of the British and American documents would have seemed "just and fitting—an affirmation of the faith in

which this nation was conceived." As MacLeish watched the public attendees gather around the Magna Carta, a document that most scholars believed formed the philosophical underpinnings for Western
democracy, he realized that a day like this made him grateful he had
agreed to become the Librarian of Congress.

He needed the reminder: in recent months the good days had been
rare. Librarians across the country had howled in protest when President Roosevelt nominated him, claiming correctly that MacLeish was
not a "professional librarian" and, perhaps not so correctly, that his lack
of certification would lead to his abject failure. The fact that he "knows
books, loves books, and makes books," as one of his supporters pointed
out, did little to temper the criticism. The president of the American
Library Association huffed to the press that, using those standards,
naming MacLeish as Librarian of Congress was about the same as
"appointing a man Secretary of Agriculture because he likes cut flow-
ers on his dinner table."

In addition, many of MacLeish's fellow intellectual progressives
and literati had accused him of joining the Roosevelt administration
as a propagandist to support aggression overseas.

Such protests were ironic considering that MacLeish had wanted
no part of the job at first.

MOST PEOPLE DID NOT turn down the president of the United
States even once, but MacLeish had twice said no to Franklin Roosevelt before succumbing to the chief executive's well-known powers of
flattery and persuasion.

For his part, Roosevelt was searching for a replacement for
seventy-eight-year-old Herbert Putnam, who had told the president a
year earlier that he intended to retire. Putnam had been Librarian of
Congress since 1899 and the president was looking for a more capable,
vigorous, and politically aligned leader for the post. Putnam still ran
the library as though it were 1899; he refused to delegate and demanded a say in virtually all decisions, a style that proved totally

impractical thanks to the growth of the Library of Congress during his four-decade tenure and the diversity of its collections and its responsibilities. In that period, the library had grown from approximately 1 million volumes to just over 6 million and had acquired from the State Department the papers of the founding fathers. It had also acquired thousands of foreign volumes, pamphlets, and papers—from Russia, China, and Japan—as well as additional ancient collections. In addition, Putnam himself had established the Library of Congress classification system for books (still in existence today), an interlibrary loan system, and deeper relationships with other libraries across the country. The complexity of the current Library of Congress demanded a leader with vision, someone who could view the big picture and not become embroiled in arcane details.

Moreover, President Roosevelt believed such a leader could best handle the new administrative and political demands that could be placed on the library, from diplomats and military strategists alike, if war broke out in Europe; when he was considering Putnam's replacement in the spring of 1939, the situation across the Atlantic was perilous.

"He is not a professional librarian nor is he a special student of incunabula or ancient manuscripts," Roosevelt acknowledged. "Nevertheless, he has lots of qualifications that said specialists have not." FDR had read MacLeish's columns and articles supporting many aspects of the New Deal, and his overall grasp of FDR's programs and policies solidified his visionary credentials in the president's eyes. More pertinent to the times, MacLeish was an outspoken and vehement critic of the rising fascist tide in Germany.

Felix Frankfurter, recently appointed as associate justice to the Supreme Court, knew MacLeish from past professional associations. Frankfurter heartily endorsed MacLeish, pointing out that he had vision, imagination, and energy. He would bring a touch of modernity to the library, since he was also acquainted with the new media of radio and motion pictures. He had a diverse background—a leader at law school, an able lawyer, a onetime editor (of *Fortune* magazine), a poet—that would serve the Library of Congress well. "He would bring to the Librarianship intellectual distinction, cultural recognition the world over, a persuasive personality, and a delicacy of touch in dealing with others," Frankfurter told the president. Moreover, he would bring "creative energy in making the Library of Congress the great center of the cultural resources of the Nation in the technological setting of our time."

Frankfurter's endorsement confirmed Roosevelt's assessment and he made his initial overture to MacLeish over lunch on May 23, 1939. Honored by the offer, MacLeish nonetheless had no intention of taking the job. He initially feared that the demands of the office would leave him little or no time to write his own poetry. In his letter declining the position, he told FDR that he had wrestled mightily with the decision and "for four days . . . nothing else has been in my mind, waking or sleeping."

The fact was, the job frightened him, he told Roosevelt, because it was "pretty much a permanent job. A man would hardly be much good at it for three or four years and it would be unfair of him to leave until he had passed his apprenticeship and served for many years thereafter." Where did that leave MacLeish? "I should therefore feel, in taking [the job], that I have given up my own work pretty much for the rest of my life."

Roosevelt persisted—he relished the thrill of the chase—and invited MacLeish to a second lunch. He ultimately wore down MacLeish's resistance and finally convinced MacLeish to change his mind by focusing on the "great importance" of the work at the library: not only would the institution serve the nation if war broke out in Europe; it could also be a great and influential institution for the United States at large. FDR suggested the Library of Congress could sponsor bookmobiles to traverse large swaths of the illiterate South, and stressed the essential democracy of a national library, a place where any American could go to read a book or conduct research regardless of his or her financial wherewithal or social status. In later years, MacLeish would say, "Mr. Roosevelt decided that I wanted to be Librarian of

Congress." Indeed, FDR's power of persuasion, along with assurances from several of MacLeish's friends that he could find the time for his own writing projects, convinced the poet to accept the position. With Roosevelt's unequivocal support, the Senate overwhelmingly confirmed MacLeish's nomination, and in October 1939, the new librarian of Congress began work.

MacLeish felt that the role of all libraries, including the Library of Congress, was to educate Americans on the benefits of liberty and the evils of tyranny. The preservation of the United States depended on it, and "time is running out," he said in late October 1939, "not like the sand in a glass, but like the blood in an opened artery. There is still time left to us. But we can foresee and foresee clearly the moment when there will be none."

Even that early, MacLeish sent a note to the White House to ask whether President Roosevelt should be informed of the need for "the preparation of a safe depository for the most valuable books of the Library of Congress on the remotest chance that such a depository may be necessary. The question keeps me awake nights," he told the president, "and I hope you will forgive me for passing a bit of my insomnia on to you."

IN THE WINTER OF 1941, Lawrence Martin's recommendation—that the documents be housed in a fortress far from Washington—both intrigued MacLeish and added to his current insomnia. MacLeish thought Martin's suggestion was shrewd, though the repository was not large enough to hold the thousands of critical documents in the Library of Congress. Only an exclusive selection of the nation's records should be transported to the near-impenetrable location—the Declaration of Independence, the Constitution, and the Gettysburg Address among them.

These were the documents whose creation founded—and ultimately preserved—the American nation. These were the documents that Americans had risked everything for, had fought and died for, and which had spawned and today formed the underpinnings of a great constitutional republic. These documents embodied the freedoms MacLeish and most Americans held dear, freedoms that had been threatened in the past, and in 1941, were in danger once again.

As others before him, MacLeish was ready to act to safeguard them and the liberties they represented.

★ ★ ★

1776

★ ★ ★

2

★

"We Hold

These Truths . . ."

★

Philadelphia, July 2, 1776

Mud-spattered and drenched, still wearing his boots and spurs, Delaware's Caesar Rodney arrived at the Pennsylvania State House just as his fellow delegates were about to debate the most important issue they would face in their lifetimes.

The forty-seven-year-old member of the Second Continental Congress had endured a night of hard riding through raging thunderstorms, galloping a grueling seventy-five miles from his family plantation just outside of Dover. He may have made the trip entirely on horseback— a lone night rider slashing through the wet, lightning-illuminated countryside—or begun his journey by horse-drawn carriage before abandoning his wheeled transport for the sureness and swiftness of a saddled steed when the roads became thick with mud.

Either way, he arrived in Pennsylvania exhausted and ill, but on time, which was all that really mattered. Rodney and his fellow Delaware delegate Thomas McKean, who had frantically sent for Rodney a day earlier and met him at the front doors when he mounted the statehouse steps, hurried to join the assemblage. Then the doors were closed tight again as members of Congress carried on their work enclosed in a cocoon of secrecy.

The vast majority of Rodney's colleagues were thrilled to see him; as he entered the room, sopping wet, many delegates gathered around. Rodney encapsulated the reason for their enthusiasm in a letter he wrote to his brother two days later: "I arrived in Congress (tho detained by thunder and rain) [in] time enough to give my voice in the matter of independence."

THE DELAWARE STATESMAN AND military leader had served as a member of the colonial militia, a representative in the colonial legislature, and a member of the Stamp Act Congress in 1765. Nonetheless, Caesar Rodney was an unlikely member of the Continental Congress to have completed a heroic sojourn on horseback that some compared to Paul Revere's midnight ride more than a year earlier in Boston.

First, Rodney suffered from debilitating attacks of asthma, "smart fits," as he called them; they hindered his breathing and often sapped his strength for hours at a time.

Worse, Rodney suffered from ravaging facial cancer, a particularly horrific form of the disease which would kill him only a few years later. Eight years earlier, he had contemplated sailing to London for surgery to remove an enormous tumor from the side of his nose, until he learned that Dr. Thomas Bond, a renowned physician in Philadelphia, had treated the rare affliction in another man. Before the surgery, Rodney confessed to his brother, Thomas, that the procedure would be a "dreadful undertaking . . . that will be attendant with great danger." Thomas expressed his alarm, urging Caesar to give his decision "serious consideration, as your health and even your life may depend on the treatment." Caesar should not be worried about the medical expenses of surgery, his brother stressed, and if he were unsure about Bond's skills, he should still consider a voyage to London.

Days later, Caesar Rodney underwent the excruciating and less-than-precise surgery that was standard for his day. When the surgeon extracted the "hard-crusted matter, which had risen so high," he left a bone-deep hole in Rodney's face that extended from the corner of his eye to more than halfway alongside the length his nose. While the surgery eased his pain temporarily, the cancer proved to be "extremely obstinate . . . [and] tedious, as well as a painful business" for the rest of his life. And if his physical discomfort were not enervating enough, Rodney was also deeply self-conscious about his facial disfigurement— he usually wore a green silk scarf as a veil to cover the affected flesh.

Despite his afflictions, and despite reported warnings from his physician that an intense ride at full gallop could prove fatal, Rodney did not hesitate for a moment when an express rider, dispatched by McKean, arrived at Rodney's plantation on July 1, 1776, with a simple but urgent message: he was needed immediately back in Congress. Rodney had attended the congressional sessions in Philadelphia throughout the spring but had returned to Delaware as part of his militia duties to quell a Tory uprising in his county. Caesar Rodney, like McKean, was a firm believer in the American colonies separating from England and becoming independent, but a large minority of his fellow Delaware residents remained loyal to the Crown. Such sentiments were not unusual in the more moderate middle colonies, even at this late date, even after what Rodney and his allies considered repeated and egregious abuses by the king and Parliament.

The message from McKean was simple and straightforward: unless he made his way back to Philadelphia forthwith, all they had worked for could be in jeopardy.

Caesar Rodney never recorded his thoughts about the ride that would one day make him the subject of flourishing poetry and convince Delaware leaders to issue a coin and erect statues and monuments in his honor. Perhaps his focus was on the struggle to see and breathe as wind and rain lashed his face and his veil, as his horse fought for purchase on slick, mud-clogged trails, as he rode northward through Dover, over Duck Creek to Cantwell's Bridge (now Odessa), through

St. Georges, to Tybout's Corner, and then through New Castle (then the state capital), Wilmington, Brandywine Village, Upland, and on into Philadelphia.

Yet, as he passed through forests and towns, past sweeping farms and old taverns, as he crossed over swollen rivers and creeks, likely waiting impatiently at delayed ferry crossings while sheets of rain engulfed him, Rodney must have pondered the circumstances that made this journey a necessity that, inexorably, was leading him to a rendezvous with destiny, for Delaware and for the American colonies.

WHILE WE KNOW THAT the messenger conveyed the urgency with which Rodney was needed, we don't know how much detail he conveyed about the dramatic events of recent days.

The Continental Congress had debated for most of July 1, and as the afternoon wore on, organized itself into a committee of the whole to "take into consideration the resolution respecting independency." When a preliminary vote on the issue was taken, it became clear that only nine of the thirteen colonies clearly favored separation from Britain. Four of Pennsylvania's seven delegates had opposed the motion (much to Benjamin Franklin's chagrin and to the dismay of popular sentiment in Pennsylvania). New York had abstained, awaiting new instructions from its state legislature—their twelve-month-old previous instructions allowed them to do nothing that would impede reconciliation. South Carolina, which had previously vigorously opposed many of the king's policies and generally supported the New England colonies' clamor for independence, surprisingly, voted no. And Delaware, with only two of its three delegates present, was divided—McKean ardently in favor and George Read believing it was too radical a move. The missing Delaware delegate, the state's most supportive proponent of American independence, was Caesar Rodney.

While the nine colonies in favor of independence—New Hampshire, Massachusetts, Rhode Island, Connecticut, New Jersey, Maryland, Virginia, North Carolina, and Georgia—formed a clear majority, supporters believed that such a monumental step demanded more. It required the kind of unshakeable solidarity that could only be achieved through unanimity or near unanimity. Only such a show of strength would make clear, both at home and abroad, the unshakable nature of their resolve.

As late afternoon approached on July 1, South Carolina's Edward Rutledge rescued the moment by asking that the final congressional decision be put off until the next day. Why? He implied that his delegation, though it disapproved of the motion, might vote in favor "for the sake of unanimity." John Adams of Massachusetts, one of the Congress's most passionate voices for independence, agreed. The rest of the majority concurred. It was at this point that McKean acted "without delay," dispatching the express rider to Delaware, "at my private expense," to deliver the urgent message to Caesar Rodney.

JOHN ADAMS DESCRIBED Caesar Rodney as "the oddest looking man in the world—thin and slender as a reed—pale—his face is not bigger than a large apple," but the Massachusetts delegate saw something of himself in his Delaware counterpart. For despite Rodney's strange appearance, Adams was also quick to note that Delaware's midnight rider had a "sense of fire, spirit, wit and humour in his countenance."

Adams was among the most jubilant to see Rodney walk into the Pennsylvania State House—one day it would be called Independence Hall—on July 2, 1776. The Massachusetts delegate had worked tirelessly toward this moment. Boston had been at the center of the storm between the Crown and the colonies for several years—feeling the brunt of the Stamp Act, the Intolerable Acts, the Tea Act, the opening volleys of war at the battles of Lexington and Concord in April 1775—and Adams had been both a witness and a participant. His experience fueled his philosophy about liberty, freedom, and the role of government. "The only maxim of a free government ought to be to trust no man living with the power to endanger the public liberty," he wrote in 1772, one of many diary entries on this topic.

When he arrived in Philadelphia in early February, Adams had been fired with emotion about the potential magnitude of events taking place inside the Pennsylvania State House. But he soon discovered that his grueling, two-week, bone-chilling, 400-mile trip on horseback across treacherous ice-rutted, snow-packed roads and frozen streams proved less arduous than hammering out an agreement these last few months among strong-willed, passionate, quarrelsome, and in most cases brilliant representatives from across the colonies.

Early in their debates, Adams had observed that members of the Second Continental Congress were equally divided three ways in their views about the colonies' relationship with the mother country: "one third Tories," who opposed independence from England; "and [one] third timid," who were too cautious to commit one way or another; and "one-third true blue," who wanted to declare independence quickly. To his fellow Massachusetts residents whose sympathies fell in the latter category, he implored patience. If the clamor for independence among some was to build to a crescendo among many, it would take time and the power of persuasive arguments—and for supporters of independence, political timing was everything. Proposing independence too soon would likely doom it to failure, and what message would that convey to both the Crown and the colonists? Waiting too long could see any momentum dissipate, an equally unpalatable result.

One by one, events helped Adams and the other independence advocates make their case.

IN FEBRUARY, WORD HAD arrived in Philadelphia that Parliament, in late December 1775, had voted to prohibit all trade with the colonies "during the continuance of the present Rebellion."

The measure put American vessels outside the king's protection, declaring all colonial vessels, whether in harbor or at sea, forfeit to the

Crown. Orders issued in the king's name essentially made American ships, ports, and sailors targets of the British Royal Navy. Further, Parliament denounced as traitors all Americans who did not uncondi- tionally submit to the Crown; every member of the Congress knew the punishment for treason was death by hanging. The Prohibitory Act, as it was known, was a blow to those who sought some kind of negoti- ated settlement with the mother country. John Hancock, president of the Continental Congress, put it succinctly if inartfully: "The making [of] all our Vessells lawful Prize don't look like a Reconciliation."

Meanwhile, a pamphlet called *Common Sense*, by an anonymous author—later revealed as a poor English immigrant named Thomas Paine—was sweeping the colonies with its call for continued war against the Crown and for eventual colonial independence. It attacked the idea of a British monarchy and asked its readers: "Why is it that we hesitate? . . . The sun never shined on a cause of greater worth. . . . For God's sake, let us come to a final separation. . . . The birthday of a new world is at hand." It was the boldest call in print to date for Ameri- can independence. Indeed, Paine captured the imagination of many Americans when he said that war had made independence necessary and desirable.

The colonies owed it to the dead militiamen on Lexington Green and army troops elsewhere to discard the idea of reconciliation as a "fallacious dream." In Paine's words, the "blood of the slain, the weep- ing voice of nature cries, 'TIS TIME TO PART."

THE CONTINENTAL CONGRESS DROVE its first major stake into the ground on May 15, 1776; coincidentally, so did the colony of Virginia, although the latter's news would not reach Philadelphia for another two weeks. This one-two punch in favor of independence all but slammed the door on any chance of full reconciliation between Great Britain and the American colonies and laid the groundwork for all that followed.

In Williamsburg, the Virginia Convention approved a resolution in- structing its delegates to the Continental Congress in Philadelphia to

propose that the American colonies declare themselves free and independent, "absolved from all allegiance to, or dependence on, the Crown
or Parliament of Great Britain." The convention then adopted George
Mason's resolves—sixteen articles of freedom known as the Virginia
Declaration of Rights—and in the following days and weeks developed
a new independent government for Virginia, with Patrick Henry as
the newly elected first governor of the Commonwealth of Virginia.

It was not that the Virginia Convention was the first to take up the
issue of colonial independence; other colonies had endorsed the idea.
What made the Virginia vote so important was that it was the first such
measure to *order its delegates to propose independence* before the
Continental Congress.

Meanwhile, in Philadelphia, congressional delegates, still unaware
of the Virginia vote, adopted their own May 15 resolution, drafted by
John Adams, recommending that the various colonies assume all the
powers of government, "to secure the happiness and safety of their
constituents in particular, and America in general." In a preamble to
a resolution that left no room for reconciliation with Great Britain,
Adams wrote that the "exercise of any authority" by the Crown should
be "totally suppressed" by the colonies in response to the "hostile invasions and cruel depredations" of the mother country. The power and
uncompromising nature of Adams's language left some delegates, even
those who generally supported independence, feeling that Congress
was acting prematurely. Pennsylvania's James Wilson asked, after two
days of acrimonious debate: "Before we are prepared to build a new
house, why should we pull down the old one, and expose ourselves to
all the inclemencies of the season?"

Adams was having none of it. His motion was risky, yes, but America
had no choice but to proceed with boldness; timidity was a sign of weak-
ness and would only encourage the king to further trample on colonial
rights. Thanks to the force of Adams's will and determination, Congress
on May 15 approved the preamble and the resolution. The Massachusetts delegate was elated. Congress, Adams declared immodestly, had
"passed the most important resolution that was ever taken in America."

Other delegates agreed. Caesar Rodney, prior to returning to Delaware, wrote to his brother Thomas of the May 15 vote: "Even the *cool considerate men* think it amounts to a declaration of independence." Massachusetts delegate Elbridge Gerry predicted that "a final Declaration . . . of independency is approaching with great rapidity." Gerry had also noticed that the mind-set of Pennsylvania residents had switched toward independence. "The spirit of the people is great," he said.

AS IF THE SEPARATE but intertwined May 15 events in Williamsburg and Philadelphia did not provide enough drama in the story of the republic's birth, a third storyline emerged almost simultaneously that would shape the Congress and the country. A thirty-three-year-old Virginia delegate, who had left the Congress the previous December to care for his family, rode into Philadelphia on May 14 after a strained, one-week journey from his beloved home. He returned to Pennsylvania in an "uneasy, anxious state"—mourning the death of his mother who had succumbed to a stroke less than two months earlier; battling debilitating migraines; and struggling with uncertainty about his upcoming role in Congress. He had missed much while he was away.

What lay in store for him?

Thomas Jefferson would soon find out.

A PHILOSOPHER, A STATESMAN, and a brilliant thinker; a scholar, a slaveholder, and a voracious reader; a gifted writer, a poor public speaker, an insatiable seeker of knowledge—the full complexity of Virginia's Thomas Jefferson would soon be known to the world. The noted lawyer and member of the Virginia House of Burgesses, the master of his Monticello plantation, would wield his pen to become the defining voice in the creation of a new nation.

Both an idealist and a pragmatist, Jefferson enjoyed learning and discussing lofty theories of politics, government, science, music, mathematics, philosophy, culture, and the arts, while understanding that the essence of leadership is the ability to translate complex theory into simple and practical solutions. He visualized both the big picture and the devil in the details in ways most men did not and could not. Among the Continental Congress delegates, Jefferson was reputed to be a man of deep political acumen; he was regarded as a champion of colonial rights and individual freedom and a gifted writer able to employ both evocative rhetoric and simple language with great effectiveness.

His most important literary contributions to the colonial cause to this point had come in the summer of 1774. In May of that year, Virginia newspapers announced the passage of the Boston Port Act, parliamentary legislation that closed the city's port until restitution was made for losses incurred during the Boston Tea Party the previous December. Virginians, including Jefferson, Richard Henry Lee, and Patrick Henry, were furious. "We must boldly take an unequivocal stand in line with Massachusetts," Jefferson said.

He drafted a paper setting out instructions for Virginia delegates who would attend the First Continental Congress in Philadelphia, scheduled to begin in September. His nearly 7,000-word treatise, entitled *A Summary View of the Rights of British America*, was printed in pamphlet form and circulated widely without his advance knowledge. A precursor to future writings, he urged King George not to allow his name "to be a blot in the page of history," and proclaimed that in no way should "our properties within our territories . . . be taxed or regulated by any power on earth but our own." He then added: "The God who gave us life gave us liberty at the same time; the hand of force may destroy, but cannot disjoin them." While Jefferson included a condition of loyalty ("It is neither our wish nor our interest to separate from" Great Britain), for many in 1774, his language remained far too intemperate.

Others, though, concurred with the tone of Jefferson's message. In August of that year, George Washington bought several copies of what he called "Mr. Jefferson's Bill of Rights." John Adams later called the

Summary View "a very handsome public paper" that clearly demonstrated Jefferson's "happy talent for composition." The work propelled Jefferson into the vanguard of the colonial cause for freedom, placing his intellectual thinking far ahead of many colonists.

After the Battle of Bunker Hill in Boston in June 1775, Thomas Jefferson had written: "As our enemies have found we can reason like men, so now let us show them we can fight like men also."

A year later in Philadelphia, Thomas Jefferson found himself at the center of the grandest fight of all.

IT WAS NOT THOMAS JEFFERSON, but another Virginian—delegate Richard Henry Lee—on instructions from his home-colony assembly, who, on June 7, 1776, proposed to the Continental Congress the most profound resolution in American history.

Eight years earlier, while hunting on his property in Virginia, Richard Henry Lee had lost four fingers on his left hand when his musket exploded. After the wounds were cauterized to stop the bleeding, Lee would cover his gnarled hand with a black silk handkerchief. The hunting accident—which resulted in what Lee called an "unhappy wound"—was the beginning of a year of deep despair. In December of that same year, his first wife, Anne, died of acute pleurisy, leaving Richard Henry with four children under the age of ten. Lee remarried a year later (her name was also Anne, she had also lost a spouse, and together the couple would have five children) and also began to strengthen his reputation as one of Virginia's leading advocates for colonial independence.

As his responsibilities and public persona broadened, Lee discovered that the black handkerchief, a symbol of the physical and emotional pain he suffered in 1768, became an asset during his public speeches, adding a theatrical flair to his gestures, captivating audiences as he punctuated his points with repeated slashes of his gloved hand.

Now, as he rose to speak to his fellow delegates on June 7, 1776, a sunny morning in Philadelphia, forty-four-year-old Richard Henry Lee was about to employ his oratorical skills and gesticulations of the black handkerchief in the most dramatic moment of his public life.

No Continental Congress record exists of any preamble uttered by Lee before he offered his resolution, but it is likely that he did speak, and forcefully so. Just five days earlier, he had written angrily of the Crown: "Contrary to our earnest, early and repeated petitions for peace, liberty and safety, our enemies press us with war, threaten us with danger and slavery . . . force on his [King George III's] part & submission on ours is all he proposes." It should be presumed that many of these sentiments were still top of mind when Lee stood before the delegates on June 7.

Whatever the true content and length of his introductory remarks preceding the motion, the powerful language contained in Lee's historic resolution is not a matter of speculation; it is contained in the *Journals of Congress* as the last item the delegates dealt with on June 7. Lee's motion contained three separate clauses, the first of which, especially, would soon reverberate like a thunderclap far beyond the walls of the Pennsylvania State House:

> That these United Colonies are, and of right ought to be, free and independent States, that they are absolved from all allegiances to the British Crown, and that all political connection between them and the State of Great Britain is, and ought to be, totally dissolved.

Lee's resolution continued:

> That it is expedient forthwith to take the most effectual measures for forming foreign alliances.

And:

> That a plan of confederation be prepared and transmitted to the respective Colonies for their consideration and appropriation.

To no one's surprise, John Adams quickly seconded the motion. Then, as though to reflect on the momentous nature of Lee's resolution, the delegates voted to table the proposal until the following day— Saturday—when the debate would begin in earnest. The resolution postponing the debate ordered members to return on June 8 "punctually at 10 o'clock."

The delegates would have one night to collect their thoughts.

OVER THE NEXT FEW days, not only did the Continental Congress engage in a spirited debate over Richard Henry Lee's resolution, but members made their opinions known in letters back to their home colonies. On the first day, June 8, candles were brought into the Pennsylvania State House as the debate continued well past dark. There was no doubt that men such as Adams, Jefferson, Lee, McKean, and a majority of others would be supporting the resolution for independence. But a strong minority—Pennsylvania's John Dickinson and James Wilson, New York's Robert Livingston, and South Carolina's Edward Rutledge among the leaders—opposed the idea, at least initially. Some believed that the colonies needed a confederated government in place before announcing to the world that they were declaring independence from Great Britain. Others, while "friends of the measure," as Thomas Jefferson recalled years later, were reluctant to vote in favor until "the voice of the people" drove them to it.

As the debate continued on June 8, 9, and 10, it became clear that many delegates from the middle colonies—far more moderate than the New Englanders—were reluctant to vote in favor of independence without additional time to consider the matter, to exchange correspondence with their home-colony assemblies, and to hear directly from the people in their colonies. Thomas Jefferson, in his notes written years later, said they were "not yet ripe for bidding adieu to British connection, but that they were fast ripening, and in a short time, would join the general voice of America."

On Monday, June 10, Edward Rutledge moved that the vote on

Lee's resolution be delayed for twenty days, until July 1, to allow recal-
citrant delegates from the middle colonies—Maryland, Delaware, New
York, New Jersey, even Pennsylvania—to further gauge the reaction of
their citizens and receive additional instructions. Delegates agreed;
even those who favored independence saw the wisdom in a delay to
help sway votes. Jefferson even speculated that if Congress had proceeded against the wishes of the moderates, then certain colonies
"might secede from the union."

Still, since it appeared that Congress was leaning toward approving Richard Henry Lee's resolution when it eventually reconsidered
the measure, delegates appointed a five-member committee to draft
a declaration of independence. The Committee of Five, as it became
known, consisted of John Adams, Thomas Jefferson, Benjamin Franklin, Robert Livingston, and Connecticut's Roger Sherman. Jefferson
was the youngest, at thirty-three; Franklin, at seventy, by far the oldest
and struggling with health issues.

It was up to these men to decide the next big questions: What would
be the nature of the content of the Declaration? And who would draft
the document that the committee would present to the full Congress
in less than three weeks?

DECADES LATER, AS OLD MEN, John Adams and Thomas Jefferson
differed widely in their recollections of how the Virginian became
the drafter of the Declaration of Independence. The Committee of
Five met several times to consider the content of the document, and
no one other than Adams and Jefferson was considered as a potential
author; Benjamin Franklin was battling a severe attack of gout, and neither Roger Sherman nor Robert Livingston were considered especially
gifted writers or lofty thinkers. It is at this point, however, that the
divergence occurs between Adams's and Jefferson's account of events.

Adams, whose account is by far the more intriguing, maintains that
the decision to delegate the writing task to Jefferson had its roots in a
private conversation Adams had with delegates almost two years be-

fore, at the First Continental Congress. At that point, Adams warned that no one should ever "utter the word independence" because it was too soon, but if and when the time came, Virginia should have the honor of taking the lead in the effort. "It is the most populous State in the Union," he noted, but more important, "they are very proud of their ancient dominion, they call it; they think they have a right to take the lead, and the Southern States and Middle States too, are too disposed to yield it to them." Massachusetts, on the other hand, had a reputation as a rabble-rousing state that was too far out front of the prevailing sentiment in the colonies.

An aging Adams recalled that Jefferson urged him to write the Declaration draft, but Adams declined. When Jefferson asked why, Adams responded: "Reason first, you are a Virginian, and a Virginian ought to appear at the end of this business. Reason second, I am obnoxious, suspected, and unpopular. You are very much otherwise."

Was there a third reason? Yes, Adams said to Thomas Jefferson: "You can write ten times better than I can."

According to Adams, Jefferson replied: "Well, if you are decided, I will do as well as I can."

Jefferson's account, well after the fact, maintains that Adams's advanced age (Adams was eighty-seven when he recounted the story, while Jefferson was eighty) had dulled his memory and led him "into unquestionabl[e] error." He recalled no such exchange with Adams, remembering only that the committee met and "unanimously pressed" him to write the draft. "I consented; I drew it [up]."

The end result was the same. Thomas Jefferson would draft the Declaration. With the independence issue still not resolved, Adams knew there would be political advantage in a Virginian taking the lead on the document, just as there had been symbolic merit in selecting Virginia's George Washington to lead the Continental army. In addition, he admired Jefferson's way with words, which were "remarkable for the peculiar felicity of their expression." In short, Adams said: "I had a great opinion of the elegance of his pen, and none at all of my own. I therefore insisted that no hesitation should be made on his part."

*

JEFFERSON TOOK ADAMS'S ADVICE.

Alone in his second-floor rooms at the corner of Seventh and Market streets, several blocks from the center city, he worked fast and sure on the draft of the Declaration. He had moved there shortly after his arrival in Philadelphia because it afforded him some relief from the noise and distractions of the center city, yet he could still walk comfortably to the statehouse. And while he complained about horseflies from a nearby stable finding their way through his open window, here he was removed from the horse-and-carriage traffic that clattered along the pebble-stoned streets; away from the story swapping and political arguments of fellow delegates at taverns and coffeehouses; undisturbed by the farmers from the countryside who drove their huge wagons to market to sell produce, chicken, pigs, and cattle; and otherwise oblivious to the noise created by the 30,000 inhabitants who lived in America's largest and most cosmopolitan city.

Jefferson had thought about independence and liberty for some time and he knew the task at hand. As one historian would later note, Jefferson's primary purpose was not to *declare* independence but to proclaim to the world the reasons for declaring it: "it was intended as a formal justification of an act already accomplished," although a final vote had not taken place. Jefferson described his responsibility to "place before mankind the common sense of the subject, in terms so plain and firm as to command their assent."

Jefferson claimed he "turned to neither book or pamphlet" while preparing his draft, though he had formulated similar ideas in his own 1774 *Summary View*, and in his recently drafted preamble to the Virginia Constitution. He also borrowed liberally ideas about freedom, the dignity of the individual, and the virtues of self-governance that had been propounded by philosophers and documents of times past— John Locke, David Hume, and Montesquieu; St. Augustine and Sir Isaac Newton; Cicero and Aristotle; the Magna Carta—and refined by contemporaries such as Thomas Paine, Pennsylvania's James Wilson, and his fellow Virginian, George Mason, a strong proponent of individual rights who had embedded the concept into his draft of the Virginia Declaration of Rights. The document was in circulation among the delegates in Philadelphia in early June of 1776 and had attracted wide attention. Jefferson called Mason "one of our really great men, and of the first order of greatness," making it a near certainty that Jefferson had Mason's work at the top of his mind as he drafted his own Declaration.

Jefferson made no apologies for drawing on the thinking of others; on the contrary, his intention was to set down ideas with which the colonists had become familiar in the debate of recent years. Making the case for independence—one that would generate support from the delegates, from undecided Americans, and from potential European allies—required a restatement and reemphasis of concepts that the people understood and accepted, at least in principle; introducing radically new ideas would have been risky. His goal was to lay out before the Congress and the world the "sentiments" of independence and the reason for declaring it. It was not originality of principles that was important, he emphasized, but the notion that the Declaration reflected "an expression of the American mind."

Jefferson performed his task brilliantly. His language was a combination of the elegant and the prosaic, a mixture of soaring rhetoric that defined the derivation and essence of human freedom and liberty, and a relentless drumbeat of facts as he built a prosecutor's case against the king to justify the colonies' break with England. His dramatic and unique cadence and flourishing literary style provided the appropriate weight and gravitas for the document that would not merely justify rebellion but literally define the ideals of a new American republic.

The ideas about governing and human liberty contained in his draft might not be new, but a nation *conceived* upon such bedrock principles certainly was.

IT IS NO ACCIDENT that his draft Declaration was far more than a recitation of grievances against the Crown—though it certainly does contain a lengthy list of such wrongs—but a treatise on the essence of the human condition and the role that freedom and self-government plays in it.

Indeed, if European allies and even American loyalists were to support the document, it needed to convey far more than the colonies' desire to rebel against the mother country. In fact, such a limited scope would have doomed the Declaration in the eyes of the world; rebellion against the king was most often viewed as treasonous, a crime that could never be sanctioned, especially by those European countries that engaged in trade and commerce with England.

The same worldwide attitude would have prevailed had the dispute between the Crown and the colonies been viewed merely as a civil war within the structure of Britain's empire. No potential ally would interfere in England's "internal" affairs.

Thus, Jefferson needed to appeal to a much higher set of ideals, a much broader vision, and a deeper set of principles to define the colonial cause.

For that reason, Jefferson does not mention Great Britain, the king, the colonies, or the specific American rebellion until almost 300 words into the Declaration. His opening arguments focus on laying out essential principles of freedom, the natural order, and God's law. His draft was more than a declaration to define the American condition; it was a statement declaring the right of *any* people to seek the most basic rights and live according to the most basic tenets of human dignity.

Jefferson's long, haunting opening sentence set the tone:

When in the Course of human events, it becomes necessary for one People to dissolve the Political Bands which have connected them with another, and to assume among the Powers of the Earth, the separate and equal Station to which the Laws of Nature and of Nature's God entitle them, a decent Respect to the Opinions of Mankind requires that they should declare the causes which impel them to Separation.

Jefferson structures the remarkable paragraph as a fait accompli of epic importance; neither its premise nor its conclusion seeks approval or concurrence from readers. Jefferson chooses his words carefully, and perhaps the most important word in this opening is "necessary"—it is simply beyond debate and inarguable that the colonies have any choice but to break with England. The wrongs America has suffered require it; it is not "desirable" or "preferable" or "beneficial" to dissolve the connective tissue between the two countries, but "necessary." Moreover, the freedom to which the colonists are *entitled*—the "equal Station"—is not bestowed by kings, parliaments, assemblies, or any other political or manmade entity, but by the "Laws of Nature and of Nature's God." Jefferson's powerful tone-setting opener declares as a given that the people were entitled to a concept of freedom that went far beyond the power of men to grant.

Jefferson's eloquent and iconic follow-up sentences—those that would be most often quoted, studied, debated, and analyzed in the succeeding centuries—distill the universal truths about the sanctity of the individual, his natural-order right to self-govern, and his central role in his relationship to government. It was individuals—the people—who bestowed any and all powers unto the government, rather than the other way around. Jefferson outlined a general philosophy of government that was universal in tone and scope, a thesis that, as one historian noted, makes "revolution justifiable, even meritorious." He wrote:

> We hold these truths to be sacred and undeniable [later changed to "self-evident"], that all Men are created equal, that they are endowed by their Creator with certain unalienable Rights, that among these are Life, Liberty, and the Pursuit of Happiness— That to secure these Rights, Governments are instituted among Men, deriving their just Powers from the Consent of the Governed, that whenever any Form of Government becomes destructive of these Ends, it is the Right of the People to alter

or to abolish it, and to institute new Government, laying its Foundation on such Principles, and organizing its Powers in such Form, as to them shall seem most likely to effect their Safety and Happiness.

Thus, in the first 200 or so words of his draft, Thomas Jefferson clearly and concisely articulated two concepts that had taken previous thinkers and writers thousands of words to explain: the essential reasons that require people to dissolve the ties that bind them to an oppressor and the indisputable right of those newly freed people to govern themselves.

In doing so he elevated the political dispute between the American colonies and England into something far more than a civil war—but rather, an epic battle between the essential dignity of the individual and the power of the state.

ONLY AFTER THIS PREAMBLE laying out universal principles did Jefferson turn his attention to reciting, point by point, the "injuries and usurpations" inflicted by King George upon the colonies; he referred to them as facts for a "candid world" to consider. In this section, Jefferson assumes the role of prosecutor, laying out the king's crimes for a worldwide jury. His prose is less elegant here, much harsher, but no less effective: Among the king's despotic actions that Jefferson hammered home:

He has plundered our Seas, ravaged our Coasts, burnt our Towns, and destroyed the Lives of our People.

He has dissolved Representative Houses repeatedly, for opposing with manly Firmness his Invasions on the Rights of the People.

He has affected to render the Military independent of and superior to Civil Power.

A portion of Jefferson's indictment moves away from the "He has" or "He is" construction and chastises the king:

> For quartering large Bodies of Armed Troops among us;
> For cutting off our Trade with all parts of the World;
> For imposing Taxes on us without our Consent;
> For depriving us, in many Cases, of the Benefits of Trial by
> Jury . . ."

Immediately after his searing point-by-point attack, Jefferson emphasized that, despite the king's malfeasance and cruelties toward the colonies, the Americans had tried their best to reason with him and his emissaries along the way, but to no avail:

> In every stage of these Oppressions, we have Petitioned for
> Redress in the most humble Terms; Our repeated Petitions
> have been answered only by repeated Injury.

Jefferson also called the British people to task, pointing out that the colonies had "warned them from Time to Time" of attempts by their legislature to "extend an unwarrantable Jurisdiction over us." Yet, despite repeated warnings, most British subjects had been "deaf to the Voice of Justice and of Consanguinity." Under current circumstances, the colonists would hold their British brethren to the same standards as they would hold the rest of the world—"enemies in War, in Peace, Friends."

Jefferson then reached the crescendo, penning the stirring concluding paragraph to America's Declaration of Independence, likely the first reference ever to the "United States of America":

> We . . . the Representatives of the United States of America . . .
> solemnly Publish and Declare, that these United Colonies are,
> and of Right ought to be, Free and Independent States; that

they are absolved from all Allegiance to the British Crown, and
that all political connection between them and the State of
Great Britain, is and ought to be totally dissolved.

Jefferson closed with the solemn oath that bound him and his
fellow delegates together as they embarked on an undertaking that
was, at once, a most brazen act of treason and a most noble and risky
adventure—the creation of a new nation:

And for the support of this Declaration . . . we mutually pledge
to each other our lives, our fortunes, and our sacred honor.

THE COMMITTEE OF FIVE made several edits to Jefferson's "Rough
Draught," though it is difficult to determine exactly how many and
precisely who made them. Perhaps the most important change, small
but telling, was the substitution of the words "self-evident" in the
second paragraph in place of Jefferson's original "sacred and undeni-
able." The revised sentence thus began, "We hold these truths to be
self-evident, that all men are created equal . . ." The new phrase established the equality clause as indisputable; beyond a matter of political
debate and essentially etched into the laws of nature, as undebatable as
gravity or the tides.

One other section of Jefferson's Declaration was bound to cause
controversy when the paper was submitted to the delegates. It was the
last of his charges against the king, what John Adams called the "vehement philippic against negro slavery."

As a privileged Virginian, a landowner and a slaveholder, Thomas
Jefferson was a product of his time and his geography. Of the 2.5
million people who lived in the American colonies in 1776, perhaps
as many as 500,000 were slaves; some 200,000 of those resided in
Virginia, the largest slaveholding colony. All members of the Virginia
delegation to the Continental Congress owned slaves. Throughout his
life, Jefferson owned a total of approximately 600 slaves, perhaps as

many as 200 at any one time. Later in his life, he would reportedly engage in a relationship with one of his slaves, his late wife's half-sister, Sally Hemings, with whom he would sire children.

And yet, intellectually if not emotionally, Jefferson possessed a predisposition against the institution of slavery. Early in his career as a member of the Virginia House of Burgesses, he recalled: "I made one effort . . . for the permission of emancipation of slaves which was rejected." His proposed legislation would have given slave owners the right to free their slaves based on "meritorious service," a bill the House swiftly defeated. Later, in court, he represented the grandson of a mixed-race couple and argued that the man should be free despite a Virginia law requiring that he be held in servitude until the age of thirty-one. On behalf of his client, Jefferson wrote that "everyone comes into the world with a right to his own person and using it at his own will." In language that would foreshadow similar thinking in his current draft of the Declaration, he added: "This is called personal liberty, and is given him by the author of nature, because it is necessary for his own sustenance."

He lost the court case.

Rebuked so early in his career in both the legislature and the courts, Jefferson—who, after those defeats, became reluctant to promote causes that he perceived as unwinnable—refrained from further efforts to abolish or even limit slavery. If abolition were to become a reality in America, future generations would have to take up the torch.

For now, for his draft of the Declaration, Jefferson trained his literary skills against the king and his support of the slave trade with one of his longest and harshest indictments. He began:

He has waged cruel war against human nature itself, violating the most sacred rights of life and liberty in the persons of a distant people who never offended him, captivating and carrying them into slavery in another hemisphere, or to incur miserable death in their transportation thither. This piratical warfare . . . is the warfare of the *Christian* king of Great Britain.

Having established the king's personal responsibility for the slave trade, Jefferson accused England's monarch of fighting to keep "open a market where MEN should be bought and sold . . . suppressing every legislative attempt to prohibit or to restrain this execrable commerce."

If Jefferson saw any inconsistency in vilifying the king for his support of the slave trade while he and his Virginia neighbors were some of the largest customers of such commerce, an irony that could hardly escape a man of his intellect, he offered no indication or explanation; this passage was his attempt to lead the Congress and the new country into more progressive intellectual territory on the issue of slavery.

This slave trade language was one of John Adams's favorite passages in the Declaration; he despised slavery and, as a matter of principle, never owned slaves. Yet he was skeptical of the reaction of the Congress to Jefferson's stinging attack on the king. "Though I knew his southern brethren would never suffer to pass it . . . I certainly would never oppose [it]," he recalled later. Nonetheless, Jefferson had written his passage on the slave trade and the Committee of Five left it unaltered. How would the full Congress respond?

On Friday, June 28, 1776, Jefferson's draft, with edits from Adams and Franklin, was reported to Congress. "I was delighted with its high tone and the flights of oratory, with which it abounded," Adams remarked. Delegates disposed of a number of minor issues and then decided to wait until after the weekend to begin debate on independence and the Declaration document. The brief and uninspiring official journal entry reads: "The committee appointed to prepare a Declaration brought in a draught which was read . . . Ordered to lie on the table."

THE PHILADELPHIA TEMPERATURE WAS already in the steamy low eighties when the Continental Congress convened at 9:00 a.m. on Monday, July 1. By 4:00 p.m., thunderstorms swollen with rain and carried on gusty winds would clear out the heat and refresh the city and the delegates. But in the morning, the statehouse was thick with humidity and tension.

John Adams tingled with anticipation. In an early-morning letter to former delegate Archibald Bulloch, he laid out the stakes: "This morning is assigned for the greatest debate of all. A Declaration, that these colonies are free and independent states, has been reported by a committee . . . and this day or tomorrow is to determine its fate." Finding it difficult to contain his enthusiasm, Adams exclaimed: "May Heaven prosper the new-born republic, and make it more glorious than any former republics have been!"

Regrettably, because of the secrecy of the proceedings, we have no official congressional account of the actual debate over independence. No transcription was made, no official notes kept by the secretary or by any delegate. The journals of Congress report only this: after the delegates handled some routine business, they broke into a committee of the whole to "take into consideration the resolution respecting independency."

However, thanks to subsequent letters from several delegates, thanks to Adams's autobiography and Jefferson's notes recorded much later, thanks to documents discovered years afterward, it is possible to piece together the dramatic events of July 1, 1776, the beginning of four of the most meaningful days in all of American history.

FIRST, PROPONENTS OF INDEPENDENCE heard some bad news: a letter from the Provincial Congress of New York instructing the New York delegates not to vote for independence was read into the record; it was dated June 11, and no further instructions to the delegates had arrived in the interim. The frustration with New York was offset by some good news: just as Congress was about to begin debate, word arrived that the Maryland convention had unanimously instructed its delegates to vote for independence. The news gave John

Adams "much pleasure." He was thankful that "Maryland . . . behaved well."

After Congress received these reports, the independence debate began in earnest and took up most of the day. Members wanted their say. Judging from delegates' recollections in subsequent letters and diaries, Pennsylvania's John Dickinson, a stalwart opponent of independence at this stage, rose first. Consistently opposed to separation, at odds with the likes of John Adams, Samuel Adams, and Richard Henry Lee, Dickinson spoke powerfully and eloquently. Dickinson's main thrust was that separation was premature. "To escape the protection we have in British rule by declaring independence would be like destroying a house before we have got another . . . then asking a neighbor to take us in," he argued. Further, separating from Britain before the colonies were fully recognized by foreign countries, especially France, would be folly. To go forth with a vote on independence now would be "to brave the storm in a skiff made of paper."

Dickinson knew his stance was unpopular, and that by remaining firm in his principles, he was jeopardizing his career. "My conduct this day, I expect, will give the finishing blow to my once great . . . and now too diminished popularity," he wrote. "But thinking as I do on the subject of debate, silence would be guilt."

WHEN DICKINSON CONCLUDED, SILENCE filled the hall. Rain had begun to fall outside, so perhaps the delegates heard drops slapping against the windows. For a time, no member rose to answer the influential Pennsylvanian in his own statehouse. Finally, "after waiting some time, in hopes that some one less obnoxious than myself" would respond, John Adams rose, "determined to speak." He recognized the importance of the moment—all that he had worked for over the past year, as "the author of all the mischief," would be resolved on this day. He began by saying that this was the first time in his life that he had wished for the "talents and eloquence of the ancient orators of Greece and Rome, for I was very sure that none of them ever had before him a question of more importance to his country and to the world."

To Jefferson, Adams was "not graceful nor elegant, nor remarkably fluent," but his Massachusetts colleague spoke "with a power of thought and expression that moved us from our seats." Years later, he would call Adams "our Colossus on the floor . . . he was the pillar of [independence's] support on the floor of Congress, its ablest advocate and defender against the multifarious assaults it encountered." Adams spoke forcefully, but rebutted Dickinson with a steady stream of facts and suggested that the Pennsylvanian's call to delay independence until "the time was right" was simply delaying the inevitable. There would be no ideal time to declare independence.

To New Jersey's Richard Stockton, Adams resembled "the Atlas of American Independence" as he stood and made the case, "the man to whom the country is most indebted for the great measure of independency."

In all, Adams spoke for perhaps two hours and the entire debate lasted nearly nine hours, the delegates exhausted by day's end. A preliminary resolution for independence was moved, and nine colonies voted in favor. Without new instructions from their assembly, New York delegates, who personally supported the resolution, were forced to abstain. Pennsylvania and South Carolina voted against it, and Delaware—minus Caesar Rodney at this time—was divided.

South Carolina's Rutledge suggested that the final vote be delayed until the next day, that perhaps, with a night to think about it, his state's fellow delegates would vote in favor for the "sake of unanimity." Adams and other supporters of independence agreed, looking to deliver a message of solidarity to the colonists, the king, and the world.

Delaware's Thomas McKean had already dispatched the express messenger to Dover to fetch Caesar Rodney.

Writing that evening, John Adams believed the independence question would pass on July 2 by a "great majority, perhaps with almost unanimity," yet he made it clear that he could not promise anything.

Virtually all that could be said on the subject had been. All that remained was a final vote.

AGAIN, CONSIDERING THE MAGNITUDE of the topic, the official congressional journals for July 2, 1776, are maddeningly sparse, all the more disappointing since they fail to record the comments of delegates on two of the most dramatic occurrences of the entire "independency" process.

The first, of course, was the stunning and timely arrival of Delaware's Caesar Rodney after his rain-soaked overnight ride from Dover. He would cast the tie-breaking vote that would record Delaware on the side of independence. His eighty-mile trek through booming thunder and crackling lightning, his entrance into the statehouse while still clad in muddy boots and spurs, his face covered with a silk handkerchief to hide his cancerous disfigurement, was emblematic of the relentless spirit of a man who would overcome any obstacle to cast his vote for independence.

The second dramatic event was one of quiet political stagecraft, and just as important as Rodney's theatrical entrance. Two vacant chairs among the Pennsylvania delegation told the story. John Dickinson and Robert Morris, ardently opposed to independence at this time but recognizing the importance of a unified Congress, had absented themselves from the hall. Of the five Pennsylvania delegates in attendance, a majority—Franklin, Morton, and Wilson—voted in favor of independence. With his absence, Dickinson, especially, had sacrificed his own deeply held personal beliefs for what he apparently believed was the greater good of Congress speaking with one voice.

With Delaware and Pennsylvania on board, Edward Rutledge and his South Carolina comrades remained true to their word and cast their affirmative vote for independence. Again, there is no record of whether they offered remarks before they voted.

Now, twelve colonies had voted in favor, with New York abstaining, still awaiting new instructions from its convention. Of those colonies that had voted, the decision was unanimous. Adams and other proponents could live with that. As much as humanly possible, the delegates had spoken with one voice in Philadelphia.

A war still needed to be won to enforce the political action, but what the Continental Congress accomplished on July 2, 1776, would ring out across America and around the world: the colonies had voted for their independence, dissolving all connection with powerful Great Britain.

With their most important vote ever behind them, the delegates agreed to meet the following day to consider Jefferson's draft of the Declaration of Independence.

IT WAS A JUBILANT John Adams who wrote to Abigail the day after the historic vote. His reputation for crankiness, impatience, and irascibility notwithstanding, the tired but resolute Massachusetts delegate poured out the depth of his elation to his wife in two long letters, declaring that he and his colleagues had reached a decision on the "greatest question . . . which was ever debated in America." In fact, "a greater, perhaps, never was nor will be decided among men," he wrote to Abigail.

Five months after Adams had arrived in Pennsylvania's capital city, he and his fellow delegates, men from different regions with markedly different personalities and priorities, had reached consensus on a remarkable Declaration that months earlier had seemed impossible.

"The second day of July, 1776, will be the most memorable epocha in the history of America," the scrappy Adams wrote on July 3 to Abigail, his dearest friend. "I am apt to believe that it will be celebrated by succeeding generations as the great Festival." Indeed, Adams believed July 2 "ought to be commemorated as the day of deliverance . . . solemnized with pomp and parade, with shows, games, sports, guns, bells, bonfires and illuminations, from one end of this continent to the other, from this time forward, forevermore."

Lest Abigail infer that he was "transported with enthusiasm" and had underestimated the perilous road forward, Adams reassured his wife in the same way he had reassured his fellow delegates during the debate. He was "well aware of the toil, and blood, and treasure that it will cost us to maintain this Declaration, and support and defend these States." Indeed, the explosiveness of the resolution that Congress had approved almost assured that the delegates had placed their own lives, liberty, and families in danger, not to mention their property and other belongings.

What these fifty-six men had done was at once astonishing, risky, brilliant—and treasonous. All were well aware that they had crossed a line from which there was no return, and while most were proud that they had done so, a sense of grave solemnity had settled over the Pennsylvania State House.

Nonetheless, nothing could dampen Adams's spirit or his resolve on this momentous occasion. Surrounded by the ravages of a violent rebellion being waged by the American colonies against their king, one that would spill additional colonial blood across multiple battlefields, he and his fellow delegates had approved a bold and unprecedented vision for a separate and independent America.

"Through all the gloom," John Adams confided to Abigail, "I can see the rays of ravishing light and glory. I can see that the end is more than worth all the means."

MUCH TO JEFFERSON'S ANGST, the delegates spent the latter part of July 2, all of July 3, and a portion of July 4 poring over his draft, editing the Declaration in a way that caused him pain, but, remarkably for a committee, shortening and sharpening his work and perhaps making it stronger. Still, the essence of the document—the power of its ideas, the eloquence of its language, the simplicity of its structure—was Jefferson's and would remain so long after the delegates finished their review.

Again, because the proceedings were shrouded in secrecy, we have no official record of the debates among delegates over the three days that they edited Jefferson's Declaration. We do know from John Adams's recollection years later that "Congress cut off about a quarter part of it, as I expected they would," though as Jefferson would write later, it was Adams who spent the debate "fighting fearlessly for every word." Adams may have submitted his own edits to Jefferson's draft, but once the document reached the floor, Jefferson said Adams was "its ablest advocate and defender against the multifarious assaults encountered."

Like many gifted writers, Jefferson did not take kindly to seeing his work edited. He painstakingly made several copies of his original draft in longhand to send to friends. A few days after the Declaration was adopted, he sent the final congressionally approved version along with his original draft to Richard Henry Lee, and asked him to "judge whether it [his original draft] is the better or worse for the critics."

As an exasperated Jefferson listened to the debate about his carefully crafted words, Benjamin Franklin related an anecdote to him about the collective ruthlessness of an opinionated group of editors. A hatter named John Thompson was about to open a shop and decided to have a signboard produced. He composed it with the words: JOHN THOMPSON, HATTER, MAKES AND SELLS HATS FOR READY MONEY, and included a picture of a hat. One by one, his friends edited Thompson's work. The first suggested he remove the word "hatter" since the phrase was redundant—"makes and sells hats" clearly demonstrated that he was a hatter. Another said to remove the word "makes," because his customers would not care who made the hat. A third suggested removing "for ready money," since it was not the custom at the time to sell hats on credit. Finally, still another editor asked why he needed "sells hats" on the sign. After all, no customer would expect John Thompson to give the hats away, and the word "hats" was unnecessary since a picture of a hat was already painted on the board. Thus, Franklin related to Jefferson, "his inscription was reduced ultimately to 'John Thompson' with the figure of a hat subjoined."

JEFFERSON'S EDITORS WERE NOT quite as tough as Thompson's, nor did the document suffer because of them. Congress made a total of about eighty edits, most of them minor. However, delegates did cut two large and significant passages from Jefferson's draft.

First, they made wholesale deletions to Jefferson's excoriation of the English people, including exorcising his language declaring that Americans must "renounce forever these unfeeling brethren" and "endeavor to forget our former love for them." The Congress thought too controversial Jefferson's passage that said America must "hold them as we hold the rest of mankind, enemies in war, in peace friends" or his harsh "we might have been a free and a great people together, but a communication of grandeur and of freedom, it seems, is below their dignity."

Not surprisingly, delegates also struck Jefferson's entire passage condemning the king for perpetuating the slave trade. Jefferson surmised years later that it was eliminated "in complaisance with South Carolina and Georgia, who had never attempted to restrain the importation of slaves, and who on the contrary still wanted to continue it." But it wasn't just the objections of Southerners, Jefferson noted. "Our Northern brethren also I believe felt a little tender under those censures, for tho' their people have very few slaves themselves, yet they had been pretty considerable carriers of them to others."

Both observations have merit, but Congress also no doubt recognized the hypocrisy of blaming the king for the slave trade and, by extension, for slavery itself in the American colonies. John Adams, who utterly opposed slavery, said the slave-trade passage was his favorite in the entire draft, but even he must have understood that Jefferson's language actually weakened the colonies' cause since it almost embarrassingly shifted responsibility for slavery away from those who should have borne it completely: American slave owners themselves. Blaming King George for American slavery was ridiculous: Adams knew it, as did the rest of the delegates. Jefferson, brilliant as he was, must have recognized it, too; his slave-trade passage was a misdirected effort to address the most glaring inconsistency of the entire Declaration— American slave owners espousing freedom and equality for all men. Jefferson's reluctance to address the subject head-on may have also been influenced by his previously unsuccessful efforts in Virginia to change the public mind-set on slavery.

Moreover, a stronger denunciation of slavery could have put congressional adoption of the entire Declaration in jeopardy, and neither Adams nor Jefferson was willing to risk it. While both men, and many other delegates, would renounce slavery later—Adams would one day call it "an evil of colossal magnitude"—it is clear that neither man believed July of 1776 was the appropriate time to join the battle, nor was the debate over the Declaration the precise moment. During his retirement at Monticello following his presidency, Jefferson would recall of the revolutionary era that the "public mind would not yet bear the proposition [of emancipation], nor will it bear it even at this day." Prophetically, he added: "Yet the day is not distant when it must bear and adopt it, or worse will follow. Nothing is more certainly written in the book of fate than that these people are to be free."

But for now, with Congress's deletions, the Declaration of Independence would not mention the issue of slavery.

Congress made one other notable change, this one to Jefferson's stirring close, adding, "with a firm reliance on the protection of divine Providence," to the concluding paragraph, which in its final form thus read:

> And for the support of this Declaration, with a firm reliance
> on the protection of divine Providence, we mutually pledge to
> each other our lives, our fortunes, and our sacred honor.

JUST AS IMPORTANT AS their edits was the agreement by the delegates on which sections should be left untouched, which sections Jefferson captured beautifully—most notably the eloquent second paragraph, the heart of the Declaration, the core language that would define its essence, and the nation's, in the years and decades to come.

Not even Jefferson, a lover of words, a connoisseur of ideas, a voracious reader, could have foreseen the long-term impact of this daring passage, one that would, from 1776 on, define America's spirit, pride, philosophy, policies, politics, culture, responsibilities, ideals, civic duty, and sense of purpose. Especially because of this passage, the Declaration of Independence would become one of the most influential documents in the world, and the most revered in all of American history. Americans would cite this iconic second paragraph, especially, to both defend and criticize their nation, to seek better lives, to right injustices, to define their place in the world, to create and build and dream and dare. It would one day form the underlying foundation of the American Constitution, and its message would influence later independence movements and revolutions in Europe, Asia, and South America.

One of Jefferson's fellow committee members, Adams or Franklin, likely added the sturdy and incontrovertible "self-evident," but the full Congress made no changes to the passage. Jefferson's fellow delegates recognized the power and timelessness of his words. The thirty-three-year-old from Virginia, sitting alone in his upstairs room in a Philadelphia boarding house, had written what would become the most important single paragraph in American history:

> We hold these truths to be self-evident, that all men are created equal, that they are endowed by their Creator with certain unalienable Rights, that among these are Life, Liberty, and the pursuit of Happiness.—That to secure these rights, Governments are instituted among Men, deriving their just power from the consent of the governed.

THURSDAY, JULY 4, 1776, BROKE COOL and pleasant in Philadelphia, but even before they arrived at the statehouse, delegates felt the intensity of this day. While war raged in the colonies, while colonial forces were retreating from superior British regulars in Canada, while Britain's General Howe was advancing toward New York with a large force, America had voted for its independence. Now, wrote New Jersey delegate Abraham Clark, "a declaration for this purpose, I expect, will this day pass Congress."

Congress had toiled on the Declaration for most of the day on July 3 and began July 4 with other matters. When members resumed their discussion of the Declaration, the *Journals of the Continental Congress* once again remained silent on the nature of the debate. John Adams and Thomas Jefferson wrote not a word about the proceedings inside the statehouse on that day. The secret journals of Congress do not even contain an entry for July 4. It appears that sometime in the late morning members finished their work on the draft and voted to approve the Declaration. Once again, as they did on July 2, twelve colonies voted in favor and once again New York abstained. Pennsylvania's John Dickinson was again absent. In addition to approving the document, a record of which is contained in the journals, Congress also ordered the Declaration authenticated and printed immediately.

By early afternoon, it was done. The Declaration of Independence, the first document of the new republic, had become a reality.

Appropriately, it was Delaware's Caesar Rodney, who had arrived just in time to take the vote on independence two days earlier, who recorded the July 4 moment in a letter to his brother that afternoon. "We have now Got through with the whole of the Declaration, and ordered it to be printed, so that you will soon have the pleasure of seeing it," he wrote to Thomas Rodney. "Handbills of it will be printed, and sent to the Armies, Cities, County Towns, etc. To be published or rather proclaimed in form."

Days later, Thomas Jefferson's friend, John Page, one of the recipients of Jefferson's recopied original drafts, captured the drama of the accomplishment and the fight that lay ahead, both for the Congress and the fledgling nation. "I am highly pleased with your Declaration," Page wrote to Jefferson. "God preserve the United States. We know the race is not to the swift nor the battle to the strong. Do you not think an angel rides in the whirlwind and directs this storm?"

3

★

"The Unanimous
Declaration"

★

For 240 years, most Americans have clung to two persistent misconceptions regarding the remarkable events that took place in Philadelphia during the summer of 1776.

The first is the incorrect notion that America declared its independence on July 4, when in reality the historic and dramatic vote occurred two days earlier. John Adams was correct when he said independence would be celebrated by succeeding generations "as the great Festival . . . commemorated with . . . bonfires and illuminations," but the Massachusetts delegate thought surely that July 2, not what is now referred to in the vernacular simply as "the Fourth," would become the country's Independence Day, "the most memorable epocha in the history of America."

The second commonly held, but incorrect, belief is that the fifty-six signatures that appear at the bottom of the handwritten-on-parchment copy of the Declaration of Independence—often called the "engrossed" copy to refer to its decorative style written in a large fine hand—were affixed by delegates at the end of the debate on July 4. This was not the case. Despite fuzzy recollections to the contrary by

both Adams and Jefferson in their old age, the historic signing ceremony, which immediately identified the delegates as traitors to the
Crown, would not occur until several weeks later. On July 4, only the
congressional president, John Hancock, and the secretary of Congress,
Charles Thomson, signed the document.

On the night of July 4, Congress's priority was to get a version of
the document printed so it could be distributed across the colonies—
"to the several Assemblies, Conventions & Committees or Councils of
Safety, and to the several Commanding Officers of the Continental
troops that it be proclaimed in each of the United States & at the head
of the Army."

TO DO THE JOB, Congress turned to John Dunlap, its official printer
and a man whose shop was located just a few blocks from the statehouse. His team worked with a sense of urgency well into the night,
and likely overnight, to set in type and then print an unknown number of copies, likely working from a corrected copy handwritten by
Thomas Jefferson (now lost to history). To save time, Dunlap's men cut
the original into as many as eleven sections so several compositors could
work on it separately, and then pasted together the typeset portions into
a single continuous document before the Declaration was printed. This
first printed version, known as the John Dunlap Broadside, carried the
title "In Congress, July 4, 1776. A DECLARATION By the Representatives of the United States OF AMERICA, In General Congress Assembled," and contained only the printed names of Hancock and
Thomson.

That hectic activity filled the inside of Dunlap's print shop is a
matter of conjecture, as is one of the more interesting questions about
the evening of July 4: Did Thomas Jefferson spend most of the night in
the print shop watching his document come to life on the printed page?
Someone had to transport the handwritten copy to Dunlap, and with
Charles Thomson still busy with his secretarial duties, it is not a leap
to presume that Jefferson took the short walk from the statehouse,

clutching the now final copy of his work as approved by his fellow delegates. He would be loath to trust a messenger to make the delivery.

From Jefferson's records, all we know is he took time off on the afternoon of July 4 and purchased seven pairs of ladies' gloves and a new thermometer. Some historians think Dunlap's broadside reflects capitalization and other idiosyncratic touches more consistent with John Adams's influence, but the stronger argument is that Jefferson was present. Jefferson—lover of words, aware of the power of the printing press, perhaps filled with adrenaline after four days of debate that had culminated in this moment—would unlikely be anywhere but Dunlap's shop at High and Market streets.

As the historian Julian P. Boyd pointed out: "Perhaps no other involved in the transaction could have symbolized so well or grasped so fully the meaning of the document that was about to come from the press and carry its message throughout the world."

And if Jefferson's motives were not so lofty, then his possible presence at Dunlap's print shop could also carry a more prosaic explanation: there is little doubt he would have wanted several printed copies for himself as soon as they came off the press, to send to friends and colleagues in Virginia and elsewhere.

IN THE DAYS THAT followed Dunlap's printing, a mixture of excitement, anxiety, and celebration raced through the colonies as copies of the Declaration were distributed by members of Congress. On July 5, John Hancock sent a copy to the Pennsylvania Committee of Safety, "to request you will have proclaimed in your Colony in the way and manner you shall judge best." Over the next few days, he sent copies to the assemblies in New Jersey, New York, Massachusetts, Virginia, and Maryland. He also dispatched copies to army generals, including George Washington, requesting to "have it proclaimed at the Head of the Army." Washington was in New York when he received the Declaration; on July 9 he ordered his men to form up on the parade grounds to hear the document read "with an audible voice."

Washington recognized somberly that anything short of full victory on the battlefield would render the Declaration meaningless. By reading the document aloud to his troops, he hoped the moment would "serve as a free incentive to every officer and soldier, to act with fidelity and courage, as knowing that now the peace and safety of his Country depends (under God) solely on the success of our arms."

Philadelphia held a massive celebration on Monday, July 8, beginning at noon in the statehouse yard with the reading of the Declaration before a large and enthusiastic crowd. Battalions of troops paraded through the city, cannons were fired and bells chimed well into the night. Across the city, bonfires blazed and people displayed candles in their windows. Inside the statehouse, revelers removed the king's coat of arms from the wall and tossed it into a huge fire.

In colony after colony, in the days and weeks that followed, residents celebrated and, with exuberance, removed as many vestiges as possible of the king and the Crown. In New York, a raucous crowd tore down a statue of George III astride a horse and "laid [it] prostrate in the dirt, the just dessert of an ungrateful tyrant!" In a New York City courthouse, the British coat of arms, carved in stone, was broken into pieces and set afire, and British arms in churches across the city were removed and destroyed. Long Island revelers hanged King George in effigy. In Providence, Rhode Island, cannon and artillery boomed, the Declaration was read, and crowds destroyed the royal coat of arms and tore down and burned the sign adorning the Crown Coffee House. In Georgia, the day-long celebration included a mock funeral procession and burial of the king. In Jefferson's Virginia, the Declaration arrived on July 20 and the Virginia Council ordered sheriffs to "proclaim the Declaration" at every courthouse. A few days later, Williamsburg "was illuminated" with bonfires, and patriotic toasts were drunk before a crowd of more than a thousand in the town square.

IN THE MIDST OF all the revelry, on July 9, the New York Convention finally approved the prior week's actions of the Continental

Congress; this meant that all thirteen colonies had now approved and ratified the Declaration of Independence.

And so it was that in Boston on July 18—after the Declaration was read from the balcony of the statehouse at 1:00 p.m. before a cheering throng—thirteen cannon were fired from Fort Hill and thirteen divisions answered with musket fire, representing the "number of American States United." Forts on Dorchester Neck and Castle Island also boomed their cannon. Bells pealed across the city, and that evening, Boston celebrants tore down the royal coat of arms and dozens of signs belonging to Tory businesses and burned them in a massive conflagration on King Street.

"Every face appeared joyful," Abigail Adams wrote to her husband in Philadelphia, as she described the bonfire that consumed "every vestige" of king and Crown in Boston. "Thus ends royal authority in this State. And all the people shall say Amen."

ON JULY 15, JOHN ADAMS and the rest of the delegates in Philadelphia received word of the New York vote, and the Continental Congress reacted to the news almost immediately. On July 19, according to the secret journals, delegates ordered that the Declaration "be fairly engrossed on parchment." With New York finally in the fold, Congress also decreed its long-hoped-for title of the document: "The unanimous Declaration of the thirteen united States of America." Once the document was engrossed, "every member of Congress" would then sign the Declaration.

Engrossing the historic document meant engaging the services of an artistic engraver or calligrapher to beautifully recreate Jefferson's words in an elegant, formal, polished hand. For this task, the Congress turned to Timothy Matlack, an ardent patriot from Pennsylvania who had assisted the secretary of Congress, Charles Thomson, in his duties for more than a year and had also written out George Washington's commission as commanding general of the Continental army. Matlack, roughly forty years old (though even he was unsure of his exact date of birth), was a boisterous, swashbuckling personality, a man of eclectic tastes who loved horse racing, cockfighting, brawling, and beer. He had been excommunicated by the Quakers for his rowdy behavior, his failure to repay creditors for business debts, and his "negligence in attending religious meetings."

On the other hand, he was a man of intellectual vigor, a fine writer and public speaker, and a colonel in the Pennsylvania rifle battalion, as emotionally invested as any delegate in the cause of independence. Matlack's "patriotic ardor" convinced Congress to select him as Thomson's clerk. Described as "robust in health, brimful of animal spirits and vigor, virile, pugnacious, undauntedly courageous," and an unabashed lover of liberty, Matlack developed and maintained a friendship with Thomas Jefferson that would last for years.

For the task at hand, Matlack possessed a critical skill—he was a master calligrapher. With pen, ink, and a parchment sheet that measured 24¼ by 29¾ inches, he set his steady hand to his historic work. Across the top, he boldly penned the words: "In CONGRESS, July 4, 1776."—a heading that would lead to vast confusion in later years as to the actual date the delegates voted on the question of independence and signed the parchment. This was followed by the title that Congress had ordered: "The unanimous Declaration of the thirteen United States of America." Matlack chose to engross a flourishing capital "T" on "the" and "D" on Declaration. The word "unanimous" remained lower case, though the same general size as "The," "Declaration," and "States of America." Matlack depicted the words "of the thirteen united" in much smaller calligraphy, and added a bold comma at the end of the title, which thus read in its entirety:

𝕿𝖍𝖊 𝖚𝖓𝖆𝖓𝖎𝖒𝖔𝖚𝖘 𝕯𝖊𝖈𝖑𝖆𝖗𝖆𝖙𝖎𝖔𝖓 of the thirteen united 𝕾𝖙𝖆𝖙𝖊𝖘 of 𝕬𝖒𝖊𝖗𝖎𝖈𝖆,

Matlack then proceeded to pen the entire declaration in one block of elegant handwriting, inserting dashes and flourishes at various strategic places. The first word—"When"—is inked with bold authority, the left tip of the W preceded with a curlicue line that hints at the importance of the words to come. In the final paragraph, Matlack also reinforces the opening words, "We, therefore" and "United States of America" and, later, "free and independent." The first word in the final statement is larger, bolder, and the words "Declaration," "Providence," and the collective three components of the pledge, "Lives," "Fortunes," and "Sacred Honor," are all capitalized for emphasis. Thus the final powerful closing sentence:

And for the support of this Declaration, with a firm reliance on the protection of divine Providence, we mutually pledge to each other our Lives, our Fortunes, and our Sacred Honor.

The same question arises about Matlack's work as historians have posited about John Dunlap's print shop on the night of July 4: were any delegates looking over his shoulder as he labored? If so, no record exists in any letters or memoirs to tell us; however, if anyone did visit—and perhaps influence—Matlack as he toiled with pen and parchment in late July 1776, document experts have asserted that the pattern of capitalization, punctuation, and dashes throughout the document indicate again that it was Jefferson. The kinship between the two makes this an even stronger likelihood.

When he had finished his work, Matlack had produced a stunningly beautiful document, without question the most important accomplishment of his career. It is Matlack's engrossed copy of the Declaration of Independence on parchment that Americans are most familiar with. This is the document that was nearly lost and then protected and preserved in the earlier days of the republic; that is today displayed in an environmentally controlled casement under the watchful eyes of guards in the National Archives rotunda; that was copied over and over again, perhaps millions of times through the decades, and hung in homes, classrooms, government offices, and community centers across the country.

The Philadelphia engrosser had no idea that his work would become the version Americans recognized as *the* copy of the Declaration of Independence. All he knew was, once his work was finished, Congress had mandated that its members permanently ink their signatures at the bottom of the parchment.

Danger or no, it was time for the delegates who voted for independence to finally identify themselves.

OF ALL THE MOMENTOUS days along the road to American independence in the late spring and summer of 1776—including Richard Henry Lee offering his famous resolution on June 7, Congress naming the Committee of Five on June 11, Jefferson's draft submitted to the full Congress on June 28, or what would become four world-shaking days starting July 1—it is Friday, August 2, signing day, that holds a unique place in these annals.

As delegates gathered at the Pennsylvania State House for the signing ceremony, they were well aware that they could not turn back, and even if they were so inclined, they could no longer hide or obscure their actions. Once they signed Timothy Matlack's superb engrossed version of the Declaration of Independence, their defiant and brazen act of treason against the Crown would be complete—and visible for all to see.

August 2 was notable for another reason, one that had become part of the Congress's practice throughout its controversial debates: on that day and in succeeding days, virtually nothing was recorded about the historic signing ceremony. No newspaper carried a story. We have only Charles Thomson's note in the secret journals to tell us: "Aug. 2, 1776. The Declaration of independence being engrossed & compared at the table was signed by the Members."

Yet, we do know from later writings that delegates were well aware of the drama of the moment. Pennsylvania's Benjamin Rush, most vivid in his recollections years after the signing, recalled the "silence and gloom of the morning." He reminded John Adams of the "pensive and awful silence which pervaded the house when we were called up, one after another, to the table of the President of Congress to subscribe what was believed by many at that time to be our own death warrants."

Rush's letter notwithstanding, perhaps it was the lack of contemporaneous documentation that clouded the memories of Adams, Jefferson, and others in later years who mistakenly recalled that the document was signed on July 4. In addition to the secret journal, letters show that several delegates who voted for independence returned home after July 4 and then made the trip back to Philadelphia to sign the Declaration. Others were absent on August 2 and returned to sign later. At least one delegate who signed was not even seated when the vote for independence was taken on July 2. While most delegates signed on August 2, it took a full four months for the entire list of fifty-six names to finally appear at the bottom of Timothy Matlack's engrossed Declaration.

Apparently things went smoothly inside the statehouse on this historic Friday. John Hancock, president of the Congress, signed first and largest, affixing and underscoring his name at the center of the document, a bold gesture that would forever make his name synonymous with the word "signature." We cannot verify whether Hancock, who already had a price of 500 pounds on his head, said of his enormous signature: "There. Now His Majesty can read my name without spectacles, and may now double his reward for my head. That is my defiance." Whether Hancock uttered those words or something similar, as some historians have recounted, or the words were apocryphal, they are believable because they were in character for the Massachusetts patriot.

After Hancock, the other delegates lined up to sign according to custom, with the names arranged geographically, starting on the upper right-hand side of the signature area with delegates from the Northeast and ending on the bottom left with the Georgia delegation. New Hampshire's Josiah Bartlett was first following Hancock; slightly further down, John Adams of Massachusetts signed in his neat, compact hand, and Elbridge Gerry, who was absent on August 2 and signed later, lightly inked his name. Directly below Gerry, Rhode Island's sixty-nine-year-old Stephen Hopkins, suffering from a "shaking palsy" that had affected him for years, signed his name as "Steph Hopkins" in an unsteady hand.

Some delegates later said Hopkins gamely proclaimed as he signed: "My hand trembles, but my heart does not."

AND SO IT WENT.

Thomas Jefferson abbreviated his first name to "Th," and Benjamin Franklin signed as "Benj. A Franklin, nestling the small *A* adjacent to the top-piece of his large, decorative *F.* Caesar Rodney underlined both his first and last names, and his fellow Delaware delegate, George Read—the only signer who actually voted against independence—wedged his name close to Rodney's, perhaps to leave ample space for the third Delaware delegate, Thomas McKean, to sign. McKean appears not to have signed until January 1777, making him the last delegate to affix his name. Virginia's Richard Henry Lee, author of the famous resolution for independence, was also absent on August 2 and signed later, just above Jefferson, with a neat, almost dainty touch. South Carolina's Edward Rutledge, whose resolution tabled the vote on independence for three weeks, punctuated his signature by inserting a slash and a period after his name.

Each delegate knew the risk and that knowledge is reflected in the stories that accompany the signing. We do not know for sure whether Franklin joked, "We must all hang together, or most assuredly we shall hang separately." And Jefferson loved the story of an exchange that occurred later between portly Benjamin Harrison of Virginia and reed-thin Elbridge Gerry of Massachusetts. Apparently Harrison quipped: "Gerry, when the hanging comes, I shall have the advantage; you'll kick in the air half an hour after it is all over with me!" Benjamin Rush recalled the story too, noting that Harrison's remarks "procured a transient smile, but it was soon succeeded by a solemnity with which the whole business was conducted."

Fortunes, too, were at stake. Maryland's wealthy Charles Carroll, whom John Adams once described as "a gentleman of independent fortune, perhaps the largest in America," was not yet seated in Congress when the vote for independence was taken. He arrived in Philadelphia on July 18, in plenty of time to sign the Declaration. Some accounts say that after he signed, one of the delegates shouted: "There goes a few millions," and most delegates agreed that few risked more in terms of material wealth than Carroll.

The Maryland delegate actually signed his name as "Charles Carroll of Carrollton"—the story has it that one delegate supposedly reminded him in jest that other Charles Carrolls hailed from Maryland, and that he would risk little unless he clearly specified his identity. Other historians sniff at the story as mere legend and note that Carroll had added "of Carrollton" after his name for years.

BY THE CLOSE OF Congress's business on August 2, arguably the most remarkable two-month political period in American history had concluded. From Richard Henry Lee's resolution offered on June 7 to the signing of the Declaration on August 2, the delegates in Philadelphia had transformed a call for separation and independence into a full-fledged blueprint for freedom and liberty. In just under sixty days, they had declared the American colonies free of Great Britain's yoke and forged a new republic, actions that required enormous courage under any circumstances and astounding risk in a time of war against the world's mightiest power.

How would America fare? That would now depend on the performance of its generals and their armies on the field of battle. But this much was clear to the delegates in Philadelphia, and soon would become apparent across the colonies and the world: more than anything else, it was the Declaration of Independence that would inspire soldiers and farmers, merchants and seamen, lawyers and clerks. It would serve as the bedrock foundational document that embodied the spirit and the promise of a grandiose and unprecedented experiment in the most turbulent and uncertain of times.

For this document, the delegates had pledged to each other and their new country their lives, their fortunes, and their sacred honor.

For this document, they had risked everything.

THE FIFTY-SIX DELEGATES WHO signed the Declaration of Independence were driven by the courage of their convictions, and they based their support of the Declaration in part "on the protection of divine Providence." But they also grasped the realities of the situation and were not interested in pursuing a death wish.

Things were going badly for the colonial army in the late summer and fall of 1776. In fact, on December 12, threatened by the British army in Philadelphia, the Congress adjourned, fled, and reconvened in Baltimore five days before Christmas. The engrossed and signed declaration was transported to its temporary Maryland home in a light horse-drawn wagon.

Thus, it was not until the Americans had won hard-fought victories at Trenton and Princeton that they ordered the second official printing of the Declaration of Independence, this one containing the signatures of delegates. On January 18, 1777, Congress agreed that "an authentic copy of the Declaration of Independency, with the names of the members of Congress subscribing to the same, be sent to each of the United States, and that they desired to have the same put upon the record." The Congress turned to newspaper editor and printer, and Baltimore's postmaster, Mary Katherine Goddard, to undertake the second printing of the Declaration of Independence—the first printing from Matlack's original that included the signers' names. An ardent proponent of American independence and liberty, Goddard's newspaper had long championed separation from Britain.

Now Goddard would print the broadside that would, for the first time, reveal the identities of the Declaration's signers—the delegates' treasonous act would be complete and public.

*

IN THE END, NONE of the signatories were hanged for treason, though several endured extreme hardships, as did their family members in some cases. Historians have long debated whether these sufferings were ministered in direct retaliation for signing the Declaration or as part of the privations and misery meted out in the natural course of war; the most accurate interpretation is that there is truth in both theories.

Among the most heartbreaking and poignant stories involves Elizabeth Lewis, wife of New York signer Francis Lewis. In the autumn of 1776, with Francis still in Philadelphia, the British attacked Long Island and a battleship fired on the Lewis home while Elizabeth and her servants were inside. Shortly afterward, British soldiers entered the house and began plundering it and destroying belongings—books, furniture, kitchenware—and arrested Elizabeth, who was in her late fifties and in poor health. She was transported to a New York City prison, where she was not allowed a bed or extra clothing and was fed only meager rations. Intent on making an example of Mrs. Lewis because of her wealth and prominence—and perhaps because her husband was a signer of the Declaration—the British held her captive in a damp, filthy, unheated cell for nearly three months. At one point, one of her servants learned about her location and smuggled her a few extra rations, but her health deteriorated dramatically while she was held captive.

The Continental Congress repeatedly demanded better treatment for Elizabeth, but their pleas fell on deaf ears until General George Washington arrested the wives of two prominent British officials in Philadelphia and threatened them with similar treatment if the British did not release her. The two sides negotiated an exchange and Elizabeth was freed from prison, but she was not allowed to leave New York until months later, when she finally joined Francis in Philadelphia. But her time spent in a gruesome British prison had taken its toll and she would never fully recover. In early 1779, two years after his wife's release, Francis took a leave of absence from the Continental Congress to care for Elizabeth, whom he regarded, in the words of a descendant, as "Heaven's best gift."

In June of that year, she contracted a fever and severe consumption and died within days, with Francis at her side.

New Jersey's Abraham Clark also likely had loved ones persecuted because of his treason. His two sons, Aaron and Thomas, both officers in the Continental army, were captured during the war. Thomas was imprisoned and subjected to brutal treatment—some reports say he was tortured—on the notorious and barbarous prison ship *Jersey*, which housed thousands of American prisoners and served as a breeding ground for smallpox, dysentery, and other contagious diseases. Aaron was held captive in a solitary cell in a New York dungeon, where he received barely enough food to keep him alive. Some accounts say that fellow prisoners passed him bread and other scraps of food through a keyhole. The British reportedly offered to free both sons if their father would recant his support for the Declaration and announce his support for the king and Parliament, but he refused. Both of Abraham Clark's sons were later released, but Thomas, who died in 1789 at age thirty-four, suffered with health problems for the rest of his life.

Ironically, the signer who may have suffered most grievously for his treasonous action was the one delegate who eventually recanted his support of the Declaration. Richard Stockton, also of New Jersey, was betrayed by loyalists, and one night, while he slept, he was captured and dragged to prison—first in Perth Amboy, New Jersey, and then New York City. He was subjected to short rations and deliberately exposed to frigid weather. Meanwhile, his estate, Morven, was ransacked, much of his livestock were killed, his library was burned, and his house was used as a headquarters by British officers. Stockton spent months in prison and was finally released when he signed a document swearing allegiance to the Crown and promising to cease his war efforts. He returned to Morven sick, exhausted, and humiliated in the eyes of his fellow rebels. While his prison stay did not kill him, it certainly weakened him. He developed cancer shortly after his release, and after a few years of struggle, died in 1781 at the age of fifty-one.

Whether other signers who suffered losses were specifically

targeted or were simply victims of war's excesses is difficult to say, but either way, their sacrifices were real. New York's William Floyd had his estate on Long Island confiscated, and British troops commandeered his house as a barracks for several years, subsisting by slaughtering Floyd's livestock and harvesting his produce. South Carolina's Arthur Middleton and Edward Rutledge were serving with the militia in Charleston when British troops destroyed their plantations. After Charleston fell to the British in 1780, Middleton and Rutledge were transported to St. Augustine, Florida, and incarcerated on one of the horrific British prison ships until they were exchanged at the end of the war. The home of Georgia signer Lyman Hall was burned and his property was confiscated by British troops.

Years later, delegate Benjamin Rush reminisced about the numerous sacrifices the signers had made for the cause of American independence, risking life and property, and he lamented that many Americans had minimized or overlooked their contributions. "The military men ran away with all the glory of the day," he wrote to John Adams after Independence Day festivities in July 1811, thirty-five years after the two had forged a friendship in Philadelphia and the Continental Congress delegates had formed a new American nation. "Scarcely a word was said of the solicitude and labors and fears and sorrow and sleepless nights of the men who projected, proposed, defended, and subscribed the Declaration of Independence."

AS FOR THE DOCUMENT itself, the original signed and engrossed copy of the Declaration of Independence accompanied a peripatetic Congress in the early years of the new republic, the country's parchment of freedom often rolled up and stuffed in a linen bag or the back of a wagon as it traveled from city to city—New York, Trenton, Annapolis, Philadelphia. Its own journey was reflective of the unsettled early years of the fledgling nation.

These travels, plus constant unrolling and rerolling of the parchment each time the Declaration was used, took its toll on the ink and on the parchment surface through abrasion and flexing. While there were some benefits to the constant rolling—the National Archives reports that the "acidity inherent in the iron gall ink used by Timothy Matlack allowed the ink to 'bite' into the surface of the parchment, thus contributing to the ink's longevity"—constant handling in this manner presented hazards to its overall condition. The natural wear and tear on the Declaration in the early years of the republic resulted in deterioration that American government officials would not deal with for nearly half a century.

In July 1789, the first Congress (created under the new Constitution ratified two years earlier at the Constitutional Convention) made a decision that would change the custodial home of the Declaration. Congress created the Department of Foreign Affairs and directed that its secretary should have "the custody and charge of all records, books, and papers" kept by the department of the same name under the old government. On July 24, venerable Charles Thomson retired as secretary of the Congress, and upon the order of the new president, George Washington, surrendered the Declaration to Roger Alden, deputy secretary of foreign affairs.

In September, the name of the department was changed to the Department of State. In March 1790, the new nation's first secretary of state, Thomas Jefferson, assumed his duties after returning from France. The author of the Declaration of Independence was now its steward and its protector.

NEITHER JEFFERSON NOR THE rest of the nation yet regarded the Declaration as the sacred political document it is today, but there were annual July 4 celebrations even before the war had ended. With the tide of battle swinging in 1778, Congress ordered the Fourth of July to be celebrated as a holiday and urged Americans to give three cheers for the "Perpetual and Undisturbed Independence of the United States of America."

In the midst of one of these celebrations, in July 1790, Congress provided for a permanent capital to be built amid the swamps and marshlands bordering the Potomac River. In the meantime, Congress ordered that "all offices attached to the seat of the government of the United States" should be relocated once again to Philadelphia by the close of 1790. Finally, in 1800, with the "federal city" complete in the District of Columbia—land carved from the states of Maryland and Virginia that would eventually be named after General Washington—President John Adams ordered the Declaration of Independence and other government records moved from Philadelphia to America's new national capital.

As the National Archives points out: "To reach its new home, the Declaration traveled down the Delaware River and Bay, out into the ocean, into the Chesapeake Bay, and up the Potomac to Washington, completing its longest water journey."

For more than a decade, the Declaration of Independence remained undisturbed and largely unnoticed in what became known as the "federal city" or "Washington City" in the District of Columbia. America's cornerstone document, and many other precious records and documents, would only become top of mind when the fledgling nation once again found itself at war with Great Britain.

Well before that, though, years before the creation of the federal city as America's capital, the next crucial chapter in the American story shifted back to Philadelphia and then to the individual American states.

In the summer of 1787, a federal convention, this time with nearly a whole new set of delegates, created the laws and articulated the government structure that codified the ideals and principles set forth in the Declaration of Independence and secured the future of the nation. When they adjourned in September of that year, their remarkable finished product redefined the framework for the American government; laid out that government's authority, power, and limits in relation to its states and its citizens; and set the course for America's direction and destiny for generations to come.

★ ★ ★

1941

★ ★ ★

4

★

"The Preservation
of National
Morale"

★

Washington, D.C., mid-December 1941

Archibald MacLeish and his wife Ada spent the morning of December 7, 1941, in Sandy Spring, Maryland, where they had met friends for a picnic. The MacLeishes left early in the afternoon so Archie could keep an appointment in Washington. Fifteen minutes into the drive to the capital, the radio program they were listening to was interrupted with news that the Japanese had attacked Pearl Harbor.

The following day, President Roosevelt made what would become one of the most famous speeches in American history—the "date of infamy" address seeking—and receiving—a declaration of war from Congress. Four days later, Hitler's Germany declared war on the United States.

It's hard to comprehend the palpable and widespread fear in the days following Pearl Harbor that the American mainland, and particularly New York and Washington, would be next. Not since 1814 had the capital city faced such danger from a foreign power. "I hold the view that we are in very grave danger in Washington," declared a prominent member of the Committee on Conservation of Cultural Resources at a December 11, 1941, meeting, four days after Pearl Harbor and the very day Germany declared war on the United States. "I feel that we are going to be bombed in Washington and we may be bombed very, very much and it might be very, very soon."

Archibald MacLeish's massive undertaking now seemed entirely worthwhile; because of his team's tremendous efforts during the previous eight months, the Library of Congress was ready.

THE PREVIOUS SPRING, UNDER MacLeish's direction and with the full support and encouragement of President Franklin D. Roosevelt, 700 Library of Congress volunteers had worked more than 10,000 hours over ten weeks to identify, inventory, collect, and carefully pack the nearly 5,000 boxes of irreplaceable documents, music, maps, rare books, and artifacts that now needed moving. Workers took meticulous notes on the records that had been packed and cross-checked those with the box numbers in which documents were stored for easy reference later.

Then, in the early summer, MacLeish had dispatched Alvin W. Kremer, the Library of Congress's keeper of the collections, on a mission to find suitable locations for the vast majority of library documents. This had come about only after MacLeish and his team had searched in vain for an appropriate storage location in the Washington, D.C., area and had been unsuccessful in convincing Congress to fund construction of a bombproof, waterproof, climate-controlled underground shelter within the borders of the capital.

MacLeish had discussed with President Roosevelt and Supreme Court justice Harlan F. Stone the possibility of linking a shelter with the planned construction of a memorial garden dedicated to the late governor Oliver Wendell Holmes Jr. MacLeish had proposed that a large shelter be constructed beneath the Holmes Garden and linked by an underground passage to the Supreme Court and Library of Congress buildings, which were already connected by tunnel.

Among the benefits of such a plan, MacLeish believed, was that the vault "could be used without the knowledge of its use being brought to the attention of the public or press to further aggravate public tension." Also, by keeping the documents in close proximity, Library of Congress staffers could examine them regularly to assess their condition. Further, by linking the cost of the Holmes Garden and the underground shelter, MacLeish thought Congress would be more amenable to funding the entire project.

Unfortunately, the elaborate project did not see the light of day—legislators had balked at the potential cost of subterranean storage, especially since the United States was not at war at the time.

Thus, MacLeish needed to look elsewhere to store the library's documents.

IN TOTAL, KREMER VISITED more than thirty locations in Virginia, West Virginia, and Kentucky. He selected three spots as most favorable: the University of Virginia at Charlottesville and, in Lexington, Virginia, the Virginia Military Institute and Washington and Lee University. The Lexington locations, especially, were ideal, Kremer reported, since they were "situated less than 200 miles from Washington, in the Shenandoah Valley, practically surrounded by mountains," making an approach by enemy bombers difficult. Further, the population of the town was only 3,000 people, and "there are no industries of any importance," meaning Lexington was unlikely to be regarded by the enemy as a strategic target. Military officials had assured Kremer that the Lexington locations "contained no objectives upon which aircraft attacking this country from abroad might be expected to center their attentions." In addition, all of the buildings at the University of Virginia and at the Lexington locations were "excellent" in terms of storage facilities, "fireproof, with ventilation by automatic fan control," though none were actually air-conditioned, Kremer noted.

MacLeish had also sought a legal opinion from the attorney general to confirm that he had the authority to move the documents without congressional approval. If that turned out the way he and FDR thought it would, the library staff would begin the daunting task of relocating the documents. He viewed this as a national priority, every bit as important as the military ramp-up for war.

IF AMERICA'S KEY DOCUMENTS were damaged or destroyed, so, too, would be its national morale. But what of the Declaration of Independence, the Constitution of the United States, the Gettysburg Address? If these priceless, irreplaceable documents were lost to the enemy, would this not only shatter the national psyche, but its essence, its very identity?

For those, MacLeish agreed with his staff executive, Lawrence Martin, who recommended that America's most precious documents be relocated to perhaps the safest place in the country: America's recently constructed gold bullion depository vault at Fort Knox.

"The fort lies southwest of Louisville and far enough inland from the Ohio so that the river would not be a guide for invading bombers," Martin informed MacLeish. Not only would the underground steel and concrete vaults be impervious to bombing attacks, "the permanent military protection would obviate the necessity of such a force of guards as we would have to place at any other refuge."

MacLeish hadn't thought of Fort Knox, but he found it an ideal spot for documents that he considered far more valuable than gold bullion. In the early summer, he requested and received approval from treasury secretary Henry Morgenthau to use about sixty cubic feet of Fort Knox, roughly the size of a stand-alone home freezer, a mere fraction of what the Library of Congress would need to house all of its records but ample space for its most important documents.

For MacLeish, there were "two aspects" to the preparations to remove precious records from the Library of Congress in Washington to distant locations: "the preservation of cultural treasures and the preservation of national morale."

★

MEANWHILE, WASHINGTON WAS ABUZZ with war preparations by mid-December.

In the capital, a flurry of plans and ideas were floated or put in place to protect the White House, the Capitol, and the president, some more practical than others. Among those that were suggested but not implemented included the recommendation to paint the White House black to make it less visible (though many windows *were* painted black); to move the seat of government away from the coast and farther inland; and to literally change the directional flow of the Potomac and Anacostia rivers to prevent bomber pilots from using the waterways to draw a bead on the White House. "No camouflage of the White House is practical while the confluence of these rivers remains a mile from the mansion," noted the head of President Roosevelt's security detail. "A pilot would find it quite simple to hit the White House by flying up either river and getting his 'fix' at the confluence."

Many steps *were* implemented, however, and quickly. America's military planners reinforced buildings, placed antiaircraft guns on strategic roofs, and conducted air-raid drills at all hours. By December 8, 1941, U.S. Army, Navy, and Marine guards stood at twenty-four-hour posts around Washington's government buildings, including the White House and Capitol; this had not happened since the U.S. entry into World War I in 1917—and before that, not since 1865. By December 10, the White House and the Capitol were darkened for the duration of the war; the floodlights that had illuminated the great buildings for years were turned off.

By December 15, eight days after the attack—Bill of Rights Day, 1941—the White House was in lockdown.

"Papers and passes were demanded," author Craig Shirley wrote. "Cops and military police roamed ubiquitously stopping everyone, guns bristling. On the White House grounds, guard towers had been built and one-inch steel cables ran every which way, controlling the flow of foot traffic." By Christmas, just as the Declaration of Independence and the Constitution were being prepared for transfer to Fort Knox, members of Congress were required to carry photo identification to enter the Capitol. "Washington [now] was ground zero for a world war zone," Shirley said. "The town was radically altered, forevermore."

Later, the Secret Service created ten safe houses in Washington where they could take FDR in the event of an attack, installed bullet-proof glass on the windows of the Oval Office directly behind the president's desk, and, in the most ambitious move, constructed an underground tunnel connecting the White House to a large subterranean vault under the Treasury Department that could serve as a temporary bombproof refuge for Roosevelt and staff members.

The Treasury vault, once used to store contraband opium and currency, was supported by walls constructed of heavy armored plates and reinforced with concrete. The Secret Service oversaw the construction of an office and a bedroom for the president, a large outer office for the staff, and the installation of bunk beds and emergency telephone facilities. The 761-foot-long tunnel, built in a zigzag route from the White House to the vault to lessen the impact of concussion in the event of a direct or near-direct hit, was stocked with water, food, beds, blankets, first-aid kits, and a portable toilet.

To this day, the Secret Service does not permit the release of classified photos of the tunnel.

FDR questioned the need for highly visible extreme-security measures, fearing they would turn the White House into a fortress and convey a sense of panic to the American people. He felt the same way about the hidden tunnel. He joked to the treasury secretary, Henry Morgenthau: "I will not go down into the shelter unless you allow me to play poker with all the gold in your vaults."

SECRET SERVICE AGENT Harry Neal was assigned to record the progress of the Treasury tunnel's construction for historical purposes. With the help of a Treasury Department document expert, Neal "made photos of the entire protective area." He noted that "certain rooms in the vault area were reinforced with steel, then plastered and painted for use as offices and staff sleeping quarters."

Neal's thoroughness and attention to detail would not have surprised his colleagues or superiors. He was considered one of the finest agents in the Secret Service—thorough, meticulous, relentless, loyal, and focused on detail; but also strategic, brave, highly principled, and occasionally rebellious. His skills and professionalism had helped him become one of Secret Service chief Frank Wilson's most trusted agents.

Neal had been transferred from the Secret Service's New York City office to its Washington headquarters in early December 1939. It was a difficult time; his father was quite ill from complications of a heart attack and related circulatory issues. Wishing to bring his wheelchair-bound father along, Harry consulted with his doctors, who assured him that his dad "could withstand a train trip to Washington, and might even enjoy it after being cooped up for a long while."

The elder Mr. Neal did indeed survive the train trip, but his illness would soon catch up with him. On Christmas Eve, 1939, Harry insisted that Helen attend a party with her family while he stayed with his dad. Harry's father died that night. "I remember only that I sat on the bed, held one of my father's hands, and cried," he wrote later. The Neals spent a somber Christmas Day at a Washington undertaker's parlor making arrangements to transfer Harry's father's body back to Pittsfield, Massachusetts, for a home-town funeral service. After the funeral, Harry, just thirty-three years old when his father died, returned to Washington to resume his Secret Service career.

This was not Harry Edward Neal's first trip to Washington, D.C. The path that led him to a career as a Secret Service agent began in a most unorthodox manner. He had started his working life as a stenographer with General Electric in Pittsfield. At the age of nineteen, he took a civil service exam and accepted a similar job with the Post Office Department at an annual salary of $1,320. He was assigned to the post office in the nation's capital. "When I walked out of the Union Station in Washington, I was transfixed and awed by the sight of the lighted dome of the Capitol," he recalled. "I just stood and looked at it for probably four or five minutes. Not only did I feel proud and excited, but I also felt as though I were now beginning some kind of great adventure." He met his future wife, Helen Armstrong, during his stay in D.C. They were married on May 8, 1929.

A year after arriving in Washington, Harry, bored with work at the post office, applied for a stenographer's position with the Treasury Department's Secret Service division. A month later, he was told he could have the job if he was willing to transfer to the Albany office, which was only about thirty-five miles from Harry's hometown. There, he was assigned to work for the agent in charge, James H. Brady, for an annual salary of $1,800, and visited Helen in Washington whenever he could.

Harry spent his days taking dictation from the agents, who made detailed reports of their daily activities, writing special reports on counterfeiting and forgery investigations, and handling correspondence for senior agents. One day, he was asked if he would be willing to participate in a raid on a counterfeiting plant in Yonkers. When Harry accepted, the agent gave him a revolver and asked, "Ever used one of these?" When Harry said no, the agent replied: "Well, I don't think you'll have to, but it's just as well to be prepared." The Yonkers raid was the first of several on which Harry accompanied agents.

In January 1931, Harry joined a midnight raid on a Brooklyn row house. As Harry stood shivering in the darkness, waiting with agents to burst in the back door of the house, another contingent of agents prepared to smash through the front door. On a signal, both groups stormed the house. Harry heard a woman shouting "Cops! Cops!" Just then, the inside basement door flew open and Harry saw a man rush to the furnace in the corner, open the boiler door, and toss something onto the glowing coal embers. Instantly, Harry opened the door and reached for the object, burning his gloved hand. When he pulled it out, he and the other agents saw that it was a photographic negative used to make counterfeit bills; it would turn out to be the most important piece of evidence in the case.

Harry received accolades from his fellow agents and superiors and was immediately recommended for a promotion. Washington approved it without hesitation.

Five years after joining the Secret Service as a stenographer, Harry Neal became a full-fledged agent, earning $2,500 a year. The story of the fearless stenographer who thrust his hand into a coal-fired furnace to retrieve evidence became the stuff of Secret Service legend.

IN THE PAST DECADE, Harry Neal had enjoyed a meteoric rise in the service and achieved senior agent status, his reputation burnished by sound thinking and hard work. The respect with which he was viewed can be seen in his assignments; he was given responsibility for the security detail that protected the king and queen of England when they visited the New York World's Fair in 1939 (where the Magna Carta was exhibited). He led the Secret Service's efforts against counterfeiters, traveled west to arrange for the service's exhibit at the San Francisco World's Fair in 1940, was the lead inspector for Secret Service offices in California and Texas, and became the service's lead budget preparer.

He was so committed to the Secret Service and so convinced of its capabilities that he also began the effort that eventually led to the service's independent jurisdictional authority as the U.S. Secret Service, outside what Harry Neal considered the less prestigious status as a division of the Treasury Department.

Now, with Christmas approaching and the United States at war, Frank Wilson assigned Neal another mission that would not only add to his cachet among fellow agents and assure his place in the proud annals of the Secret Service, but also number him among the stalwarts of American history who helped create, preserve, and protect the nation's most important national treasures.

★ ★ ★

1787–1791

★ ★ ★

5

★

"Suspended
upon a
Single Hair"

★

June 24, 1788, Richmond, Virginia, Late Afternoon

Even the gods seemed to be listening to Patrick Henry.

As the fiery statesman boomed his opposition to the U.S. Constitution before a rapt audience in a packed theater on Richmond's Shockoe Hill, he told his fellow Virginians that he saw "beings of a higher order, anxious concerning our decision." He looked "beyond the horizon that bounds human eyes" and saw "intelligent beings which inhabit ethereal mansions" sitting in judgment of the decisions Virginia would make on this day. As if on cue, the afternoon grew dark, a summer storm arose, and strong wind slammed the doors "with a rebound like a peal of musketry," according to one delegate in attendance. "The windows rattled; the huge wooden structure rocked; the rain fell from the eaves in torrents, which were dashed against the glass; the thunder roared."

As the crowd stirred, Henry recognized the drama of the moment and continued his oratory, his voice soaring above the crash of thunder and roar of the wind. He warned of the "awful immensity of the dangers" presented by a constitution that called for a strong central government and lacked a strong citizens' bill of rights. As the darkness swallowed the theater, Henry appeared to be "rising on the wings of the tempest," as he "seized upon the artillery of heaven and directed its fiercest thunders against the heads of his adversaries." The suddenness of the storm, on the heels of Henry's visions of "beings of a higher order" had a profound impact on his audience, causing "every nerve [to] shudder with supernatural horror . . . the spirits whom he had called seemed to have come at his bidding." Later, Henry's son-in-law said the scene had the effect of bestowing upon Henry "the faculty of calling up spirits from the vasty deep." Soon, the storm became too violent for Henry to continue. Delegates and much of the crowd fled to the center of the building, away from the windows, until the wind and rain passed.

Among those seeking shelter was another Virginian who disagreed profoundly with Patrick Henry's point of view. James Madison had worked tirelessly over the past year to ensure the ratification of the Constitution. But as magnificent as it was, as important as it would eventually become to all Americans, the Constitution approved in Philadelphia the previous September was merely an advisory document until the states approved it. And that had been far from a foregone conclusion.

MADISON WATCHED AS EIGHT of the nine states needed for ratification approved the sweeping document (he did not know yet that New Hampshire, the ninth state, had ratified just three days earlier). But he also knew that Virginia's endorsement was critical to the nation's long-term success, as was New York's, whose decision he and other supporters also awaited. If Virginia rejected the Constitution, New York would follow suit. North Carolina might also reject it. And Rhode Island, which had not even sent delegates to the convention, would remain opposed. A constitution with a bare majority of support would be imperiled from the start—Americans would doubt its effectiveness, foreign governments its validity. Madison and his 169 fellow Virginia delegates held the fate of a nation in their hands. All he could do at this point was wait for the final vote, which, unlike in other states that had ratified, he expected to be close. Only days earlier, he had written: "I dare not positively decide," when he was asked how the vote would go. His fellow delegate Archibald Stuart agreed: "The fate of Virginia is thus suspended upon a single hair."

In many ways, the Virginia vote—the entire ratification debate— would be the culmination of work that began a dozen years ago with the adoption of the Declaration of Independence in Philadelphia. The principles of freedom, equality, and self-governance espoused in the nation's founding document were first secured through hard-fought victories on the battlefield, and then, in late summer of 1787, codified into a framework of laws and governmental structure when delegates had debated and approved the new Constitution. To complete their task, they had returned to the Pennsylvania State House made famous by the work of the Continental Congress in 1776.

Over the last weeks and as late as this day—just prior to Patrick Henry—the thirty-seven-year-old Madison had labored to convince his home-state countrymen that the Constitution was America's best hope and that their worries were unfounded. Point by point, he had explained the benefits of the document and the government it would implement. But his efforts had taken their toll: "My health is not good," he wrote to New York's Alexander Hamilton, "and the business is wearisome beyond expression." In another letter to George Washington, he said: "I find myself not yet restored and extremely feeble."

Yet his performances on Shockoe Hill were stellar, even inspirational. One letter writer said Patrick Henry's "declamatory powers" were "vastly overpowered by the deep reasoning of our glorious little Madison." Archibald Stuart, a supporter of the Constitution, summed up Madison's efforts in a letter to a friend: "Madison came boldly forward and supported the Constitution with the soundest reason and most manly eloquence I ever heard." With admiration, he added: "He understands his subject well and his whole soul is engaged in its success."

Madison had plenty of practice. For several years, he had thought about and championed a strong national government, recognizing that the Articles of Confederation were insufficient to govern a new nation, and he had supported his overall goal with persuasive arguments, brilliant essays, subtle arm-twisting, and indefatigable conviction.

In many ways, he seemed the least likely statesman to undertake such an effort. At just under five feet, six inches tall, with a sharp nose and a receding hairline, he was neither physically imposing nor a gifted orator. One observer said the diminutive Virginian was no bigger "than half a piece of soap." He often spoke in such a low voice during meetings that attendees asked him to speak up or repeat himself. He suffered from chronic ailments, including gastrointestinal problems, fevers, and debilitating seizures that he described as "somewhat resembling epilepsy, and suspending the intellectual functions." He had a "constitutional liability" to these sudden attacks, which proved most distracting to prolonged work and often drove him to despair. At the age of twenty-one, Madison had written: "I am too dull and infirm now to look out for any extraordinary things in this world, for I think my sensations for many months past have intimated to me not to expect a long or healthy life."

Despite his physical infirmities, James Madison was a brilliant strategist, a tireless reader, a lover of deep thinkers and philosophers, a man who was most comfortable delving into history and the classics, and constructing and deconstructing ideas about government and its relationship to people. In 1776, while the Continental Congress was debating the Declaration in Philadelphia, Madison, age twenty-five, was helping to draft Virginia's state constitution. When he joined the Continental Congress in 1780, he was its youngest member. There he worked with Thomas Jefferson and others, articulating his passion for religious freedom and his dedication to human liberty.

All this preparation served James Madison well in May 1787, when he began in earnest the most important intellectual and political pursuit of his life. One day Madison would become president of the United States, but even that heady responsibility could not compare with the charge and the prospect of creating a new American government.

He relished the challenge. Madison plunged into the work of the Federal Convention immediately upon his arrival in Philadelphia—and he had not stopped thirteen months later.

May 1787

UNLIKE REVOLUTIONARY WAR HERO George Washington, who entered Philadelphia by troop-escorted carriage on May 13, 1787, amid a dramatic crescendo of church bells and cheering crowds, James Madison had arrived quietly and alone by stagecoach a week earlier from New York, where he had represented Virginia in the country's Confederation Congress.

He was determined to prepare for and prevail in a debate that he believed and hoped would dramatically alter America's expectations for and view of its future. Essentially, he and a handful of others hoped to launch the second revolution in American government in fewer than a dozen years.

Madison certainly was not alone in his feeling that the Articles of Confederation, which had been adopted in 1781 in an attempt to implement some sort of central government, were woefully inadequate to govern the fledgling and ambitious nation. But he was among the most outspoken. The articles granted the government no real taxing authority, he argued, and little ability to provide for the nation's defense. They provided insufficient power to regulate commerce on land or when foreign ships sailed into American ports, offered no way to handle accords and treaties, and delineated no clear path to settle disputes among the states. For example, the articles had left the nation largely incapable of forcing the British to live up to the terms of the 1783 Treaty of Paris that had ended the Revolutionary War. "It is not possible that a government can last long under these circumstances," Madison warned.

In the past few years, Madison had witnessed all the drawbacks of a weak central authority. The federal treasury was depleted and the country was in danger of defaulting on loans from both private creditors and European nations such as France and Holland. Individual states balked at the confederation's efforts to impose tariffs on top of their own. Paper money—printed by states to help them pay off debts, meet their pension obligations to veterans, and assist farmers in covering their mortgages—flooded the country, causing rampant inflation and a financial crisis. As a result, small businesses and farmers continued to struggle, merchants were thrown into jail unable to pay their debts, and many owners had their farms or shops confiscated and sold to pay debts or back taxes.

The economic conditions led to violence in 1786, when Daniel Shays, a former captain in the Continental army, led an insurrection of armed, defiant, and impoverished farmers in Northampton, Massachusetts. The men who took part in what is today known as "Shays' Rebellion" blocked western Massachusetts courts from sitting and ordering further foreclosures and threatened to seize muskets and other arms in the nearby arsenal in Springfield. In Northampton, Taunton, Worcester, and Great Barrington, mobs took over courthouses, threatened judges, and even fired upon citizens who had business with the courts. Although the rebellion was put down by state troops, the incident highlighted in stark terms the fear of many that a weak central government could lead to anarchy.

And while Shays and his men were responsible for the most violent uprising of the period, other places felt the undercurrent of unrest. "There are combustibles in every state," wrote George Washington, "which a spark may set fire to. . . . Who, besides a Tory, could have foreseen, or a Briton predicted them?" Later, he wrote to Madison: "Wisdom and good examples are necessary at this time to rescue the political machine from the impending storm."

Madison had articulated the problems with the Articles of Confederation in a long treatise entitled *Vices of the Political System of the United States*. In it he talked of the "encroachments by state on federal authority," the "trespasses of the states on the rights of each other," and "violations of the law of nations and of treaties," all glaring prob-lems that the weak Articles of Confederation had fostered.

Was this what America had fought for in seeking independence from Britain?

Contrary to the perception of many Americans who feared, in the wake of the revolution, that a large central government would threaten their liberty, Madison fervently held the opposite view—American lib-erty and freedom were far more likely *imperiled* by an impotent fed-eral government, unable to protect the country from foreign predators and helpless to offset state excesses and disputes.

Writing to his friend Thomas Jefferson in Paris, Madison said that a strong federal government would not only "guard the national rights and interests against invaders," it would also serve to "restrain states from thwarting and molesting each other." In April 1787, he explained to George Washington that he had "sought middle ground" that could be palatable to all, a plan "which may at once support a due suprem-acy of the national authority, and not exclude the local authorities wherever they can be subordinately useful."

MANY WOULD SOON DISAGREE vehemently with Madison that his desire for a strong central government constituted "middle ground." Indeed, he must have understood that the phrase stretched even the loosest definition of compromise. In his letter to Washington, he pro-posed that the national government "should be armed with positive and complete authority in all cases which require uniformity," includ-ing the regulation of trade and the right to tax exports and imports. He proposed that "national supremacy" be extended to the judiciary, that the national legislature be divided into two branches, and that a na-tional executive be included in the federal structure.

He also believed it was "absolutely necessary" for the national government to supersede the legislative authority of states. Without a federal check on state power, "the States will continue to invade the

National jurisdiction, to violate treaties and the law of nations, and to harass each other with rival and spiteful measures dictated by a mistaken view of interest."

These commercial and trade disputes among states threatened peace and economic recovery. For example, New York and Vermont often imposed restrictions and usurious taxes on interstate commerce, while Virginia and Maryland argued over navigation rights on the Potomac River.

In an attempt to settle these disputes, Virginia and Maryland asked the Continental Congress to invite states to discuss whether a more "uniform system" of trade regulations would satisfy their common interests. Congress responded by calling a meeting in Annapolis in 1786, but delegates from only five states—New York, New Jersey, Pennsylvania, Delaware, and Virginia—attended, all of whom favored a stronger central government. Without a quorum, they had no authority. But the delegates—among them Madison, Alexander Hamilton of New York, and John Dickinson of Delaware—recommended that Congress call for a federal convention in Philadelphia to determine what action could be taken to "render the constitution of the federal government adequate to the exigencies of the Union." Virginia again took the lead in appointing delegates, and other states followed suit. In February 1787, Congress endorsed the idea but was deliberately cautious in its resolution, calling on the Federal Convention to gather "for the sole and express purpose of revising the Articles of Confederation."

Most delegates who would trek to Philadelphia for the gathering would do so believing their task was to do exactly that: to modify the articles in places, to strengthen and broaden them in others, to adapt them to meet what was a clear need for an expanded role for the federal government.

Madison had other ideas. He and a handful of other great thinkers—including fellow Virginian Edmund Randolph, Alexander Hamilton of New York, Pennsylvania's Gouverneur Morris, Robert Morris, and James Wilson—had come to Philadelphia not to alter the articles but to abolish them. Assisted by the support, guidance, shrewdness, reputation, and wisdom of George Washington and the sagacious Benjamin Franklin, these men would direct the convention toward a plan for a federal union that was unforeseen by most of their peers or the general population.

"It is an unsettling but inescapable fact," one historian wrote, "that several of the principal authors of the U.S. Constitution . . . would never have made it to Philadelphia if their constituents had known their real intentions."

MADISON WAS GRATEFUL FOR Washington's support and, more than anything, desired the great general's attendance at the Philadelphia convention. No one in the new nation was more beloved and more respected than Washington. For the convention itself and for any document produced by its delegates to carry credibility with the American people, Washington's gravitas, wisdom, and virtue were essential.

Pennsylvania's Benjamin Franklin would lend a certain level of prestige and celebrity to the gathering—outside of Washington, he was perhaps the most famous American in the world—but it was George Washington's attendance that was a prerequisite to the convention's success. As early as December 1786, Virginia's governor, Edmund Randolph, urged Washington to attend the Philadelphia convention, so that "those who began, carried on, and consummated the revolution can yet rescue America from impending ruin." This, Randolph said, was the "one ray of hope" that shone through the nation's "gloomy prospects."

Washington was reluctant at first. Fiercely protective of his esteemed reputation, he saw two potential pitfalls of lending his prestige to the convention. On the one hand, he did not want to attend if the convention had little or no chance of success; any association with a failed convention, or even one that fell short of its goals, could sully Washington's image in the eyes of the American public. On the other, if he did attend, he feared being perceived as an opportunist who would exploit his own reputation to achieve personal gain, particularly since some advocates were suggesting he would be selected by acclamation to lead the convention. He also wondered about the legality of a federal convention whose goal was to significantly alter the Articles of Confederation.

Madison and others persisted. Without Washington's presence, they argued, the very thing he feared—a failed convention—was likely a foregone conclusion. Conversely, Washington's very presence as a prominent member of the Virginian delegation would convince other states to send their most competent and respected statesmen, which in turn increased the odds of the convention's success. Greatness would attract greatness, in other words, and Washington was the lynchpin, the sturdy axis on which a productive convention would turn.

To further nudge Washington, Madison even sent him a list of some of the prestigious names who would be attending: Elbridge Gerry of Massachusetts, a Declaration signer; John Rutledge, governor of South Carolina, a member of one of the state's most powerful families, and brother to Edward Rutledge, also one of the signatories of the Declaration; and Washington's protégé, former senior aide-de-camp, and confidant, the irrepressible, opinionated, and brilliant Alexander Hamilton of New York.

Washington weighed his options: the danger that an inept or feeble convention would fail to create a government that could cure the nation's ills versus the argument that the Philadelphia convention could represent the last best chance for the new nation's future success. This was a nation for which Washington had fought and led men on the battlefield, in many cases watching them suffer terribly or die from British fire, starvation, or prolonged exposure to bone-numbing cold. He was steadfast in his opposition to the Articles of Confederation, writing in 1784 that they saddled the nation with "a half starved, limping Government that appears to be always moving upon crutches, tottering at every step."

Still, he hesitated.

*

FINALLY, WASHINGTON TURNED TO one of his most trusted friends and courageous officers from the revolution, General Henry Knox of Boston. The Virginian outlined his dilemma and asked Knox "to inform me confidentially, what the public expectation is on this head—that is, whether I will, or ought to be there?"

Washington trusted Knox implicitly. The former Boston bookstore owner had served with immense distinction during the revolution from the moment Washington had plucked him from the ranks in late 1775 and selected him to lead a daring, high-risk, against-all-odds mission, one that provided Washington with a stunning first victory and infused the Americans with a deep sense of confidence that the powerful British could be defeated.

With boldness, vision, imagination, and inexhaustible perseverance—and with Washington's pleas for haste ringing in his ears— Henry Knox and his brother led the successful mission to transport nearly sixty cannon from Fort Ticonderoga on Lake Champlain in New York to Continental army emplacements outside British-occupied Boston. This improbable 300-mile trek in the dead of winter had made Knox a hero and forever solidified his relationship with Washington. Knox transported the heavy artillery—which weighed 120,000 pounds in total—on an unprecedented and perilous three-month journey that would come to be known as the "noble train of artillery." He and his men hauled the artillery pieces, strapped to more than forty ox-drawn sleds and horses fitted with thick rope harnesses, across frozen Lake George, ice-encrusted streams, and rutted roads in upstate New York, and through narrow and sometimes treacherous mountain passes in the Berkshires and snow-draped forests in western Massachusetts, unbowed and undeterred on their march toward Boston.

Historians have called Knox's march one of the great logistical achievements in military history. He finally arrived in Boston in early February, his "precious convoy" a welcome sight to Washington, whose men mounted the cannon on Dorchester Heights, just south of the city of Boston. On March 2, after replenishing their supply of gunpowder, Knox's men relentlessly bombarded the British, whose ships, with great ceremony, evacuated Boston on March 17, 1776, a sight that "amazed" Abigail Adams as she watched.

When a victorious Washington rode triumphant into Boston, Knox was at his side, and for the rest of the war, he remained there. Washington put Knox in charge of field artillery, including men, ammunition, and cannon; he played a key command role when the Continental army crossed the Delaware on Christmas Eve in 1776, and the repeated bombardment from Knox's heavy guns was critical in bringing about Cornwallis's surrender at Yorktown, ending the Revolutionary War.

Now, six years after the war's end, Washington asked his dear friend whether his "non-attendance" at the Federal Convention would be "considered as a dereliction to republicanism," something that would bring him profound embarrassment. With an unbreakable bond between them, Washington would value and weigh Knox's opinion most of all.

Should he go to Philadelphia?

KNOX'S RESPONSE WAS SWIFT and unequivocal, confirming the argument that others had made: Washington's presence by itself would lend the convention the serious weight it needed to accomplish its goals.

"Were the convention to propose only amendments, and patch work to the present defective confederation, your reputation would suffer," Knox posited. However, he urged his friend to consider the more optimistic scenario: "But, were an energetic and judicious system to be proposed with Your signature, it would be a circumstance highly honorable to your fame, in the judgment of the present and future ages." In addition, Washington's attendance at such a gathering would "doubly entitle" him to the "glorious . . . epithet—The Father of Your Country."

In the end, persuaded by the arguments of Knox and other men he respected, and bound by a sense of duty to the new republic he had been so instrumental in forging, Washington decided he would travel to Philadelphia for the convention. His journey and the country's again were destined for entwinement.

Immediately upon his arrival on May 13, 1787, Philadelphia basked in the aura of his presence. The next day, the *Philadelphia Packet* reported on the enthusiasm that engulfed the city: "Yesterday His Excellency General WASHINGTON, a member of the grand convention, arrived here. He was met at some distance and escorted into the city by the troops on horse, and saluted at his entrance by the artillery. The joy of the people on the coming of this great and good man was shown by their acclamations and the ringing of bells."

In midsummer, after the convention was well underway, James Monroe wrote to fellow Virginian Thomas Jefferson of Washington's impact on the delegates. It was obvious, Monroe noted, that "the presence of General Washington will have a great weight in the body itself . . . and that the signature of his name to whatever act shall be the result of their deliberations will secure its passage thro' the union."

JAMES MADISON WAS THE first delegate outside of Pennsylvania to reach the city, ten days before anyone else and nearly three weeks before a quorum of seven states was achieved on May 25. He had hoped his fellow Virginians would have arrived as well, suggesting to Governor Randolph that Old Dominion delegates "ought not only to be on the ground in due time, but to be prepared with some materials for the work of the Convention." He asked Randolph to arrive more than a week before the convention began.

Madison's desire to begin work on a new way of governing the nation had been heightened by his mounting frustration in the past months with a decided lack of action in Congress. Time and again, legislation had stalled, debates had gone nowhere, individual states had erected roadblocks to any sort of congressional authority, and their representatives often seemed paralyzed and despondent at their inability to make progress. Even when Congress had the occasional piece of important business before it, delegates found it difficult to take their duties seriously and were often absent, rendering the body "so thin as to be incompetent," Madison lamented to Jefferson.

As May drew near, Madison's feelings about the convention's prospects for success ascended to peaks and dipped into valleys, sometimes day-to-day. The truth was, neither he nor anyone else knew what to expect. Perhaps, he admitted to his father, the best hope for success would come from the "existing embarrassments and mortal diseases" of the current Articles of Confederation. His hope was that "a spirit of concession on all sides may be produced by the general chaos."

If not, if delegates could not agree on a remedy, Madison was convinced that a "very different arrangement would ensue" to govern the country. Some people had whispered that a monarchy was needed; others that "partitioning" the nation into geographic regions would be necessary to preserve peace and a working relationship between states.

Privately, to Jefferson, Madison admitted: "What may be the result of this political experiment cannot be foreseen."

BY THE LAST WEEK of April, most states had agreed to send delegates to the convention; only Rhode Island had refused outright. The state's governor said Rhode Island lawmakers were concerned about "breaking the compact" established by the Articles of Confederation, lest "we must all be lost in a common ruin" that could result if small-state sovereignty were encroached upon by an abusive central government. Despite Rhode Island's decision, Madison believed that "the prospect of a full and respectable convention grows stronger every day."

He was pleased that delegates would gather, grateful that a debate about the tepid Articles of Confederation would finally occur, but he was also fully cognizant that the Philadelphia meeting would represent a watershed moment. The irony was not lost on Madison that the convention would occur in the same city and the same building in which America had declared its independence eleven years earlier; yet, in the same east assembly room where John Adams, Thomas Jefferson, and

Benjamin Franklin had signed the Declaration of Independence—to which they had pledged their lives, their fortunes, and their sacred honor—a failed convention could spell doom for the young nation they had created. The 1776 delegates had achieved something they believed was inspirational and eternal, and had done so with the threat of prison and death hanging over their heads. Their brave political actions had then been backed up by the valiant sacrifices of patriots who had died or suffered grievous wounds and great deprivation on the battlefield.

With the American victory settled several years earlier, the men who would gather in Philadelphia in May 1787 faced no such risk; how grave a disservice to their courageous predecessors, then, if mere pettiness, stubbornness, hubris, regionalism, or factionalism led to the end of the brief American experiment without a single enemy shot having been fired.

Madison felt the burden of his charge and the weight of the task ahead. As the convention date loomed, he confided to a friend: "The nearer the crisis approaches, the more I tremble."

6

★

"Our Doors
Will Be Shut"

★

With humility and self-deprecation, the ever modest George Washington accepted his unanimous election as president of what would become known as the Constitutional Convention on Friday, May 25, 1787. In Madison's words, he "lamented his want of better qualifications" and asked the delegates for their indulgence for any "involuntary errors which his inexperience might occasion."

As his friends had predicted, Washington's leadership over the proceedings lent an instant air of prestige to the convention; and the manner in which he was chosen brought a sense of gentility to the opening session. Washington, fifty-five years old and at the height of his popularity, was nominated for the honor by Robert Morris of Pennsylvania, who informed members that he had been instructed to do so by his state's delegation. Considering, as Madison noted, that Pennsylvania's own Benjamin Franklin "could have been thought of as a competitor" to Washington, Morris's gesture "came with particular grace." In fact, Franklin himself reportedly was set to nominate Washington, but the eighty-one-year-old Pennsylvanian, weakened and wracked with pain from agonizing kidney stones and severe gout, found it difficult to move about and missed the first day's session, likely due to downpours that would have further impeded his ability to traverse Philadelphia's streets.

Washington was well known to the delegates. Thirty of the fifty-five men who eventually attended the convention had served in his army and revered him. Among them were five men who had endured the ghastly winter at Valley Forge; forty-two had sat in the Continental Congress and knew well of his leadership qualities on the battlefield.

Madison pointed out that Washington reminded delegates of the importance of their upcoming work, "of the novelty of the scene of business in which he was to act." His deference notwithstanding, Washington was a proud man, cognizant of the importance of history, tradition, and ceremony and well aware of the august position to which delegates had elected him; he was enormously touched by their confidence in him. Over the next few months, George Washington would remain virtually silent, both from the chair and when he surrendered the gavel to participate in committee of the whole, but delegates would be reassured by his quietude, bearing, and strength of leadership.

Perhaps more important, with Washington occupying the presiding chair, he would now be inextricably linked to any work, decision, and final document produced by the convention; whether explicit or by inference, his endorsement would carry enormous weight with the American people.

After the delegates elected Washington as convention president, they voted to name Major William Jackson as secretary; he had served with distinction in the Continental army, including as a member of Washington's staff. They also appointed a committee to determine convention rules and read into the record the formal credentials of the attending delegates and the states. With fatigue a factor among members, the convention adjourned until Monday to give delegates who had journeyed great distances a chance to rest, acclimate themselves to the city, acquire lodgings, and become acquainted with each other and the issues ahead.

Members did not know it then, but May 26 would be the only Saturday until late July on which they would not meet. Inside the Pennsylvania State House, and across the American landscape, there was a sense of urgency in the air.

NINE ADDITIONAL DELEGATES WERE in attendance at the state-house on Monday, May 28, so when the convention resumed business at ten o'clock in the morning, thirty-eight men were in their seats ready to conduct business.

The most noteworthy new attendee was Benjamin Franklin. The weather had cleared and cooled, making the two-block trip from his home on Market Street much easier, yet Franklin, never shy or reserved, arrived at the statehouse in the most flamboyant way anyone could re-member. Suffering from gout and in pain, Dr. Franklin was carried to the convention in a decorative sedan chair that he had shipped from Paris. Glass windows on both sides gave it the appearance of a small carriage, but instead of resting on wheels, it was supported by two poles, ten or twelve feet long, pliant enough to absorb some of the shock and vibrate only gently as the bearers carried Franklin over the cobble-stoned streets. When the carriers—who were prisoners from the nearby Walnut Street jail—reached the assembly room, delegates helped Franklin from the chair and he took his seat with the Pennsylvania delegation. The prisoners set down the sedan chair in one corner of the room and departed; they would return in the afternoon to carry Franklin home.

Franklin, the elder statesman, would lend his wisdom to the of-ficial proceedings, but he also served as the convention's unofficial host. He had his dining room enlarged for the convention, and his home became an informal gathering place for delegates,

With Franklin's spectacular arrival, both legends were now pres-ent at the convention—Washington standing tall at the front of the room and Franklin seated near the back—giving enormous dignity and a sense of unified purpose to the gathering on its first full day of work.

Outside and inside the statehouse, preparations were under way to ensure a smooth convention. Workmen had covered the cobblestoned streets with dirt and gravel to reduce the sound of disturbances in the street and the clatter of passing carriages in case the delegates chose to debate with the windows open. That would not be the case often. Even when temperatures rose to sweltering conditions later in the summer, the convention would conduct most of its business with the windows and doors shut closed.

There were two major reasons for this decision. First, when the portals remained open, delegates complained of a swarming inundation of bluebottle flies from a nearby stable. The second and more important reason cut to the heart of one of the most critical decisions the delegates would make during the summer of 1787—for this federal convention, secrecy would be the order of the day.

DELEGATES INVOKED STRICT SECRECY rules to protect the convention from the potential "licentious publication of their proceedings." As such, they agreed that no copies would be made of any journal entries without express approval of the convention, that only members would be permitted to inspect the official journal, and that "nothing spoken in the House be printed, or otherwise published or communicated without leave." No journalists or spectators would be allowed to attend. Guards were posted at the locked doors and blinds were drawn across the closed windows.

Operating in secrecy permitted delegates to argue openly, engage in uninhibited debate, float trial balloons, build consensus, and reconsider their positions without tying their positions and their votes to the record, and without fear of being accused of inconsistency and fecklessness, or worse, vacillation or outright dishonesty. "Our doors will be shut, and communications upon the business of the convention be forbidden during its sitting," wrote Virginia's George Mason, agreeing that the decision was "a necessary precaution to prevent misrepresentations or mistakes." After all, Mason explained, there was a "material difference between the appearance of a subject in its first crude and undigested shape, and after it shall have been properly matured and arranged." Years later, James Madison would acknowledge that "no Constitution would ever have been adopted by the convention if the debates had been public."

Delegates seemed to adhere to the strict secrecy rules in virtually every instance, even when corresponding with confidants and friends throughout the convention. Madison wrote to Jefferson in early June and felt comfortable only naming the delegates in attendance at that time. Even by mid-July, Madison wrote to Jefferson and confessed: "I am still under the mortification of being restrained from disclosing any part of [the] proceedings," but promised to "make amends for my silence" as soon as he was at liberty to do so.

Augmenting the secrecy provision was the agreement by delegates to meet in the more informal committee of the whole to debate key points, rather than recording every vote in a formal meeting of the convention. Rufus King pointed out that "changes of opinion would be frequent in the course of the business." Recording yeas and nays on every matter "would fill the minutes with contradictions." Mason concurred, adding that such a record of members' opinions "would be an obstacle to a change of them on conviction." If every vote was recorded, delegates would be less likely to change their mind for fear of being called to task by "adversaries" after the convention had concluded.

THE SECRECY RULES, ESPECIALLY, along with the committee of the whole decision, benefited the convention in several ways, politically and practically.

First, it allowed delegates the breathing room and the flexibility they would need as they debated individual components and considered the enormity of their overall actions.

Second, as it became clear that the debate would move well beyond the convention's charter to merely alter the Articles of Confederation, the full breadth of the delegates' intentions to create a strong central government remained within the walls of the Pennsylvania State House; otherwise there would likely have been howls of protest from political opponents, such as Jefferson (from Paris), Samuel Adams (from Massachusetts), and Patrick Henry (from Virginia). Secrecy enabled the influential proponents of a powerful national government—Madison most notably—to build momentum without outside interference.

Third, the shroud of secrecy enabled delegates to finish their audacious and monumental work without outside distractions from the press and the general public that would have indisputably bogged down and chilled the debate. Without the secrecy provision, it is virtually inconceivable that they could have completed their task in an astonishing four months' time.

Finally, the secret discussions taking place inside the shuttered doors and windows of the statehouse, the sentries posted to prevent intruders, the agreement forbidding delegates from sharing any information outside the walls of the convention—all of this enveloped the convention proceedings in an aura of awe and reverence. There could be little doubt that the delegates were working on something of great importance. This secrecy scenario may have angered some prominent dissenters and certain members of the public, but for most, it filled the convention with intrigue and mystery and magnitude. Just as significant, inside the statehouse, the secrecy pact imbued the delegates with a sense of seriousness, urgency, daring, and gutsiness as they worked. The secret proceedings, coupled with the historic statehouse location and the presence of Franklin and Washington, were not merely symbolic trappings of the convention, but components that propelled the delegates to attempt—and achieve—one of history's boldest strategic maneuvers.

Indeed, no one argued with Madison and Hamilton when they asserted that decisions made by the delegates would decide forever the fate of republican government; nor with Pennsylvania's Gouverneur

Morris when he proclaimed that "the whole human race will be affected by the proceedings of this Convention"—nor with Washington when he declared: "The event is in the hand of God."

SECRECY NOTWITHSTANDING, JAMES MADISON fully grasped the need to record the convention's work for posterity and trusted himself more than anyone to accomplish the task. The work of the convention would determine the "happiness of a people . . . and possibly the cause of liberty throughout the world," and thus deserved to have its debates and discussions recorded. Madison's goal was to "preserve as far as I could an exact account of what might pass in the convention while executing its trust."

William Jackson was the convention's official secretary, but Madison wanted more than the sparseness and constrained language that often accompanies an official record or journal. He wanted to record the speeches, the reasoning and rationale, the color with which delegates made their points and proffered their arguments. Other delegates took notes—Hamilton, Mason, Rufus King of Massachusetts, New York's Robert Yates for a time—but most of these were incomplete; none remotely approached the voluminous and exacting note-taking of Madison. To ensure that he could hear as much of the discussion as possible, he chose a seat near Washington and Jackson, with his back to the chair, so that he faced members on his left and right. "In this favorable position . . . I noted in terms legible and abbreviations and marks intelligible to myself what was read from the Chair or spoken by the members," he explained. At the end of each session, or within a day or two, Madison would then write out his notes longhand "in the extent and form preserved in my own hand on my files."

Madison's labors were all the more valuable due to his virtual perfect attendance at the convention; unlike many delegates who came and went throughout the summer, Madison noted that he was "not absent a single day, nor more than a casual fraction of an hour in any day, so that I could not have lost a single speech, unless a very short one." While he was devoted to his task, Madison found his work taxing. Battling his chronic health issues during the hot and humid summer of 1787, Madison acknowledged years later that the combined exertions of "writing out the debates," participating fully in the discussions, and attending the convention without any break "almost killed" him.

Nonetheless, as a friend of Madison's remarked well after the convention: "Having undertaken the task, he was determined to accomplish it."

Madison wrote down virtually everything, even remarks that were critical of him. He wrote to Jefferson in July: "I have taken lengthy notes of everything that has passed, and mean to go on with the drudgery, if no indisposition obliges me to discontinue it."

When New Jersey's William Paterson objected that the large states, especially Virginia and Pennsylvania, were overstepping their bounds in the initial plan for the new federal government, Madison faithfully recorded: "He complained of the manner in which Mr. M & Mr. Gov. Morris had treated the small states." Madison certainly could have omitted the reference to "Mr. M," but his scruples—or as one historian called it, "an abnormal or extravagant regard for accuracy"—prevented him from doing so. Later, Delaware's John Dickinson also chastised Madison for pushing sweeping changes that would drastically limit the power of the small states, and Madison painstakingly and accurately recorded Dickinson's objections.

His dedication to accuracy, honesty, and comprehensiveness compelled him to record the "nasty" remarks directed toward him. Virtually all of Madison's longhand accounts were derived from his own note-taking during sessions.

Ever mindful of the convention's secrecy provision, James Madison kept virtually silent about his notes until decades later, when he shared them with Thomas Jefferson. They remained unpublished until 1840, three years after his death and fifty-three years after the historic gathering in Philadelphia.

★

7

"That a National Government Ought to Be Established"

★

The Federal Convention did not ease into its work of creating a new government for the young nation; it simply plunged in without preamble or hesitation. After weeks of preplanning and informal discussions, the proponents of a strong national government, led by delegates from Virginia and Pennsylvania, chose directness over circumlocution and boldness over restraint as they launched their opening salvo in a high-stakes gamble to define a new governing direction for America.

Virginia's governor, Edmund Randolph—highly respected, his integrity above reproach, a member of one of his state's most powerful and influential families—rose after Washington recognized him on Tuesday morning, May 29, 1787, and offered remarks that would forever solidify the date as among the most important in American constitutional history.

Randolph, thirty-four years old, tall, self-assured, dignified, and a far more polished orator than Madison, would put forth most of

Madison's and the other Virginians' ideas and proposals in what would soon become known as "the Virginia Plan" to govern the country. He outlined the weaknesses in the Articles of Confederation, but was careful to praise the authors—some of whom were in attendance—for "having done all that patriots could do, in the then infancy of the science of constitutions and of confederacies." At the time, the myriad problems America now faced had yet to bubble to the surface: since then, however, "commercial discord" had arisen among many states; treaties had been violated; foreign debts had grown; and the economic crisis had led to controversy and dissonance.

The danger from all of these weaknesses was the real threat of anarchy and the dissolution of the new country a mere eleven years after the United States had declared its independence and only six years after it had defeated the British on the battlefield.

In presenting the new plan, largely the brainchild of James Madison, Randolph offered fifteen resolutions that went far beyond "correcting or enlarging" the Articles of Confederation, but effectively called for supplanting them altogether. Randolph called for establishment of a new form of national government, one consisting of a bicameral legislature, with the "first" house elected by the people and the "second" house elected by the first, both based on a state's population—the current Articles of Confederation called for a single house with members appointed equally by the states, which made their representatives mostly beholden to them rather than broader national priorities. Randolph's resolutions also called for a national executive—the Articles established no such position—a clear signal that he was proposing a stronger central government; and a national judiciary to consist of "one or more supreme tribunals, and of inferior tribunals to be chosen by the National Legislature."

Those representatives who had come to Philadelphia to amend the Articles of Confederation rather than replace them were likely shocked by Randolph's opening resolutions, but there was no strong protest when he had finished. Members apparently understood that they needed some plan upon which to debate and also recognized that

Randolph's proposals were recommendations only. Nonetheless, the Virginia Plan would come to frame the discussions and the vociferous disagreements inside the statehouse and, eventually, form the basis for the U.S. Constitution, a plan, in the words of one historian that would "be debated clause by clause in Committee of the Whole, with every resolve reconsidered, reargued, passed or discarded."

For now, as day one drew to a close, the convention agreed to adjourn and, the following day, organize itself into a committee of the whole to consider Randolph's propositions and "the state of the American union."

ANY AMBIGUITY ABOUT THE intentions of the Virginia Plan's supporters, any misplaced nuance that softened the clarity of their message, any misconstrued inference by other delegates—all these were washed away when the delegates reconvened at 10:00 a.m. on Wednesday, May 30, the day after Randolph's opening resolutions.

Did supporters of the Virginia Plan huddle overnight or at breakfast? No one knows, but it is clear they spoke at some point after Randolph's long monologue on Tuesday and concluded that his initial resolution did not articulate their message either clearly or forcefully enough. Wasting no time, on Wednesday, Pennsylvania's Gouverneur Morris jumped to his feet and suggested that Randolph replace his initial resolution from the previous day that called for the Articles of Confederation "to be corrected and enlarged." As a substitute, Morris resolved, and Randolph agreed, that because a "union of the states merely federal will not accomplish" the goal of providing the nation with "common defense, security of liberty, and general welfare," and because "no treaty or treaties among . . . the states as individual sovereignties would be sufficient" to sustain a nation, the convention should debate the following:

That a national government ought to be established consisting of a supreme Legislative, Executive, and Judiciary.

The motion by Morris and Randolph was clear and explicit. For the first time, advocates for the Virginia Plan had resolved to scrap the Articles of Confederation and replace them with a supreme national government.

THE CONVENTION WAS SILENT—the small-state delegates, especially, were perhaps stunned. A stronger central government was one thing, but a national government that was *supreme*? What were the implications of such a scheme? What powers would such a government expropriate from the states? Didn't this language fly in the face of the tenets of the Declaration, which emphasized the preeminence of the individual over the government? Didn't America revolt against its mother country precisely because its central government had grown too large, too unresponsive, too abusive? The delegates certainly were not prepared to pass the resolution, not without further debate and clarification.

South Carolina's Pierce Butler said he definitely had *not* made up his mind on the subject and said it was incumbent upon Randolph to show that a national government was necessary for the existence of states. His colleague, Charles Pinckney, was more pointed: did Randolph mean to "abolish state governments altogether?" Indeed, if the convention were proceeding down such a path, Pinckney believed "that their business was at an end." Connecticut's Roger Sherman, who had just arrived in Philadelphia and was attending his first convention session, also believed events were moving too fast and urged that Randolph's resolutions be postponed. Delaware's George Read also expressed dismay about the speed at which the convention was moving.

As debate raged, confusion reigned. How was the Virginia Plan so different from the king and parliamentary councils that had subjugated the colonies just a decade earlier? State sovereignty was a bedrock principle of federalism, of self-government, a bulwark against the excessive concentration and abuse of power.

Would not states become irrelevant under the Virginia resolutions?

No, Randolph responded vigorously, the protestors had it all wrong: there was no intention of overthrowing state governments, but rather to strengthen the national government by giving it the power to "defend and protect itself . . . and to take from the legislatures or states no more sovereignty than is competent to this end."

For certain, states would *not* wield the same power in the newly proposed government that they possessed currently. Pennsylvania's Gouverneur Morris attempted to clarify the resolution and the terms that delegates were tossing around during debate, and to draw the distinctions between these new and, in some ways, difficult concepts. A *federal* government, he explained—the current formation of the country's governmental structure operating under a confederation of states—was a "mere compact resting on the good faith of the parties." A supreme *national* government had a "complete and compulsive operation," and only the establishment of such would be capable of providing for "the common defense, security of liberty, and general welfare." And while he, too, agreed that the state governments should retain some sovereignty, there was no doubt that the national government he and his colleagues were proposing would wield preeminent power.

Morris could not conceive of a government in which "two supremes" could coexist—in America and "in all communities there must be one supreme power, and one only."

He also warned his fellow delegates that failure to establish a supreme national government would only lead to further chaos and abuses of power by factions or ill-meaning individuals in the future. "We had better take a supreme government now, than a despot twenty years hence—for come he must," Morris said.

OF THE EIGHT STATES represented at the convention on May 30, six of them voted in favor of the Virginia Plan resolution. Only Connecticut voted no outright, and New York's two delegates in attendance were divided—fervent nationalist Alexander Hamilton in favor and states-rights advocate Robert Yates opposed. Those delegates who had objected most strenuously about the notion of a supreme national government believed a reluctant vote in favor was superior to blatant inaction; perhaps amendments and details could be hammered out in future discussions.

Without question, the vote was a victory for Madison and the other Virginia and Pennsylvania delegates who had labored prior to the convention to craft the "supreme" resolutions. Madison, especially, had demonstrated yeoman-like determination and intellectual leadership on the need for a strong central government, and then he and his allies engaged in deft political maneuverings to change the debate among delegates from merely modifying and patching the Articles of Confederation to repudiating them altogether and considering the construction of a whole new government.

And they had managed to coax an affirmative vote on only the third full day of the convention's business.

In many ways, considering from whence the young nation had come in such a short time, considering the delegates' frame of reference and collective memories, the May 30 vote was an astounding one—in the words of historian Richard Beeman, delegates had, within a matter of hours, approved the concept of a government that "was closer to that of the imperial British government against which the colonies had rebelled than to the confederation of sovereign states they had created in the aftermath of the Revolution." The deficiencies of the current confederation, the strain its shortcomings had placed on the young nation, anarchistic events such as Shays' Rebellion and the fear of more civil unrest—or worse—had generated support for a strong national government that would have been impossible just a few years earlier.

But no sooner had a gratified James Madison claimed his first victory than things begin to disintegrate. Just minutes after delegates had approved the Virginia resolution, the vote and the convention itself were in jeopardy.

*

THE TROUBLE BEGAN THAT afternoon, shortly after the Virginia Plan was approved, when delegates took up the matter of how representatives would be chosen for the bicameral legislature.

Almost all the delegates—Benjamin Franklin was a notable exception—agreed that the legislature should consist of two houses. George Mason would say later that "the mind of the people of America was unsettled as to some points," but on two basic principles they agreed: "in an attachment to republican government and in an attachment to more than one branch in the Legislature." Most delegates recognized the value of a deliberative second chamber, or "upper house," somewhat insulated from the daily influences of the electorate, to consider bills and policies with more detachment than a "first" chamber, the "popular house," whose more direct ties to the people would subject it to the passions and emotions of the moment.

George Washington apparently explained the concept in simple terms two years after the convention during a reported breakfast with Thomas Jefferson, who recently had returned from Paris. Though historians debate whether the discussion actually took place, the story goes that the Declaration's author reportedly complained about the establishment of two houses in the national legislature, in particular the second house, which was referred to as the Senate. The model was far too similar for Jefferson's tastes to the Houses of Parliament, and in any case, the Senate was also too removed from the people. To a man who had spent time navigating the corridors of power in a country ruled by Louis XVI, Jefferson feared any form of government that diluted the power of citizens. Washington assured him that the sole purpose of the Senate was to act as a more sober, deliberative body: "Why did you pour that coffee into your saucer?" Jefferson replied: "To cool it." Washington responded: "We pour legislation into the senatorial saucer to cool it."

While the notion of a bicameral legislature produced harmony among delegates, the manner in which representatives would be selected caused acrimony and bitterness, perhaps the most rancorous of the convention.

★

FOR MADISON AND THE other staunch supporters of a supreme national government, there was no doubt that representation in both houses, directly or indirectly, should be apportioned according to a state's "free" population—larger states would have a greater number of representatives in the legislature than smaller states. This was the only way to assure that the people, rather than the states, held power and sovereignty. It was a dramatic departure from the current confederacy, in which each state held an equal vote, and Madison was not subtle about his intentions.

The precept of proportional representation provided the philosophical foundation of Madison's thinking. He and the other supporters of a strong national government, who would come to be known as the Federalists—ironically a term they cleverly adopted and turned on its head, since it derived from the "confederation" of states outlined in the articles—believed that power should reside in the people, not in the state legislatures. Remove the concept of proportional representation, the Federalists argued, and you once again put too much power in the hands of individual states to derail the national government. After all, Madison argued, under what reasoning could anyone justify Delaware and Virginia wielding equal power in a national government when Virginia's population was ten times greater?

Delaware's George Read was unconvinced. He favored a stronger central government but not to the detriment of the small states. He warned the assembly that if such a change "should be fixed on," Delaware delegates would have little choice but to "retire from the Convention."

There it was—a threat to walk out.

Read demanded that the vote be postponed until additional small states arrived at the convention; perhaps fearful of his threat to "retire," delegates approved his motion.

READ'S REACTION TO THE issue of proportional representation had established a tone that would carry throughout the next several weeks of debate and beyond. His threat to withdraw Delaware's delegates had sent a message to all members that it was appropriate and acceptable to raise dissent that might be bubbling beneath the surface. Battle lines would be drawn on issues that were rooted in, and in some cases transcended, the debate between proportional representation and state sovereignty.

Over the days and weeks to follow, the walls of the Pennsylvania State House would reverberate with the countervailing arguments between those who feared and despised a strong central authority for the potential abuses it could impose, and those who believed a strong national government—with the appropriate checks and balances— was the most effective way to manage a large, dispersed republic. Within this overarching struggle, divisions would also emerge on many key issues: between those who favored a strong national executive to lead and unify the new nation and those who were terrified of a return to monarchical despotism; between those who ardently advocated for the power of the majority and those who sought concrete protections of minority rights; between those who argued that the interests of the more populous large states were paramount and those who feared the destruction of small-state sovereignty; between free states and slave states; between those who saw America as thirteen states only and those who gazed westward and envisioned its vast expansionist possibilities.

At the core of these debates, notwithstanding the rapid passage of the Virginia Plan, was the philosophical struggle between those delegates who clung to the past and favored a tepid tinkering at the edges as the best way to modify the current government and those who foresaw the need for something radically different to preserve the future.

It would be difficult. It would be messy. The delegates would quarrel and compromise and, in the moments of their greatest struggle, they would draw strength from the two principles that united them from the beginning: the inadequacies of the Articles of Confederation meant that *some form* of modified government structure was essential; and, regardless of what form that structure took, individual freedom and liberty must be preserved above all else.

At the end of business on May 30, the route they would take was still very much up in the air, made more circuitous by Delaware's balking. That evening, George Washington wrote to Thomas Jefferson, and—ever mindful of the convention's secrecy rules—revealed only that "the business of this convention is as yet too much in embryo to form any opinion of the conclusion."

Washington sensed in the wake of Delaware's resistance that the road ahead would be difficult. A week later, concerned about the summer crops at his plantation, he wrote to his nephew with instructions on how to proceed at Mount Vernon, making it clear that, "there is not the smallest prospect of my returning home before the harvest, and God knows how long it may be after it."

8

★

"We Are
Now at a
Full Stop"

★

"New Jersey will never agree to the plan," thundered delegate William Paterson as the convention resumed on Saturday, June 9. "She would be swallowed up!"

Speaking during a contentious committee of the whole session, Paterson was referring to the Virginia Plan for proportional representation in both houses of the national legislature. Paterson declared that he would "rather submit to a monarch, to a despot, than to such a fate"—such a plan would render his home state powerless against abuses of power by the large states. New Jersey, with a population of just under 140,000 people, was ninth in the order of states. Give large states—in this category, Paterson listed Virginia, Massachusetts, and Pennsylvania—"influence in proportion to their magnitude" and the consequences would be dire: "Their ambition will be proportionally increased and the small states will have everything to fear."

For the nationalists, who viewed the nation's future power in the hands of the people rather than within a confederation of states, population was the one and only way to determine representation. Paterson scoffed at this notion. In his view, the states had a crucial role to play in balancing and checking the interests of the majority, and each state deserved an equal vote in the same way property-owning citizens each deserved an equal vote, regardless of the amount of property they owned, "or there is an end to liberty." Let the large states unite, if they please, "but let them remember that they have no authority to compel the others to unite."

In fact, Paterson warned his colleagues, not only did he vigorously oppose the Virginia Plan here in Philadelphia, but during the ratification process that followed, he "would return home [and] do everything in his power to defeat it there."

THOUGH NEW JERSEY'S DELEGATES had initially shown a willingness to discuss the Virginia Plan, Paterson's salvo would be the most forceful early objection to it, and his remarks set the tone for the next several weeks of debate, each side fighting on the grounds of deep principle and each resolute that its truth was the only truth.

The nationalists—Madison, Morris, Washington, Wilson, and others—were dejected at the reaction of the smaller states. Not only did they strongly believe in the concept of proportional representation as the best way to create a government closest and most responsive to the people, from a practical standpoint they knew the divisive issue cut deep enough to derail the convention; perhaps no other disagreement would pose such a threat.

Paterson and his small-state allies considered proportional representation as "striking at the existence of the lesser states," as a disappointed Madison described in his notes.

Connecticut's delegation, led by Roger Sherman, sought a compromise on the issue, proposing proportional representation in the lower house and equal state representation in the upper house, or what he called the Senate. The plan was similar in most respects to what would later be called the Connecticut Compromise, the agreement that ultimately emerged from the convention and governs the structure of Congress to this day. But at the time of Sherman's motion, the delegates were not ready to consider it; to both sides, the idea appeared awkward, convoluted, and ill-conceived, an attempt to shoehorn a misshapen puzzle piece into place simply to convey the illusion that the overall picture was complete.

Obdurate, unwilling to embrace the compromise proposal that Sherman had put forward, the delegates thus were destined to embark on a contentious multiweek journey, with each side digging in its heels on the issue of representation. Back and forth they battled, large-state nationalists and small-state anti-Federalists, each convinced of their righteousness. "Can we forget for whom we are forming a Government?" bellowed James Wilson for the nationalists. "Is it for *men* or for imaginary beings called *States*?" But Connecticut's Oliver Ellsworth accused Wilson of grandstanding, pointing out that Sherman's compromise allowed for proportional representation in the lower house, which should satisfy the need for the people to be well represented.

In fact, Ellsworth argued, the nationalists' insistence on obliterating states' rights and sovereignty was not a solution to the limitations of the current national government, but simply a structure that would create a different set of problems.

"We are running from one extreme to another," Ellsworth argued. "We are razing the foundations of the building, when we need only repair the roof."

DURING THE HEATED DEBATES on proportional representation, different delegates put forth ideas, some meritorious and others misguided, some with a genuine desire to break the impasse, others to restate their own positions even though they knew these had little chance of adoption.

The standoff continued.

On June 29, the Connecticut delegation, led by Oliver Ellsworth, once again put forth the motion that had been dismissed earlier as unwieldy: proportional representation would exist in the first branch, or lower house, and in the Senate—the upper house—each state would have an equal vote.

The following day delegates debated the plan in language that was among the most personal and acerbic of the entire convention.

James Wilson suggested calling the bluff of the small states that had threatened to leave if full proportional representation became a reality. "If a separation must take place, it could never happen on better grounds," he declared. Delaware's Gunning Bedford, in the most bombastic language he could muster, retorted to the nationalists: *"I do not, gentlemen, trust you.* If you possess the power, the abuse of it could not be checked; and what then would prevent you from exercising it to our destruction?" Be forewarned, he told the large states—if you dissolve the confederation of states, "the small ones will find some foreign ally of more honor and good faith, who will take them by the hand and do them justice."

Bedford's threat was shocking, even explosive—the notion that the small states would threaten to align with foreign powers to form their own union provided the strongest and most evocative evidence yet of the depth of their feelings about state sovereignty.

Emotions were running as high as they ever had and nerves had frayed. Delegates adjourned for the day and returned on Monday, July 2. The Connecticut Compromise was put to a vote, and it failed in a stalemate: five states in favor, five against, and one—Georgia—divided. The division in the large-state Georgia delegation was a new development, and it convinced Madison and other nationalists that momentum was swinging to the small-state point of view. In any case, the deadlocked vote had illustrated with stark reality that the two sides were at a critical impasse.

"We are now at a full stop," declared Roger Sherman of Connecticut, and he then backed a motion for the convention to establish a Grand Committee, consisting of one representative from each state, which would attempt to reach a compromise. "It seems we have got to a point that we cannot move one way or the other. Such a committee is necessary to set us right." Elbridge Gerry concurred that cooler heads must prevail, and for reasons that transcended the convention. "Something must be done, or we shall disappoint not only America, but the whole world," he said. Unless the delegates could find a way out of this predicament, the future of the American nation would be imperiled.

Despite objections by Madison and James Wilson, the convention—including many large-state delegates—voted in favor of this conciliatory gesture and the measure passed. The Grand Committee was established with Gerry as its chairman. More disappointing for Madison and his allies was this: not a single strong federalist was selected by his state to serve on the committee. Those members chosen who leaned toward the formation of a nationalist government consisted of moderates who were more likely to conciliate and accommodate; on the other hand, several ardent states' rights advocates were named. Madison must have seen the handwriting on the wall as soon as the makeup of the committee was announced: his plan for proportional representation in both houses was in jeopardy

Weary and discouraged, skeptical that the Grand Committee could achieve workable results, the delegates adjourned for a three-day holiday to celebrate the Fourth of July.

This fortuitous coincidence of the calendar went a long way toward saving the convention, the Constitution, and the country.

IT WAS NOT MERELY that delegates needed a recess from the grinding and divisive debates they experienced while cooped up inside the statehouse assembly room—though a break *was* essential. More to the point, the stirring celebrations that occurred in Philadelphia and around the country on July 4, 1787, served to remind members of the nobleness of their task; of the sacrifices and heroism that had made this date—and this convention—possible; of the common threads that bound them rather than the philosophical differences that divided them.

For most delegates, the eleventh anniversary of the country's declaration of independence was far more than a historical holiday, it was a tribute to their own legacies; they had been integrally involved in the new nation's valiant and at times desperate struggle to break from England.

Despite the fact that several notables were absent—John Adams, Thomas Jefferson, and by this time, Alexander Hamilton, who had left Philadelphia on June 30 in a fit of pique after delegates responded negatively to his speech praising the British form of government—the July 4, 1787, celebration in Philadelphia took place in the midst of perhaps the greatest gathering of prominent Americans before or since, including the first Fourth of July in Philadelphia in 1776.

Of course, the incomparable Washington—who had been absent eleven years earlier while he commanded the Continental army—was the most famous, and Franklin claimed his exalted place as unofficial convention host and founder emeritus. Other delegates were part of an esteemed collection of military heroes, many of whom were also absent from independence discussions in 1776; then, they were risking their lives on the battlefield. Several members of the convention had participated at Valley Forge and Yorktown, and more than half had served in state militias or the Continental army. Further, among the delegates in attendance on July 4, 1787, were six signers of the Declaration of Independence, including Franklin and Sherman, who were members of the Committee of Five designated to draft it. Of the fifty-five delegates who would attend the 1787 Federal Convention at various points, three-quarters had represented their states in the Continental Congress during the Revolutionary War.

For these men, the patriotic atmosphere in Philadelphia on the Fourth of July would resonate: they would hear with clarity the stirring call of duty when the celebrations began before dawn with the assembling of the state militia and artillery regiments; with the late-morning firing of cannon and ringing of bells; with the afternoon procession of troops accompanied by fife and drum; with the spectacular display of fireworks after dark.

And when many convention delegates joined a late-morning

patriotic oration at the Reformed Calvinist Church, they would take to heart the lofty expectations and the unbridled hope of the citizenry when one speaker predicted "the stately fabric of a free and vigorous government rising out of the wisdom of a Federal Convention."

For the delegates toiling in Philadelphia in the summer of 1787, who literally held America's destiny in their hands, the Fourth of July was a sacred and powerful symbol of the sacrifices that had led them and their nation to this moment, the solemn burden before them, and, perhaps more significant than anything else, the unthinkable consequences of failure.

THE HEARTFELT AND EMOTIONAL Fourth of July observances may have appealed to the delegates' patriotism and redoubled their commitment to succeed when they returned to the Pennsylvania State House on July 5, but no bolt of lightning struck the building infusing it with a sudden change of heart or a burst of instant conciliation.

It was obvious from the start that progress, if it occurred at all, would lurch forward in a ragged and painstaking manner.

Events began dramatically enough, when Elbridge Gerry rose to offer the proposal of the Grand Committee, which had been working over the July 4 break to hammer out a workable compromise. Members were fully aware that this was likely their last chance; failure to convince their fellow delegates of the merits of their proposal would lead to a failed convention. And then what?

Gerry laid out the proposal, which contained components of the original Connecticut plan and additional contributions suggested by Franklin: in the first branch of the legislature, each state would be allowed one representative for every 40,000 people, the proportional representation that nationalists favored; but in the second branch, the Senate, each state would have an equal vote, the representative formula favored by the small states. The committee added incentives it believed would mollify the nationalists—for example, all bills and spending appropriations would originate in the lower house, whose representatives were closest to the people. It wasn't perfect, Gerry acknowledged, but committee members hoped that "some ground of accommodation" might be achieved by the proposal.

Nationalists were not surprised by the proposal, but they minced no words expressing their fury. Madison declared that the convention had "departed from justice" to pacify the small states and the minority of people of the United States at the expense of the majority of people who resided in the large states. The outspoken Gouverneur Morris was even blunter in his objections. Employing language that was defiant and truculent, even contemptuous of his small-state colleagues, he argued that proportional representation was the *only* formula that was "reasonable and right" and "all who have reasonable minds and sound intentions will embrace it." The large states saw the justice in this approach; that the small states could not was due to their own myopia, limitations, and self-serving attempts to retain power. "This country must be united," the dynamic Morris warned. "If persuasion does not unite it, the sword will."

Moreover, foreign powers would revel in the confusion such a representation plan would create. Had not the committee even considered that? No, he supposed not; in fact, he did not think the committee's proposal was "in any respect calculated for the public good."

UNFORTUNATELY FOR THE NATIONALISTS, Morris had overplayed his hand.

In the view of the small-state delegates, his verbal belligerence and bullying, along with Madison's refusal to even consider a compromise, symbolized perfectly the potential abuses of power that larger states could exert if both branches of a federal legislature were populated based solely on proportional representation. Morris's overbearing language was a harbinger of the oppression large states would bring to bear on small states. If Madison and Morris were unafraid to hide their rigidity and intolerance now—while debate was still under way and they presumably were trying to convince small states of the righteousness of their position—how arrogantly would they and other large-state representatives behave once the small states had yielded on the issue of representation?

William Paterson complained vigorously about Morris's language and the general lack of respect with which Morris and Madison had treated the smaller states in their remarks. Delaware's Gunning Bedford, in defense of the equal-vote proposal for the second branch, explained that "the lesser states have thought it necessary to have . . . security somewhere." He also demanded an apology from Morris for his suggestion that "the sword is to unite."

Just one day after the Fourth of July respite, the convention was again fully embroiled in rancorous uproar, and the small-state, large-state stalemate continued.

After the vitriolic debate on the Grand Committee's proposal had subsided, and perhaps to give tempers a chance to cool once again, delegates put aside the thorny issue of equal representation in the Senate. Instead, they took up the practical elements of an issue that generated its own contention, one whose moral implications would transcend the convention, divide the nation for the next several decades, and eventually consume it in a bloody and terrible war.

Delegates decided to plunge into the controversial debate on how each state's population would be determined for representation in the lower house—more specifically, which inhabitants would be counted in each state, and how.

NO DELEGATE COVERED HIMSELF in glory during any of the several instances that the Constitutional Convention took up the issue of slavery.

For the most part, delegates tiptoed and skirted around the moral essence of human bondage; those who even considered such an argument or were personally opposed to slavery fully realized the resistance they would meet, especially from the Carolinians and the Georgians, and perhaps from some of the other delegates who may have agreed about the evils of slavery but believed it would and should die a natural death within a decade or two. In this belief, delegates shared the mainstream point of view in America. Even those religious organizations opposed to slavery—Quakers primarily—focused their energies on halting the importation of slaves into North America, rather than on the abolition of slavery itself. The declaration's promise that "all men are created equal" was simply not part of the constitutional debate.

Late in the convention, delegates did reach an eventual compromise on the slave trade, brokering an agreement between those states, the Carolinas and Georgia among them, that wanted Congress to have no authority over it and those that wanted Congress to end it. Virginia was included in the latter group, despite the fact that several of its delegates, including Washington, currently owned slaves. Initially, the convention agreed that Congress would have no authority over the slave trade until 1800, and subsequently could take steps to limit or abolish it; however that date was later amended to 1808. Delegates approved the amendment despite Madison's objection that "so long a term will be more dishonorable to the national character than to say nothing about it in the Constitution." Not only did delegates from the Deep South support the extension to 1808, but Connecticut, New Hampshire, Maryland, and Massachusetts did also.

Of all the delegates, Gouverneur Morris delivered the most stinging remarks in opposition to the overall institution of slavery, calling it "the curse of heaven on the states where it prevailed." When the convention approved the slave-trade language, the resolution gave the states the right to admit "such persons . . . as [they] shall think proper to admit." In the interest of forthrightness, Morris wanted the word "slaves" substituted, so there could be no doubt about the convention's meaning. Madison objected, perhaps out of his own discomfort and even shame, saying that he "thought it wrong to admit in the Constitution the idea that there could be property in men." This view prevailed—the word "slavery" would not appear in the Constitution until the Thirteenth Amendment abolished it in 1865.

As Delaware's John Dickinson would write in his private notebook: "The omitting [of] the WORD will be regarded as an Endeavor to conceal a principle of which we are ashamed."

In the words of one historian, euphemisms helped delegates rationalize the contradiction between the fact that slavery existed and the fervent desire to create a new governing document based on fundamental freedoms; but the euphemisms also helped "create a document suitable for a time when it [slavery] would not [exist]." Or, as political scientist Robert Goldwin observed, convention delegates created a constitution for a society that would offer more justice than their own.

Put simply, in the summer of 1787, most delegates were unwilling to risk the fate of the entire convention, perhaps the future of the country, on the overarching and emotional issue of slavery. Thomas Jefferson's recollection of the 1776 mind-set among delegates debating the Declaration was still applicable in 1787: the "public mind would not yet bear the proposition [of emancipation]. . . . Yet the day is not distant when it must bear and adopt it, or worse will follow."

For now, members of the Federal Convention focused only on the narrow and intractable issue of representation—should slaves be counted when considering a state's total population?

IN REALITY, TWO QUESTIONS dominated the debate: Were slaves considered people or property? And, regardless of the answer, should their numbers be counted in a manner equivalent to freemen for the purposes of proportional representation?

The southern states, particularly, faced a conundrum of logic as they argued their case. There was no doubt that southern slaveholders viewed their slaves as property, and treated them as such. Slaves, especially young black males, were considered prime assets when plantation owners determined their total wealth; and when slave owners died, their slaves were included in their owners' estates, usually identified by name in last wills and testaments. Yet there was grave concern on the part of Southerners that if slaves were not counted as equivalent to freemen for the purposes of representation, then the northern states would dominate them in the lower house. For the southern argument to work, the value of slaves needed to be counted as equivalent to that of freemen, despite the slaves' classification as "property."

Southern delegates made the argument by emphasizing that people *and* property should factor into the representational formula, since the new government would be responsible for protecting both. In the words of South Carolina's Charles Pinckney and Pierce Butler, "wealth was the great means of defence and utility in the nation." They argued that "the labor of a slave in South Carolina was as productive and valuable as that of a freeman in Massachusetts." Did it not stand to reason that slave "property" should be counted *equally* in determining representation? Mere numbers did not measure value.

But wait, Elbridge Gerry said, such logic ran afoul of common sense. Southerners treated slaves exclusively as property. "Why then," he asked, "should the blacks who were property in the South be in the rule of representation more than the cattle and horses in the North?" In an even more pointed jab at his southern brethren, New Jersey's William Paterson wondered, "if Negroes are not represented in the state to which they belong, why should they be represented in the General Government?"

Pennsylvania's James Wilson, too, objected to the principle of equality for other reasons. He agreed with Morris, who, despite his forceful language against slavery in general, believed that the citizens of Pennsylvania would "revolt at the idea of being put on a footing equal with slaves," a sentiment certainly shared by both Northerners and Southerners. Virginia's George Mason, even while acknowledging that equal representation of slaves in the counting process would benefit his large slave-holding state, stiffened at the idea of equal representation: "I cannot regard them as equal to freemen and cannot vote for them as such," he said.

For days, the delegates engaged in debates rich with irony; southern delegates demanded that their slaves be counted equally with whites, and northern states argued that slaves—because Southerners considered them property—should not be counted at all. Southern delegates were fearful and angry that Northerners would attempt to run roughshod over them because the North appeared unwilling to consider people and property as equally virtuous and important.

IN THE END, WITH the help of numerous delegates—Randolph, Madison, Ellsworth, Pinckney, and George Washington among them—the convention agreed on a compromise for counting slaves that made no one entirely happy and would, for the next seventy-five years, epitomize the deep and dark divisions between North and South, the gulf between blacks and whites, and the unfulfilled promise of the Declaration of Independence: that "all men are created equal."

Just before the delegates adjourned on July 13, they reached a shaky consensus on a formula for representation and direct taxes in the lower house of the new Congress: the three-fifths compromise. Representation would be apportioned based on a periodic census of the "number of whites and three-fifths of the blacks." Put another way, three of every five slaves would be counted to determine a state's population and, thus, the number of representatives it would have in the lower house. Based on this formula, each state would be entitled to one representative for every 40,000 inhabitants (this would later be amended to 30,000). The formula would also apply to new states admitted to the union.

As incomprehensible as it seems by today's standards, the three-fifths compromise was seen as the most equitable solution to deal with the issue of assessing the "relative value" of slaves in comparison with a state's free residents. When the vote was tallied, the accord was approved by nine of the ten states in attendance. (New York's remaining delegates, as well as Hamilton, had departed by this point; New Hampshire's representatives had still not arrived; and Rhode Island had continued with its steadfast refusal to send delegates to Philadelphia.)

Unwilling to grapple with the larger moral questions, the convention had disposed of the slavery issue.

America's long battle with it had just begun.

9

★

"The People
Are
the King"

★

In the more than two centuries since delegates gathered in Philadelphia to form a new government for America, most historians have considered Monday, July 16, 1787, as the decisive day of the Constitutional Convention. For a day so momentous, for a vote so important, the proceedings had an almost anticlimactic feel.

In a lengthy soliloquy the previous Saturday, Madison had strenuously argued in favor of proportional representation in both houses. He addressed and rebutted the small-state arguments one-by-one, pleading with delegates to see the injustice in equal representation in either branch of the new legislature. Using an argument he had voiced before, Madison declared: "No one would say that, either in Congress or out of Congress, Delaware had equal weight with Pennsylvania." Debate had been long, tiring, and circular as other nationalists desperately fought for a cause they knew in their hearts was hopeless.

Now, Maryland's Luther Martin, wasting little time, moved that the entire report of the Grand Committee, "as amended and including the equality of votes in the second branch," be approved by the convention. On a narrow vote of five in favor, four opposed, and Massachusetts divided, the motion carried—it would soon become known as the Great Compromise. North Carolina joined Connecticut, Delaware, New Jersey, and Maryland in the majority. Rejecting the proposal were Virginia, Pennsylvania, South Carolina, and Georgia. Divided Massachusetts delegates Elbridge Gerry and Caleb Strong supported the motion, albeit unenthusiastically, while staunch nationalists Rufus King and Nathaniel Gorham voted in the negative.

That quickly it was over—in the second branch of the legislature, the Senate, each state, large or small, would have an equal vote. Senators would be chosen by the state legislatures and serve for six years, two structural components that would assure the upper chamber was removed from the political passions of the moment; the "cooling" that Washington had described to Jefferson over breakfast (one of these elements was abolished in 1913 when the Seventeenth Amendment provided for direct elections of senators by the people). Each senator would have one vote and each state would be represented by two senators.

THE NATIONALISTS WERE SO dejected by the Senate vote that the next morning, before the formal convention commenced, a number of large-state delegates gathered to determine what they should do. But it was clear their will to fight on had ebbed.

Some delegates—tenacious nationalists such as Madison, Morris, King, and Randolph—believed the large states should press on and propose a method of governing that benefits "the principal states and a majority of the people of America." Others, though, perhaps less offended by the small-state position, were also less willing to jeopardize the convention's work.

In the end, nothing came of the large-state threat to take further action.

Thus, each state, large and small, would have an equal number of votes in the U.S. Senate—state sovereignty, a bedrock principle of the

American experience, remained strong. More to the point, the country would be governed by a solution that was at once deliberately difficult to navigate and delicately ingenious in the manner in which it balanced power: one that historians have referred to as "part national" and "part federal," with the "people" represented according to their numbers in one branch, and the "states" represented with their own power in the other. The more populous states would have an advantage in the lower house, and the Senate's makeup would ensure that smaller states, and thus the rights of the minority of the population, would not be trampled.

Stung by the loss, James Madison nevertheless kept up appearances in a letter to Thomas Jefferson written one day after the impromptu large-state gathering. While Madison could not share details, he had "little doubt that the people will be as ready to receive as we shall be able to propose—a government that will secure their liberties and happiness."

IF THE BATTLE BETWEEN large states and small states over the issue of Senate representation proved anything, it illustrated that nothing in Philadelphia during the summer of 1787 was preordained or predestined. The struggle to create a new government—a new constitution—was arduous, suspenseful, fraught with anxiety and peril, and for weeks during the Senate debate, compromise appeared futile and resolution hopeless. For all of June and half of July, the delegates faced the strong possibility—even likelihood—that the convention would dissolve without consensus or any lasting agreement.

The formation of a new country, the very future of that country, had been in jeopardy for weeks.

The struggle to determine the makeup of the Senate had a sobering effect on delegates; teetering so close to the precipice had taught them a lesson and strengthened their resoluteness to succeed. In the succeeding days, they moved quickly, and while debates and disagreements continued, members made rapid progress without the bitter rancor that the Senate debates had produced.

There is no doubt that the *Pennsylvania Packet and Daily Advertiser* engaged in hyperbole in its July 19 edition when it reported rumors that delegates were in "great unanimity" at the convention, so united "that it has been proposed to call the room in which they assemble Unanimity Hall."

But it is not an exaggeration to say that once members had disposed of the controversial and bitter Senate representation issue, they never looked back.

THERE WERE DISPUTES, FOR certain, but delegates never again approached the anger and animosity generated by the Senate battle.

They disagreed for a time on the role of the chief executive, as well as the way such an executive would be selected. Some delegates favored a three-man chief executive office while others favored a single individual. In the end, the single-person faction prevailed—and that person would have extensive powers—mostly because of the presence, virtue, and leadership of George Washington, whom most delegates believed would be the nation's first chief executive. South Carolina's Pierce Butler, who worried deeply about an oppressive chief executive, felt that delegates put too much stock in the fact that Washington would likely become the nation's first—what would happen in the future, long after Washington was gone?

There were also long debates on how the executive—delegates would eventually settle on the term "president"—would be elected and for how long he would serve. Some delegates favored his election by the national legislature, arguing that he should be little more than an agent carrying out the legislature's will. Others feared that such a process would limit his independence and violate the principle of separation of powers by making the president beholden to the legislature rather than the people.

A few delegates favored the president's election directly by the people, but most opposed this method, believing in some cases that ordinary Americans did not possess the intellectual capability to make a proper choice, or—the more common objection—that America's vast expanse would make it impossible for the people to know about good candidates in distant locales. In that case, they would be more likely to vote for the candidate they knew rather than the best leader for the country; this would reduce the presidency to a local rather than a national office.

It was James Madison who helped delegates to decide; initially, Madison's Virginia Plan favored the legislature choosing the president, but this was before the makeup of the Senate had changed. Madison instead proposed that state legislatures decide how electors in each state would be chosen, with the number of electors equivalent to the state's combined number of senators and representatives in Congress. This "electoral college" would choose the president. Moreover, to discourage provincialism, Madison proposed that each elector cast two votes, one of which had to be for someone from outside his home state. In this way, the vice presidency came into being—the person with the most electoral votes would become president, and the man with the second highest number would become vice president. The vice president would be first in line of succession and serve as president of the Senate, but he would only cast a vote in the event of a tie in the upper chamber.

Thus, the president and vice president would be independent from the national legislature; state legislatures could opt to have voters choose the electors, which assured that both states and the people were involved in the president's selection; and large states were provided with an appropriate advantage in the electoral college because their populations assured they would have a larger number of representatives in the legislature's "first branch."

Madison's plan, with minor changes, was similar to the electoral college system we have today, and while unwieldy, contained benefits for everyone.

★

AS FOR THE PRESIDENT'S length of term, delegates also differed, but their views were not intractable.

One delegate suggested the president serve for life so long as he exhibited "good behavior," a notion that horrified those who feared the similarities to a monarchy and the potential abuses that could accompany it; in fact, trepidation about granting the president the powers of a king permeated the debates. Other members argued that one term would be sufficient; in fact, a proposed single seven-year term appeared on its way to approval until very late in the convention. There were lengthy discussions on the power of the office and how the president could be removed or impeached.

In the end, of course, delegates settled on a four-year term for the president, with no restrictions on reelection. (This would only change in 1951 with the passage of the Twenty-second Amendment, which reads, in part, that "no person shall be elected to the office of the President more than twice"; it was put forth in response to President Franklin Delano Roosevelt's tenure—he was elected four times.)

Through all of the discussions about a chief executive, the delegates operated on the fundamental principle that the president's powers should be limited: checks and balances between the president and the legislature should be locked into place; and the legislature, the body closest to the people, should retain the lion's share of the influence in the new government. The president would administer and "faithfully execute" the laws passed by Congress, would serve as commander in chief—though only Congress could declare war—and could appoint judges and make treaties, but only subject to the Senate's "advice and consent." Legislation passed by Congress—and only Congress could do so—would not become law until the president signed it, and he could veto proposed legislation with the stroke of his pen. However, his veto could be overridden if two-thirds of the Congress in each house agreed. And ultimately, it was the legislature who could try, convict, and remove—impeach—a president for treason, bribery, or "other high crimes and misdemeanors."

Gouverneur Morris, though an outspoken advocate for a strong national president, nonetheless reminded his colleagues of the importance of providing the people, through their legislators, with appropriate checks and oversights on the president. "This magistrate is not the King," he said, "but the prime-minister. The people are the King."

DELEGATES ALSO AGREED WITH the concept of a national judiciary but struggled to fully define its powers and its relationship with the other branches of government—part of the convention's constant tug to find equilibrium between the simultaneous concepts of checks and balances and separation of powers.

In some ways the creation of a judiciary was almost a constitutional afterthought; delegates believed that establishing the roles of the legislature and executive were far greater priorities. Ultimately, Article III of the Constitution created a single Supreme Court and "such inferior courts as the Congress may from time to time ordain and establish." The federal judiciary would have jurisdiction over all cases "arising under this Constitution." Article III also made clear that, with the exception of impeachment proceedings, the "trial of all crimes . . . shall be by jury."

Much more fuzzy, however, and certainly not delineated in the Constitution's section on the judiciary, was whether the Supreme Court would have the right to declare federal or state laws unconstitutional or contrary to the law of the land. Many delegates adhered to this principle, but several vocal ones feared judicial overreach. Nathaniel Gorham of Massachusetts argued that judges did not possess any special expertise that would give them the right to veto legislation. Luther Martin of Maryland added that "a knowledge of mankind, of legislative affairs, cannot be presumed to belong to a higher degree to the judges than to the legislature." Others had faith in a strong, independent judiciary and saw it as essential to checking the power of Congress or the president. Connecticut's Oliver Ellsworth offered a harbinger of the future role of the judiciary. He wrote "that if the united

States . . . make a law which the Constitution does not authorize, it is void, and the judicial power, the national judges, who to secure their impartiality are to be made independent, will declare it to be void."

Delegates, however, included no direct language about the judiciary's ability to declare a law unconstitutional. Such power would emanate from the judiciary itself, but not until 1803, when the Supreme Court ruled for the first time that one of Congress's laws was unconstitutional in the landmark *Marbury v. Madison* case.

THE CONVENTION WELCOMED THE long-awaited New Hampshire delegation on July 23, and three days later, members decided they were far enough along to refer all of their work to a five-member Committee of Detail, whose responsibility would be to organize the various resolutions into a coherent document. The committee was not charged with writing a final document, but with integrating and collating the decisions of the past seven weeks, or to frame "a constitution comfortable to the resolutions passed by the Convention." Once the committee was named, the convention adjourned for two weeks and the other delegates rested.

When members reconvened on August 6, the Committee of Detail had prepared a draft, and delegates further debated new issues and revisited old ones, all of which generated additional changes to the Constitution: slavery, impeachment, the powers and limitations of the presidency, the relationship between the House and the Senate, the powers of Congress, and even where the seat of government would be located. For the latter issue, they agreed, but only after intense debate, to create a ten-mile-square "federal district" that would not be part of any existing state. In addition, delegates settled on nine states as the number needed to ratify any finished Constitution.

In mid-September, Virginia's George Mason raised the issue that the draft Constitution did not include a bill of rights, wishing that such an enumeration of government's limits and the people's rights "had prefaced" the document. He said such a listing of rights would "give great quiet to the people, and, with the aid of the state Declarations, a bill might be prepared in a few hours." Shockingly, not a single state delegation supported the idea. Delegates did not address the reasons why at the time, though later, during ratification discussions, Pennsylvania's James Wilson defended the convention's decision, asking, "Who will be bold enough to undertake to enumerate all the rights of the people?" The danger of trying to do so, he said, was that "if the enumeration is not complete, everything not expressly mentioned will be presumed to be purposely omitted."

James Madison was also dismissive of Mason's concerns, arguing that because most states had their own bills of rights, a federal guarantee of constitutional rights would be redundant. There were several reasons why George Mason declared late in the debates that he would "sooner chop off my right hand than to put it to the Constitution as it now stands," and the omission of a bill of rights ranked high on the list.

Eventually, during the ratification debates, Madison and others who opposed the addition of a bill of rights would see the error of their ways; the promise of a strong bill of rights would become critical, not only to ratifying the Constitution but to preserving it—and the American government—against threats to weaken or overturn it. For now, the delegates were coming down the home stretch of their work and were uninterested in getting sidetracked on such an enormous and potentially controversial undertaking.

By the second week of September, the Constitution needed a "last polish," in the words of one delegate, and the convention assigned the task to a five-member Committee of Style and Arrangement to essentially write the final document. Members selected Madison, Gouverneur Morris, Rufus King, and Alexander Hamilton (who had returned just days earlier)—among the most influential men at the convention— and they were joined by Connecticut's William Samuel Johnson.

Of this esteemed group, Pennsylvania's Morris would make the most memorable contribution of all.

*

SOMETIMES A MAN'S LEGACY is immortalized with a single action or event rather than an entire body of work.

Such a man was Gouverneur Morris—the delegate with the unusual first name (his mother's maiden name), whose pronunciation even today is debated by historians (Abigail Adams, who often spelled phonetically, wrote his name as "Governeer," which is as close as we are likely to get). Morris was as complex and multidimensional as any member of the Constitutional Convention. Full of brashness and brimming with intelligence, Morris possessed great wealth, good looks, a piercing wit, a quarrelsome disposition, a gift for oratory, a flair for writing, a mischievous sense of humor, and a reputation as a swashbuckling philanderer (the last of which he did nothing to discourage).

On the other hand, his unabashed patriotism lent a serious air and a passion to his work. He loved his country deeply and always had. During the Revolutionary War, while a member of the New York Convention prior to his move to Pennsylvania, he was separated from his dying mother, who was still loyal to the Crown. "I would like to be able to console you in your old age—the duty toward a dear mother commands it," he wrote to her, "but a task of a higher order binds me to the service of my fellowmen." In addition, the fact that Morris had lived through his own painful physical ordeals often inspired him—his wealth and station in life notwithstanding—to assist the downtrodden and offer a sympathetic ear to others who were suffering through troubles.

And yet, for the many layers that made up his personality, Morris is remembered most for three small words that flowed from his quill, words that generated admiration and controversy in 1787. Along with "all men are created equal" and "life, liberty, and the pursuit of happiness," these words are today among the most oft-referenced that Americans use to define the essence of their democracy and their constitutional republic form of government.

Morris would have agreed that his decision to pen the words "We the People" was a major step in the development of the new nation. He likely would have also argued that the four words that followed—"of the United States"—demonstrated his true political brilliance and had an equally transformative impact on the nation's future.

AT AGE THIRTY-FIVE, Gouverneur Morris would become one of the most admired delegates at the convention and the most vocal of all, speaking more than 170 times during the summer of 1787. "No man has more wit—nor can any one engage the attention more than Mr. Morris," exclaimed South Carolina's William Pierce.

For certain, Morris commanded attention for his words, his ideas, his startling audacity, but also for his physical appearance, which was a reminder to delegates of what he had overcome. When Morris was just a boy, he had tipped a kettle of boiling water onto his right side, burning his arm badly. Doctors, who feared gangrene, managed to save the arm, but the limb was badly disfigured. Then, at age twenty-eight, he was mounting a carriage in Philadelphia when the horses bolted. Morris was thrown and his left leg was caught in the spokes of the wheel, crushing his ankle and fracturing bones in his leg. The two physicians who treated him—Morris's own doctor was out of town—recommended immediate amputation as the only means to save his life, and they removed the leg below the knee. Neither Morris's burned arm nor his wooden peg leg slowed him down, "except when he occasionally slipped on muddy cobblestones," noted his biographer, Richard Brookhiser. Rather, the injuries "reminded him what he lacked." The "inescapable mark of two heavy blows" enabled Morris to adopt a philosophy of compassion toward others and an ability to enjoy life to its fullest—no one knew what lurked around the next corner.

Morris's humor was an outgrowth of this thinking. When a friend visited him the day after the amputation and offered Morris a lengthy pep talk on how the loss of his leg could actually build his character and strengthen his moral fiber, Morris replied: "My good sir, you argue the matter so handsomely and point out so clearly the advantages of being without legs, that I am almost tempted to part with the other." Morris also never fully refuted and likely took delight in the apocryphal story that circulated after his accident—that he had damaged his leg jumping from a bedroom window, narrowly escaping his lover's incensed husband.

Quipster or not, serving on the convention's Committee of Style and Arrangement was serious business, and Morris, who handled the bulk of the organizing and polishing, did his job well. He led the committee as they transformed the resolutions into words, and he did the lion's share of the work, impressing his colleagues. "The finish given to the style and arrangement of the Constitution fairly belongs to the pen of Mr. Morris," said James Madison. "A better choice could not have been made."

Arranging and editing the work of the entire convention was a major task, but most of Morris's efforts to scrub clean the prose in the main body of the Constitution did not require sustained creativity and did not employ his original words.

The document's preamble was another story. Morris sensed the importance and profound meaning that Americans would attach to the opening words of this historic document.

For that reason, while he incorporated some words written by others, Morris took it upon himself to make the preamble his own—and he did not disappoint.

TO START, MORRIS DISCARDED the original preamble developed by the Committee of Detail. Like other introductions to documents and treaties that Congress had approved under the Articles of Confederation, the initial draft preamble in the Constitution mentioned "the people" but only as a means to highlight their relationship to individual states. Thus, the Committee of Detail's draft preamble began: "We the people of the States of New Hampshire, Massachusetts . . . etc.," continuing in a north-to-south geographic order all the way to Georgia. It then continued: "do ordain, declare, and establish the following Constitution for the Government of ourselves and our posterity."

Morris opted for a lengthier preamble, one that captured the full meaning of what the Constitution was intended to accomplish, and one that immediately established from whence the new government derived its legitimacy and power:

> We the People of the United States, in Order to form a more perfect union, establish Justice, insure domestic Tranquility, provide for the common defence, promote the general Welfare, and secure the Blessings of Liberty to ourselves and our Posterity, do ordain and establish this Constitution for the United States of America.

Morris's decision to omit the names of the individual states and replace them with "United States" accomplished the near-impossible: the successful meshing and blending of the priorities of the two major factions and points of view at odds throughout the convention. At first blush, the preamble seemed to advance the nationalists' point of view. Whereas the Committee of Detail had vested power in the individual states through their residents, Morris's preamble appeared to vest authority in the people of the entire nation.

Or did it?

ON SECOND LOOK, MORRIS'S opening words were just vague enough to also placate the states' rights advocates at the convention; in fact, the preamble's brilliance lay in its opening ambiguity. When Morris wrote, "We the People of the United States," was he talking about a brand-new sprawling country called the "United States" to whom the people pledged their fealty? Or was he talking about a confederation of states that was "united" in its efforts to create a new government—hence, the "United States"—perhaps better interpreted as "States United"?

Certainly Morris, Madison, Washington, and others would have preferred that delegates embraced the former interpretation, but the vagueness of the language also allowed states-rights' advocates to call the preamble their own.

In fact, whether deliberate or not, Morris's simple and powerful opening words embody the delicate balance between national and state power that provoked such passions during the Senate discussion and remain a cornerstone of our constitutional republic today. In his eloquent defense of the Constitution in *The Federalist Papers*, James Madison would later describe the Constitution as being "neither a national nor a federal constitution, but a composition of both," and Morris's preamble captured this concept in the opening seven words.

Even so, Morris's "We the People of the United States" phrase would prove controversial and set some tempers aflame during the state ratification debates that followed the approval of the Constitution. "Who authorized them to speak the language of 'We the People,' instead of 'We the States'?" an angry Patrick Henry asked during Virginia's ratification convention.

But it was clear, as the convention neared its end in Philadelphia, that Morris had captured the essence of the delegates' thinking. He had spoken the words during the debate on the presidency and his preamble dramatically illustrated the point: "The people are the King."

IN THE REMAINDER OF the remarkable preamble, Morris articulates the major themes of the convention and the major goals of the new government with bold clarity. "To form a more perfect union," a phrase often misinterpreted in contemporary times, meant simply to improve upon the disastrous and largely unworkable Articles of Confederation. The word "perfect" did not carry the absolutist connotation it has today; thus, a "more perfect" union was an understandable and aspirational concept that simply meant America would strive to improve.

"Establish justice" referred not only to the establishment of a national set of legal principles that the courts would enforce; it also signified a level playing field for trade and an overall concept of fairness and human dignity that the Constitution would promote. Morris had the recent memories of Shays' Rebellion and other civil unrest in mind when he referred to the "domestic tranquility" the Constitution would help ensure.

And when Morris penned the words "provide for the common defence," delegates recognized the phrase as a way for the national government to protect its citizens against foreign invaders—something no state could do individually—several of whom had either explicitly or, in a veiled way, threatened the young nation's shores and sovereignty.

To Morris and the other delegates, to "promote the general Welfare" was the culmination of everything that had come before in the preamble—the welfare of the people was the reason for justice, tranquility, and defense. Such "welfare" was defined as establishing the framework for an equitable and peaceful domestic environment, which included the prospects for a robust economic and commerce system that would benefit as many Americans as possible.

Finally, Morris's powerful last clause, to "secure the Blessings of Liberty to ourselves and our Posterity," summed up the most important concept that delegates discussed in Philadelphia in both 1787 and eleven years earlier during the debates over the Declaration of Independence. A document that would "secure the Blessings of Liberty" would codify the Declaration's promise of ensuring the unalienable rights of "life, liberty, and the pursuit of happiness." Above all else, in both documents, individual liberty and freedom would be the bedrock upon which the new government would rest. All power the government derived would emanate not from the courts or the president or even the national legislature—but, again, from "We the People."

Thus, Morris's preamble—a poetic introduction to the new Constitution that lacked the legal authority of the document itself—signaled clearly that not only had delegates created a comprehensive blueprint for governing the young nation, but in so doing, they had fulfilled the promise of the ideas and ideals expressed in America's sacred founding scripture, the Declaration of Independence.

10

★

"Approaching
So Near to
Perfection . . ."

★

September 15, 1787

As the late-afternoon summer shadows lengthened on the Convention's last Saturday of work, Virginia Governor Edmund Randolph made one last desperate attempt to delay the passage of a new constitution.

It had been a long, tense, exhausting day, a microcosm of the summer. Delegates had worked through the document, debated, made small changes, considered each article again. As the day wore on, Randolph and his fellow Virginian, George Mason, grew more dissatisfied, as did Elbridge Gerry of Massachusetts.

Randolph began offering caustic criticism of the Constitution, especially "on the indefinite and dangerous power given to Congress." His words carried weight and his latest objections must have perplexed some delegates; it was Randolph, after all, who only four months earlier had put forth the Virginia Plan calling for a strong central government. Resolute in his objections, he offered a change to the amending process: amendments to the new Constitution should be offered by the state conventions, which, in turn, would be "submitted to and finally decided" by yet another general national convention. Should his motion be disregarded, Randolph said, "it would be impossible [for] him to put his name to this instrument."

Virginia's George Mason and Elbridge Gerry of Massachusetts agreed: if another convention were approved, they could affix their signatures; otherwise they would decline.

Delegates held their collective breath.

Two prominent defections such as Mason and Randolph could influence the other Virginia delegates as well as members from other states. Yet the notion of a second convention after such an exhausting summer sounded preposterous, especially to the strong nationalists such as Washington, Madison, and Hamilton, who had already seen their initial vision diluted during the Senate debate. Another convention could reopen the argument over representation, and could perhaps jeopardize proportional representation in the House. It was a risk they could not afford to take.

Charles Pinckney of South Carolina objected to the idea also. While he respected Randolph and Mason, he thought their proposals were utterly unworkable and the idea of a second convention foolhardy.

If any other delegates responded to the three dissenters, no one recorded it; perhaps Pinckney had spoken for the rest of the supporters. Many still had questions and concerns about the proposed Constitution, but the notion of a second convention to revisit all the issues of the past summer simply was anathema to most delegates.

When the roll was called on Randolph's motion for a second convention, "All the States answered—no," Madison recorded.

Then it was time for the vote that would mark the culmination of the entire summer's work and change the course of the United States. It happened swiftly and without further debate. In his most anticlimactic language, Madison recorded it as follows: "On the question to agree to the Constitution as amended, All the States aye."

With Mason and Randolph voting against the Constitution, George Washington was forced to cast the deciding vote in favor for Virginia.

Without further discussion, the convention then ordered that the Constitution be engrossed, and delegates then adjourned—agreeing to return on Monday, September 17, for a review of the final document.

WHILE MOST OF THE delegates spent Saturday evening and Sunday relaxing after their grueling ordeal—Washington spent Sunday at the Morris family estate—one man toiled long and hard over the remainder of the weekend. Jacob Shallus, assistant clerk to the Pennsylvania legislature, was given the task of engrossing the completed Constitution on parchment.

Considering the limited time he had, Shallus did a superb job with his quill pens and inks, meticulously inking 4,000 words across four large sheets of parchment. Shallus recognized the importance of the first three words of the Constitution (or else he was informed by one or more delegates)—the calligraphic words "We the People" are inked in large, bold letters at the top of the first page, by far the most prominent phrase in the entire document.

Viewing the four pages provides a quick assessment of the contents and emphasis of the new Constitution. Article I, which defines the powers of the Congress, is the longest section, covering nearly two entire parchment pages to enumerate the lengthy powers of the legislative branch. The powers of the presidency are outlined in Article II and begin at the bottom of the second page, concluding two-thirds of the way down page 3. The judiciary section, described in Article III, is significantly shorter, covering nearly the bottom third of the third page. Articles IV, V, VI, and VII—dealing with citizenship, the admittance of new states to the union, the amendment process, debts, treaties, and finally, asserting that the approval of nine states would be required to ratify the Constitution—are much shorter. Shallus began Article IV at the bottom of page 3 and squeezed the remaining articles onto a bit more than half of page 4.

If the delegates decided to sign the Constitution on Monday, September 17, Shallus had left them ample room to do so.

Despite Shallus's tireless and admirable efforts over the weekend, the rushed project did result in mistakes that he would spend time correcting on Monday. Several errors were omissions of words that he then inserted carefully between the lines. He used a penknife to scrape away an extra line of text near the bottom of page 1 that left behind a band of gray. There are also several ink splotches on page 1 that must have been unavoidable; working so quickly with quill pens presented its own challenges. On the Constitution's final sheet of parchment, Shallus inscribed a record of his changes and insertions so there could be no mistake that the modifications were legitimate.

Shallus would make one more change to the Constitution, but this was not his error or a corrected smudge. When delegates arrived at the statehouse for the final day of the convention, presumably to approve and sign the final engrossed copy of the document, they realized they weren't quite finished.

MONDAY, SEPTEMBER 17, 1787, broke clear, cool, and sunny, a day of promise and anticipation for most of the delegates as they made their way to the statehouse. Perhaps a touch of nostalgia was also in the air. For most delegates, this would be their last day on Chestnut Street: their final time gathering inside the familiar chamber; the final day the sentries would stand guard in front of the locked doors; the last time prisoners would carry Benjamin Franklin, seated in his sedan chair, into the chamber. These men had begun the summer with an ambitious goal, seen their work and the new country nearly derailed several weeks into the convention, and then recovered and emerged with a new constitution and a new government. Any self-satisfied sense of accomplishment was certainly earned and warranted.

Yet, not all delegates would have a spring in their step; the dissenters—Gerry, Mason, and Randolph—entered the convention's final day with a sense of profound disappointment. This was not the Constitution they had hoped for.

To begin the day's drama, the convention secretary, William Jackson, read aloud the engrossed Constitution. Then, appropriately enough, it was Benjamin Franklin who stood first, speech in hand, and whose words would open this auspicious day. Tired and enfeebled, the near eighty-two-year-old Pennsylvanian handed the pages to his colleague, James Wilson, and asked if Wilson could read his words.

Franklin's speech began with a conciliatory tone aimed at those who had doubts about the document before them; he himself had some issues with the Constitution. But he took heart that so many delegates had worked so hard on the document and provided their best thinking, and clearly a majority of them supported the Constitution—that counted for something.

Franklin said he agreed to the Constitution, "with all its faults, if they are such," because a strong national government was necessary to place the country on a solid footing. Delaying a vote on the issue any longer, or deferring to a second convention at some undeclared time in the future, were unappealing options. "I doubt too whether any other Convention we can obtain can make a better Constitution," he said. With so many factors at play, "from such an assembly can a perfect production be expected?" Considering those factors, Franklin said he was "astonished" to find the Constitution "approaching so near to perfection as it does." This convention had proven the naysayers wrong—delegates had produced a finished product and it was a constitution worthy of the people. "I consent to this Constitution because I expect no better," Franklin said, "and because I am not sure that it is not the best."

For any delegate who still harbored objections, Franklin asked if he could "doubt a little of his own infallibility—and to make manifest our unanimity, put his name to this instrument." He then offered an official motion, prepared by Gouverneur Morris, that the Constitution be signed and finally approved "by the unanimous consent of *the States* present the 17th of September." By focusing on the states, Morris's language offered individual delegates the opportunity to dissent.

It was a moving speech, and though its text was not read aloud by Franklin, Wilson had done the great man justice. As the convention's senior statesman, Franklin's ideas carried enormous influence; there is little doubt that his remarks about reconsidering his own infallibility set an example that would help delegates quell their potential doubts. Perhaps Franklin's patented wisdom revealed the truth—perhaps this convention had produced a constitution that was "approaching so near to perfection."

Nathaniel Gorham of Massachusetts had one last-minute recommendation that he believed would nudge the document ever so much closer to that ideal.

GORHAM RECOGNIZED THE LATENESS of his proposal, but he hoped his fellow delegates would indulge him. With the hope of "lessening objections to the Constitution," would Washington entertain a motion to reduce—from 40,000 to 30,000—the number of inhabitants an individual congressman would represent in the House of Representatives? Rufus King of Massachusetts and Daniel Carroll of Maryland quickly seconded the motion. Gorham's proposal seemed innocuous, but in reality, it touched on the area that had been the subject of long debates throughout the convention—reducing the ratio between representatives and people, thereby increasing the number of representatives in the lower house, clearly benefited the larger states with greater populations.

All eyes turned to Washington, and, shockingly, the convention's president spoke for one of the few times of the entire summer. He acknowledged that his leadership post had "hitherto restrained him from offering his sentiments" on these matters and reminded delegates that they should make "as few as possible" changes to the Constitution at this late hour. However, he felt strongly about this issue and was compelled to speak on and support Gorham's motion. The "smallness of the proportion of Representatives" had been an objection of many members of the convention, and had provided "insufficient security for the rights and interests of the people." To Washington personally, the ratio had "always appeared . . . among the exceptionable parts of the plan," and, late in the proceedings or not, this issue was of such great consequence to him that "it would give him much satisfaction to see it adopted."

The eleventh-hour timing of Gorham's proposal, which discouraged dissent from the weary delegates, coupled with Washington's endorsement—the only time in the convention when he had ventured an opinion—offered more than enough to sway the delegates. Gorham's amended proposal was agreed to unanimously, a collective result that had proved elusive through most of the convention.

Jacob Shallus used his tools and inks to alter the "40,000" to "30,000" in the engrossed copy and made a note of the change on the final page of the parchment.

For all intents and purposes, the historic document was finished.

The final debates were over. Benjamin Franklin's motion to approve and sign the United States Constitution was passed, with ten states in favor and South Carolina divided (two of the Palmetto state delegates thought the "equivocal form" of Franklin's motion was inappropriate). Without a quorum of delegates, New York could not cast a vote, and Rhode Island had continued its refusal to send delegates to Philadelphia.

At about three o'clock on September 17, 1787, the signing ceremony began. James Madison recorded the momentous event with a simple declarative sentence: "The members then proceeded to sign the instrument."

A TOTAL OF THIRTY-NINE of the fifty-five delegates who participated in the Constitutional Convention throughout the summer of 1787 signed the document that would govern the young nation, assuming at least nine states ratified it in the coming months. With the exception of Mason, Randolph, and Gerry, all the delegates in attendance on September 17 signed the engrossed Constitution. Actually, forty signatures found their way onto the parchment; Secretary William Jackson signed the document also, his name preceded by the word "Attest," basically identifying him as a witness to the proceedings.

The convention president, George Washington, signed first (also noting he was a "deputy from Virginia"), and again, the remaining signatures are grouped in two columns by states listed in geographic order from north to south, with New Hampshire listed at the top right column and Georgia concluding the written roll call of states at the bottom of the left column.

As with the Declaration of Independence, the Constitution's signatories represent a collection of men who would go on to become some of America's most preeminent historical figures—George Washington, Benjamin Franklin, Alexander Hamilton, James Madison—and additional individuals whose names carried enormous prestige in 1787 such as James Wilson, Gouverneur Morris, Roger Sherman, and Charles Pinckney. Six of the signatories—Franklin, Sherman, Wilson, George Clymer, Robert Morris, and George Read—had signed the Declaration of Independence eleven years earlier.

The signatures would serve two main purposes during ratification. First, they would prevent the delegates who signed from withdrawing their support of the Constitution, or even equivocating, during their state ratification gatherings. More to the point, the stature and prestige of the signers would certainly enhance the chances for ratification. For those potential ratifiers who were unsure or even unknowledgeable about the intricacies of the Constitution, the imprimaturs of many prominent statesmen would serve to reassure them to support the document.

Of all the names, Washington's and Franklin's carried the greatest influence and prestige, and if these were ranked, Washington's would be most important to the Constitution's ultimate approval at the convention and ratification afterward. Federalists, especially, who supported a strong national government, were eager to tout the support of Washington and Franklin for their point of view.

In a letter to Washington shortly after the convention, Gouverneur Morris said: "I have observed that your name [associated with] the new Constitution has been of infinite service. Indeed, I am convinced that if you had not attended the convention, and the same paper had been handed out to the world, it would have met with a colder reception, with fewer and weaker advocates, and with more and more strenuous opponents."

AS EACH DELEGATE STEPPED up to sign the Constitution on September 17, 1787, his sense of pride at this epochal moment must have been tempered by a tentative reality. In the words of one historian: "They all believed they had framed a document that would create 'a more perfect union,' but no one believed they had achieved perfection."

The ardent nationalists, Madison and Morris especially, and Washington too, still believed the Senate structure provided the states with too much influence; the strong states-rightists still believed the national government was too powerful and the lack of a people's bill of rights was a dangerous omission. Virginia's George Mason would leave Philadelphia "in an exceedingly ill humor" because of this, Madison pointed out. The southern states believed the more populous northern states would leave them at a disadvantage in Congress, especially when it came to approving regulations and taxes that could threaten their agricultural economies; yet some northern states believed southern states had wielded disproportionate influence on slavery protections and advantages that were built into the Constitution, including the three-fifths compromise and the provision allowing the slave trade to continue for another two decades.

Differences aside, the momentousness of the occasion was not lost on Franklin, who would have the last word inside the statehouse. It was past three o'clock when members began signing, and as the last delegate approached the table—Georgia's Abraham Baldwin—a still weakened Franklin made reference to the half-sunburst carved on the back of the chair that Washington had occupied all summer. Speaking quietly to delegates around him, he confided that "I have often . . . in the course of the session, and the vicissitudes of my hopes and fears as to its issue, looked at that behind the President without being able to tell whether it [the sun] was rising or setting."

At this moment, as the last delegate signed the Constitution, Franklin said, the meaning of the carving had become clear and gratifying to him: "Now, at length, I have the happiness to know that it is a rising and not a setting sun."

WITH THE SIGNING COMPLETED, the delegates' work was finished. The future of the new Constitution was now in the hands of the individual state ratification conventions—nine states would have to vote yes for the Constitution to take effect.

Major William Jackson, secretary of the Federal Convention, was instructed to depart the following morning for New York to transfer the original, signed, engrossed copy of the Constitution to the secretary of the Confederation Congress.

Meanwhile, Philadelphia printers John Dunlap—who printed the Declaration of Independence—and David Claypoole would spend the night producing approximately five hundred copies of the Constitution, some to be given to delegates as they left Philadelphia, others to be delivered to the Confederation Congress and the states. The original printed copies did contain the correct "thirty thousand," the last-minute change made by the convention in assigning the number of inhabitants each congressman would represent in the lower house. But it did contain one error: in Article V, in the clause that forbade any amendment affecting the slave trade before 1808, the date was written as "one thousand seven hundred and eight," in reality, a century earlier. While this incorrect version appeared in a few newspaper printings of the Constitution, in Philadelphia and New York, these were soon replaced by correct versions and the mistake faded into history.

On September 19, the *Pennsylvania Packet and Daily Advertiser* became the first newspaper to publish the Constitution; though the paper could not reproduce the actual signatures, the names of the signers were printed in the typewritten version. This practice would be replicated in many American newspapers—the injunction of secrecy was lifted quickly after approval and the signers' names were made public.

In his notes, James Madison describes the end of the remarkable and unprecedented four-month convention with understated terseness: "The Constitution being signed by all the Members present except Mr. Randolph, Mr. Mason, and Mr. Gerry who declined giving it the sanction of their names, the convention dissolved itself by an Adjournment."

IN HIS LETTER TO Congress that would accompany the engrossed Constitution, George Washington stressed that the hope, belief, and "ardent wish" of the delegates was "that it [the Constitution] may promote the lasting welfare of that country so dear to us all, and secure her freedom and happiness."

Yet, it would not be until months later, in February 1788, as the Constitution was making its way through the ratification process, that Washington had gained enough perspective to express his full sense of pride for the convention's accomplishments. In a letter to his dear friend, the Marquis de Lafayette, Washington wrote: "It appears to me, then, little short of a miracle, the Delegates from so many different States (which States you know are also different from each other), in their manners, circumstances, and prejudices, should unite in forming a system of national Government, so little liable to well founded objections."

Benjamin Franklin recognized the achievement of the convention as well, choosing a brief quip over eloquence in his initial explanation of the delegates' work and the future of the country and its government. Maryland delegate James McHenry said that he had overheard Franklin in conversation with a woman outside the statehouse shortly after adjournment: "The lady asked Dr. Franklin, 'Well, Doctor, what have we got—a republic or a monarchy?'" Franklin's response: "A republic, if you can keep it."

NO ASSESSMENT OF REACTION would be complete without also examining the feelings of James Madison, who would become known as the "Father of the Constitution," whose Virginia Plan and outline for a strong national government sparked most of the convention's debate before it became the foundation of the new document and the new government. Disappointed as he was about the Senate outcome, Madison spent the next several months speaking and writing in support of the Constitution and the delegates' efforts. After spending four months in close contact and constant meetings with his fellow delegates, perhaps he appreciated the motives that drove even those with whom he fervently disagreed.

He most eloquently articulated these thoughts late in his life in one long sentence, an unabashed tribute to the men who gathered in Philadelphia in the summer of 1787, a paean to the work he had begun and his fellow delegates had completed in triumph:

"I feel it is my duty to express my profound and solemn conviction," he wrote, "that there never was an assembly of men, charged with a great and arduous trust, who were more pure in their motives, or more exclusively or anxiously devoted to the object committed to them, than were the members of the Federal Convention of 1787 to the object of devising and proposing a constitutional system which should best secure the permanent liberty and happiness of their country."

June 25, 1788, Richmond, Virginia

ONE DAY AFTER PATRICK HENRY'S "thunderstorm" speech shook the walls of the theater on Shockoe Hill, a weary but determined James

Madison stood to urge members of the Virginia ratification convention to approve the United States Constitution.

He was well aware of how critical the upcoming vote would be to the nation's future. Virginia had already been upstaged by New Hampshire, which days earlier had become the ninth and deciding state required to ratify the country's new governing document. Still, Virginia's assent was vital not only because of its potential influence on New York's vote scheduled in mere weeks, but for important symbolic reasons also. Changes to the Senate's structure notwithstanding, it was the Virginia Plan, after all, that essentially defined the blueprint for the new Constitution—and it had been two of Virginia's most respected statesmen, Washington and Madison, who were most closely associated with its success. A no vote on ratification in their home state would constitute a major political defeat and personal embarrassment for both men.

Without doubt, the forces arrayed against ratification were formidable: they included Bill of Rights stalwart George Mason; John Tyler (whose son would become the nation's tenth president); James Monroe (who would become the country's fifth president); and most influential of all, the irrepressible and incomparable Patrick Henry, whose oratory skills and "give me liberty or give me death" speech thirteen years earlier had earned him revered status among his fellow Virginians. At the heart of the Virginia opponents' protestations about the Constitution were two related issues: the document's lack of a "people's bill of rights," and the refusal by proponents to consider amendments *before* ratification. Assurances by the Federalists that amendments could and would be proposed and submitted to Congress following ratification did nothing to mollify opponents.

Madison laid out the argument eloquently for the proponents. Nine states had already ratified the document, several unanimously and others by wide margins. Proposing "conditional" amendments at this time, even a bill of rights, would render the other states' decision to ratify null and void and require them to revisit a revised constitution. Such a tactic presented the "extreme risk of perpetual disunion." The Constitution provided an amendment process, and "reasonable amendments" could be approved after ratification. Using some of the strongest language of the entire constitutional era, Madison warned of the alternative: "If, on the other hand, we call on the states to rescind what they have done, and confess that they have done wrong, and to consider the subject again, it will produce such unnecessary delays, and is pregnant with such infinite dangers, that I cannot contemplate it without horror."

For Madison, the choice was clear—could opponents not see it? "There are uncertainty and confusion on the one hand, and order, tranquility, and certainty, on the other," he said. "Let us not hesitate to elect the latter alternative."

Madison's arguments in favor of ratification continued to ring strong inside the theater. One French diplomat in attendance wrote home that Madison was "always clear, precise, and consistent in his reasoning, and always methodical and pure in his Language." Time and again, contemporaneous accounts of the Virginia ratification convention cited Madison's strength of reasoning and clear, cool, difficult-to-refute logic as the antidote to Henry's fire and brimstone. It was clear to the delegates that Madison, the man who had put forth the initial plan for a new constitution, had intricate knowledge of its benefits and virtues.

It was no wonder. For, despite his deep disappointment after the Constitutional Convention had altered his dream for full proportional representation in the Congress, James Madison had almost immediately embarked on perhaps the greatest intellectual pursuit of his lifetime—penning a series of masterful essays to convince Americans to fully support and embrace the new Constitution and their new form of government.

Put simply, over the last several months, he had had plenty of practice defending the United States Constitution.

WHEN HE FIRST BEGAN writing his share of *The Federalist*—later colloquially referred to as *The Federalist Papers*—James Madison likely had no inkling that his work would become part of what most historians believe is among the most brilliant and incisive political writing of all time; in the eyes of one scholar, "the most important work in political science that has ever been written, or is likely ever to be written in the United States."

It is also, without dispute even today, the single most indispensable resource for interpreting the Constitution.

Consisting of a series of eighty-five essays by Madison, Alexander Hamilton, and John Jay, *The Federalist Papers* defended and explained the new Constitution and the intricacies of the constitutional form of government. The collection of essays was Hamilton's brainchild and they were first published as letters to the public in New York newspapers. Concerned that the Constitution faced stiff opposition in his home state, Hamilton enlisted the aid of the two other ardent nationalists and published the work under the pseudonym Publius; the first essay appeared on October 27, 1787, just weeks after the Constitution was approved in Philadelphia. The essays were still appearing in March 1788, when the first thirty-six were issued in a collected edition. A second volume containing essays 37 through 85 was published in late May of the same year. Jay had fallen ill in the autumn of 1787, leaving the bulk of the writing to Hamilton and Madison.

It was in these essays that Madison solidified his reputation as a brilliant political scientist and legal scholar. *The Federalist*, in the word of one historian, bore few "marks of immortality" at birth. What began as a propagandist effort by Hamilton to convince New York residents to support the Constitution was transformed by the words that flowed from Madison's quill. The essays became a groundbreaking compendium on the virtues of the republican form of government and the foundation of personal liberty and freedom upon which they rested.

The Federalist not only discusses the Constitution but offers insights on a variety of existential topics: greed, human nature, ambition, and power. It is because of all of these, Madison argued, that the new Constitution must be approved, a unique document defining a government unique in the world. With their remarkable essays, Hamilton and Madison created a blueprint to understand and interpret the Constitution, one that presidents, Supreme Court justices, academics, journalists, students, and all Americans have been referring to for more than two centuries.

IT WAS IN *THE FEDERALIST NO. 47* that Madison introduced the theory of separation of powers, wherein each branch of government imposed a system of "checks and balances" on the others. Indeed, it was a delicate balancing act; each branch had to be strong and independent enough to carry out its tasks and duties, but also connected to the other branches to prevent the misuse of power. Hence, the fact that the president could nominate judges, but the Congress had to approve them; that the Congress could pass laws, but the president could veto them—and yet another level of power check, the Congress could in turn override the presidential veto. This clear separation of powers, Madison wrote in his magnificent *Federalist No. 51*, was "essential to the preservation of liberty."

The veto override example also illustrates another crucial precept of the Constitution—the legislature, because it is closest to the people, is meant to possess predominant power. It is the only branch that can pass laws, impose taxes, declare war, and remove officials from the other branches through impeachment. Further, Congress is the only branch of the federal government that can propose amendments to the Constitution; the executive and the judiciary were deliberately omitted from this process. But precisely *because* of its broad power, Congress required its own internal checks: the two houses represented different constituencies (the people via legislative districts in the lower house and the people by way of the individual state legislatures in the Senate); and the assent of both houses was required for Congress to pass anything.

Indeed, the separation of powers and checks and balances occurred throughout the new government—between the federal government and the states; the branches of government; and within the legislature. Such a system was created, Madison noted, so "that its several constituent parts may, by their mutual relations, be the means of keeping each other in their proper places."

It was this general wariness of power, and the need for "concurrence" of both houses of Congress, that also made it deliberately difficult to pass legislation and create laws. Some legislation would be required, but the Constitution and *The Federalist* were skeptical of the idea of a multitude of new laws. As Hamilton stated, "The injury which may possibly be done by defeating a few good laws will be amply compensated by the advantage of preventing a number of bad ones."

To employ modern-day parlance, not only was the potential for gridlock woven throughout the Constitution by design, the framers overwhelming *favored* gridlock over the dangers posed by an overreaching and oppressive government. While the Constitution was developed in large part to rectify major problems with the Articles of Confederation—which had promoted near paralysis and impotence—the point of the new document and governmental structure was not "efficiency first."

Rather, it was the creation of independent branches with substantial powers that would move deliberately, but virtuously, because of interlocking checks and balances that would force the government to proceed slowly and focus on the common good for the broad society.

As such, this "extended republic," as Madison referred to it, also reduced the potential for abuses by individual "factions" with malicious or self-serving agendas. Because power was distributed across the government, because no one branch could proceed on its own, only those laws that had widespread appeal, especially among the people, had the potential to bubble to the surface and garner approval. It was a government that had never before been implemented, but Madison urged anti-Federalists not to use this fact as a criticism. "Why is the experiment of an extended republic to be rejected merely because it may comprise what is new?" he asked. America had "accomplished a revolution which has no parallel in the annals of human society." Thus, it should come as no surprise that "they reared the fabrics of governments which have no model on the face of the globe."

AT ITS HEART, THE Federalists argued, the Constitution existed to provide a governing structure for the new nation while ensuring the basic "unalienable rights" of freedom and human liberty that the Declaration of Independence professed. Indeed, never before had men fashioned such a government, one in which power flowed from the governed—the *people*—to the government, rather than the other way around. The Constitution, above all else, needed to protect and fortify that principle.

As Madison observed in *Federalist No. 51*, perhaps the most famous words that have endured from these great essays: "If men were angels, no governments would be necessary. If angels were to govern men, neither external nor internal controls on government would be necessary." Since men were not angels, controls and limitations on government were needed to ensure that the people's will was served and their freedoms preserved.

In the words of one modern historian, the message of *The Federalist* is: "no happiness without liberty, no liberty without self-government, no self-government without constitutionalism, no constitutionalism without morality—and none of these great goods without stability and order."

Madison likely received all the praise he needed when his friend, Thomas Jefferson, wrote in November 1788 that *The Federalist* was "the best commentary on the principles of government which was ever written."

THE VIRGINIA VOTE WAS close but not razor-thin.

Madison's forceful and cogent arguments in favor of the new Constitution won the day—June 25, 1788. Virginia actually took two separate votes, with the first signaling the final outcome; delegates first rejected a motion, by a vote of 88 to 80, to attach a "Declaration of rights" to the Constitution as a condition of ratification. And then, on the main motion, one member crossed over, and the Commonwealth of Virginia ratified the new U.S. Constitution by a vote of 89 to 79. Patrick Henry, George Mason, and James Monroe stood firm in their opposition, unable to support a document that contained no bill of rights.

Virginia had not put the Constitution over the top—that honor belonged to New Hampshire, which had ratified just days earlier—but the weight of Virginia's approval reverberated across the state and across the nation.

Two days later, the evening stagecoach brought word to Alexandria that the Constitution had been approved, and the townspeople—with cannon firing in celebration—went to Mount Vernon to invite George Washington to partake in the following day's festivities and revelry.

★

11

"Tis Done! . . .

We Have

Become a Nation"

★

The entire process of creating a new constitution for the United States had occurred with stunning, even unimaginable, swiftness. James Madison first arrived in Philadelphia for the Federal Convention in May 1787 and the Constitution had been fully ratified before the end of June 1788. The initial framework of a new government, the debates that followed, the modifications, the drafting, the redrafting, the preamble, final approval, the publication of most of *The Federalist*, and the ratification by the requisite number of states—all of it had been accomplished in a little more than thirteen months. The "miracle" that George Washington had alluded to after the Constitutional Convention continued throughout the ratification process.

A few days after an enormous July 4, 1788, celebration in Philadelphia—what the city's residents labeled the Grand Procession to celebrate both Independence Day and the Constitution's ratification—Philadelphia physician and declaration signer Benjamin Rush wrote to a friend in New Jersey and described the glorious event.

When he finished his detailed account of the day, Rush took a moment to triumphantly sum up his feelings and the thoughts of Americans with simple words that have echoed down through the decades:

"Tis done! . . . We have become a nation."

But quick-moving events thereafter made it clear that the nation needed one more important document.

DURING THE RATIFICATION DEBATES and in the months afterward, Madison and other Federalists had seen and heard enough to know that a people's bill of rights would need to be added to the Constitution quickly. Otherwise, support and momentum for the national government would erode, and, just as important, some states would push for a second federal convention to address the Constitution's shortcomings, a gathering that could threaten the entire document.

Powerful voices clamored for a bill of rights. Madison had witnessed the passionate arguments of Patrick Henry, George Mason, and James Monroe during the Virginia ratification debates. In Massachusetts, opponents criticized the Constitution and accused proponents of undermining the achievements of the American Revolution. Mercy Otis Warren, a poet and essayist who traced her roots back to the *Mayflower* and whose family had been active revolutionary leaders, published her scathing *Observations on the New Constitution* under the pseudonym "a Columbian Patriot." In a brilliant piece of anti-Constitution writing, she articulated eighteen specific deficiencies of the new document, including her claims that there were no "well-defined limits" on the judiciary; the executive and legislative branches were "dangerously blended" and a cause for alarm; one representative for every 30,000 inhabitants is "very inadequate"; and most egregiously, there was no provision for a bill of rights "to guard against the dangerous encroachments of power in too many instances to be named." Warren criticized the Constitutional Convention for "shutting up the doors . . . and resolving that no member should correspond with gentlemen in different states." Such secrecy, she said, led to the "annihilation of the independence and sovereignty of the thirteen distinct states."

Warren's treatise was among the most influential and powerful anti-federalist rhetoric during the ratification process. Massachusetts eventually ratified the Constitution, but the vote was relatively close: 187 in favor to 168 against. That vote was followed by neighboring Rhode Island's rejection of the Constitution by popular referendum.

Then, on July 26, 1788, strategically and geographically important New York ratified the Constitution on a close vote, 30 to 27, but also agreed unanimously to send a "circular letter" to the other states calling for a second convention to consider amendments. In early August, North Carolina adjourned its convention without ratifying, with anti-Federalists expressing strong dissatisfaction that amendments were not included prior to the ratification vote. The North Carolina decision plus the New York circular letter energized anti-Federalists elsewhere, especially in Virginia, where Patrick Henry was also rallying support for a second convention. Henry had told his fellow Virginians during ratification that no less an "illustrious citizen" than Thomas Jefferson "advises you to reject this government, till it be amended, and Jefferson's opinion had not changed." In Madison's view, the notion of another convention was dangerous to the Constitution's future, a "signal of concord and hope to the enemies of the Constitution everywhere." Amendments aside, a second convention could bring down the entire Constitution and, possibly, the Union. Unless the first Congress approved amendments—specifically a bill of rights—anti-Federalist sentiments for a second convention would likely prevail.

Madison pondered the Bill of Rights even as the new government took shape.

On September 13, Congress formally announced that the Constitution had been ratified by the required number of states and set the first Wednesday in January 1789 for appointing presidential electors in the eleven states that had ratified it and the first Wednesday in February for electors to vote for a president in their respective states. The "present seat of Congress"—New York—was established as "the place for commencing proceedings under the said Constitution" during the first week of March.

On April 14, 1789, the Congress's secretary, Charles Thomson, arrived in Mount Vernon and notified George Washington that every elector had cast a ballot for him as the nation's first president—he had won unanimously—a decision that was not unexpected but was significant nonetheless.

After a triumphant journey north, where he was greeted by cheering thousands, Washington was inaugurated on April 30 in New York, where cannon again boomed and church bells pealed across lower Manhattan. More than 500 soldiers led the parade procession to Federal Hall, where Washington took the oath of office to become the first man in American history to answer to the salutation "Mr. President."

Always the reluctant orator, and admitting the "greater anxieties" that filled him as he was about to embark on this new journey, Washington nonetheless struck the right chord in his twenty-minute inaugural address when he reminded Americans of their national purpose: "The preservation of the sacred fire of liberty, and the destiny of the republican model of Government, are justly considered, perhaps as *deeply*, as *finally*, staked on the experiment entrusted to the hands of the American people."

On the first full day of the new federal administration, May 1, 1789, the New York *Daily Advertiser* proclaimed: "Good government, the best of blessings, now commences under favorable auspices. We beg to congratulate our readers on the great event."

JAMES MADISON, WHO HAD defeated James Monroe by 300 votes to win one of Virginia's ten seats in the House of Representatives in the First Congress, had promised voters during the campaign that, if elected, he would work to convince his colleagues to recommend amendments to the states for ratification. "It is my sincere opinion that the Constitution ought to be revised," he had said during the campaign, "and that the first Congress meeting under it ought to prepare and recommend to the states for ratification the most satisfactory provisions for all essential rights." These should include, "particularly, the rights of conscience in the fullest latitude, the freedom of the press, trials by jury, security against general warrants, etc." He believed that a bill of rights, "pursued with a proper moderation and in a proper mode," would satisfy "well-meaning opponents" and provide "additional guides in favor of liberty."

Madison kept his campaign promise. On May 4, 1789, he informed his fellow representatives in the House that, within three weeks, he "intended to bring on the subject of amendments to the Constitution." He stressed to lawmakers, particularly the Federalists, that his goal was to make the Constitution "as acceptable to the whole people of the United States as it had been acceptable to a majority of them." He also believed the two holdout states—North Carolina and Rhode Island—would be more inclined to ratify the Constitution and come into the union once amendments were added.

Madison drafted nineteen amendments to the Constitution, which he presented to Congress on June 8, 1789. The House reduced this number to seventeen and sent them along to the Senate. The Senate whittled the number to twelve and the House agreed. On September 25, the twelve approved amendments were sent to the states for ratification. The states rejected the first two: the original "first amendment" dealt with apportioning representation in the House of Representatives and would have made the size of the House unwieldy as the country's population increased; the second prevented members of Congress from voting to increase their own pay. Any pay hike passed by a particular Congress would not take effect until the next Congress was seated. (Ironically, this original second amendment was finally added to the Constitution 200 years later, in 1992, as the Twenty-seventh Amendment.)

THE TEN AMENDMENTS THAT we know today as the Bill of Rights were fully ratified on December 15, 1791, and they became part of the

Constitution. Like the Declaration of Independence and the Constitution before them, the ten amendments were engrossed, this time on a single parchment page by a congressional clerk, William Lambert. The Bill of Rights was signed by House Speaker Frederick Augustus Muhlenberg, and the president of the Senate, Vice President John Adams.

Together, the amendments form a bulwark on behalf of the people against government encroachment and overreach and are built upon the foundation of the Constitution by protecting what people then—and now—consider among their most precious liberties: freedom of speech, religion, assembly, the due process of law, the sovereignty of the state, and the power and sanctity of the individual.

None of the amendments grant powers to the people; rather, the citizenry was—and is—presumed to already possess the rights, powers, and privileges referred to in the amendments. The Bill of Rights enjoins the government from ever abridging or repealing these rights, and the manner in which they are written—not articulating what a citizen *can do* but what the government *cannot do*—reflects this principle.

In essence, the Bill of Rights was a furtherance of the "We the People" principle captured by Gouverneur Morris in his stirring preamble, and the "unalienable rights" to "life, liberty, and the pursuit of happiness" concept so boldly stated by Thomas Jefferson in the Declaration of Independence. Ironically, of course, it was the opponents of the Constitution, those who fought ratification unless a bill of rights was included, who ultimately forced Madison and the other Federalists to draft and approve the first ten amendments. Madison never would have campaigned for Congress on the promise of proposing amendments to the Constitution if Monroe had not pushed him during the pair's battle for election to the nation's first House of Representatives; the battle between the two future presidents for a congressional seat was just as surely a battle for the future of the Constitution.

Another irony: the Bill of Rights, omitted from the original document, initially opposed by the new government's strongest proponents and supported by its staunchest foes, is today—perhaps along with Morris's preamble—the most recognized and cherished portion of the entire Constitution.

The Bill of Rights did not come easily; ratification debates in the states were nearly as contentious and rancorous as the arguments over the Constitution. But Madison, who had drafted the bulk of the amendments, kept his word to also push them to passage, fighting the apathy of some, the diffidence of others, and the outright hostility of obstructionists. Without Madison, the Bill of Rights never would have become law: the father of the Constitution was also the father of the Bill of Rights, though on the latter, Madison's opponents forced his hand.

One other by-product occurred with the approval of the first ten amendments to the Constitution. When the two states that had not ratified the Constitution saw that the process had begun to incorporate a bill of rights, they finally came into the fold and joined the union: North Carolina ratified on November 21, 1789; and Rhode Island—which had stubbornly refused to even send delegates to the Constitutional Convention—voted to ratify by a narrow two-vote margin on May 29, 1790.

Even Patrick Henry, still not enamored with the Constitution or the strong central government as a whole, ended his active opposition.

Because of the Bill of Rights, there would be no need for a second convention. The Constitution was saved. On the amended document and the new republic that it governed, America's original thirteen states had finally spoken with one voice.

IN THE YEARS FOLLOWING its ratification, the engrossed copy of the United States Constitution remained in "custody and charge" of the State Department. Thomas Jefferson accepted his appointment as secretary of state on February 14, 1790, and on March 21, he arrived in New York to begin his tenure. He likely viewed firsthand the document he now called "unquestionably the wisest ever yet presented to men."

From that moment until the early 1920s, the original Constitution, usually stored in desk drawers and office cabinets, never passed out of the secretary of state's custody, was never put on exhibition, and suffered virtually no deterioration.

The travels of the State Department, however, kept the parchment sheets on the move. From 1790 to 1800 alone, they followed the department and the government through several offices in the new capital of Philadelphia; only from August to November of 1789 did the secretary of state's office leave Philadelphia—fleeing a devastating yellow fever epidemic—and relocate briefly to the statehouse in Trenton, New Jersey. In 1800, the federal district created from portions of Maryland and Virginia, and the federal city—Washington City, or Washington—became the permanent seat of the American government. On May 27, 1800, Jefferson described the letters and papers of his office as "being packed up for removal to the City of Washington."

When the Constitution parchments, the Declaration of Independence, and the other papers first arrived in Washington, carried by vessel to Lear's Wharf on the Potomac, they were placed first in the Treasury, the only building sufficiently completed to receive them. In late August 1800, they were moved to one of the "Seven Buildings" at Nineteenth Street and Pennsylvania Avenue, and in May 1801, the Constitution and the Declaration of Independence were relocated to the War Office, a large brick building on Seventeenth Street.

There, both documents would remain until 1814, when they—along with the new government they defined and emblemized, the capital city of Washington, and the fledging United States of America—faced the threat of permanent destruction.

On the day after Christmas 1941, three weeks after Pearl Harbor, Librarian of Congress Archibald MacLeish (center) and Assistant Librarian Verner Clapp, with help from a guard, seal and secure the original signed and engrossed Declaration of Independence in preparation for its relocation to a safe and secret location to protect it from a feared enemy attack on Washington, D.C. (*Library of Congress*)

In the spring of 1941, 700 Library of Congress staffers had volunteered more than 10,000 hours to identify, inventory, collect, and carefully pack nearly 5,000 boxes of irreplaceable documents, music, maps, rare books, and artifacts that would be moved to safe havens after Pearl Harbor. (*Library of Congress*)

Secret Service agent Harry E. Neal (left), who supervised the relocation of America's most important documents, insisted on accompanying them to Union Station on the night they left Washington. *(United States Secret Service)*

Agent Neil Shannon, who often guarded President Franklin D. Roosevelt, was among the agents who accompanied the Declaration of Independence, the Constitution, and the Gettysburg Address on the overnight train ride en route to their secret hiding place. *(United States Secret Service)*

In the days and weeks after the attack on Pearl Harbor, Washington, D.C., was in full-blown war mode, which included a blacked-out White House. *(Library of Congress)*

In a sign that times were indeed different, British Prime Minister Winston Churchill delivers his historic and unprecedented address to the United States Congress on December 26, 1941. *(Library of Congress)*

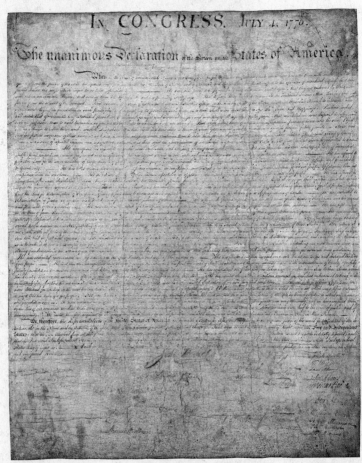

Among the country's most important documents moved out of Washington for safekeeping was the original—signed and engrossed (that is, inked in a calligraphic, flourishing style), albeit faded—Declaration of Independence, adopted on July 4, 1776, engrossed in the succeeding weeks, and signed by most delegates on August 2, 1776. *(National Archives)*

The original, engrossed United States Constitution was also relocated for safekeeping on December 26, 1941. In December 1952, after nearly two centuries of itinerancy—during which they were subject to deterioration and wear and tear, as well as heroic rescue efforts—both the Declaration and the Constitution were enshrined in the National Archives, where they remain today. *(National Archives)*

One of two original copies of the Gettysburg Address in Lincoln's hand, which
was moved to an impenetrable secret location on December 26, 1941;
the first page was written on White House stationery before the President
left for Gettysburg, and the second inked on a sheet of foolscap after he
arrived. The Library of Congress holds the original Gettysburg Address.
(*Library of Congress*)

ted to the great task remaining before us—
that, from these honored dead we take increased devotion to that cause for which
they here, gave the last full measure of devotion— that we here highly resolve these
dead shall not have died in vain; that
the nation, shall have a new birth of freedom, and that government of the people by
the people for the people, shall not perish from the earth.

The Library of Congress also relocated several "next tier" documents to several safe havens in early 1942. Among them were the so-called Dunlap Broadside version of the Declaration of Independence that was printed on the night of July 4, 1776 (left); and the "exact facsimile" of the signed, engrossed copy, replicated by William Stone over three years and unveiled on July 4, 1823—the version that established the Declaration's visual image for generations of Americans.

Also relocated were (opposite page), Pierre Charles L'Enfant's original layout of Washington, D.C.; Samuel Morse's first-ever telegraph message, transmitted in 1844, entitled "What Hath God Wrought?"; George Washington's October 1781 diary entries recording the British surrender at Yorktown; and (left) Queen Victoria's April 29, 1865, letter of condolence to Mary Todd Lincoln after President Abraham Lincoln's assassination. (*Library of Congress and National Archives*)

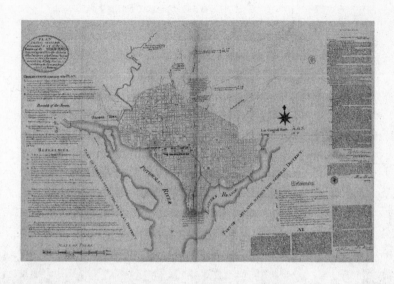

This Content was written from Washington by me at the Baltimore Terminals at 8 h 45 min on Sunday All A.M.

W h a t h a

Defensor — 1781.

of each of the Captured redoubts
were opened upon the enemy about
5 o'clock in the afternoon —

16th

About four o'clock this morning
the enemy made a Sortie upon our
Second parallel and spiked four
French pieces of artillery & two of
ours but the Guards of the Trenches
advancing quickly upon them they
retreated precipitately — The Sally being
made upon that part of the parallel
which was guarded by the French troops
they lost an Officer & 12 men killed and
Officer taken prisoner — The American
loss was one Serjeant [Artillery]

In 1817, in the midst of a patriotic revival in America, Congress commissioned artist John Trumbull to create four large paintings to commemorate the American Revolution; of these, the most important was his depiction of the signing of the Declaration of Independence.

At the nation's Centennial Exhibition in Philadelphia in 1876, Richard Henry Lee—grandson of the Virginia delegate who a century earlier offered the resolution for independence in the Continental Congress—read the original, engrossed copy of the Declaration of Independence to a crowd of thousands. Lee's reading was highlighted on the cover of Frank Leslie's "Illustrated" newspaper. (*Library of Congress and Architect of the Capitol*)

Painting above depicts Dolley Madison's efforts to save Gilbert Stuart's portrait of General George Washington as British regulars approached the White House during the invasion of Washington, D.C., in 1814. While President James Madison was in the field with American troops, Dolley also rescued her husband's voluminous notes from the Constitutional Convention of 1787, which virtually no American knew existed.

Hours after Dolley Madison's heroic actions (see above), the British burned much of the American capital, including the White House. (*The White House Historical Association*)

A pleased President Herbert Hoover watches workers lay the cornerstone for the National Archives on February 20, 1933. He dedicated it in the name of the people of the United States and said: "There will be aggregated here the most sacred documents of our history—the originals of the Declaration of Independence and the Constitution of the United States." It would be nearly two decades before the documents were finally enshrined in the National Archives in 1952. (*The National Archives and the Library of Congress*)

President Franklin D. Roosevelt prepares to address a crowd of more than 5,000 people at the dedication of the Jefferson Memorial on April 13, 1943, the 200th anniversary of Thomas Jefferson's birth. "Today, in the midst of a great war for freedom, we dedicate a shrine to freedom," he told audience members, who were required to purchase official tickets to attend the event.

To bolster national morale during the war, FDR ordered the original, engrossed Declaration of Independence removed from its secret storage location and displayed at the base of its author's new memorial for one week under heavy Marine guard. (*Library of Congress*)

Library of Congress executives view
Jefferson's rough draft of the Declaration
of Independence after it is returned from
hiding in September 1944. From left:
David Mearns, director of the reference
department, Librarian of Congress
Archibald MacLeish, and Verner Clapp,
director of acquisitions, anxiously examine
the document.

With a Marine guard looking
on, a family views the
original Bill of Rights
aboard the Freedom
Train, which criss-crossed
America for sixteen
remarkable months during
1947–49, carrying 127
of the most important
documents in American
history (though the
original Declaration and
Constitution were deemed
too irreplaceable to risk
travel). The train covered
37,000 miles and visited
326 communities in all 48
states at the time; along
the way, more than 3
million Americans waited
hours in line to view
documents.

Americans' interest in viewing and preserving the country's priceless documents has been a constant throughout our history. In 1951, photographers record a technician from the National Bureau of Standards encasing the Declaration of Independence in a helium-filled airtight case to prevent further deterioration. *(Library of Congress and National Institute of Standards and Technology Digital Archives)*

On Saturday morning, December 13, 1952, Pennsylvania Avenue in Washington, D.C., was the scene of spectacular pageantry as the original Declaration of Independence and United States Constitution were transferred under heavy guard from the Library of Congress to the National Archives. Twelve members of the Armed Forces Special Police carried the documents through a cordon of eighty-eight servicewomen.

Two days later, on December 15, 1952, Bill of Rights Day, President Harry Truman delivered the main address during the enshrinement ceremony, when the documents were placed on permanent display in the rotunda of the National Archives. (*National Archives*)

★ ★ ★

1941

★ ★ ★

12

★

"A Place
of Greater Safety"

★

December 26, 1941, Washington, D.C., Night

The train that Harry Neal watched depart from Union Station, accompanied by two of his finest agents, would chug overnight through the mostly rural and dark sections of West Virginia and southern Ohio and then skirt the sparsely populated border of southeastern Indiana and northwestern Kentucky, before completing its 675-mile journey in Louisville. There, it would be met by a team of Secret Service agents who would guard the document cases on the final leg of their journey to the United States' recently constructed gold bullion depository at Fort Knox, far from the coast and virtually impervious to bombing attacks.

Hundreds of trains had made the same trip, but none had ever carried what Archibald MacLeish characterized as "the documentary history of freedom in our world."

Aboard the train, sealed with precision, were the documents that MacLeish's assistant, Verner Clapp, had described in his memo to Harry Neal:

- Case 1: **Gutenberg Bible** (St. Blasius–St. Paul copy), 3 volumes
- Case 2: **Articles of Confederation** (original engrossed and signed copy), 1 roll
- Case 3: **Magna Carta** (Lincoln Cathedral copy), one parchment leaf in frame; **Lincoln's Second Inaugural Address** (original, autographed copy, 1 volume); **Lincoln's Gettysburg Address** (first and second autographed drafts, 1 volume)

Perhaps most important were the contents of the final container, the one MacLeish worried about most of all:

- Case 4: **Constitution of the United States** (original, engrossed and signed copy, five leaves); **Declaration of Independence** (original, engrossed and signed copy, 1 leaf)

In addition to the documents relating to the founding and preservation of the American republic, the Library of Congress had designated as "utterly irreplaceable" the Gutenberg Bible (printed in 1455) and the Lincoln Cathedral original copy of Britain's sacred Magna Carta (from 1215). MacLeish had informed the British ambassador that morning that the Library of Congress was moving the Magna Carta out of Washington "to a place of greater security in another part of the country." So intent was MacLeish on maintaining the total secrecy of the mission that no one at the British embassy knew where the Magna Carta, a document once called "the starting point of the constitutional history of the English race," was heading. Later, MacLeish would personally inform the British ambassador that the Magna Carta had reached Fort Knox, but he asked that the identity of the secret location be conveyed no further.

In fact, in a letter to the dean of Lincoln Cathedral in England, MacLeish said only that the church's copy of the Magna Carta was shipped from Washington "to a point farther inland on the continent."

*

WHILE HARRY NEAL AND Archibald MacLeish worked in secret to move the Charters of Freedom—as the Declaration of Independence and the Constitution had come to be called—a far more public event occurred on December 26, something that signaled to Americans that the war had changed their world: Britain's prime minister, Winston Churchill, delivered an unprecedented address to a joint session of the U.S. Congress.

While many senators and representatives had gone home for Christmas, both houses had surprisingly large delegations in attendance. The public was barred from the ceremony owing to limited seating.

Churchill, who had traveled to the United States to meet with President Roosevelt to discuss the "grand alliance" between the two English-speaking countries, already had addressed the American people from the White House on December 24. More than 20,000 Washingtonians had gathered, three weeks after Pearl Harbor, filling the lawn in the December twilight, to bear witness to a Christmas tradition on the most untraditional of Christmases. First, President Roosevelt lit the tree, reminding the pensive crowd that it was for our "sons and brothers, who serve in our armed forces on land and sea . . . who serve for us and endure for us—that we light our Christmas candles now across this continent from one coast to the other on this Christmas evening."

It was Churchill, addressing the crowd next, who captured the feeling of many in the United States when he said, "This is a strange Christmas Eve. Almost the whole world is locked in deadly struggle. . . . Here, in the midst of war, raging and soaring over all the lands and seas, creeping nearer to our hearts and our homes—here, amid the tumult, we have tonight the peace of the spirit in each cottage home and in each generous heart." Churchill urged his new allies: "Let the children have their night of fun and laughter. . . . Let us grown-ups share to the full in their unstinted pleasures before we turn again to the stern task and the formidable years that lie before us, resolved that by our sacrifice and daring, these same children shall not be robbed of their inheritance or denied their right to live in a free and decent world."

The prime minister's words had served as an inspiration to Americans, even as panic, uncertainty, and fear gripped families from coast to coast during the Christmas season of 1941. Every American's life had changed nearly three weeks earlier when the Japanese attack had catapulted the United States into World War II. On December 25, as families visited houses of worship and opened gifts at home, Americans everywhere wondered which of their sons, brothers, husbands, and fathers would not be around for Christmas the following year.

The Pearl Harbor attack triggered a wave of new feelings across the country. The day before, December 6, 1941, Americans viewed the war as a distant event playing out across the Atlantic in Europe or across the Pacific in Asia. Isolationist sentiments ran deep across the country. After Pearl Harbor, however, these feelings dissipated overnight. Thousands of men enlisted within days of the attack. In a mere three weeks since December 7, Americans—now on a war footing—had been introduced to price controls, rationing, censorship, bond drives, scrap-metal drives, rubber drives, and air-raid drills. It was as though a switch had been thrown and the country's pre–Pearl Harbor collective mind-set had vanished forever. Now, Americans viewed the situation as perilous.

Fears of a German or Japanese attack—or sabotage—on Washington, D.C., consumed the public, military strategists, and political leaders.

INSIDE THE CAPITOL BUILDING on December 26, Winston Churchill tapped into this new reality when he addressed the Congress. The air was electric when he stepped to the podium amidst a gaggle of microphones from CBS, NBC, and other broadcast networks. The fiery British prime minister, who could trace his heritage on his mother's side "through five generations from a lieutenant who served in George Washington's army," felt confident and "quite at home . . . more sure of myself than I had sometimes been in the House of Commons." Churchill viewed the U.S.–British relationship as an "all-conquering alliance," and his family's roots in America steeled him with a "blood-right to speak to the representatives of the great Republic in our common cause."

As for the Japanese, their assumption that an unprovoked attack on an American navy base would lessen American and British resolve was miscalculated.

"What sort of people do they think we are? Is it possible that they do not realize that we shall never cease to persevere against them until they have been taught a lesson which they and the world will never forget?" he asked, receiving thunderous applause from the American Congress. In Washington, he had found an "Olympian fortitude," he said, which was the "mark of an inflexible purpose and the proof of a sure, well-grounded confidence in the final outcome."

Churchill concluded by promising that "in the days to come, the British and American people will . . . walk together in majesty, in justice, and in peace." As he finished, he received a rousing standing ovation and the noise became deafening as Churchill flashed the V for victory sign while exiting the Senate chamber.

It was fitting that on that same day Archibald MacLeish and Harry Neal huddled with their teams to finalize plans to protect the historical documents that symbolized the "great republic" of which Churchill spoke.

LATER ON THIS BUSY December 26 in Washington, British and American senior military officers—including Sir Dudley Pound, Britain's admiral of the fleet; Field Marshal Sir John Dill; Admiral Ernest King, commander in chief of the U.S. Fleet; and General George C. Marshall, the U.S. Army's chief of staff—held a strategy session at the Federal Reserve Building, their first face-to-face gathering since the United States entered the war. The Chiefs of Staff Conference, as it was called, then moved to the White House to brief Roosevelt, Churchill, and senior civilian advisers. The White House session focused on general conditions in various theaters of the war and the best use of American resources in the short term: assisting in an invasion of

North Africa, relieving British troops in Iceland and Northern Ireland, the dire situations in Singapore and other areas of Southeast Asia, the arrival of German U-boats off the East Coast of the United States.

After the formal meeting—at about the time MacLeish and Harry Neal were preparing to remove the Declaration of Independence and the Constitution from the Library of Congress—FDR, Churchill, and their senior advisers had tea at the White House, followed by dinner. To relieve some of the pressure of the long day, FDR ordered a movie shown after dinner: *The Maltese Falcon,* starring Humphrey Bogart.

Shortly after, Churchill retired to his room to work on a speech he was scheduled to deliver to the Canadian Parliament before the New Year recess. As he attempted to open a window, he became "short of breath. I had a dull pain over my heart. It went down my left arm." Then the discomfort abated and he went to bed. The next morning Churchill talked with his physician, Dr. Charles Wilson, and said: "It didn't last very long, but it has never happened before. What is it? Is my heart all right?"

Wilson did not reveal his visit to treat Churchill until twenty-four years later, shortly after Churchill's death at the age of ninety, when the doctor's diary was published. In 1941, he informed the prime minister: "Your circulation is a bit sluggish." Later, in his diary, Wilson revealed that Churchill had survived an angina attack. "I did not like it, but I determined to tell no one," the doctor wrote. Ordering bed rest for Churchill was impractical considering the current state of war, nor did Wilson believe there was any sound medical reason to do so. "You needn't rest in the sense of lying up," he told Churchill during his exam, "but you mustn't do more than you can help in the way of exertion for a little while."

HOURS AFTER WILSON LEFT Churchill, on Saturday afternoon, December 27, 1941, one day after the Declaration of Independence, the Constitution, and the Gettysburg Address left Washington, Harry Neal waited until the Library of Congress documents reached Fort Knox and then typed a long report marked "Secret" to Secret Service chief Frank J. Wilson.

It was an extraordinary recap of his most intriguing forty-eight hours.

The mission Neal would remember for the rest of his life began with a Christmas Day meeting with Wilson and Assistant Chief Joseph E. Murphy, where Neal was informed that he would meet with MacLeish the following day to arrange for the transfer of "priceless historical documents" from the Library of Congress to Fort Knox, "because of the possibility that in Washington they might be destroyed or damaged in the event of air raids by the enemy." Because Neal's presence in Washington was deemed critical, agents Daniel Moriarty and Neil Shannon would accompany the documents to Kentucky; both were assigned to the Washington field office for special duty.

On December 26, Neal huddled with MacLeish and Verner Clapp, and requested a description of the contents of the cases. A simple understanding was reached: the Secret Service would assume responsibility for the shipment until its delivery into the Fort Knox vaults, at which point, Clapp—who would also travel to Kentucky—would be given a receipt for the packages. "I requested Mr. MacLeish to have each package carefully sealed," Neal reported. Then, for security reasons, "at the suggestion of Agent Shannon, I asked that each be then wrapped in plain wrapping paper, tied with cord, and not be marked in any way." MacLeish complied, ordering the documents first sealed in a specially prepared locked bronze container that had been heated for six hours to a temperature of about 90 degrees to "drive off any moisture." The container was then embedded in mineral wool and placed in a large wooden case, secured with screws, wires, and padlocks on each side, then sealed with lead.

His meeting with the librarians completed, Neal then went about making security arrangements and planning logistics for the rest of the day: driving three different routes between the Library of Congress and

Union Station to determine traffic patterns and identify potential sites for an ambush; arranging for an armored truck and two armored guards from the Bureau of Engraving and Printing to convey and escort the documents; designating a contingent of armed agents to quietly accompany the baggage cart from the Union Station storage room directly to the train; and confirming that a second cadre of armed agents would meet the train upon its arrival in Louisville to take custody of the cargo and transfer it to Fort Knox.

At 5:15 p.m., as the late-afternoon gloom enshrouded Washington, Neal met MacLeish and Clapp at the Library of Congress Annex, at which point "four wrapped packages were loaded onto the armored truck" bound for Union Station, separated from the Library of Congress by expanses of greenery and rows of trees. The truck made its way through a Washington that was thronged with men in uniform, military vehicles, and civilian workers who had flooded the city to staff the bureaucracies of wartime agencies. Military police guarded government buildings and gun emplacements lined the rooftops. Motivational posters (LOOSE TALK IS DANGEROUS IN WARTIME and BUY WAR BONDS) adorned lampposts and tavern windows.

An hour later, agents quietly removed the packages from the baggage room at Union Station and boarded the National Limited, led by Neal, who inspected the car, and placed the packages into Compartment B in Car A-1. All of this was done with utmost discretion and without attracting the attention of the uneasy crowds that flooded Union Station. After reviewing the next phase of the plan with his agents and Clapp, Neal left the train, which departed Union Station at 6:47 p.m.

Neal had little left to do but wait. He resigned himself to a long and pensive night.

THE TRAIN HAD RUMBLED inland overnight without incident, and the Baltimore & Ohio Limited arrived in Louisville at 9:50 a.m. the next morning, where—as Harry Neal described in his memo—it was met by Secret Service agents, including supervisor Alonzo A. Andrews, who accompanied the packages by armored car the forty-five miles to Fort Knox. Harry Neal had already arranged with the director of the U.S. Mint to set the time lock on the massive twenty-two-ton door protecting the gold vault to open shortly after 10:00 a.m. The intricate time-locking mechanism required several people to reset it.

R. J. Van Horne, the clerk in charge of the U.S. Bullion Depository, provided Agent Andrews with a receipt that read:

> Receipt is acknowledged of four (4) sealed cases bearing marks identifying them as the property of the Library of Congress and numbered respectively from one (1) to four (4). In accordance with arrangements previously made, these cases have been deposited in the space assigned to the Library of Congress in the U.S. Bullion Depository, Fort Knox, Kentucky, and will be held subject to withdrawal upon order of the Librarian of Congress.

Van Horne made no mention of the contents of the packages—no mention of the original Declaration of Independence, Constitution, or Gettysburg Address—because he did not know what was inside.

Aside from the president of the United States, the secretary of the Treasury, the chief of the Secret Service, the librarian of Congress and his top aides, Harry Neal, and a cadre of hand-picked agents, no one else knew either.

OF ALL THE POTENTIAL secret storage locations, Fort Knox was most appropriate for the Charters of Freedom, both for the practical purposes of security and suitability and for symbolic historic reasons that linked the Kentucky fort with the Declaration and the Constitution.

Completed in December 1936, the Treasury Department's bullion depository was a fortress of steel, concrete, marble, and granite, as well as the sentries, soldiers, systems, and security procedures that made it one of the world's most impenetrable storage facilities. The United States had constructed it as a protected inland central depository for its burgeoning gold supply; expansion of other mints was considered either too costly or impractical because of space limitations. The exterior of the two-story building measured 105 feet long, 121 feet wide, and 42 feet high. The outer wall of the depository was constructed of 16,500 cubic feet of granite lined with 4,200 cubic yards of concrete, and strengthened by 750 tons of reinforcing steel and nearly 700 tons of structural steel. Within the building was a two-level steel and concrete vault divided into four compartments; its casing was constructed of steel plates, I beams, and cylinders laced with hoop bands and encased in concrete. No one person was entrusted with the combination to the vault door, which weighed more than twenty tons.

Four guard boxes connected to the four corners of the building and sentry boxes guarded the entrance gate. Soldiers from the nearby army post could provide additional protection if needed. The depository was equipped with its own electric and water supplies.

The United States began transferring billions in gold bars to the Treasury Department's new depository in January 1937, and the government was very public about the shipments. While exact shipment schedules and routes were kept secret, U.S. officials informed the press when gold arrived at Fort Knox and even when it left other mints. The FDR administration conveyed the clear message, in the midst of a Depression, that the U.S. monetary system rested solidly on a gold standard and that the gold was in the safest possible location. "It is the greatest treasure of all time," noted an article in *Popular Mechanics*, "the strongest, best guarded, least expensive, most sensible strongbox owned by any nation." The *Literary Digest* called the new depository "a memorial to the gold standard and an emblem of managed money." One publication noted that any potential invaders would have to "fight their way across the Appalachians" to reach the fort and when they arrived, they would still face an impregnable obstacle. Other articles reported on the fort's bombproof roof, hinted at booby traps, and even mentioned an emergency flooding system that had been installed at the depository; whether all the accounts were true or simply rumors intended to solidify the image of Fort Knox as a fortress, the Treasury Department seemed content to allow the stories to stand. Even Henry Morgenthau answered a reporter in a cryptic way when he was asked why Fort Knox had been selected as the site for the new depository, hinting that there were security reasons that went well beyond what the Treasury Department had made public: "We thought Fort Knox would be a safe place," he said. "You know what I mean—*safe*."

More than $200 million in gold bars arrived by train on January 13 from the Philadelphia mint. They were then offloaded by derrick into enormous trucks, which lumbered to the depository, all under the watchful eyes of soldiers armed with sidearms and submachine guns. Another shipment valued at more than $120 million—about 120 tons— moved out of New York's financial district on January 18 under heavy police escort. By June 1937, the end of the first wave of gold bullion relocations, some $4 billion in bars had been moved to Fort Knox, all of it "guarded more carefully than royal potentates," according to one news account. And by the end of 1941—at about the time the Library of Congress transferred its documents—the Fort Knox depository was filled with nearly 650 million ounces of gold, close to $23 billion, the peak level of holdings in its history.

There was little doubt that the U.S. Bullion Depository would provide the safety that befitted the Library of Congress documents. Bombers were unlikely to reach that far inland without being stopped, and even if they did, the underground vault itself was considered virtually impervious to any known Axis bomb. The vault's superior construction and the depository's location on an army base would make sabotage next to impossible.

Safety and security were the primary reasons Fort Knox made sense for the Library of Congress documents. But the historic symbolism of the location was also striking. That the fort was named for Henry Knox, the revolutionary general, trusted friend, and confidant of George Washington, gave it a direct connection to the Declaration of

Independence and the Constitution. Knox's daring mission to transport sixty cannon from Fort Ticonderoga to Boston in 1776 helped make the very notion of a Declaration of Independence thinkable. Eleven years later, of course, Henry Knox convinced George Washington to attend the Constitutional Convention, arguing that Washington's prestige would bring enough cachet to the gathering to increase its chances of success.

It is quite possible that without the efforts of Henry Knox, the Declaration of Independence and the Constitution of the United States would not exist. Now, in one of history's fateful moments, the fort that bore his name would provide their protection from possible enemy attack.

THE LIBRARY OF CONGRESS was not the only institution to protect its precious collections after Pearl Harbor. At a December 29 meeting— just two days after the train carrying the documents arrived at Fort Knox—the National Gallery of Art trustees authorized the staff to evacuate nearly 80 pieces of art, prepare 130 additional pieces for evacuation in case of air raids, and implement protective measures for the building.

On New Year's Day of 1942, staff members accompanied works by Botticelli, Raphael, Titian, Donatello, Goya, Rembrandt, and many others to Biltmore House in North Carolina, whose storage areas were controlled for temperature and humidity. In March 1942, the State Department asked the National Gallery to also assume custody of more than 150 paintings from the Louvre, other French museums, and private collections that had been sent to the United States in 1940 as part of a traveling exhibition; French officials considered it unsafe for the works to be returned to Europe, since they would likely fall into Nazi hands. Paintings loaned by the Belgian government were also retained in the United States for safekeeping.

Elsewhere, the U.S. National Museum found space for its artifacts in Shenandoah National Park near Luray, Virginia. The National Archives evacuated its nitrate and acetate film to Fort Hunt, Virginia, and also arranged to occupy space at the Illinois State Archives in Springfield if further evacuations were necessary. The New York Public Library examined caves in upstate New York, where one official found "ice on the ceiling and dripping water," and a mine in Dover, New Jersey, as possible storage places, before evacuating $20 million worth of rare holdings to local bank safes and a stalwart building in Saratoga. The director of Boston's Museum of Fine Arts reported that museum directors across Massachusetts were buying sandbags, microfilming their materials, and purchasing packing materials in preparation for relocating their collections. And the Houston Public Library relocated the majority of its newspaper holdings to the bomb-resistant quarters of the San Jacinto Monument.

Just as fear of attack was palpable across the United States, concern ran deep about damage and destruction to America's priceless documents and artistic treasures.

IN A DECEMBER 30 NOTE, MacLeish thanked Henry Morgenthau for the Secret Service's help in relocating the library's documents to Fort Knox—though he did not mention the location, referring to it only as "a place of greater safety." He admitted that the responsibility of relocating the documents had weighed heavily on him for many months, but "never as heavily as on the night when the shipment left the Library of Congress." He complimented the Secret Service's professionalism—the care they provided was "conscientious" and "intelligent" and "scrupulous"—particularly with the stakes so high. "I suppose it is quite literally true that no shipment of a value even remotely approaching the value of this shipment was ever made in this country," he wrote to Morgenthau.

It was not the first time that the threat of war had forced the relocation of America's most important documents from the nation's capital.

★ ★ ★

1814

★ ★ ★

13

☆

"Take the Best
Care of the Books
and Papers . . ."

☆

Monday, August 22, 1814

Secretary of State James Monroe had seen enough and knew what was coming next. The only question was whether it was too late for him or anyone else to stop it.

For nearly three days, accompanied by a contingent of twenty-five cavalrymen and with the blessings of the president, James Madison, Monroe had scouted the Maryland countryside on horseback, seeking to determine the strength of the British force that had come ashore at Benedict and the number of enemy ships that had entered Chesapeake Bay. More than two years after the United States had declared war against Great Britain, the enemy was bearing down on the nation's capital.

Initially, Monroe sought to survey the scene from atop a hill nearly three miles from Benedict; from there he could see British ships in the Patuxent River. But lacking a spyglass, he could not get an accurate count from that distance. "We shall take better views in the course of the evening, and should any thing be seen, material, I will advise you of it," he had written to Madison a day earlier. He felt compelled to share with Madison the rumors and conjecture that were swirling: that the British were "still debarking their troops, the number of which I have not obtained any satisfactory information of," and, "that Washington is their object." But at that point, Monroe, who was an experienced military man and Madison's eyes and ears in the field, would not engage in speculation, willing only to say, "of this I can form no opinion at this time."

The situation changed quickly the next day. Monroe received word that an American artillery unit, transporting cannon on barges, had slipped further upstream, and "that it is probable that a [British] force by land and water had been sent against the flotilla." In response, Monroe directed his men toward Nottingham, about fifteen miles upstream, where the American cannon were sheltered. Horseback riding was hard, hot, and dusty. The late-August Maryland heat and humidity were stifling—it was the hottest summer in memory. Monroe's small group arrived in Nottingham before the British, and at first, Monroe spotted only a moderate number of British barges transporting troops. "The enemy are now within four hundred yards of the shore," he wrote in a note to Brigadier General William Winder. "There are but three barges at hand and the force in view is not considerable. If you send five or six hundred men, if you could not save the town, you may, perhaps, cut off their retreat."

Before he could complete his note, Monroe realized his mistake—he had spoken too soon and vastly underestimated the size of the British flotilla. "P.S.," he scribbled, "ten or twelve more barges in view. There are but two muskets in town and a few scattering militia."

And then, by five o'clock that afternoon, Monroe added: "Thirty or forty barges are in view."

The British were landing in huge numbers and marching into Nottingham virtually unopposed.

*

IF JAMES MONROE HAD been his adversary in 1787 and 1788 over the Bill of Rights, President Madison had come to appreciate his secretary of state's considerable talents. He was, in fact, the ideal person to handle the reconnaissance Madison needed so desperately.

After the fight over the Constitution, the two Virginians had patched up their relations and become close friends. At six feet tall, Monroe towered over the diminutive president, and some observers had taken to calling them "Big Jim" and "Little Jim." Monroe, age fifty-six, brought a wealth of experience in politics and the military. After losing the election to Madison to sit in the first national House of Representatives, the current secretary of state had served as a U.S. senator, as governor of Virginia, twice as a minister to France—including under President Jefferson to negotiate the Louisiana Purchase—and as an envoy to both Britain and Spain. Monroe had distinguished himself in the Revolutionary War, fighting in several important battles, including Trenton, Monmouth, and Brandywine. He had crossed the Delaware with Washington, and at the Battle of Trenton he suffered a near fatal wound to his shoulder when he was struck by a cannonball.

Madison appreciated Monroe's considerable overseas experience and diplomatic skills, which was why he selected him as secretary of state in 1811. During the current crisis, however, it was Monroe's military background—and his knowledge of the British—that earned Madison's confidence.

With such a deep background, Monroe knew exactly what information Madison needed, both for military and political reasons, and how and when to report it. The president had received a great deal of criticism for involving the United States in this latest war, and both Madison and Monroe were well aware that the young country entered the conflict woefully undermanned and underprepared. Now more than ever, the president and the country needed accurate intelligence; hence Monroe's initial caution in his early dispatches.

By this morning, though, caution and hesitation were no longer options. Monroe estimated that 6,000 British troops had landed and they were encountering limited resistance from, at most, 2,200 disorganized and inexperienced American soldiers. There was now no doubt about the destination of the invading force; Monroe could now verify that the conjecture had been accurate, though Madison's own secretary of war had scoffed at the rumors for weeks. "The enemy are in full march for Washington," Monroe wrote in a dispatch to President Madison. "Have the materials prepared to destroy the bridges."

In yet another postscript he added: "You had better remove the records."

James Monroe arguably contributed as much as anyone to the founding of America and the development of the early republic. And perhaps because of all he did as soldier, senator, secretary of state, and president, few people know of this six-word postscript—of his crucial role in preserving America's founding documents.

THE WAR OF 1812, a conflict that some historians call the second war for American independence, started officially when President James Madison signed the declaration of war against England on June 18, 1812. But tensions between the two countries had been simmering for years.

From the U.S. perspective, Americans had resented British condescension almost from the beginning of the nineteenth century, expressed in the years leading up to the war by seizing U.S. sailors and forcing them to serve in the British Navy—known as "impressments"—and encouraging Indian tribes to attack settlers in the American interior. In his request to Congress for the declaration of war, Madison objected to the "crying enormity" of impressment; the "avidity of British cruisers" as they harassed American ships in American territorial waters, and recent blockades by the British that violated the "neutral rights of the United States." Such actions, Madison said, resulted in a "spectacle of injuries and indignities which have been heaped on our country." James Monroe, during his tenure in England, had tried unsuccessfully to convince the British to cease impressments.

Madison also cited the role of Great Britain in "the warfare just renewed by the savages" in the Northwest Territory, blaming English provocateurs for Indian unrest. Matters came to a head when William Henry Harrison, governor of the Indiana Territory, called for the further expansion of white settlements and had been opposed mainly by Tecumseh, a Shawnee chief. Federal troops pushed the Indians back at a bloody battle on the Tippecanoe River in November 1811, but the Shawnee and other tribes continued attacks on white settlements. Senator Andrew Jackson of Tennessee decried the Indian violence, exclaiming that the "blood of murdered heroes must be revenged." There was little doubt, he added, that "this Hostile band, which must be excited to war by the secret agents of Great Britain, must be destroyed."

From the British point of view, the War of 1812 began as almost an annoyance and was a direct result of England's total war against Napoleon and the French Empire, its most detested and powerful rival. Britain had established numerous economic blockades to defeat France and was furious when American merchant ships—citing neutrality—attempted to breach the blockade and deliver merchandise. The British introduced new laws—Orders in Council—to block the trading between the United States and France and used the laws to carry out impressment against American sailors. The United States was further caught in the Anglo-French crossfire when France announced that it would seize any British cargo found on American ships, retaliatory action that the United States blamed squarely on British aggression on the high seas. Napoleon seemed intent on provoking a war between the United States and England to ease the pressure on his own forces. Even though the French Navy had seized many American ships, Napoleon promised to cease the high-seas action if the United States imposed trade restrictions against the British. Thomas Jefferson wrote of the United States: "Never since the battle of Lexington have I seen the country in such a state of exasperation."

With every transgression that Americans perceived as bullying from Old World powers, U.S. defiance heightened, no place more than in the halls of Congress. Bold young lawmakers from the west and south, such as Henry Clay of Kentucky and John C. Calhoun of South

Carolina, not only inspired other members with their oratorical skills; they also infused Congress with a sense of "impetuous nationalism," in the words of historian Anthony Pitch. They had been born after the Declaration of Independence and raised in a free and sovereign nation. "What was tolerable for older Americans would be insufferable for the young war hawks," Pitch wrote. "War . . . was the only honorable course for a people claiming to be free and independent."

Not everyone agreed. Many Americans, especially from the New England states, believed war would be madness, that fighting the British would result in devastating seaport blockades that would cripple maritime economies. Their fears would be realized: by 1814, the U.S. economy had collapsed, and while nationalism and anti-British sentiments remained strong, opponents of the war blamed Madison for the country's economic woes.

IN SHEER GEOGRAPHICAL SCOPE, the War of 1812 covered thousands of square miles, engulfing land and sea, from Canada—once in the war, the British goal was to prevent the United States from taking any part of Canada—to the Gulf of Mexico, from the Great Lakes to the Potomac, from Detroit and other western outposts to Washington. The participants in the struggle included some of American history's legendary names and its next generation of presidents: Dolley and James Madison, Monroe, Tecumseh, Andrew Jackson, William Henry Harrison, and Zachary Taylor. The U.S. Navy came of age during this war, and the country's East Coast–centered economic and demographic power shifted westward.

The war also featured some of the greatest battles in American history, including the September 1814 British bombardment of Fort McHenry in Baltimore Harbor that inspired an emotional Francis Scott Key to write "The Star-Spangled Banner." Just a few months later, Major General Andrew Jackson would launch a spectacular and decisive victory at the Battle of New Orleans, thwarting a British effort to capture the city and separate Louisiana from the rest of the United States.

No event, however, angered Americans and steeled their resolve more than the devastating British attack on Washington in August 1814. Starting on August 24, British troops set fire to much of the city, including the White House and the Capitol building, forcing President Madison and his wife, Dolley, to flee, and instilling fear in Washington residents that the republic itself was in jeopardy.

WHEN WAR BROKE OUT, Madison—our first wartime American president—faced the daunting task of battling a powerful Royal Navy and British regulars who were seeking to avenge England's defeat in the American Revolution and destroy the fledging nation just a few decades into its existence.

In early 1813, American forces invaded the British territory of Canada and won a major battle at York—present-day Toronto. After winning the battle, and in retaliation for an explosion ignited by retreating British troops, U.S. troops plundered the city, looting tea, sugar, whiskey, and other goods and torching several buildings, including the provincial parliament building—along with the records housed there—a courthouse, a library, and the governor's residence. What was a major military victory for the Americans was marred by the looting and burning.

The British didn't forget.

By 1814, England had won several key battles against Napoleon (the French emperor would face his ultimate defeat in June 1815 at Waterloo). As a result, thousands of British soldiers were freed up and redeployed against the United States.

The British move against the American capital would be the ultimate revenge for York, though it surprised many in the American command structure. Madison had received an anonymous letter from an American sympathizer aboard a British ship warning him that English troops planned to lay waste to Washington. Calling himself "A friend to the United States of America," the seaman, who claimed he had been captured by the enemy and "compelled against his will to fight" onboard a British vessel, warned that "your enemy have in agitation an attack on the Capital of the United States." The British intended to land their men, move quickly to Washington, "batter it down and then return to their vessels immediately." They planned to employ upwards of 7,000 men in the attack. The letter writer implored Madison to take his warning seriously. "You had better be prepared for such an event," he said. "Do not repose under a too fallacious belief of security; for by so doing, you may fall into the hands of your enemy."

The president found the anonymous warning credible—and indeed, it would prove to be remarkable for the accuracy with which it outlined the British plans. He turned it over to Brigadier General William H. Winder, who commanded the military district that included Washington and Maryland. But most of Madison's military strategists gave the letter minimal credence and employed only cursory precautions to protect Washington. Most in the military command structure saw little in the way of strategic importance in the bleak, swampy city. The secretary of war, John Armstrong, was adamant in his refusal to believe that Washington was at risk. "They certainly will not come here!" he declared in a letter to the head of the District of Columbia militia. "What the devil will they do here? No! No! Baltimore is the place, Sir. That is of so much more consequence." Nearly blinded by his stubbornness, Armstrong seems never to have considered the symbolic importance of the nation's capital.

But the British certainly did. Baltimore—with its thriving port and providing a gateway to Washington and the interior—*was* on England's target list, but so was Washington, which the British viewed as the most valuable of symbolic prizes. The British commander in chief of the North American station, Admiral Sir Alexander Cochrane, believed an attack on the U.S. capital would give the Americans "a complete drubbing." Such a gambit would do far more than avenge the American excesses at York. If British troops could capture and occupy the city, it would embarrass the United States; if they could imprison President Madison in chains, it would humiliate all Americans; and if they could destroy America's most precious governing documents, the nation of laws would be perceived as impotent.

The experiment would be over. Chaos and anarchy would reign and the young country would be brought to its knees—perhaps to disintegrate entirely, perhaps forever.

NOW, ON AUGUST 22 AND 23, Washingtonians scrambled frantically to flee the nation's capital ahead of the impending arrival of the British. Word had spread quickly that the largely unprotected city was the next target of enemy troops fast-marching from Maryland. Residents loaded their belongings on carts and wagons, saddled horses, or simply escaped town on foot over hot, dusty dirt roads, leaving their belongings to be collected by slaves or abandoning them altogether. The pandemonium soon resulted in clogged egress roads from Washington; many other refugees poured into the wooded countryside, preferring to take their chances in the wild rather than risk encountering enemy troops on the roads.

House clerk J. T. Frost, desperate to save important papers, ordered three messengers to scour the countryside looking for wagons to serve as transport. But they were too late—most of the carts and wagons had already been procured and most were piled up with personal belongings. Frost's messengers returned with a single cart and four oxen, apparently purchased from a man who lived several miles outside of Washington. They loaded many House papers into the cart and drove nearly ten miles from Washington, but still they were frustrated. Frost believed he could have saved all the House documents, and even the volumes in the Library of Congress, if only he had a sufficient number of wagons.

Senate clerks John McDonald and Lewis Machen also acted quickly in the midst of what Machen called "doubt, confusion, and dismay" all around them. They were able to get their hands on a single wagon by threatening the owner with impoundment if he did not turn it over voluntarily. McDonald and Machen then loaded the most important Senate documents onto the wagon, including what Machen said later was the only copy of the Senate's quarter-century of executive history and secret positions and troop strengths of all American military forces. One broken wagon wheel later, followed by an accident in which their transport overturned, the two men made their way safely to Montgomery County, Maryland, out of the path of the advancing British. More than twenty years later, when recalling the swift decision to relocate the Senate documents without a directive from a superior, Machen pondered the consequences of inaction: "What would have been the feelings of every intelligent individual . . . had the Executive History of the Senate for a period of twenty-five years been blotted forever from the knowledge and memory of man?"

The House and Senate documents that the clerks were able to save were valuable to Congress and to America's national record to that point.

But it was State Department senior office clerk Stephen Pleasonton, resisting protests from a cabinet official who believed the British threat to Washington was exaggerated, who led the effort to evacuate documents far more critical to America's past, present, and future.

WHEN A MOUNTED SCOUT arrived at the secretary of state's office with Monroe's warning about the impending British arrival, Pleasonton sprang into action. The rider advised him and the other department clerks "to take the best care of the books and papers of the office which might be in our power." Monroe wanted the nation's precious national documents and records secured quickly.

Pleasonton, who had worked as a government clerk in Washington since the capital city was organized in 1800, wasted little time. He and a few of his fellow clerks hurried out to purchase coarse linen fabric, which they cut up and fashioned into large bags. Into the makeshift sacks they stuffed the founding documents: the original signed and engrossed copies of the Declaration of Independence and the Constitution, the Articles of Confederation, the papers of the Continental Congress—including the still unpublished secret journals—international treaties, and the correspondence of George Washington, including his famous letter resigning his commission at the end of the Revolutionary War.

As they worked in a passageway between the War Department and the State Department, John Armstrong, the secretary of war, passed them on the way to his office; still in denial about the danger of the situation, he scolded Pleasonton and the other clerks for raising "unnecessary alarm." In Pleasonton's words, "he did not think the British were serious in their intentions of coming to Washington." Undeterred, Pleasonton, a mere clerk, stood his ground against the cabinet official. "I replied that we were under a different belief, and let them [the British] be what they might, it was the part of prudence to preserve the valuable papers of the Revolutionary Government," he recalled years after the fact.

When the bags containing the documents were loaded onto carts, Pleasonton and the clerks crossed the Potomac by the Chain Bridge and stopped at an abandoned Virginia grist mill about two miles "above Georgetown," where they unloaded the wagons and hid the papers. But Pleasonton had second thoughts the next morning when he realized the mill was close to a large foundry that manufactured cannon and shot, and would almost certainly be targeted by the British. Not only could an explosion and conflagration at the foundry possibly spread to the mill and consume the documents, but "some evil disposed person"—a traitor or spy—could lead the British to the hiding place. Finding such treasures together in one group would exceed the enemy's wildest expectations.

On the morning of August 24—the date the British would arrive in Washington—Pleasonton reloaded the precious cargo and set out again, visiting several farmhouses in the Virginia countryside to procure wagons. This time, he drove the teams thirty-five miles inland to Leesburg, where, according to his account, he found an empty house. Inside he "safely placed" the bags of documents, "locked the door," and turned the keys over to the "Rev. Mr. Littlejohn," one of the collectors of internal revenue—essentially the country sheriff. Pleasonton and Littlejohn then parted ways, leaving the Declaration of Independence, the Constitution, and the other irreplaceable American documents stored in a small abandoned farmhouse in Virginia, while every American in the area awaited Washington's fate.

Wearied by his efforts, Pleasonton checked into a nearby inn on the evening of August 24 and went to bed early.

14

★

"Such Destruction —
Such Confusion . . ."

★

Thursday, August 25, 1814

The next evening, shivering and exhausted, the president's wife
pounded on the wooden door of a tavern, seeking refuge in an establishment whose angry occupants had denied her entrance just an hour
earlier. They were angry because they blamed President Madison for
thrusting the United States into the war with England; with him absent, Dolley became the target of their ire. Twilight had arrived and
with it the resumption of the furious thunderstorms and hurricane-
force winds that had raged all day and turned the dusty roadways into
barely passable mud-clogged swamps. Dolley Payne Madison and her
companions, drenched, needed food and a warm fire.

Dolley had traveled sixteen miles from Washington in the miserable weather, fleeing just ahead of the rumored onslaught of British
soldiers. She'd faced harrowing danger over the past two days. With
enemy troops advancing on Washington, she had remained at the White
House as long as she could, desperate for James to return from the front
lines so they could seek safe harbor together. The president had left
three days earlier on horseback to join American militiamen marching

to confront British soldiers who longed to capture Madison and destroy the White House. James and Dolley both believed the president's presence would steel the resolve of the American troops. Before his departure, James had chosen this tavern as a meeting place if Dolley were forced to evacuate the president's house before his return.

Although James had penned an initial letter to her two days earlier, declaring that American troops were "in high spirits & make a good appearance," the situation deteriorated rapidly. She received two additional dispatches from James by messenger, each written in pencil; the second she found "alarming, because he desires I should be ready at a moment's warning to enter my carriage and leave the city; that the enemy seemed stronger than had been reported and that it might happen that they would reach the city, with intention to destroy it."

She had acted swiftly after that, filling trunks with cabinet papers and other government documents, including her husband's voluminous notes from the Constitutional Convention of 1787, which virtually no American knew existed. She decided that all the trunks should fit into a single carriage and thus made the decision to sacrifice their personal property. Late Tuesday night, she vowed to remain in the White House until James returned and could accompany her. She feared for his safety, not just from British soldiers but from disgruntled Americans angry about the war with the British and now the humiliating invasion of Washington. "I hear of much hostility towards him," Dolley had written in a letter to her sister. "Disaffection stalks around us."

With the exception of her steward, John Pierre Sioussat, or "French John," and a few other White House servants and staff members, Dolley was alone in the White House Tuesday night. "My friends and acquaintances are all gone," she wrote, and even a contingent of 100 troops left behind to guard her and the house had fled.

At dawn on Wednesday, August 24, 1814, she climbed to the roof of the White House and began looking through her spyglass in every direction, "watching with unwearied anxiety" and searching for James and his fellow riders. To her dismay, she saw instead scores of disorganized American troops, "wandering in all directions, as if there was a lack of arms, or of spirit to fight for their own firesides!" By three o'clock that afternoon, she heard the roar of cannon from the nearby battle, and still, she recounted, "Mr. Madison comes not; may God protect him." Two dust-covered messengers arrived and begged Dolley to leave, but again she refused, holding out hope that James would return. She oversaw the loading of the wagon with the documents, state silver, and other White House valuables, and sent it on its way to the Bank of Maryland. "Whether it will reach its destination . . . or fall into the hands of British soldiery, events must determine," she wrote.

Finally, a close family friend, Major Charles Carroll, arrived and announced that the situation had become too perilous for Dolley to remain at the White House; reluctantly, she acquiesced to his insistence that she vacate the premises. "I must leave this house, or the retreating army will make me a prisoner in it, by filling up the road I am directed to take," she wrote. It was bad enough for the country's psyche that the chief executive's house was imperiled by British troops, but Dolley realized the far more deleterious symbolic impact that the president's captured wife—the woman who would eventually provide the nation with the term "First Lady"—would have on the American will to fight.

She undertook one final task before rushing to the carriage, annoying Carroll with her delays. She ordered servants to remove and secure the full-length Gilbert Stuart portrait of General George Washington from the wall. She would not leave it to be mocked and desecrated by the enemy—not Washington, the greatest American hero of all. When it became apparent that unscrewing the large frame would be too time-consuming, Dolley ordered the frame broken and the canvas removed. At about this time, two more friends arrived at the White House to offer help, and Dolley entrusted the painting to them, urging them to conceal it from the British at all costs; they would transport the portrait by wagon across the Potomac to safety.

With her final task completed, Dolley and her small group finally left the White House. French John locked the house and deposited the key with the Russian ambassador, whose nearby house was protected from destruction by his country's flag.

"When I shall again write to you, or where I shall be tomorrow, I cannot tell!" Dolley had written to her sister.

James Madison would serve as president for another two and a half years, but never again would the Madisons live in the White House.

THE BAND OF MORE than 150 jubilant and rowdy British soldiers found the White House unguarded. Ever thorough, they ransacked the house from cellar to attic, smashing windows and piling furniture in the center of various rooms. Outside, they methodically soaked rags in oil, draped them on poles, set them alight, and proceeded to throw them through the openings where windows had once been. Within minutes, the White House was consumed in flames and the night sky was aglow with smoky orange light. "I shall never forget the destructive majesty of the flames as the torches were applied to the beds, curtains, etc.," reported Captain Harry Smith, junior adjutant to Major General Robert Ross. "Our sailors were artists at the work." What was artistry to the British was horrifying to Washingtonians. Resident Margaret Bayard Smith, describing the White House as being "wrapt in flames and smoke," related her reaction and that of her companions: "The spectators stood in awful silence, the city was light and the heavens redden'd with the blaze!"

Within hours, the president's house was a gutted ruin, the walls "still white except for great licks of soot that scarred the sockets that had been windows." An architect's report later despaired that the White House had "suffered immensely, particularly in the superstructure of the external walls," and predicted that "any means taken to prevent this Building from receiving further injury by the weather, would be ultimately useless." British soldiers also spotted an abandoned coach outside the White House. "The soldiers amused themselves by knocking this coach to pieces with the but-ends [sic] of their muskets," noted a report by one British lieutenant. Another soldier took President Madison's "fine dress sword" from the White House.

But the British didn't stop there. They moved next to the twin buildings of the Capitol—the Senate to the north and the House to the south. The central part of the Capitol was not built; the two wings were linked by a covered hundred-foot-long wooden walkway. British troops lit bonfires inside the Capitol, fueled by piles of furniture and gunpowder, which destroyed artwork and burned so intensely that more than one hundred panes of plate glass skylights melted and the outer stone columns fell off the building. The Library of Congress—and its more than 3,000 volumes of rare books—was consumed by fire.

To add to the fiery spectacle, the Americans had set ablaze their own nearby navy yard to prevent the British from capturing it—the secretary of the navy would later report this order "was not issued without serious deliberation and great pain"—and in the process had destroyed ships and ignited vast ammunition stores, sending flames roaring high into the night sky. "It would be difficult to conceive of a finer spectacle than that which presented itself," noted Lieutenant G. R. Gleig, who was with the British forces at the nearby Battle of Bladensburg. "The sky was brilliantly illuminated by the different conflagrations; and a dark red light was thrown upon the road, sufficient to permit each man to view distinctly his comrade's face."

THE FOLLOWING DAY, AS Dolley and her bedraggled entourage ventured through the countryside toward the tavern, with the hope of rendezvousing with the president, the British continued their destruction, burning the Treasury building, the structure that housed the State and War departments, and several other public buildings.

Then, as if by providence, torrential rains and fierce winds roared through Washington and the surrounding area; one report called it "the most tremendous hurricane ever remembered by the inhabitants." Roofs of houses were torn away and "carried up into the air like sheets of paper, while the rain which accompanied it was like the rushing of a mighty cataract rather than the dropping of a shower." The raging winds destroyed other buildings, burying civilian inhabitants and American soldiers beneath the ruins. In the midst of the chaos, a powder magazine exploded, killing nearly a hundred British soldiers. Mercifully, the disaster and the severe weather caused most of the redcoats to retreat from Washington and regroup.

Occupants of the tavern finally admitted Dolley, and that night she watched lightning crackle against a black sky, split trees in the distance, and illuminate the faces of her exhausted companions. After hours of anxious waiting, Dolley saw President Madison and his friends ride up on horseback; the sixty-three-year-old president had been in the saddle for the better part of four days. Marveling at her husband's stamina, Dolley urged him to sleep. As midnight approached, a breathless courier arrived and warned the tavern occupants that a contingent of enemy soldiers had discovered a clue to the president's hiding place and were on their way to capture him. The Americans relocated Madison to a miserable hovel deep in the woods behind the tavern, where, with the storm still exploding around him, as "the boughs moaned and sobbed," he spent the remainder of the night. All the while confined to his cramped and cold shed, the president of the United States expected "at any moment, to hear the tread of the British soldiers as they passed, or perhaps halted and searched for the coveted prisoner."

AFTER DAYBREAK, WORD REACHED the tavern that the British had evacuated Washington, and James Madison returned to the capital, insisting that Dolley remain in Virginia until the city was safe. On August 28, she rejoined her husband and visited the charred White House. Smoke still rose from the ashes and the blackened timber and walls; a despondent Dolley, "sick at heart," was forced to turn away from the painful sight. For several days, friends reported that she was tearful and morose. When her friend visited her, she found Dolley "much depressed. She could scarcely speak without tears."

President Madison was not faring much better. As he toured Washington, inspecting the devastation, he not only saw a White House in ruins but a devastated Capitol building—particularly the House of Representatives—punctuated by the collapse of the magnificent domed roof into the cellar, where it lay smoldering from the searing fire. In addition, homes around the government buildings had been looted and destroyed, and the carcasses of dead horses were strewn around the city. Madison would later condemn the British troops for the wanton destruction and their failure to spare "those monuments of the arts and models of taste with which our country had enriched and embellished its infant metropolis." For now, though, one witness described the president as "miserably shattered and woebegone. In short, he looks heartbroken."

Months later, Dolley Madison wrote of her return to Washington: "I cannot tell you what I felt on re-entering [the city]—such destruction—such confusion. The [British] fleet full in view and in the act of robbing Alexandria!"

But because of her quick thinking and resourcefulness, Dolley had rescued one particularly priceless document, her husband's still unpublished notes from the Constitutional Convention, a gift that she would one day place "before Congress and the World."

Like the Declaration of Independence and the Constitution, the only surviving written account of the highly secretive Constitutional Convention was safe for now.

DESPITE THE BRITISH EVACUATION of Washington after the storm, Americans were not celebrating. Rumors were spreading that the enemy was preparing for a second invasion to finish what they had started—to reduce the city to rubble. For now, Stephen Pleasonton—who returned to Washington on August 26—and James Monroe decided they would keep the Declaration of Independence, the Constitution, and the other important state papers hidden in the Virginia farmhouse.

The documents would remain there for three weeks, returning to Washington only when the British fleet finally departed the waters of the Chesapeake after the Battle of Baltimore in mid-September. In the interim, Pleasonton made several trips to Leesburg to sift through the linen sacks and find "particular papers to which the Secretary of State had occasion to refer in the course of his correspondence." With its capital burned, with its most important governing documents stored in an abandoned farmhouse, the business of the United States carried on.

Stephen Pleasonton would one day go on to become superintendent of lighthouses, a position he would hold for more than thirty years. Without a doubt, though, Pleasonton's most valuable contribution to the United States was his almost single-handed rescue and subsequent protection of the original engrossed copies of the Declaration of Independence and the Constitution. His initial decision to save these documents, his defiance of Secretary Armstrong's rebuke, his quick thinking to remove the documents from Washington and then to relocate them to the abandoned farmhouse in Leesburg—these stand as his immemorial legacy of the preservation of America's heritage.

In one way, at least, Pleasonton's patriotic actions were not surprising; indeed, such resourcefulness and honor ran in his family. Pleasonton was the grandnephew of Delaware's Caesar Rodney, whose grueling midnight ride nearly forty years earlier, in the face of great physical peril, allowed him to cast the crucial vote in favor of American independence on July 2, 1776.

THE DESTRUCTION OF WASHINGTON left physical, emotional, and symbolic scars on the young nation. As one historian described it, America, "proud of its bold beginnings, had been humbled, and a profound vision would be required to lead the nation back from the abyss." Washington residents were furious, at the British, yes, but also with Madison initially, and later with Secretary Armstrong. Monroe termed the anger "a tempest of dissatisfaction at the late events here, [which] rages with great fever." Margaret Bayard Smith described the scene in the nation's capital as "gloomy" and added: "I do not suppose Government will ever return to Washington."

But the devastation wrought by the British on Washington also galvanized the citizens of the young country. By September of 1814, more than 15,000 volunteers marched into Baltimore to repel the British, while Fort McHenry withstood bombardment from the enemy flotilla. Francis Scott Key, a Georgetown lawyer, observed the battle from a British hostage ship in Baltimore harbor; the "rockets' red glare" and the "bombs bursting in air" inspired Key to write the lines to "The Star-Spangled Banner," which would become America's national anthem.

In the fall of 1814, Congress crowded into one of the few surviving public buildings, the Patent Office (now the National Museum of American Art), and debated whether the capital should be moved someplace else, perhaps inland, to a location "with greater security and less inconvenience." One New York congressman suggested it be moved closer to Wall Street so government could be nearer its creditors. New Englanders also wanted the capital relocated. Those who favored relocation not only sought a place that could be more easily defended; they believed suitable accommodations already existed that would save the country untold dollars in renovations and rebuilding. Congressmen who supported remaining in Washington argued on more defiant symbolic grounds. "I would rather sit under canvas in the city than remove one mile out of it to a palace," declared Samuel Farrow of South Carolina. Or, as Nathaniel Macon of North Carolina warned: "If the seat of government is once set on wheels, there is no saying where it will stop."

In the end, by a narrow vote, the emotional and steadfast arguments against moving won the day. Congress voted that the U.S. capital would remain in Washington. After the Treaty of Ghent ended the war in early 1815, rebuilding began in earnest. As part of the restoration effort, Congress agreed to an offer from Thomas Jefferson to purchase the former president's extensive library collection to replace the volumes destroyed in the 1814 fire; Jefferson's volumes would form the core holdings of the new Library of Congress. Across its landscape, Washington rose from the ashes, and the most visible symbol of national unity and resilience—the restored White House—made its public debut on New Year's Day in 1818. Its first occupant would be the new president, James Monroe, who, as secretary of state, had issued the warning to secure the nation's records as the British approached Washington.

With its second war for independence over and its capital rebuilt, with its government intact and its most important national records and documents preserved, America faced the early nineteenth century with a newfound sense of purpose, pride, and respect for its accumulated sacrifice and its stirring four decades of history.

★ ★ ★

1942

★ ★ ★

★

15

"The Library
of Congress
Goes to War"

★

At the end of January 1942, with the nation and the Library of Congress on full war footing, Archibald MacLeish dispatched the keeper of collections, Alvin Kremer, on another long road trip.

A month earlier, the library had begun transferring the first of its 5,000 boxes to the university repositories—staff members loading large moving vans and panel trucks, mostly at night and in the early-morning hours, braving freezing cold and winter storms to remove the library's documents, books, maps, and artifacts to safety. MacLeish expected the entire process to take until May. It was becoming clear quickly, however, that the three locations Kremer had secured the previous spring would not contain sufficient space for the entire inventory of items scheduled for transfer. Plus, MacLeish and his staff members worried that the library's collection was concentrated in too few locations and in the same state; one or more additional storage locations had to be found.

To this point, the relocation process had gone relatively smoothly, with one scare. After arriving at Washington and Lee University with the second and third truckload of the collection, an assistant librarian at the school casually mentioned to Library of Congress staffer Edward Waters that one of the local newspapers in Lexington, Virginia, wanted to do a story on the transfer. Sensing potential danger, Waters "deemed it advisable to talk with the young lady."

The young lady in question was Guy Nelson Forrester, managing editor of the *Rockbridge County News* in Lexington, a respected journalist with a master's degree from the Columbia School of Journalism in New York City. As Waters later told MacLeish, "I found Miss Forrester to be a very intelligent person, naturally anxious to secure a good story, but sympathetic to our point of view."

Forrester told Waters that the arrival of the library materials in Lexington "was perhaps the biggest event in the history of the town." She also pointed out that as soon as the first truck had opened its doors, the stenciled legend on every box—PROPERTY OF THE LIBRARY OF CONGRESS—had "proclaimed the news to the town at large." Finally, there was word-of-mouth and gossip that had—or would—potentially spread the news. "The two trucks I accompanied south were unloaded by about a dozen Negroes of the college janitorial staff in addition to several white men," Waters stated. Forrester concluded, rightly or wrongly, that the "sisters, wives, and sweethearts of the Negroes were employed in many homes in Lexington and that they would promptly spread the news as rapidly, perhaps less accurately, than a newspaper account."

Nonetheless, Forrester agreed to refrain from publishing until Waters could supply her with an official statement from the library.

Waters urged MacLeish to agree to Forrester's request. "I believe that a sober unvarnished account of the Library's evacuation efforts would be of value both to us and to the residents of Lexington," he said. "It is no more than a Declaration of our awareness of responsibility and an expression of confidence in the chosen repository." Waters acknowledged that it would be wise to be "entirely non-committal" about the types of materials arriving from Washington, "so that no one could essay a guess regarding the contents of every single box." Such a compromise would demonstrate the library's willingness to be informative "without being indiscreet." A well-written story would make the residents of Lexington *properly* aware of the treasures in their midst."

MacLeish received Waters's letter on January 8, and not only was he unconvinced by his arguments—he was stunned and furious that Waters had even considered sharing information with a journalist. MacLeish had stressed repeatedly to his staff the need for utmost secrecy; there could be no room for leaks where the nation's irreplaceable documents were concerned. Contrary to Waters's desire, the last thing MacLeish wanted was for residents of Lexington to be aware of the treasures in their midst; the entire Library of Congress relocation plan was predicated on secrecy. Townspeople and workers who saw the Library of Congress boxes being unloaded might very well wonder what their contents contained. Perhaps that could not be helped because of logistical limitations; but that was a far cry from revealing the secret relocation project to a journalist

The very next day, MacLeish phoned Forrester, declined her request, and asked her to keep secret the Library of Congress work in Lexington.

No story ever appeared.

ALVIN KREMER AND HIS assistants set out on January 29 in search of one or more additional locations, their ten-day automobile odyssey this time taking them to thirty-four locations in Virginia, North Carolina, South Carolina, Georgia, Tennessee, Kentucky, and Ohio.

The search for storage locations had specific parameters. "Chief factors [we] considered were distance from areas of strategic significance, freedom from danger of damage by floods, freedom from likelihood of excessive atmospheric humidity, or pollution by noxious smokes or gases," Kremer reported. The additional locations also had to have fireproof construction, proper ventilation, sufficient capacity, accessibility, and an absence of "plumbing pipes or fixtures from which steam or water might escape." In his lengthy February 11 report to MacLeish, Kremer detailed his visits and reasons for his recommendations, though he acknowledged that the number of places visited and their scattered locations made it difficult to gather "more than fundamental and essential facts concerning storage conditions."

Still, he was able to dismiss several potential facilities. Roanoke College in Salem, Virginia, for example, offered a private and fireproof gymnasium building basement, but the room was adjacent to a swimming pool, "which could possibly be a source of humid atmosphere unless controlled by guard." The Veterans Administration Hospital in Oteen, North Carolina, had "exposed pipes overhead," a potential disaster for the documents if one burst. Clemson's Agricultural College offered a possible location, but its basement was "unfloored" and a new concrete floor would cost $872, Kremer noted. The Library would have to consider the cost and the time to install flooring. The library at Bowling Green College in Kentucky was well-ventilated and dry, "but some signs of termites had recently been observed in the corners of one of the rooms." College officials were planning to call in an exterminator, but time was of the essence for Kremer and Mac-Leish. Both men were mindful of an assessment from the Committee on Conservation of Cultural Resources that "those areas of the continental United States within roughly 100 miles of any coast or border [would be] exposed to attacks." Indeed, the report continued, such attacks on large coastal cities and other prominent military objectives near the coast "are *likely* to occur."

In the end, Kremer and MacLeish decided on one additional suitable location: Denison University in Granville, Ohio, about 400 miles from Washington.

Ultimately, more than 1,200 boxes—about 25 percent of the total number relocated—were moved to Denison. Included in these treasures were Samuel Morse's first telegraph paper-tape recording of his historic "What hath God wrought?" message, transmitted on May 24, 1844; two Stradivarius violins that had been donated by private collector Gertrude Clarke Whittall in 1935; and perhaps most valuable of all, George Washington's diaries and other papers, including the entries that recorded the British surrender at Yorktown in 1781, "their Drums in front beating a slow march, Their colours furl'd and Cased," as the defeated enemy troops marched through a gauntlet of American and French troops. In Washington's eyes, "the sight was too pleasing to an American to admit description."

THE PRECAUTIONS TAKEN BY the Library of Congress and other repositories were based on credible intelligence and military events suggesting that an attack on the American mainland, and particularly on Washington, was not only a distinct possibility but a likely one. Unlike several of James Madison's advisers in 1814, Roosevelt and his administration took them seriously in 1942.

Adolf Hitler had long expressed a desire for Germany to develop long-range bombers and rockets that could reach North America from Europe or from U-boats in the Atlantic. After Germany had conquered and occupied Denmark, Americans feared that the Danish territory of Greenland—located a few hundred miles from northern portions of Canada and perhaps 2,000 miles from New York City—might also be used as a staging and refueling area for German and Italian bombers. In April 1941, the United States occupied Greenland to defend it against a possible invasion by Germany.

For his part, President Roosevelt was well aware of the potential for an attack on the United States. At a February 1942 press conference, while the Library of Congress was searching for additional storage locations, Roosevelt told the nation that the enemy "can come in and shell New York tomorrow night, under certain conditions. They can probably . . . drop bombs on Detroit tomorrow night under certain conditions." During the first six months of 1942, German U-boats crept perilously close to the East Coast of the United States, and, with impunity, sank more than 600 merchant ships, many as horrified coastal residents looked on. Roosevelt and his advisers worried about German saboteurs reaching North American shores after being dropped off by

U-boats. (Indeed, this did happen in June. Their efforts were thwarted by law enforcement; they were captured and imprisoned, and several were executed.) The Japanese floated balloon bombs over the West Coast. Japanese ships shelled the coast near Santa Barbara in February and Fort Stevens, Oregon, in June; some damage occurred but there were no casualties. Japanese troops did take two islands in the Aleutians, the only actual occupation of American soil in World War II. Meanwhile, the Germans were working furiously to mount bombing raids against the U.S. East Coast, particularly against war factories and larger ports.

American fears of attack and saboteurs on U.S. soil reached their peak during the first few months of 1942. From strengthening the country's intelligence-gathering operation, to air-raid drills at all hours, to rooftop patrols to watch for overhead bombers—American cities, including Washington, D.C., were on full war footing.

MACLEISH AND THE Library of Congress also swung into action.

In June 1940 MacLeish had wept when a colleague informed him that the Nazis had marched into Paris, goose-stepping their way down the Champs-Elysées, and it infuriated him that even now—even after, "in country after country, it was the intellectuals, the artists, the writers, the scholars who were searched out first" by the Nazis "or left to rot in concentration camps"—even now, some of his fellow writers and intellectuals still clung to the fiction that "the world of art and learning was a world apart from the revolution of our time."

MacLeish ignored them. In addition to relocating America's documents, the Library of Congress, under MacLeish's leadership, played a critical role in the war efforts—from providing military planners with extensive world maps; to staffing FDR's Office of Facts and Figures (OFF) and, later, the Office of War Information (OWI); to answering questions from reporters, diplomats, and members of the military; to leading the efforts of the CCCR, whose mission was to protect and preserve irreplaceable documents, paintings, photographs, and other "essentials of culture" in the United States.

"The Library of Congress goes to war," was the theme of many press and academic accounts in late 1941 and throughout 1942.

Even as the critical documents were being trucked away from the library, MacLeish and his team created an air defense collection that included course outlines for air wardens as well as handbooks on fire-fighting, poison gas, first aid, and protection of buildings. Along with libraries across the United States, the Library of Congress also established war information and civil defense reference services to assist the military and civilians who had questions. "What is the formula for blackout paint for windows?" one curious patron asked the Cleveland Public Library. Many libraries also became air-raid shelters. Dozens of academic libraries followed suit, creating special collections of war information. For example, the University of North Carolina's library became a busy conduit for civil defense information for the entire state, mailing out kits of civil defense materials on a daily basis in 1942.

All of these efforts were front-of-the-house activities in plain view of the general public each and every day. Behind the scenes, MacLeish and his staff assisted the country's early intelligence networks by collaborating with the Office of Strategic Services (OSS). With MacLeish's blessings, more than fifty Library of Congress staff members became spies when they went to work for William "Wild Bill" Donovan, the first OSS director, a story largely untold as part of World War II history. These Library of Congress personnel, many of them scholars, served in OSS's research and analysis section and analyzed intelligence reports from overseas to determine Axis strengths and vulnerabilities.

MacLeish also recruited several leading East Coast academics to serve in the OSS section and helped organize them into a unit that eventually gave OSS its renown as a "brain bureau." Donovan recruited the president of Williams College, Dr. James Phinney Baxter, to head the bureau, and he quickly built a staff of historians, geographers, political scientists, and economists to analyze a steady stream of vital intelligence throughout the war. MacLeish would write in 1945 that the role the library played in the area of military intelligence was "a matter of public interest, but limited public knowledge."

Thus, Archibald MacLeish not only led the effort to safeguard America's important historical documents, but he converted the machinery of the Library of Congress to meet the information demands of the war effort in no less a fashion than American factories transformed themselves to meet the industrial and production demands of war. He believed libraries, academics, writers, and thinkers had a duty to resist fascism and to promote the virtues of American democracy.

It was for this reason, along with his disdain of Nazism, that MacLeish had been President Roosevelt's selection for the librarian's job in the first place.

BY EARLY MAY, ALL of the thousands of boxes that had been stacked in the Library of Congress basement had been moved. In the end, more than 1,000 boxes were shipped to the University of Virginia, more than 1,300 to Washington and Lee University, nearly 1,400 to the Virginia Military Institute, and nearly 1,200 to Denison. Subsequently, officials decided that unexpected dampness at VMI could damage the documents, so they relocated the boxes at VMI to Washington and Lee. Another 800 storage cases were moved to higher floor levels at Denison "because of the threat from possible humidity-laden atmosphere."

In the three final locations—Denison, the University of Virginia, and Washington and Lee University—four guards monitored the documents day and night, prepared daily reports, and took regular atmospheric readings of each storage area using instruments provided by the library. Alvin Kremer said the library received "unlimited cooperation" from authorities at the repositories, and from "many other officials at other institutions covered in surveys for national repositories." Librarians at the repositories regularly reviewed reports prepared by the guards "and have frequently written to inform us of certain matters deserving our attention."

Kremer also marveled that "during days of actual shipment of materials, officials at one repository used to remain up until early morning hours for no other reason than to offer hospitality to our weary convoyees; in most cases storage was not undertaken until daylight."

Archibald MacLeish wrote that the relocation of documents was "the most extensive, laborious, and significant series of operations . . . perhaps in the Library's history." He reported that the collections had been examined "piece by piece," and that "dummies were ready to be placed on the shelves in place of the items" removed. One historian would later call the effort "Herculean" and the relocation of documents "unprecedented in American library history."

And, of course, MacLeish wrote that "suitable depositories had been located and secured" for the library's documents. He added: "To these custodians—who cannot of course be named now—the Library is very deeply indebted for the facilities thus granted."

By housing the priceless documents, these university libraries had donned the mantle as stewards of American democracy.

★ ★ ★

1826–1860

★ ★ ★

16

★

"I Had Flattered Myself
That He Would
Survive the Summer"

★

July 9, 1826

After making a note in his diary of the 4:39 a.m. sunrise, President John Quincy Adams wasted no time departing the White House. By 5:00 a.m., he was gripping the reins and directing the four-horse team that pulled his private carriage, accompanied only by his twenty-three-year-old son, John II (named after his famous grandfather). The previous day had been the hottest of the summer, and the Adams men were hoping to make headway on their long journey northward while a light easterly breeze cooled the early morning.

The president had decided only a day earlier to leave Washington, so he'd been forced to make preparations quickly. He'd sent his servant ahead separately, laden with heavy storage trunks to load onto a stagecoach, believing he and his son could travel more rapidly in the horse-drawn carriage. The impetus for his haste occurred with the arrival of the White House mail on July 8: John Quincy had received three letters from family members in Massachusetts informing him that his father, John Adams, was nearing death. The venerable former president and signer of the Declaration of Independence, just a few months shy of his ninety-first birthday, was "rapidly sinking," according to John Quincy's brother Thomas. His doctor thought Adams would "probably not survive two days, and certainly not more than a fortnight," in the words of John Quincy's niece Susan Clark. The elder Adams had "suffered much." The situation was so dire that the president's family had sent an express for John Quincy's eldest son, George, who was in Boston at the time, with the hopes that he would arrive in nearby Quincy "in time to receive his [grandfather's] last breath."

The news from Boston left John Quincy Adams shaken. On the night of July 8, he "was up, in anxiety and apprehension, till near midnight. The suddenness of the notice of my father's danger was quite unexpected." Indeed, his brother had written weeks earlier informing John Quincy that their father's health was declining, "though not so as to occasion immediate alarm." The president had planned a visit in August. "I had flattered myself that he would survive this summer, and even other years," he confided to his diary.

It was a time of much emotion for President John Quincy Adams. He had learned two days earlier that Thomas Jefferson had died on July 4, fifty years to the day that the Declaration of Independence had been adopted by the Continental Congress in Philadelphia. John Quincy's relationship with the Declaration's author was mixed and had changed with time. As a young man, Adams declared Jefferson "a man of great judgment" on political matters. When the Adams and Jefferson families would visit each other, Thomas Jefferson took an interest in John Quincy's educational progress; the two talked about books, school, philosophy and other topics. Later, though, and especially during the contentious presidential contest between John Quincy's father and Thomas Jefferson in 1800, the relationship between the two families had frayed. As Jefferson and the senior John Adams aged, the two had resumed correspondence, and their relationship had become more cordial, if not overly friendly. John Quincy and the rest of the Adams family had adopted a similar outlook in their relationships with Jefferson.

John Quincy Adams's secretary of war had brought word on July 6 that at midday on the Fourth of July, while Americans across the country were celebrating the Jubilee to mark fifty years of independence, Jefferson had passed at Monticello at the age of eighty-two. His time of death—around 1:00 p.m. on July 4, 1826—came on the same day and at roughly the same time that the Declaration had been adopted a half century earlier. That the Declaration's primary author had expired on the document's fiftieth anniversary was "a strange and very striking coincidence," John Quincy Adams noted in his diary.

As he departed Washington on the morning of July 9, the president, literally, didn't know the half of it.

PRESIDENT ADAMS AND JOHN II stopped for a half-hour refreshment break between 7:00 and 8:00 a.m., and reached Merrill's Tavern in Waterloo, Maryland, at approximately 11:00 a.m. It was then that proprietor John A. Merrill, who had visited Baltimore earlier that morning, interrupted their breakfast to deliver bad news. He'd received word by messenger from Massachusetts that the president's father had died on July 4 at about six o'clock in the afternoon.

Later, a family friend would write to the president that at the moment of John Adams's death, a violent thunderstorm that had shaken the house subsided, the rain stopped, and the early evening sun emerged, "bursting forth . . . with uncommon splendor at the moment of his exit . . . with a sky beautiful and grand beyond description." Now, at Merrill's Tavern, John Quincy Adams wrestled with his emotions. "From the letters which I had yesterday received, this event was so much expected by me that it had no sudden and violent effect on my feelings." He adopted a philosophical tone, noting that "my father had nearly closed the ninety-first year of his life—a life illustrious in the annals of his country and of the world. He had served to great and useful purpose his nation, his age, and his God." John Quincy could only hope that he "may live the remnant of my days in a manner worthy of him from whom I came."

That both his father and Thomas Jefferson, the leading proponents of American independence, had perished on the fiftieth anniversary of the Declaration's adoption struck John Quincy Adams not as mere coincidence but as "visible and palpable marks of Divine favor, for which I would humble myself in grateful and silent adoration before the Ruler of the Universe." The date's special meaning extended even further for the president: his son, John II, who sat beside him in his carriage as they trekked northward, had been born on July 4, 1803, assuring that future independence days would conjure a wide range of emotions for John Quincy. Later he would call the July 4, 1826, departures of the two former presidents and signers of the Declaration of Independence a dual event that was "unparalleled in the history of the world."

As details emerged about the last days and moments of Thomas Jefferson and John Adams, the nation would interpret their deaths in the same manner.

IN THE FIFTY YEARS since the adoption of the Declaration of Independence, the nation had undergone monumental change—its size, population, and advancements in technology, transportation, and international clout would have made it barely recognizable to those who helped found it in 1776.

The nation's population had quadrupled in fifty years and now approached 12 million people residing in twenty-four states, two of which lay beyond the Mississippi River. Thomas Jefferson's audacious Louisiana Purchase in 1803 had doubled the nation's territory, and John Quincy Adams's successful efforts while secretary of state to establish joint occupation of the Oregon Territory with the British meant that, in one capacity or another, America actually stretched from sea to sea.

Concurrently, Americans were inventing ways to overcome these vast distances. The 365-mile Erie Canal, which reduced from three weeks to eight days the length of time it took to haul goods from New York City to Buffalo, opened up boat traffic from the Atlantic Ocean to the Great Lakes and the great Northwest. Built over eight years by tens of thousands of workers, the canal had been dedicated in the fall of 1825, and by July 1826, one publication boasted that "three or four hundred boats" now passed through the booming city of Utica every week; in addition, more than 100 canal projects were under way across the country. And Gridley Bryant of Scituate, Massachusetts, had started work in April 1826 on the nation's first commercial railroad, which he designed to transport huge granite blocks from a quarry in Quincy, Massachusetts, to the Neponset River just a few miles away. The blocks would be needed to erect the Bunker Hill Monument in Charlestown, which Bryant had the contract to build and whose cornerstone had been laid in June 1825. Bryant, whose railroad design was met with ridicule by many and skepticism by many more, had ushered in a powerful transportation force that would reshape America over the next century and beyond. Seeing the potential for passenger travel, Baltimore journalist Hezekiah Niles wrote in May 1826: "A person may now breakfast with his family in Baltimore, or Philadelphia, and take tea with his neighbor in Philadelphia or New York, respectively."

In his 1825 annual message to Congress, President John Quincy Adams announced that in the preceding two years, more than a thousand new post offices had been established in the United States. He also called for a system of federal roads and canals, a national university and observatory, an expedition to explore the Northwest, and the creation of a Department of the Interior. He urged Congress to approve big ideas and projects that would benefit the people, and not to turn its back on "the bounties of Providence and doom ourselves to perpetual inferiority."

Internationally, the United States supported Latin American peoples in their efforts to achieve independence, and recognized in 1822 the republics of Mexico, Colombia, Chile, and Peru. President James Monroe's doctrine of December 1823 declared that any intervention by a European power in the Western Hemisphere could be viewed only "as the manifestation of an unfriendly disposition to the United States."

In the midst of this national transformation, Americans would finally take stock of their heritage and history in the decade following the War of 1812, after years of overlooking or ignoring both.

AMERICA'S LACK OF INTEREST in its history had troubled the aging founders.

In 1815, Thomas Jefferson had asked in a letter to John Adams: "On the subject of the history of the American revolution, you ask who shall write it? Who can write it? And who will ever be able to write it?"

In Jefferson's view, records alone were insufficient to capture the spirit and depth of the behind-closed-doors discussions and debates that led to independence. He believed that for years the country had neglected those who could have enriched the nation's heritage with colorful first-person stories. "These, which are the life and soul of history, must forever be unknown," he lamented, except to those who were present. The nation was running out of time—Jefferson, Adams, and Charles Carroll of Maryland were the last remaining signers of the Declaration of Independence, and all three were over seventy; Adams was eighty. John Adams worried as early as January 1817 that his country had forgotten its historical precedents: "I see no disposition to celebrate or remember, or even Curiosity to enquire into the Characters, Actions, or Events of the Revolution."

Indeed, as the *North American Review* of 1826 explained it, the founders themselves had little time to reflect on their history because they were so busy making it. After the Revolutionary War, "the whole country was miserably exhausted by the exertions and sufferings incident to the arduous struggle, and all became engaged . . . in repairing their wasted fortunes." The revolutionists faced other daunting challenges, including the creation of a new government, threats from European nations that hoped to intimidate the new republic, internal party squabbles as the United States established its domestic footing, and finally, of course, the War of 1812 and the brazen British invasion and burning of Washington.

For those reasons, the magazine pointed out, "we are not to look at the early years of our national progress . . . for any very intense interest in the history of the revolution."

However, with the near destruction of Washington fresh in their minds, Americans experienced an upwelling of national pride, a decade-long reawakening of the achievements of the revolutionary generation. After the Treaty of Ghent ended the War of 1812, Americans were ready for "the principles, causes, events, and characters of the revolutions" to claim "their just share of public attention." As John Adams and Thomas Jefferson grew older, the new generation paid greater heed to their bequests to America. In the ten-year period leading up to the 1826 Jubilee, Americans took stock of their contemporary status and tied their accomplishments, successes, and good fortune to the achievements and the sacrifices of the revolutionary generation—the founders and the framers. It was as though their successful efforts to turn aside the British for a second time established for Americans their permanent place in the world; and the near destruction of Washington reminded them of the blessings of freedom and liberty that they might have taken for granted and come so close to losing.

This attitude was manifested most prominently in American feelings toward the Declaration of Independence and other revolutionary era records, as well as to the men who had created them, the founding generation, those who had risked everything—their lives, their fortunes, their sacred honor—to bring forth a new nation.

SHORTLY AFTER JOHN ADAMS expressed his disappointment in 1817 that Americans had lost touch with their history, Congress commissioned artist John Trumbull to create four large paintings to commemorate the American Revolution; the paintings would hang in the rotunda of the new Capitol building. Of these, the most important was his depiction of the signing of the Declaration of Independence, which he exhibited to large and enthusiastic crowds in Boston, Baltimore, and Philadelphia before delivering it to Washington. "Indeed," wrote historian Pauline Maier, "of all the paintings [Trumbull] completed for the Capitol, the *Declaration of Independence* was the greatest popular success."

Americans' enthusiasm also extended to written documents and records from the revolutionary era, and the founders themselves joined in the excitement. In 1815, while James Madison was president, Thomas Jefferson finally became the first person outside of Madison's family to read and review the chief executive's Constitutional Convention notes. Jefferson marveled at their thoroughness. "Do you know," he wrote to John Adams, "that there exists in manuscript the ablest work of this kind ever yet executed of the debates of the constitutional convention of Philadelphia in [1787]? The whole of everything said and done there was taken down by Mr. Madison, with a labor and exactness beyond comprehension."

Jefferson was certainly correct that the written word alone could not convey the entire story of the country's founding. Yet, precisely because the first-hand stories of the secret sessions and the men who participated in them would soon be lost to history, the written records were essential to build the historical foundation of the United States. If the country had neglected to capture and preserve the recollections of the founders themselves, it would not make the same mistake with the documentary trail of America's creation. After the burning of Washington, Americans had become acutely aware of the need to refer to, organize, protect, and preserve the documents that literally defined their nation and government. Perhaps enemy attacks were not the greatest danger after the Treaty of Ghent, but fear of natural disasters and the most destructive force to written records—fire—were top of mind.

In March 1818, Congress directed the publication of the journal of the Constitutional Convention (not Madison's copious notes, but the rather sparse official journal), along with the secret journals and the foreign correspondence of the Continental Congress from the first meeting to the date of the ratification of the peace treaty between Great Britain and the United States. The resolution authorized the president to "suppress such parts of the foreign correspondence as he might con-

sider improper at the time to publish." John Quincy Adams, then secretary of state, was already negotiating with Boston printer Thomas
Wait to publish the papers. Wait had proposed "to print, and deliver at
the city of Washington, the Journals of the convention which formed
the Constitution, also the Secret Journals of Congress and its correspondence with foreign powers prior to the treaty of peace of 1783, at two
dollars for a volume of five hundred pages in strong leather binding."

Adams accepted the proposal, and Wait first printed the journals
of the Constitutional Convention. On November 25, 1819, he shipped
500 copies of the printed book to Washington aboard the schooner
Adams, and by the second week in December, he had produced 500
more. Next, the printer went to work on the secret *Journals of the Continental Congress*, and in October 1821, he sent John Quincy Adams a
"bill of lading of the four volumes" (1,000 copies) for the heretofore unpublished journals.

INTEREST IN THE DECLARATION OF INDEPENDENCE also
soared.

In 1818 and 1819, two enterprising engravers, Benjamin Owen
Tyler and John Binns, saw a commercial opportunity and engaged in a
bitter competition to produce the first engraved facsimile of the historic document. Tyler finished first, producing a version in 1818 with
the initial lines of text formed in a decorative arched heading, and a
number of phrases in bold lettering different from the remainder of
the text. However, while the Tyler engraved text was not in facsimile,
the signatures below were full-sized reproductions in the arrangement
seen on the original document.

In 1819, Binns published his engraving, with a text reduced in size
and full-size facsimile signatures, rearranged to fit inside the oval
border that encircled the text. The border included circular medallion
portraits of George Washington, John Hancock, and Thomas Jefferson
surrounding the top half of the text and the seals of the thirteen original states around the lower half.

Both versions sold well, but both Binns and Tyler continued their feud as to which facsimile was "official"—although *neither* was an exact replica of the original. In addition, prior to completing his version, Tyler had, in 1817, requested acting secretary of state Richard Rush—son of signer Benjamin Rush—to attest to the accuracy of his work by comparing it to the original engrossed and signed Declaration. In the lower left corner of Tyler's facsimile, Rush wrote his endorsement, but also included a cautionary phrase: "The foregoing copy of the Declaration of Independence has been collated with the original instrument and found correct. I have myself examined the signatures to each. Those executed by Mr. Tyler are curiously exact imitations, so much so, that it would be difficult, if not impossible, for the closest scrutiny to distinguish them, were it not for the hand of time, from the originals."

Rush's "hand of time" allusion implies that the years had not been kind to the founders' signatures on the original version of the Declaration. That fact, along with the brisk sales of the Binns-Tyler facsimiles and the ongoing spat between the two engravers over who should be credited with the official facsimile version, convinced John Quincy Adams to take action.

In 1820, he commissioned Washington engraver William J. Stone to create on a copper plate an "exact facsimile" of both the engrossed declaration text and the signatures. The copies ultimately produced from Stone's work would establish the visual image of the Declaration of Independence for generations of Americans to come.

But in the process, Stone may have done further harm to the original.

WILLIAM STONE SPENT THREE full years painstakingly replicating the original, creating the first and only exact facsimile ever produced in time for the Fourth of July celebrations in 1823. On June 5, the *National Intelligencer* in Washington reported that "Mr. William J. Stone, a respectable and enterprising Engraver of this City, has, after a labor of three years, completed a *fac simile* of the original of the Declaration of Independence, now in the archives of the government; that it is executed with the greatest exactness and fidelity; and that the Department of State has become the purchaser of the plate."

The 200 official parchment copies produced from Stone's plate carry the identification "Engraved by W. J. Stone for the Department of State, by order" in the upper left corner, followed by "of J. Q. Adams, Sec. of State July 4 1823," in the upper right corner. According to the National Archives, unofficial copies struck later do not carry the identification at the top of the document. Instead, Stone identified his work by engraving "W. J. Stone SC, Washn." near the lower left corner and burnishing out the earlier identification.

Congress ordered the original 200 copies distributed: Jefferson, Adams, and Carroll of Carrollton each received two copies, as did President James Monroe, Vice President Daniel D. Tompkins, former President James Madison, and the Marquis de Lafayette. The House of Representatives and the Senate each received twenty copies and the various departments of government each received twelve copies. The remaining copies were sent to governors and legislatures of the states and territories and various colleges and universities in the United States.

If Stone's facsimile ensured that future generations would be able to view an exact replica of the Declaration of Independence, it may have also contributed to the deterioration of the original. Historians and document experts have long debated whether Stone employed the common eighteenth-century practice of making a "wet-press copy" of the Declaration. Such copies were produced by placing a damp sheet of thin paper on a manuscript and pressing it until a small portion of the ink was transferred. The thin paper copy was retained in the same way as a carbon copy, and the ink was reimposed on a copper plate, which was then etched so the copies could be run off the plate on a press. This so-called wet-transfer method may have been used by Stone and could have lifted ink from the original version.

Others have argued that Stone meticulously traced the original during the three years the Declaration was in his shop and did not use the wet-transfer method, and some evidence bears this out. Acting Secretary Rush's 1817 "hand of time" comment about the Tyler facsimile indicates that the original declaration had deteriorated prior to Stone's work. In addition, the second half of the *National Intelligencer* story in June 1823 points out that the newspaper was thankful that Stone's exact facsimile had been completed, "for the original [Declaration] which ought to be immortal and imperishable, by being so much handled by copyists and curious visitors, might receive serious injury." Stone's facsimile "rendered further exposure of the original unnecessary."

Secretary of State John Quincy Adams was no "copyist" or "curious visitor," but he also handled the original parchment copy when he borrowed it from William Stone's shop in the summer of 1821.

He needed it to punctuate what would become his most memorable speech and one of the nation's most defining foreign policy addresses.

AS ADAMS MOUNTED THE speaker's platform and approached the rostrum in the House of Representatives on July 4, 1821, he carried with him the original signed and engrossed copy of the Declaration of Independence.

His first task, assigned by the House, was to read the Declaration aloud in its entirety; his second, to comment upon it. "Two topics struck me as preeminently involved in it," he wrote later, "the cause of *man* and the cause of our *country*." He admitted that he had little time to prepare his remarks, and was concerned that the content of his speech would be perceived as official American policy—when he first received the invitation he believed he might be "tongue-tied by my place." But after "brooding" about the request, "I made up my mind to risk it and take the consequences."

Adams spoke from his heart. In a fiery speech, he drew on the Declaration of Independence to accomplish several goals: to extol the virtues of his country and its founders; to discourage America's intervention in ongoing revolutions in South America and Europe; to set the stage for the Monroe Doctrine, which warned European nations that interference in North and South American affairs would be viewed as acts of aggression against the United States; and to respond to British criticism of America's lack of contributions to the world by drawing sharp contrasts between the former's reliance on power and the latter's dedication to liberty. Perhaps rebuking England was impolitic, but it was unavoidable and inevitable since America's independence and founding were so tied to the behavior of its former mother country. It was impossible to point out the genius of the Declaration—"which distinguishes it from any other public document ever penned by man"— without drawing contrasts with other countries, touching upon "topics of peculiar delicacy," and "coming into collision with principles which the British government itself might disclaim."

And most recently, Adams reminded his audience, was Great Britain's unjust swipe at the United States, when several English officials had asked: "What has America done for the benefit of mankind?"

AMERICANS AND THE WORLD needed to remember, Adams said, that the document he now held was "the first solemn Declaration by a nation of the only legitimate foundation of civil government. It was the cornerstone of a new fabric—destined to cover the surface of the globe."

What the Declaration of Independence accomplished, what his father and the other signers had achieved, "demolished at a stroke the lawfulness of all governments founded upon conquest. It swept away as all the rubbish of accumulated centuries of servitude." Most of all, he thundered, it "announced in practical form to the world the transcendent truth of the unalienable sovereignty of the people" and produced a compact between the people and their government that was "no figment of the imagination, but a real, solid, and sacred bond of the social union."

What happened on July 4, 1776, Adams explained, could be stated with poetic and profound simplicity: "A nation was born in a day."

What had America done to benefit mankind? The United States would not presume to compete with Britain "for the prize of music, painting, or sculpture," Adams said, nor could we contend with Britain's "chemists . . . or the ardent gaze of your astronomers." What America's greatest contribution has been is to proclaim to mankind the "inextinguishable rights of human nature, and the only lawful foundation of government." America has "uniformly spoken . . . often to *disdainful ears*, the language of equal liberty, equal justice, and equal rights."

And it had done so at home and abroad, he emphasized. In nearly half a century, Adams stressed, "without a single exception," America has "respected the independence of other nations, while asserting and maintaining its own." Unlike Great Britain, it "has abstained from interference in the concerns of others." In perhaps his most memorable passage of the entire speech, Adams set the tone for U.S. foreign policy for years to come when he stressed that while his country would sympathize with other nations seeking independence—with "her heart, her benedictions, and her prayers"—outright interference, even in the cause of liberty, would *contradict the principles of the Declaration*.

America, Adams proclaimed, "goes not abroad in search of monsters to destroy. She is the well-wisher to the freedom and independence of all. She is the champion and vindicator only of her own." America would champion freedom only "by the countenance of her voice, and the benignant sympathy of her example." Her commitment was to freedom, to the power of the idea. Unlike Great Britain and the other nations of Europe for centuries heretofore, "her march is the march of mind, her glory is not dominion, but liberty."

As his audience applauded, Adams pressed on.

The best way for the nation to honor its forebears who had created the Declaration of Independence, and the nearly half century of American sovereignty, was to adhere to these principles in matters of foreign affairs. America's actions had set a shining example for the world in 1776, and the world would judge the nation by its actions in 1821. The Declaration of Independence "stands, and must forever stand alone, a beacon on the summit of the mountain, to which all the inhabitants of the earth may turn their eyes for a genial and saving light . . . a light of salvation and redemption to the oppressed."

John Quincy Adams was reinforcing the philosophy that America's example, not its interference, was the best way to spread freedom around the world. America would remain a beacon by strengthening its own constitutional republic and defending its home front.

In international affairs, its interests—and the universal ideal of human liberty—would best be served by its restraint rather than its aggression.

ADAMS WAS SURPRISED BY the publicity his speech generated, and he expressed his gratitude that the "hasty composition" had commanded his audience's "unremitting, riveted attention, with more than one occasional burst of applause." Adams made it clear that the "sentiments were indeed exclusively my own," and did not reflect official U.S. policy, but he had no reason to believe President Monroe or anyone else in the administration would "disclaim" his ideas.

In fact, John Quincy Adams had used the Declaration of Independence not only to honor his father's generation and vindicate the colonies' separation from Great Britain but also as the rationale for America's future foreign policy. He had chosen July 4, 1821, the forty-fifth anniversary of the Declaration's adoption, not as an occasion "for flinching from . . . our peculiar and imperishable principles," but "to avail myself of the opportunity of *asserting* them."

Five years later, on July 4, 1826, the United States celebrated those imperishable principles during its fifty-year Jubilee, the last day on earth for both John Adams and Thomas Jefferson.

★

17

"No Government
upon the Earth
Is So Safe as Ours"

★

The 1826 Fourth of July celebration in Washington was most notable for the *absence* of the leaders who had made the annual celebration possible.

On June 14, Mayor Roger C. Weightman had written invitations to the four living former presidents—Adams, Jefferson, Madison, and Monroe—as well as Charles Carroll of Carollton, the only living signer of the Declaration of Independence besides Adams and Jefferson. He asked, with the "highest respect and veneration," that they "favor the city with your presence," and offered to dispatch a special entourage to accompany them to Washington and then back to their homes.

All five men apologetically and humbly declined.

Adams, now ninety years old and living in Massachusetts, was "grateful for this mark of distinguished and respectful attention" but hoped Weightman would understand that the "present state of my health forbids me to indulge the hope of participating." Madison, too, while complimenting Weightman for offering him the opportunity to reflect on the past and anticipate the future of the country, cited the "instability of my health" as a reason for failing to make the trip from Virginia. He assured the mayor that July 4 would forever be honored as the day "which gave birth to a nation, and to a system of self-government, making it a new epoch in the history of man." For James Monroe, who did not receive the invitation until June 28, pressing personal engagements prevented him from traveling to Washington, a disappointment for him since he had "devoted my best efforts, through a long series of years, to the support of that great cause." He would ultimately be honored in Richmond on July 4. Carroll, at age eighty-nine, did not specifically refer to his health but did point out that he had declined a similar invitation from the city of New York and thus could not, "with propriety," attend the celebration in Washington.

Jefferson's reply to Weightman was most moving.

In the last letter he would ever write, this man whose brilliant quill had smoothed and shaped and burnished the rough edges of political theory to create a gleaming, powerful, enduring testament to self-government, would again achieve the soaring eloquence he had demonstrated a half century earlier. In a June 24 letter from Monticello, which was reprinted in newspapers across the country, the eighty-three-year-old statesman thanked Weightman for his kind invitation, regretted that "ill health" forced him to decline, and acknowledged that it added to "the suffering of sickness" to be deprived of participating in the "rejoicing of that day." This was particularly true, because he was one of the surviving signers "of an instrument, pregnant with our own and the fate of the world."

The Declaration of Independence had established a tone for freedom and liberty that had infused the nation with confidence for fifty years; Jefferson had still higher hopes. "May it be to the world what I believe it will be (to some parties sooner, to others later, but finally to all), the signal of rousing men to burst the chains . . . and to assume the blessings and security of self-government. . . . All eyes are opened or opening to the rights of man." The Declaration provided the "grounds of hope for others" to secure those rights, he added. "For ourselves, let the annual return of this day forever refresh our recollections of those rights, and an undiminished devotion to them."

These were Jefferson's last words to a nation he had helped found. On the same day he took pen to paper to answer Weightman, Jefferson, in pain and losing strength, wrote to his doctor to call on him at Monticello. His physician confined him to bed. Thomas Jefferson— member of the Virginia House of Burgesses, author and signer of the Declaration of Independence, secretary of state, minister to France, president of the United States, and founder of the University of Virginia—now had but one final goal.

He wanted desperately to survive until the Fourth of July.

JEFFERSON SUCCEEDED, BUT ONLY barely, drawing his final breath just before 1:00 in the afternoon on Tuesday, July 4, 1826, significant not only because it coincided with the time the Declaration had been approved fifty years earlier but because it aligned with virtually the exact moment that the secretary of war, James Barbour, was appealing to Jubilee participants in Washington to contribute to a fund established to pay Jefferson's extensive debts. Neither Barbour nor the rest of Washington would become aware of Jefferson's death for another two days.

Jefferson, who, on the night before he died had refused any further medication from his doctor ("No, doctor, nothing more," he said), died owing creditors more than $100,000, or as much as $2 million in today's dollars. Barbour explained that "late rains [had] done immense and irreparable damage" to Jefferson's estate; flooding in Virginia, followed by drought, over a period of several years had ruined the crops of many planters. There were other reasons for Jefferson's woes, too, including a large loan that he had advanced to a friend who later defaulted, and—the down side of the country's resurgent interest in its history and founders—the expense of providing food and drink to the thousands of people who had visited Monticello to pay homage to the third president. In the words of one historian, the Monticello throngs "ate up the substance of the philosopher who lived there."

Barbour made his appeal on behalf of Jefferson in the House chamber after the formal Jubilee ceremonies had concluded. According to the *National Intelligencer*, a large number of citizens and government officials—led by President John Quincy Adams—stepped forward to sign the "subscription paper" to support the fundraising effort. No public dinner or event was scheduled as part of the effort to pay Jefferson's debts, "experience being rather unfavorable to such, as involving a good deal of trouble with very little compensation in the nature of enjoyment."

ASIDE FROM BARBOUR'S SOBER appeal to assist Jefferson, Jubilee festivities in Washington were full of pomp, pageantry, and patriotism.

Cannon salutes began at sunrise, with guns pounding from the navy yard, the Capitol, even the front lawn of the president's house. Attorney General William Wirt's teenage daughter, Catharine, awoke early in the day and could not get back to sleep. "The cannons were roaring around me in every direction," she wrote to her sister. President Adams joined a military assemblage as they processed to the Capitol. The *U.S. Telegraph* reported that the floor of the House was "filled to overflowing" when they arrived, with ordinary citizens, members of the military, and foreign guests. The main Fourth of July address was delivered by attorney Walter Jones, who was married to the granddaughter of Richard Henry Lee, signer of the Declaration and the delegate who, on July 2, 1776, had offered the resolution to separate from Great Britain. Afterward, President Adams opened up the executive mansion to the general public as part of the celebration.

Similar celebrations occurred around the country, as millions of Americans cheered their country's fiftieth anniversary—in Philadelphia, Boston, Albany, Newark, and New York City, where a huge banquet table was set to feed eight hundred residents. The *New York*

American reported that oxen, roasted whole, were served as the main dish, while celebrants also enjoyed "an endless quantity of hams and loaves of bread, interspersed with barrels of beer and cider on tap." Elsewhere, pelting rain did not dampen Jubilee celebrations in Cincinnati, or Salem, Indiana, or Lexington, Kentucky, or hundreds of other small towns across the nation.

Across the land, Americans toasted their fundamental freedoms and the bravery of those who had come before them. The Jubilee was also a celebration of Americans' renewed knowledge of their history and an interest in the foundations of their government, and the safety and well-being that such knowledge and interest could promulgate. As the *Ohio Oracle* noted, "No government upon the earth is so safe as ours" because "no other people are so well informed."

PRESIDENT JOHN QUINCY ADAMS finally learned the circumstances of his father's death on July 12.

After four grueling days on the road from Washington—"the weather was all the time fine, but the heat intense," he wrote in his diary—he and his son arrived in Boston and checked in to the Hamilton Exchange Hotel. The president's other son, George, who resided in Boston, joined them and stayed until one o'clock in the morning recounting the story of his grandfather's last moments and his funeral. George arrived at John Adams's side just before his grandfather died—Adams recognized his grandson and made an effort to speak to him but without success. "George received his expiring breath between five and six in the afternoon," John Quincy wrote.

John Adams's physician later told the president that when town leaders had asked his father on June 30 for a Fourth of July toast, he had declared: "Independence forever." Asked if he would like to add something more, he replied, "Not a word." On the day of his death, when Adams had been informed that it was the Fourth of July, he had responded, "It is a great day. It is a good day," and was quiet for a time.

But then, around one o'clock in the afternoon, just a few hours from his death, John Adams reportedly whispered in a voice loud enough to be heard by those present in the room: "Thomas Jefferson survives."

Whether John Adams actually spoke the final word is a matter of conjecture. John Quincy Adams's diary acknowledges that his father's physician heard the words "Thomas Jefferson," but recalled that the word "survives" was "indistinctly and imperfectly uttered." Regardless, John Quincy's July 21 diary entry—in which he quoted his father's deathbed words as "Thomas Jefferson survives"—soon became part of the already amazing story of the juxtaposed deaths of Adams and Jefferson. Whatever word Adams spoke after "Thomas Jefferson," the reference to his fellow Declaration signer escaped his lips at nearly the exact time of Jefferson's death hundreds of miles away, a fact that only added to the founders' legend and legacy. Their lives had been intertwined for half a century; their accomplishments and contributions on behalf of their nation were unparalleled save perhaps by those of George Washington.

John Adams had spoken no more, his son learned, until moments before he passed. Finally, to his granddaughter, Susanna, who was sitting vigil at his bedside, he whispered his final words: "Help me, child. Help me."

John Adams, a giant in the movement for America's independence and the country's second president, died at about 6:20 in the evening on July 4, 1826. He was ninety.

His son, President John Quincy Adams, was comforted by his physician's assessment that "his death was the mere cessation of the functions of nature by old age, without disease."

THE PRESIDENT LEARNED THAT as many as 4,000 people had attended his father's funeral on July 7 in Quincy, including the governor of Massachusetts, the president of Harvard, many members of the legislature, and Congressman Daniel Webster. Cannon fired and bells pealed as the solemn procession made its way from the Adams house to the First Congregational Church.

The death of his father affected John Quincy in ways that surprised him. Despite his resigned acceptance of John Adams's demise when he first learned about it from the tavern owner in Maryland, the president's arrival in Quincy elicited a far deeper and more profound response. When he entered the family homestead and walked into his father's bedchamber, the place John Quincy had "last taken leave of him and where I had most sat with him at my last two yearly visits to him," the president was wracked with grief. "That moment was inexpressibly painful, and struck me as if it had been an arrow to my heart," he confided to his diary. "My father and my mother have departed. The charm which has always made this house to me an abode of enchantment is dissolved—and yet, my attachment to it, and to the whole region round, is stronger than I ever felt it before."

Later, the president attended a service at the family church and was again touched, this time by the ghosts of his parents' presence. "I have at no time felt more deeply affected by that event than on entering the meeting house and taking in his pew the seat which he used to occupy," John Quincy wrote. "The memory of my father and mother, of their tender and affectionate care, of the times of peril in which we then lived, and of the hopes and fears which left their impressions upon my mind, came over me, till involuntary tears started from my eyes."

John Quincy Adams remained in the Boston area until October before returning to Washington. During that time, the fifty-nine-year-old president thought often about his own mortality, encountered a cousin he had not seen in fifty years, conducted as much state business as he could away from the capital, attended numerous sermons and memorial services in honor of his father, and nearly drowned when a ferry in which he was traveling almost capsized in a raging rainstorm. Of these, he found the eulogies were most emotionally exhausting; the speakers all meant well, of course, and the general public found them appropriate to express its affection to the departed John Adams. But for John Quincy, the recurring homage paid to his father was a constant reminder of his aching grief.

"I have received high though melancholy gratification from these performances," the president noted, "but found myself much, too much, overcome with fatigue."

AS NEWS SPREAD ACROSS the country of the July 4 deaths of John Adams and Thomas Jefferson, Americans everywhere expressed sentiments similar to John Quincy's: the loss of the two great statesmen went far beyond coincidence and entered the realm of "divine favor."

In his dazzling August 2 speech at Harvard, before a crowd of 4,000 ("a greater concourse of people than I ever witnessed in Boston," John Quincy Adams noted), Congressman Daniel Webster exemplified the spiritual tone of virtually every eulogist in the land. He inspired and moved the crowd when he said, "The tears which flow, and the honors that are paid, when the founders of the republic die, give hope that the republic itself may be immortal." The gifts bequeathed by Adams and Jefferson "leave the world all light, all on fire."

They had ensured the success of the revolution, "one of the greatest events in history." They had brought forth free representative government. It's no wonder, then, Webster opined, that the conjunction of their deaths on the nation's fiftieth birthday was a "special dispensation" from the deity, "proof that our country, and its benefactors, are objects of His care."

Again and again, speakers and citizens looked to the deaths of Adams and Jefferson on July 4, 1826, as divine intervention in the nation's affairs. As Caleb Cushing of Newburyport, Massachusetts, intoned in his eulogy: "Had the horses and chariot of fire descended to take up the patriarchs, it might have been more wonderful—but not more glorious."

The deaths of Adams and Jefferson reawakened the nation to the ideals of liberty, equality, and self-government that the two patriots had stood for throughout the revolutionary period and, indeed, for their entire lives. The Declaration of Independence embodied those ideals; that the two greatest contributors to the sacred document had died on the fiftieth anniversary of its adoption meant that those ideals, and the

Declaration itself, contained the blessings of a higher power. It was "the venerated instrument that declared our separation from Great Britain," one speaker in Philadelphia said. It was the document that defined "*the native equality of the human race* as the true foundations of all political, of all human institutions," offered another orator.

The Declaration, a Virginia speaker pointed out, was the manifesto that awakened a "mighty spirit" that "walks upon the earth," and during its travels will "tramp thrones and scepters in the dust."

If Americans needed any more validation to support their new-found reverence for the Declaration, they received it when word circulated around the country of Thomas Jefferson's epitaph chiseled upon the obelisk that marked his grave at Monticello. Jefferson had clearly specified his wishes, and he ignored any reference to most of his lofty accomplishments. Instead, Jefferson wished most to be remembered for eternity for his work on behalf of both academic and governmental freedom. The inscription reads:

HERE WAS BURIED
THOMAS JEFFERSON
AUTHOR OF THE DECLARATION OF INDEPENDENCE,
OF THE STATUTE OF VIRGINIA FOR RELIGIOUS FREEDOM,
AND FATHER OF THE UNIVERSITY OF VIRGINIA

THE PROVIDENTIAL AURA OF the Fourth of July did not end with the 1826 Jubilee.

Former president and Revolutionary War hero James Monroe, who as secretary of state had warned President Madison to "remove the records" prior to the 1814 British attack on Washington, died on July 4, 1831, exactly five years after Adams and Jefferson—fifty-five years after the adoption of the Declaration of Independence.

John Quincy Adams, by then a member of Congress (the only former president to become a congressman), delivered a long and stirring eulogy in Boston, noting the legacy that Monroe and other revolutionaries had left their nation. "It remains for you," Adams told the audience, "only to transmit the same peerless legacy, unimpaired, to your children of the next succeeding age."

A LITTLE MORE THAN one year later, on November 14, 1832, Charles Carroll, the last living signer of the Declaration of Independence, died in Baltimore at the age of ninety-five. His eulogist, Philadelphia statesman John Sergeant, noted that his signature upon the Declaration was the highest honor he could ever achieve. "As he was for many years the single representative on earth of the Congress of 1776, his grave seems to be the grave of the whole," Sergeant said. "It is finally closed, and we are assembled around it for the last time."

What the Declaration signers had left, Sergeant said, "is now entirely ours—ours to enjoy, and ours, be it remembered, with the favour of Providence, to preserve."

JAMES MADISON DID NOT quite reach the Fourth of July.

He died on the morning of June 28, 1836, at home in his Montpelier estate in Virginia. On the morning of Madison's death, Paul Jennings, his manservant, reported that the father of the Constitution and the former president had difficulty swallowing his breakfast. Minutes later, "his head instantly dropped, and he ceased breathing as quietly as the snuff of a candle goes out."

Fittingly, perhaps, Madison was the final Constitution signer to die—he outlived all the other founders and framers.

In March 1837, fifty years after the Constitutional Convention and nine months after Madison's death, the U.S. Congress agreed to purchase most of his papers from his wife Dolley for the sum of $30,000. For years prior to her husband's death, Dolley had worked closely with James to prepare the papers for publication. After Madison passed, Dolley believed it was her "deep and sacred charge" to publish her husband's papers; indeed, the "important trust" sustained her in the weeks and months following his death. She devoted herself to the task, writing that the publication of Madison's papers "will form the surest evidence of his claim to the gratitude of his country and the world."

Madison himself had come under some criticism for altering portions of the notes in later years, in part to more accurately reflect the official Constitutional Convention journal and, in part, for the less noble reason of aligning the older records with his evolving stance on the dangers of an overreaching federal government, his support for a bill of rights, and other topics. For the most part, though, his notes and recollections are an accurate, amazing, and valuable literary tour de force, one of the great contributions to American history. What the nation frustratingly lacks from the 1776 Continental Congress's Declaration of Independence debates, Madison bequeathed to the nation from the Constitutional Convention of 1787—a full accounting of the arguments, speeches, and rationale of delegates as they formed the opinions that would lead to their final decisions.

Madison's notes provide a day-by-day account of the most remarkable summer in the nation's existence, when, in just 120 days, delegates created a government unlike any other in history.

Dolley Madison recognized the importance of her husband's papers when she wrote to President Andrew Jackson in August 1836, shortly after Madison's death: "I am now preparing to execute his confidence reposed in me—that of placing before Congress and the World what his pen had prepared for their use, and with the importance of this Legacy, I am deeply impressed."

Fifty-three years after the delegates had debated in Philadelphia, James Madison's Constitutional Convention volumes were published in 1840 under the direction of Henry D. Gilpin, solicitor of the U.S. Treasury and, later, attorney general of the United States.

A YEAR AFTER MADISON'S papers were published, in June 1841, Secretary of State Daniel Webster made a fateful decision about the original engrossed and signed copy of the Declaration of Independence.

Webster's intentions were noble—his goal was to display the precious document for visitors to Washington to view and enjoy—but the impact of his actions did further physical harm to the nation's founding document. Webster did not comment on his reasoning, but perhaps Madison's death—the de facto end of the revolutionary and constitutional era—prompted him to keep the spirit of the founders and framers alive in the hearts and minds of Americans.

In any case, on June 11, Webster wrote to the commissioner of patents, Henry L. Ellsworth, who was then occupying a new building in Washington (now the National Portrait Gallery), a white stone structure at the corner of 7th and F streets. The Patent Office was a bureau of the State Department, and Webster had learned that "there is in the new building, appropriated to the Patent Office, suitable accommodations for the safe-keeping as well as the exhibition of various articles now deposited in this [State] Department." The new location would be suitable to display certain documents, and thus, Webster said to Ellsworth: "I have directed them to be transmitted to you." An inventory accompanied Webster's letter. Item 6 was the Declaration of Independence.

Workers at the Patent Office mounted the Declaration and George Washington's commission as commander in chief together in a single frame and placed it opposite a tall window where both documents were exposed to the "chill of winter and the glare and heat of summer." Both documents remained on exhibit for the next thirty-five years—until 1876—even after the Patent Office separated from the State Department and became part of the Interior Department. The prolonged exposure to sunlight, especially, accelerated the deterioration of ink and the parchment of the Declaration, which, by the end of this period, would be approaching 100 years of age.

As early as 1856, a writer for the *United States Magazine* referred to the Declaration as "that old looking paper with the fading ink." Several years later, another writer concurred: "It is old and yellow, and the ink is fading from the paper." And in 1870, *Historical Magazine* warned: "The original manuscripts of the Declaration and of

Washington's Commission . . . are said to be fading out, so that, in a few years, only the naked parchments will remain."

America's most important document, epitomizing a people's unbreakable will to live in freedom—created by the indomitable spirit of the founders, given enduring life through the bloodshed of patriots, rescued from destruction by the brave and swift action of public servants, immortalized by the Jubilee of 1826—was, as the nation approached its centennial, in grave danger from simple wear and tear.

★ ★ ★

1942–1943

★ ★ ★

★

18

"Are You Satisfied
We Have Taken
All Reasonable
Precautions?"

★

May 13, 1942, U.S. Bullion Depository, Fort Knox, 3:30 p.m.

Under the watchful eyes of Verner Clapp and two restoration experts from Harvard, guards carried the case containing the Declaration of Independence from the vault to the north room, which had been set up as a work area. Clapp inspected the case's seals and locks and found them all intact.

For the next hour, parchment expert Dr. George L. Stout of Harvard, and his assistant, Evelyn Ehrlich, prepared to undertake restorative work on the Declaration. They had traveled to Kentucky, in secret and at Clapp's request, in order to assess the impact of storage in Fort Knox on the document. Stout was one of the country's foremost experts on art conservation and restoration—he would later become one of the famous Monuments Men who traveled to Europe to retrieve and protect art treasures stolen by the Nazis.

Stout and Ehrlich spent the late afternoon opening the wooden case and preparing to open the bronze container that contained the Declaration. They unpacked their tools and supplies and laid them out carefully. Then they thoroughly vacuumed the room and recorded atmospheric conditions. "The document was then taken from the container, and found to be in apparently the same condition as when packed, with no signs of mould, or obvious evidence of further cracking," a relieved Clapp wrote.

Stout took a series of photographs of the entire document, and focused on those areas that were cracked and deteriorated.

At about 5:30 p.m., the document was placed in the bronze container and returned to the vault for the night.

Stout and Ehrlich would begin work in earnest the next day.

THE FOLLOWING MORNING, a Thursday, Stout and Ehrlich entered the workroom by 9:00 a.m. to begin their delicate task—repairing and restoring the Declaration that Timothy Matlack had so carefully engrossed 166 years earlier.

The first and most critical step was removing the Declaration from its mount, a heavy pulp board covered with paper, with a frame of green velvet glued to it. Atop the mount, a rectangular strip of tissue paper, about three-quarters of an inch wide, had been pasted—with an adhesive that consisted of part glue and part paste—the outer dimensions of which conformed to the dimensions of the Declaration. At one point, the Declaration had been pasted down at the margins on this strip, but, in 1940, it had been detached from the mount. Still, Clapp noted in his report, Stout and Ehrlich made it clear that the tissue had "readhered on the upper, side, and especially the lower margins, while in other places on these margins the tissue was left adherent to the document instead of the mount."

Worse, along the upper margin, the document had in several places "been fixed firmly into place with copious glue in an effort to stop the extending cracks," meaning that it would be more difficult to detach the Declaration from its mount. The restorers noted that "practically the whole of the detached upper right-hand corner had been glued down in this manner," as had the portion of the document "surrounding the crack above the capital letter 'S' in 'States' in the heading." Perhaps most disruptive of all, at one point—perhaps also in 1940—someone had made an attempt to "reunite" the detached upper right-hand corner of the document to the main mount by means of a strip of "scotch cellulose tape, which was still in place, discolored to a molasses color." Much to the restorers' chagrin, "in the various mending efforts, glue had even been splattered in two places on the obverse of the document."

The risk of trying to restore the document was that it might be damaged further. Tearing could occur as restorers attempted to detach the Declaration from its mount or remove glue from the document's face.

With the hands and eyes of a surgeon, Stout slowly freed the document from the mount when possible using a sharp, thin blade; when he could not accomplish this safely, he cut or sliced portions of the mount with the Declaration still adhering to it. "The whole upper right-hand corner, which had cracked away from the rest of the document and which itself contained multiple cracks, had to be thus sliced free," observed Clapp, who watched Stout work.

Under the Declaration, at the lower left corner of the mount, Stout and Ehrlich uncovered two signatures and a date, written in pencil: "L. T. Anderson and Robt. L. Bier—January 22, 1924." The two men, now deceased, had been employed by the Library of Congress respectively in the Manuscripts Division and the Prints Division repair shop; the date was mere days prior to the ceremony in which the Library of Congress enshrined the Declaration for public view. "These names and dates appear to give a clue to the mounting of the document," Clapp noted.

The hours passed and Stout and Ehrlich continued their efforts. They freed the Declaration of adherent glue, paste, and paper along the margins of the reverse side and on the entire detached upper right-hand corner. They did this by dry slicing and scraping, with the occasional use of toluene and ethyl alcohol to remove stubborn adhesive—acceptable methods even today. Also, because the Declaration had been rolled so often as a scroll from top to bottom, the area that was exposed when rolled—approximately eight inches of the lower portion of the reverse side—was badly soiled. Stout scraped this section clean as well. As they worked inside, rain fell outside, raising the humidity in the workroom and causing the Declaration parchment to "relax appreciably."

Into the evening, after they had removed most of the adhesives, they reassembled the document, obverse side uppermost, on white blotting paper, drawing the cracks together with Scotch tape, as their predecessor had. They then placed a large sheet of glass on the Declaration, weighted it down with bags of sand, and returned it to the vault.

It was 9:30 p.m. when they stopped. They had put in more than twelve hours of painstaking work, but they were far from finished.

FOR SIXTEEN HOURS OVER the next two days—Friday and Saturday—Stout and Ehrlich labored on the Declaration of Independence at Fort Knox.

Working carefully from the back side, they applied sealing lute, made from Japanese tissue moistened with rice paste, to the document's cracks. They patched two holes in the heading with vellum—one above the *m* in "America," an original hole in the parchment; and one above the *S* in "States," a hole resulting from a recent break. All the patches and repairs were tinted with watercolor to match the Declaration's hue. When they had finished, they dried the parchment, which had now relaxed due to humidity. The U.S. Army Signal Corps then came into the workroom to photograph the Declaration. During this short period of illumination, Clapp noted in his report, it was clear that the document had shrunk "perhaps as much as an eighth of an inch laterally" thanks to the drying. He pointed out that the changes he noticed in the physical state of the Declaration during "relaxing" and "shrinking"—based on humidity—were worthwhile to observe, since they were "an indication of the conditions expected in storing and exhibiting the document."

Finally, Stout and Ehrlich mounted the Declaration to a rag board that had been warmed overnight and secured the document with small expanding or pleated hinges at several places along the upper margin and at the two lower corners.

Before returning the Declaration to the vault, the two restorers examined the Constitution and found the document to be in good condition; the 1787 parchment had not suffered the same degradation as the Declaration since it was never displayed in direct sunlight or in rooms smoky from open fireplaces. Indeed, its size—five leaves, four for the document itself, plus the transmittal letter from George Washington—made it difficult to display and therefore had served to preserve the document for all these years. Stout and Ehrlich did remove the pulp board that had been used as filler in the case and replaced it with handmade Japanese blotting paper dabbed with a small amount of thymol dissolved in alcohol to aid preservation. The surfaces of both the Declaration and the Constitution were protected with a layer of Japanese tissue.

At 2:30 p.m. on Saturday, May 16, the bronze case containing the two documents was returned to the vault, together with a hygrothermograph to record temperature and humidity.

The compartment door was then securely closed "with the seal of the Chief Clerk in Charge, and of myself," Clapp reported.

On May 20, 1942, Stout and Ehrlich submitted to the Library of Congress their "notes on examination and treatment" of the Declaration. Despite their work, they reported that the Declaration's condition was "not much affected by treatment." They believed that "near the mends" they had made to the document, the Declaration "will buckle in time from changes in humidity."

But the Library of Congress was more optimistic in its annual report seven years later: "Frequent examinations have proved that the remedial measures were generally satisfactory."

*

PRESIDENT ROOSEVELT WAS ANXIOUS for an update.

On October 6, he wrote a short note to MacLeish on White House stationery entitled "Memorandum for the Librarian of Congress." Using his familiar salutation "Dear Archie," the president's memo was polite but pointed. "I have not talked to you for a long time in regard to the removal of valuable and irreplaceable books, manuscripts, etc. from the Library to places of safety in other parts of the country," Roosevelt wrote. "Are you satisfied that we have taken all reasonable precautions in regard to this?"

For MacLeish, the key word in FDR's memo was "reasonable." Certainly, he believed that Library of Congress staffers had done everything they could to properly package and catalog the records, select the repositories, develop security protocols, and, throughout the summer of 1942, visit the university locations to ensure that the documents were being guarded and cared for—and that mold, mildew, and vermin had not compromised the condition of the records.

But the situation was far from ideal. "Your question," MacLeish responded to Roosevelt in a secret memo on October 19, "goes to the heart of the matter which has concerned me, as I think you know, for about two years." MacLeish summarized the library's work to this point, including the transfer of the "principal treasures" to Fort Knox and Stout's restorative work on the Declaration. He said he was satisfied that his team had done "everything it could do with the means at [their] disposal, and that [the library's] most valuable materials are as safe as they can be without the construction of a properly located bombproof shelter."

MacLeish stressed to Roosevelt that the Committee on the Conservation of Cultural Resources had expressed a desire for the construction of one or more bombproof structures, "under adequate guard," to protect the nation's records. The relocation of records to inland repositories that were "fireproof but non-bombproof" was adequate as a temporary measure but did not "provide the best protection which could be given." Bombproof projects had reached the planning and discussion stage, but bureaucratic delays and other priorities had stalled construction. Prior to writing his response to Roosevelt, MacLeish had checked on the status of such projects with the Public Buildings Administration. "I was informed . . . that the effort to construct bombproof shelters had been discontinued because of the situation as regards building materials and manpower," MacLeish informed the president.

Simply put, the nation's efforts were focused on war priorities that were considered more pressing.

"Whether or not this discontinuation will be made final, I am unable to say," MacLeish added.

For now, MacLeish took some consolation that the library's most valuable documents—"the priceless heart of the country's greatest collection"—were safely ensconced at Fort Knox. He would continue to suffer anxiety about the security of the remaining 5,000 boxes now stored at universities in Virginia and Ohio.

19

★

"He Loved Peace
and
He Loved Liberty"

★

April 13, 1943, Washington, D.C.

On a gray and gusty Tuesday, President Franklin D. Roosevelt stood before 5,000 people at the Tidal Basin in West Potomac Park, while millions more prepared to listen to his words by way of a radio broadcast. The crowd had gathered to dedicate a memorial to America's "apostle of freedom," Thomas Jefferson, on the 200th anniversary of his birth.

"Today, in the midst of a great war for freedom, we dedicate a shrine to freedom," said Roosevelt, who faced the crowd and the gleaming white pantheon that encircled the bronze statue of Jefferson on the banks of the Tidal Basin. With the Washington Monument at his back, Roosevelt said that earlier generations could not understand what his generation knew all too well—"men who will not fight for liberty can lose it." With war raging around the globe, with millions enslaved by totalitarian regimes, honoring Jefferson and the principles of freedom he espoused was entirely appropriate. "He loved peace and he loved liberty," Roosevelt said of the nation's third president. "Yet, on more than one occasion he was forced to choose between them. We, too, have been compelled to make that choice." For the lessons Jefferson taught the young nation about freedom, self-government, and unalienable rights, "we are paying a debt, long overdue," FDR said. It was to honor Jefferson's greatest legacy—in his own words, his "eternal hostility against every form of tyranny"—that brought war-weary Americans to Potomac Park and caused them to huddle around their radios.

And for those who had found their way to the nation's capital, President Roosevelt also wanted them to partake in the glory of Thomas Jefferson's crowning achievement.

For that reason, he had ordered the original engrossed copy of the Declaration of Independence removed from its secret storage location and displayed at the base of its author's new memorial.

PLANS FOR THE JEFFERSON MEMORIAL had been on the drawing board since 1934 and ground had been broken on the monument in 1938, but the hastily organized dedication event had only come together in the previous several months. Not everyone agreed that the ceremony should go on in wartime, but President Roosevelt believed the event would bolster morale as the nation headed into its sixteenth month of war.

To enhance the magnitude of the occasion, FDR had ordered the Declaration exhibited at the memorial from the day of commemoration until one week thereafter.

For Archibald MacLeish, who had written the president's remarks for the dedication, Roosevelt's directive meant scrambling to make appropriate arrangements. In a secret memo to the treasury secretary, he once again requested Secret Service assistance in accompanying the Declaration from Fort Knox to Washington, "under conditions of security," and in assuring its safe return to the bullion depository at the conclusion of its public display. "We propose to bring it to Washington on or about April 7, and to return it to Fort Knox on or about April 20,"

MacLeish said. He also arranged with the U.S. Marines to "furnish a 24-hour guard for the document during the period of its stay in Washington."

Once again, Harry Neal was put in charge of the Secret Service end of the operation. In early March, a month before the dedication and early in the planning, MacLeish and Neal dealt with their first controversy of the event: *Life* had got word that the Declaration would be on display for the Jefferson Memorial ceremonies. The magazine, which was planning to devote considerable space in an issue to Jefferson, the memorial, and the bicentennial of the founder's birth, "asked whether it would be possible to take photographs of the journey of the object you and I are concerned with," MacLeish wrote to Neal. "I replied that it would not be possible." However, MacLeish said he would be "willing to raise the question of photographs of the arrival at the [train] station in Washington and the transport from that point to the Library and thence to the place of the exhibit." The question was one for the Secret Service to answer, MacLeish concluded, but he thought that *Life* would be willing to accept any conditions officials thought necessary.

In his careful response, Neal said that while the Secret Service had no objection to such photographs, he did not want to grant an exclusive to *Life*, but that "the three major press associations should be given the same opportunity." Further, photographers should not be informed of the date and time of the special train's arrival in Washington until the day it was slated to arrive. Finally, Neal insisted that if photos were taken, "their publication in any newspaper or magazine be withheld until *after* the material has been returned to its destination." Neal saw no room for compromise on the final point.

Nor was there a need to: MacLeish agreed with Neal on all conditions.

On April 5, MacLeish told the House Subcommittee on Appropriations of the plan, and the story became public when the Associated Press ran it in many newspapers across the country. When Walter Christian Ploeser, the representative from Missouri, questioned

MacLeish about the wisdom of risking the Declaration, a document "which in no way in the world can be replaced," MacLeish replied: "If there is any document in the United States which should be allowed to be exhibited to the people of this country, at this moment, it is that document."

MacLeish further explained that the Secret Service and the Library of Congress had agreed to exhibit the Declaration in a steel case with a "bullet-proof glass cover." Two Marines would stand twenty-four-hour guard, "one on each side of the case, which will be fitted to the steps at the foot of the statue."

On April 10, two army trucks with seven military police arrived at Fort Knox and placed the Declaration on a truck equipped with a submachine gun. Filled with contingents of MPs and Secret Service agents, the trucks made their way to the Louisville train station; by 8:30 the following morning, the Declaration had arrived safely at the Library of Congress.

The Declaration was on display at the Jefferson Memorial from 9:00 a.m. to 9:00 p.m. for a week. At night, the exhibit case was transferred to a side room where one sentry stood guard; quarters had been provided inside the memorial itself for the whole detachment assigned to the duty. Thousands of Americans viewed the Declaration during the period of its display in front of the new Jefferson Memorial.

On April 19, the Marine detachment accompanied the Declaration back to the Library of Congress, where it was removed from the exhibit case, remounted in its frame, photographed, and repackaged in the bronze container in which it had been stored at Fort Knox. After its safe return to the bullion depository on April 23, MacLeish wrote to Henry Morgenthau, again congratulating the Secret Service agents for their efforts—Neal on the Washington end and the agents who met the train in Louisville.

"We have just redeposited, in a place of utmost security, one of the fundamental constitutional documents of the United States Government after its brief period of exhibit during the Thomas Jefferson Bicentennial celebration," he wrote. "It has meant a great deal to me personally to have had complete confidence in measures taken to protect this document during its transportation to and from Washington."

ALSO DURING THE SPRING of 1943, the Library of Congress's Alvin Kremer spent another sixty days at the university storage repositories. His tasks, MacLeish reported later, included "overseeing the various guard forces, correcting conditions of humidity, and re-examining fire risks." Kremer also directed the removal of the 1,400 cases that had originally been shipped to the Virginia Military Institute; because of dampness, these were now transferred to two locations: Washington and Lee University and Denison.

Verner Clapp made at least two visits to Fort Knox to examine the library's documents, one in June and another in October. He sounded a note of caution in June, fearful that summer heat and humidity would create a "dangerous concentration of moisture within the packages." But when he arrived at Fort Knox on October 29, the situation was appreciably better. "The weather outside was warm, but dry; and I found, with pleasure, that the repository heating system was going, and that the packing room conditions were good."

In his mind, the documents were as safe as possible.

★ ★ ★

1860–1924

★ ★ ★

20

★

"Four Score
and Seven
Years Ago . . ."

★

November 17, 1863, Evening

President Lincoln was annoyed and more than a little impatient with his cabinet members.

Pressed as he was with issues related to military affairs and with preparations for his address to Congress in early December, and fraught with worry about the health of his son, the commander in chief had expected a crisper response and more judicious planning for his upcoming visit to Pennsylvania.

In the last month alone, he had advised his Union generals on Robert E. Lee's troop movements; urged another general to give up his congressional seat and focus his leadership skills on the battlefield; authorized testing of a new form of gunpowder; offered thoughts on how to deal with a state that was threatening to repudiate his Emancipation Proclamation; and ordered the secretary of war, Edwin Stanton, to appoint a New Jersey colonel to lead a colored regiment.

In recent hours, the president's ten-year-old son, Tad, had developed a rash and a high fever, and Lincoln, who had suffered the agonizing loss of his nine-year-old son Willie just a year earlier, feared that the deadly typhoid had struck again.

In the midst of these burdens, might he expect more from his senior advisers on this latest matter that had cropped up just two weeks earlier?

Abraham Lincoln had been invited to issue a "few appropriate remarks" at the upcoming dedication of a Union cemetery in just two days, and even at this late hour, final arrangements for his journey remained uncertain. He had expected to see his treasury secretary, Salmon Chase, at the cabinet meeting earlier that day to confirm his own attendance at the dedication, but Chase had missed the meeting; he eventually declined the invitation to visit the cemetery.

Secretary Stanton had later outlined plans for the eighty-mile journey, suggesting that the train depart Washington at 6:00 a.m. on the morning of the event—November 19—arrive at its destination at noon, and then return home with Lincoln and his traveling party at 6:00 p.m., thereby making the trip "all in one day." Lincoln, always prepared and meticulous in his planning, objected to Stanton's plan. With his usual common sense and good judgment, he wrote to Stanton: "I do not like this arrangement. I do not wish to so go that by the slightest accident we fail [to arrive] entirely."

LINCOLN HAD TAKEN IT upon himself earlier that evening to meet with the cemetery's landscaper, William Saunders, who worked in the Department of Agriculture. The president had summoned Saunders to the executive mansion and asked him to bring the cemetery map and plans. Lincoln wanted to fully understand the physical features of the sacred ground he was visiting, not just its symbolic significance. Saunders arrived, spread the plans on Lincoln's office table, and pointed out key landmarks and topographical locations. Saunders had explained that the careful way the graves were arranged was designed so that "the position of each [state] lot, and indeed of each interment, is relatively of equal importance."

Lincoln knew that it was far more than the layout of graves that made these grounds different from an ordinary cemetery. The Union men who had died on this land had turned the tide of the war. Their efforts, along with the near-simultaneous surrender by the Confederates of Vicksburg in the western theater—both battles, incredibly, concluding on the Fourth of July, 1863—had shortly thereafter prompted Lincoln to conclude that "peace does not appear so distant as it did. I hope it will come soon, and come to stay; and so come as to be worth the keeping in all future time."

The plans that Lincoln and Saunders reviewed definitely differed from an ordinary cemetery.

They were looking at Gettysburg.

IN NOVEMBER 1863, GETTYSBURG had yet to be identified as the greatest Civil War campaign, an iconic turning point in the nation's history. Yet Lincoln, and military commanders of both sides, recognized that Robert E. Lee's ultimate retreat from the south-central Pennsylvania crossroads battlefield marked a crucial moment in the war. While the fighting would continue for nearly two more years, never again would the South come close to victory. "Yesterday we rode on the pinnacle of success," Josiah Gorgas, a Confederate soldier, wrote in his diary three weeks after the battle. "Today . . . the Confederacy totters to its destruction."

On both sides, the cost of Gettysburg was staggering—the more than 50,000 total casualties, 23,000 on the Union side, convey the scope of the epic battle but do not begin to describe the ghastliness of the suffering. Three horrific days of cannon fire and in-close fighting in the intense July heat had left the battlefields stained red with blood and littered with the broken, swollen, fermenting bodies of men and horses. More than 5,000 horses and mules were burned for hygienic reasons. Comrades of the dead, fighting swarms of bluebottle flies, tried in vain to bury the remains of their fellow soldiers; weeks after the battle more than 8,000 human corpses still lay scattered across Gettysburg's fields, or under a thin coating of hastily turned ground, or barely covered in shallow trenches. Late in July, Gettysburg banker and civic leader David Wills wrote to Pennsylvania's governor, Andrew Curtin: "In many instances arms and legs and sometimes heads protrude and my attention has been directed to several places where the hogs were actually rooting out the bodies and devouring them."

Curtin asked Wills to take control of organizing the burials, and the banker did so with passion and great reverence. He convinced the federal government to ship thousands of coffins to Gettysburg, took title to seventeen acres for the new cemetery, and hired companies to rebury the bodies—whenever possible, to identify where the fallen had hailed from and arrange the graves according to states. He knew early in the process that he wanted to dedicate the ground where so many valiant men had fallen. In the words of one historian, Wills "felt the need for artful words to sweeten the poisoned air of Gettysburg."

Wills turned to one of the country's great orators, Edward Everett, to deliver the dedication. Everett had the reputation of mesmerizing audiences for lengthy periods, and the dedication of Gettysburg would require at least a two-hour speech to do the occasion justice. Everett agreed and said he needed time to research the battle and prepare his lengthy remarks. Wills agreed to hold the ceremony on November 19, a Thursday.

On November 2, Wills wrote to President Lincoln, inviting him to "participate in these ceremonies, which will doubtless be very imposing and solemnly impressive." Lincoln needn't concern himself with preparing any major speech, since, as Wills explained, the "Hon. Edward Everett will deliver the oration." Wills's desire was for Lincoln's role to occur after Everett's address, when, "as Chief Executive of the nation, [you] set apart these grounds to their sacred use by a few appropriate remarks."

Wills implored the president: "I hope you will feel it your duty to lay aside pressing business of the day to come here to perform this last sad rite to our brave soldiers dead."

LINCOLN'S FRIEND AND SOON-TO-BE attorney general James Speed said years later in an interview that the president told him "the day before he left Washington he found time to write about half of his speech." Likely, due to his preparation habits and attention to detail, Lincoln had formulated the remainder of the content in his mind before he arrived in Gettysburg. Lincoln's secretary, John Nicolay, and many others have discounted the popular fiction that Lincoln wrote the address or even made notes on the journey between Washington and Gettysburg. Nicolay pointed out that the "rockings and joltings" of the train, as well as "ordinary courtesy" that required Lincoln to converse and mingle with staff and passengers would have made thoughtful writing impossible.

Lincoln would finish and reread his address once he arrived in Gettysburg. He knew he needed to strike a balance. He was well aware of the power of rhetoric to move people and of the import of words spoken by the president. Yet, he was not the featured speaker. He presumed Everett's address would be lengthy, which meant that his needed to be both brief and inspirational, a challenging task.

The place to start, then, was the source from which he had often drawn his own inspiration and intellectual stimulation—from the founding fathers and the works they had created. "Let us revere the Declaration of Independence," he once said, and on a different occasion: "Let us readopt the Declaration of Independence, and with it, the practices and policy which harmonize with it."

What better themes were there to begin his remarks at the Gettysburg cemetery? His opening lines, written in Washington, looked back on the nation's founding and all the qualities that the event represented. Stirring, eloquent, somberly lyrical and immensely powerful, Lincoln's opening words would one day ring across the land and echo down through the decades:

"Four score and seven years ago, our fathers brought forth on this continent, a new nation, conceived in liberty, and dedicated to the proposition that all men were created equal."

ABRAHAM LINCOLN WAS SEVENTEEN years old when John Adams and Thomas Jefferson died on July 4, 1826; he was a young man in his late twenties when James Madison, the last of the founders, died. Yet the influence of these men on Lincoln was profound.

Perhaps because he had studied the founders and their philosophies, perhaps because he came of age during the resurgence of interest in America's revolutionary generation—perhaps a combination of both—for virtually all of his political life, Lincoln relied on the strength and wisdom of the creators of the Declaration of Independence and the Constitution, and the ideas embodied in each document. He did so for the foundation that supported his philosophy, for the sustenance that fueled his politics, for the courage that helped him overcome personal and political adversity, and for the moral compass that guided his decision making. He drew on them for inspiration, for the rhetorical flourishes that became his trademark, for the intellectual depth that defined his greatness.

And for the biggest crisis he faced, he summoned the founders back to life and made them and their documents allies in his struggle to convince the nation of the need to end the scourge of slavery.

AS EARLY AS 1838, shortly after Madison's death, Lincoln worried that the passing of the founding fathers would leave a void, and it was incumbent upon a new generation of Americans to carry on their legacy. "They were the pillars of liberty," he said in a speech, "and now, that they have crumbled away, that temple must fall, unless we, their descendants, supply their places with other pillars." Lincoln revered George Washington, admired Thomas Paine, and quoted scripture to emphasize his belief in the ideas of freedom and equality expressed by

Jefferson in the Declaration ("an apple of gold," Lincoln called it, citing Proverbs) and Madison and Morris in the Constitution ("the picture of silver" framed around the apple). From early boyhood, when he had read a popular biography of George Washington, Lincoln steeped himself in the history of the founders and in the philosophical roots of the nation's creation. He had come to believe that the concept that "all men are created equal," that they are "endowed by their creator with certain unalienable rights"—to life, liberty, and the pursuit of happiness—was the "Father of all moral principal." Indeed, these were "the definitions and axioms of a free society."

During his career as a congressman and a lawyer, through the great slavery crises of the day—the Compromise of 1850, which imposed the strict Fugitive Slave Act; the Kansas-Nebraska Act, which introduced the notion of "popular sovereignty," by which voters could decide whether a state would be slave or free; and southern secession—during the Civil War and throughout his presidency, Abraham Lincoln time and again sought guidance and clarity from the principles espoused in the founding documents. They were the documents that defined and unified a cause eighty years earlier. Lincoln was convinced that they could bring a nation together in the 1850s, and even after he was proven wrong and war commenced, he believed the principles in the Declaration and the Constitution could eventually help bind the country's wounds.

LINCOLN WAS ON A pre-inaugural trip to Washington when he stopped in Philadelphia on February 22, 1861, George Washington's birthday. Speaking at Independence Hall, Lincoln found himself "filled with deep emotion" standing in the place where "collected together [were] the wisdom, the patriotism, the devotion to principle, from which sprang the institutions under which we live." Any chance he had to restore peace to a "distracted country" would come from the wisdom and inspiration of the founders. "I have never had a feeling politically that did not spring from the sentiments embodied in the Declaration of Independence," he told his audience, which responded with great cheers. "I have often pondered over the dangers which were incurred by the men who assembled here and adopted that [document]."

Lincoln said he had often asked himself what great principle had kept the Union together for more than eighty years. "It was not the mere matter of separation of the colonies from the mother land; but something in that Declaration giving liberty, not alone to the people of this country, but hope to the world for all future time," he said to thunderous applause. The fundamental and unshakeable promise of the Declaration was that "in due time the weights should be lifted from the shoulders of all men, and that all should have an equal chance."

As his speech concluded, Lincoln wondered whether the country could be saved upon the principle of "equal chance." If so, "I will consider myself one of the happiest men in the world if I can help to save it." If not, "it will be truly awful."

For him, the principle was worth fighting and dying for. Lincoln admitted that if the country could not be saved without giving up the principle of "equal chance," was it a country worth saving at all? In a prophetically chilling declaration to the audience, he proclaimed his dedication to this core principle:

"I would rather be assassinated on this spot than to surrender it."

TO LINCOLN, SAVING the Union was the nation's only option to preserve the fundamental principles of liberty, self-government, and equal opportunity. A shattered America would demonstrate to the whole world that the great experiment had failed, that a constitutional republic was unworkable.

Which people in what country would have the courage to ever try such a gamble again?

Further, the establishment of a separate slaveholding Confederacy would violate the essential equality theme woven through the Declaration and the Constitution. "This issue embraces more than the fate of these United States," said Abraham Lincoln. "It presents to the whole family of man, the question, whether a constitutional republic, or a democracy . . . can or cannot maintain its territorial integrity." The government of the United States was created to "elevate the condition of men . . . to afford all an unfettered start, and a fair chance in the race of life." For that reason, more than any other, the Union must be preserved.

For Lincoln, the Declaration and the Constitution were inseparable; the first the end and the second the means. The Declaration embodied the principle of liberty for all; the Constitution was the set of laws to make it so, the document that "framed" the government according to the principles of the Declaration. In his metaphor of the apple and the frame, Lincoln pointed out that the "picture"—the Constitution—"was made for the apple—not the apple for the picture." The ideas enshrined in the Declaration served as the guideposts for the framers of the Constitution, but both documents were required for the nation to flourish. "So let us act that neither the picture [n]or apple shall ever be blurred or bruised or broken," Lincoln wrote.

Nor was Lincoln deterred from his admiration of the founders— whom he called "the wisest and best men in the world"—because of the fact that most were slave owners. He understood the inconsistency, in some cases was deeply troubled by it and in others offered little more than excuses, but he recognized also that the founders and framers were in many ways bound by their time and place in history. Many had expressed their hostility to slavery, but most recognized that vigorous attempts to abolish it amidst the debates over the Declaration and the Constitution would have jeopardized both documents and the formation of the new nation. Their declarations of equality and liberty, in and of themselves, had begun the process of slavery's extinction, Lincoln believed, and for that, the founders had demonstrated courage and vision.

He insisted over and over again that, in a new century, the "all men are created equal" clause in the Declaration applied to blacks, that the founders would have agreed "that there is no reason in the world why the negro is not entitled to all the rights enumerated in the

Declaration of Independence—the right of life, liberty, and the pursuit of happiness." He also argued that the absence of the word "slave" or "slavery" from the Constitution was evidence both of the framers' embarrassment by it and their reluctance to tackle it head-on lest the entire document—and country—disintegrate. "The thing is hid away in the constitution," Lincoln said, "just as an afflicted man hides away a wen or a cancer, which he dares not cut out at once, lest he bleed to death."

Symbolically at least, Lincoln had begun the process of excising the cancer when he issued the Emancipation Proclamation at the beginning of 1863. On July 7, after Union victories at Gettysburg and Vicksburg, Lincoln had spontaneously addressed a throng of thousands that had gathered outside the White House, and again had referenced the glorious place July 4 had in American history. Indeed, he said referring to Gettysburg, the "great battle" was fought on the "first, second, and third of July." Was it just coincidence that "on the *fourth* the enemies of the Declaration that all men are created equal had to turn tail and run?"

There was little doubt that the tide of the war had shifted to the North's advantage. There would be more fighting, to be sure, but Lincoln and the Army of the Potomac were that much closer to removing the cancer of slavery and preserving the Union that the founders had established.

Victory was far from assured, and perhaps a compromise would be required to finally end the bloodshed, but now, in November 1863, Lincoln's fervent hope was that the nation had stared into the abyss and would survive; that it had faced an epic challenge and, battered and bruised as it was, would endure.

AS IT TURNED OUT, Lincoln's order to depart for Gettysburg the day before the commemoration was the right decision.

No particular mishap or delay occurred, but the special train from Washington did not chug into the station until nightfall. Coffins were stacked nearby awaiting burial. David Wills had invited Lincoln, along with Governor Curtin and Edward Everett, to dine and board at his home. "The hotels in our town will be crowded and in confusion," Will had predicted, and he was correct. From far and wide, people came, as if on a pilgrimage. "Except during its days of battle the little town of Gettysburg had never been so full of people," John Nicolay recalled. "After the usual supper hour the streets literally swarmed with visitors." Indeed, streets throughout Gettysburg were clogged, one newspaper reporter wrote, as "citizens from every quarter . . . in every kind of vehicle—old Pennsylvania wagons, spring wagons, carts, family carriages, buggies, and more fashionable modern vehicles, all crowded with citizens—kept pouring into the town in one continual string." The crowds were joined by regimental bands and soon people broke into celebratory song.

It is likely that Edward Everett showed Lincoln the galleys of his address, which he had with him, that night in Wills's home. Everett often previewed his written orations with friends and acquaintances to hear their opinions, and it would have been a breach of protocol for Everett not to share his remarks with the chief executive who would follow him to the rostrum. Did Everett's speech influence or even inspire Lincoln as he pondered the remainder of his own talk? The president's speech was still only half-written and Lincoln was tired after his long trip and dinner with Wills and his companions.

Perhaps he made a few revisions on the portion of the address he had completed, but he went to bed soon after ten o'clock. He would finish his remarks and recopy them in the morning. Whether Everett's speech helped Lincoln fill in the edges of his own oration is unknown, but this much is clear: the president had been thinking about the major themes for virtually his entire life.

21

★

"Of the People,
by the People,
for the People . . ."

★

After breakfast the next morning, around nine o'clock, Lincoln returned to his room to complete his remarks, accompanied by his private secretary John Nicolay, who stayed with him while he wrote and recopied the address in pencil.

The president had about an hour to work, since the formal procession to the cemetery was scheduled to begin promptly at ten o'clock. He had followed his lofty opening sentence—which rang with phrases such as "a new nation, conceived in Liberty" and "dedicated to the proposition that all men are created equal"—with a scene-setting section that outlined the challenges and defined the purpose of the day:

"Now we are engaged in a great civil war, testing whether that nation, or any nation so conceived and so dedicated, can long endure. We are met on a great battle-field of that war. We have come to dedicate a portion of that field, as a final resting place for those who here gave their lives that that nation might live. It is altogether fitting and proper that we should do this."

Lincoln knew, however, before he took his place on horseback in the procession, that the epic nature of Gettysburg, of the war, of the cause of the Union, would make it truly difficult to do justice to the men who fought at places like Little Round Top and Seminary Ridge. He wrote next:

"But, in a large sense, we can not dedicate—we can not consecrate—we can not hallow—this ground. The brave men, living and dead, who struggled here, have consecrated it, far above our poor power to add or detract."

The president, who paid attention to cadence, language, and delivery, likely collected his thoughts and mentally reviewed his remarks as he awaited the start of the procession under a bright November sky in which "the sun shone out in glorious splendor," according to one Gettysburg resident. Was it humility or earnestness that had prompted him to craft the next passage in his speech? "The world will little note, nor long remember, what we say here," he wrote—a phrase among the most ironic in all of American history considering that Lincoln's speech would become one of the most memorable orations ever—"but it can never forget what they did here." The crowds pressed closer, eager to shake his big gauntlet-clad hands as he reached down from his perch in the saddle, but Lincoln did not seem to mind. Nicolay noted that the procession marshals "had some difficulty in inducing the people to desist and allow him to sit in peace upon his horse."

The presidential procession finally wended its way to the cemetery and arrived at the platform at about eleven o'clock; Everett, the featured orator, arrived a half-hour later, without apology for keeping the president waiting

When Everett began his speech at noon, he reviewed much of the battle, day by day, pointing out *exactly* what soldiers did here, impressing the audience and holding its attention rapt with his rich, sonorous voice and his command of the subject matter. When he finished the crowd cheered and the band played.

The main event concluded, people grew restive awaiting the next component of the program—Lincoln's "dedicatory remarks." Ward Hill

Lamon, as grand marshal, introduced "my friend, the President of the United States." Lincoln rose and stepped slowly to the front of the platform. One observer noted that he moved "with his hands clasped behind him, his natural sadness of expression deepened, his head bent forward, and his eyes cast to the ground." Ohio journalist Robert Miller reported that he "never before [had] seen a crowd so vast and restless, after standing to [sic] long, so soon stilled and quieted." Men in the audience removed their hats, Miller wrote, "and all stood motionless to catch the first words he should utter." Lincoln stood silent in this position for a few seconds, then pulled a sheet or two of paper from his pocket, in sharp contrast to Everett's text, which had required a stack of pages.

The president adjusted his spectacles, and in "a sharp, unmusical, and treble voice," but one that resonated with strength and clarity, began to speak to the thousands gathered before him and the world beyond.

YEARS LATER, NICOLAY RECALLED the audience's reaction to Lincoln's words.

The throng was expecting the "mere formality" of the cemetery's official dedication, a "few perfunctory words." After all, it was Everett who was supposed to deliver the "thought and feeling of the hour." Lincoln was there as a "mere figure-head." As a result, he recounted, "they were therefore totally unprepared for what they heard, and could not immediately realize that *his* words, and not those of the carefully selected orator, were to carry the concentrated thought of the occasion like a trumpet peal to farthest posterity."

Lincoln's 272-word oration took less than three minutes; some spectators said he barely exceeded two. He spoke with conviction and authority, his delivery rhythmic, his inflections expressive. From the strength of his opening—"a new nation, conceived in liberty" and "all men created equal"—to his conviction that these soldiers gave their lives so that "their nation might live," to his belief that no speech could properly "dedicate, consecrate, or hallow" this ground since the "brave men, living and dead" had already "consecrated" it beyond any measure, he paid tribute to the soldiers who had fallen and the principles of the nation's founding.

Then, Lincoln launched into the powerful main theme and memorable conclusion to his speech, the responsibility of all Americans to carry on the work of those who had given their lives at Gettysburg:

"It is for us the living, rather, to be dedicated here to the unfinished work which they who fought here have thus far nobly advanced. It is rather for us to be here dedicated to the great task remaining before us—that from these honored dead we take increased devotion to that cause for which they gave the last full measure of devotion—that we here highly resolve that these dead shall not have died in vain—that this nation, under God, shall have a new birth of freedom—and that the government of the people, by the people, for the people, shall not perish from the earth."

LINCOLN CONCLUDED SO QUICKLY that many in the crowd were caught unaware. A photographer was still fumbling with his camera and tripod setup when the president returned to his seat. One observer later recalled "that there was surprise that his speech was so short." Lincoln's brevity may explain, at least partially, why history is replete with contradictions about the immediate reaction of the 15,000 to 20,000 people in attendance, and just as unclear about the countenance of the president and those around him on the platform when he had concluded his remarks.

In the most matter-of-fact way, assistant personal secretary John Hay—his in-the-moment account differing dramatically from Nicolay's recollection written years later of a "trumpet peal to farthest posterity"—wrote blithely in his diary: "The President, in a fine, free way, with more grace than is his wont, said his half dozen words of consecration, and the music wailed, and we went home through crowded and cheering streets." Hay saw no reason to elaborate: "All the particulars are in the daily papers," he wrote.

And indeed, there are contradicting reports about the entire speech. Some attendees would say that Lincoln barely glanced at his notes; others, that he carefully read every word. A few personal accounts of those on stage say he was unhappy with his remarks and the audience's reaction to them, and that some on the platform—including Everett—believed the speech was a failure; yet other recollections insist that Lincoln believed he had accomplished his goals and, his trademark modesty notwithstanding, was more than satisfied with the results.

As for the audience, reports range from reactions of unbridled enthusiasm to total silence, and perhaps in a way, both responses would have been a testament to the power of Lincoln's remarks. There are far too many reports of the deep emotions the president's remarks elicited to discount or doubt them, but it is not hard to believe that those emotions were expressed in different ways. Cheering was one way to acknowledge agreement with and enthusiasm for a speaker's words and the emotional power of his message, but thoughtful reflection—even stunned silence—especially at a cemetery dedication, was another. Gettysburg was a place where thousands had died and thousands more had suffered; its bloodstained ground *had* been consecrated by Lincoln, regardless of the lines in his speech claiming this was impossible. This battlefield was sacred ground, and as much as uproarious cheering is out of place in a church, even after an inspirational sermon, so, too, might such a display have seemed inappropriate to the thousands in the crowd.

"It was a sad hour," said a Gettysburg man. "Any tumultuous wave of applause would have been out of place." Reporter W. H. Cunningham maintained that Lincoln's words were met only with total silence and that he heard "not a word, not a cheer, not a shout."

Tough men were moved to tender reflections. One Union army officer, who had been wounded at Gettysburg, was brought close to tears during Lincoln's speech, realizing that the audience stood "almost immediately over the place where I had lain and seen my comrades torn in fragments by the enemy's cannonballs—think then, if you please, how these words fell on my ears." For him, and for many others, Lincoln's words "an immortal dedication" had a lasting and profound spiritual impact.

Another army captain sobbed openly, according to a reporter who saw him, and "lifted his eyes to heaven and in low and solemn tones exclaimed 'God Almighty, bless Abraham Lincoln.'" Another officer, when Lincoln uttered the phrase "but it can never forget what they did here," lost all restraint, and "burying his face in his handkerchief, he sobbed aloud while his manly frame shook with no unmanly emotion." A minister at the commemoration recalled clearly twenty-five years later that Lincoln's words cast a spell over the audience. "The great assembly listened almost awe-struck as to a voice from the divine oracle," he said. Congressman Isaac Arnold from Illinois, a strong Lincoln loyalist, commented on his mesmerizing charisma and magnetism: "The vast audience was instantly hushed, and hung upon his every word and syllable."

While accounts of the audience's specific response to Lincoln's speech vary widely—the size of the audience almost guaranteed that those further from the stage would be unable to hear him—almost no one disputes that the president's words had a profound impact on much of the crowd in a way far beyond intellectual approbation. Whether attendees cheered, wept, or reflected in silence, Lincoln had touched a deep and patriotic chord in the thousands who heard him speak, and the power of his words, printed in newspapers across the country, would soon evoke a wellspring of passion and feelings from millions across the country.

The speech convinced an Ohio journalist that "Abraham Lincoln, though he may have made mistakes, is the right man in the right place."

IN FEWER THAN THREE hundred words, President Lincoln had accomplished so much.

In one fell swoop, he had linked the current great struggle between North and South—at its root, a war to end slavery—to the nation's founding documents and the principle of human freedom and equality. In the speech's brevity lay its genius; in under three minutes, Lincoln had rendered indissoluble the sacrifices of those who had given their lives at Gettysburg to the principles espoused in both the Declaration of Independence ("all men are created equal") and the Constitution ("a government of the people, by the people, for the people").

Without mentioning the battle itself, the words "North" or "South," or any specific reference to slavery, Lincoln made it clear that the cause for which the soldiers at Gettysburg had given "the last full measure of devotion" was a "new birth of freedom" for America—one that no longer contained the stain, the cancer, of slavery. Their deaths had made this birth possible. The "unfinished work" that they had "nobly advanced" was now the responsibility "for us the living" to dedicate ourselves to: completing the "great task remaining before us" was the best and only way to honor their memories, the only way to assure that "these dead shall not have died in vain."

In the view Lincoln had held for his entire adult life, the Declaration and the Constitution provided clear guidance. It was not the documents that were flawed, but the men—then in the eighteenth century and now in the nineteenth century—who had interpreted them too narrowly. The Declaration's contention that "all men are created equal," and that all are thus granted by the Creator the unalienable rights of "life, liberty, and the pursuit of happiness" was a clear testament to the founders' ultimate intent and enduring vision that slavery would disappear from the American landscape and the American psyche. That it had yet to do so was not a shortcoming of the Declaration but a result of the political prejudices of those on both sides who had sought to ignore or misread the document for their own ends. "All honor to Jefferson," Lincoln had once written, who "had the coolness, forecast, and capacity to introduce into a merely revolutionary document, an abstract truth, applicable to all men and all times."

The abstract truth of equality also applied to the Constitution; the first three words of Gouverneur Morris's preamble, "we the people," also, in Lincoln's view, meant "all the people," including blacks and black slaves.

Inherent in both documents, then, was the *promise* of America—equality and self-governance for all—and the sacrifices made at Gettysburg had gone a long way toward fulfilling that promise. There was no need to scrap the American experiment, to start over, but it was essential that a "new birth of freedom" emerge for the nation to endure—in the form of a union truly and fully "dedicated to the proposition that all men are created equal."

The formation of a new nation required more than words from Jefferson, Adams, Madison, and Gouverneur Morris; their words would have remained abstract political theory, their aspirations would have lain in tatters, if not for the sacrifices made on the battlefield. So, too, would the promise of a new birth of American freedom in a new century. Lincoln could not do it with words alone—before it was over, nearly 700,000 war dead would become part of the epic struggle to end slavery and determine the future of the United States—but the president's words at Gettysburg had redefined the stakes and the struggle.

These soldiers, he argued, had fought and died to forever enshrine and preserve the Declaration's fundamental principle that "all men are created equal." They had perished to create the "more perfect union" to which the Constitution aspires.

As Lincoln had said with reverence and pained eloquence, those who rested in the cemetery at Gettysburg "gave their lives that the nation might live."

THE FIRST INDICATION OF the full impact of Abraham Lincoln's Gettysburg Address came from the featured speaker himself, the man acknowledged as the best orator in America, Edward Everett. On the day following the commemoration, Everett, who had accompanied Lincoln back to Washington, sent him a short note. First, he thanked Lincoln for his thoughtfulness toward him and his daughter, who was also seated on the speakers' platform at Gettysburg. Then he praised the president for "such eloquent simplicity and appropriateness at the consecration of the cemetery." And then, saving his highest praise for last, Everett wrote: "I should be glad if I could flatter myself that I came as near the central idea of the occasion in two hours as you did in two minutes."

It would be hard to imagine a greater compliment to Lincoln. Such an acknowledgment by an orator with Everett's sterling reputation went beyond gentlemanly platitudes or obligatory flattery. With his kind words, Everett had expressed two important points; first, that he understood the difficulty of Lincoln's task—speaking for just a few moments following a keynote address while attempting to convey the significance of the moment—and second, that the president was successful in what he had set out to accomplish. Lincoln responded with his usual humility and graciousness. "In our respective parts yesterday, you could not have been excused to make a short address, nor I a long one," the president observed. "I am pleased to know that in your judgment, the little I did say was not a failure."

As the days and weeks went by, it became clear that Lincoln's speech was anything but a failure. Those who praised it and those who condemned it disagreed politically, and disagreed profoundly on Lincoln's conclusions, but few doubted the speech's power and impact. Most members of the press, once they had a chance to digest Lincoln's words, lauded his address. "The dedicatory remarks by President Lincoln will live among the annals of man," predicted the *Chicago Tribune*. The *Providence Journal* wondered whether "the most elaborate and splendid oration [could] be more beautiful, more touching, more inspiring, than those thrilling words of the President."

Lincoln had changed the discussion, broadened the goals of the war, moved it beyond the preservation of the Union, and even the abolition of slavery. With the Gettysburg Address, Lincoln insisted that the war between North and South was an epic struggle being fought for the bedrock principle that underscored the birth of the American republic four score and seven years earlier: equality. Two years after the speech, a man who knew something about language and rhetoric, Ralph Waldo Emerson, predicted that Lincoln's address would "not easily be surpassed by words on any recorded occasion." It was perhaps the first prophecy that accurately reflected how history would ultimately judge the Gettysburg Address.

After Lincoln was assassinated on April 14, 1865, Charles Sumner, the fiercely antislavery U.S. senator from Massachusetts, eulogized him in Boston, and pointed out: "The inevitable topic to which he returned with most frequency, and to which he clung with all the grasp of his soul, was the practical character of the Declaration of Independence in announcing the liberty and equality of all men."

For Lincoln, Sumner declared, these concepts were not merely idle words, "but substantial truths, binding on the conscience of mankind."

IN THE DAYS FOLLOWING his Gettysburg remarks, Lincoln fielded several requests for copies of his speech. David Wills asked for a copy to place in the official correspondence and papers for the cemetery dedication project. To comply, Lincoln compared the version of the speech he had delivered from the platform at Gettysburg with the Associated Press report as it was printed in many prominent newspapers. As Nicolay explained, he then added his "own fresh recollections of the form in which he delivered it," and produced a new "autograph copy—a careful and deliberate revision which has become the standard and authentic text."

Nicolay believed Lincoln lettered at least "half a dozen or more" copies, more than any other document Lincoln wrote, recopying "with painstaking care to correspond word for word with his revision." Any variations were purely accidental and "against his intention." Some of those copies ended up in private hands, and Lincoln apparently retained at least two, including the original handwritten version he held at the podium at Gettysburg—the so-called battlefield copy—and a second handwritten copy he inked after the cemetery commemoration.

Eventually, those handwritten copies, part of Lincoln's papers, found their way into the hands of his secretaries, John Nicolay and John Hay—loaned to them by Lincoln's son, Robert Todd, in 1874, as part of their efforts to write a massive biography on Lincoln and to coedit the sixteenth president's collected works. By the time their work was published in the late 1880s, Nicolay and Hay acknowledged that Lincoln's speech was "exquisitely molded," so much so that "the best critics have awarded it an unquestioned rank as one of the world's masterpieces in rhetorical art."

Decades later, in 1916, the Hay and Nicolay families jointly donated the two copies of the Gettysburg Address to the Library of Congress; construction of the Lincoln Memorial was under way in Washington, and plans called for the speech to be engraved on one of the monument's walls. Accuracy, therefore, was essential.

But how the families had retained possession of these copies, how the copies were *theirs* to donate in the first place, remained a mystery, one that included the reappearance of the original battlefield copy that had been feared lost, uncomfortable allegations of theft, and embarrassing questions between the Nicolay and Hay heirs.

22

★

"The Instrument
Has Suffered
Very Seriously"

★

Tuesday, July 4, 1876, Philadelphia

Gazing at the thousands of people sprawled before him, Richard
Henry Lee—grandson of the Virginia delegate who a century earlier
offered the resolution in the Continental Congress that America's
"United Colonies are, and of right ought to be, free and independent
States"—clutched the fading, original, engrossed parchment copy of
the Declaration of Independence and prepared to read the historic document that his grandfather had signed.

It was the 100th anniversary of the adoption of the Declaration,
and the sprawling international Centennial Exhibition of 1876, the first
world's fair held in the United States, had been under way in grand
fashion since opening ceremonies on May 10. Lee was among the more
than 8 million people who would travel to Philadelphia during the
exhibition's stirring six-month run to celebrate the centennial year of
America's independence and its growth and emergence as a world
power.

Years in the planning, the massive exhibition was intended to unite the country riven by Civil War and Reconstruction by showcasing the country's industrial prowess, geographic expansion, and material and spiritual growth in the 100 years since it had adopted the Declaration of Independence. Even the opening day of the event was orchestrated to symbolize the country's progress; organizers chose May 10 since it marked the seventh anniversary of a watershed moment in American history; on that day in 1869, the presidents of the Central Pacific and Union Pacific railroads met in Promontory, Utah, to drive the ceremonial final spike into the track that connected their lines and marked the completion of the transcontinental railroad. For the first time in U.S. history, the American continent was connected through modern rail traffic. What better date to open the world's fair, whose goal was to highlight America's advancement and innovation?

More than 180,000 people attended the opening ceremonies, hosted by the president, Ulysses S. Grant, and those who thronged to Philadelphia by train, horseback, horse-drawn carriage, or steamboat on the Schuylkill River beheld the vast exhibit halls spread over more than 450 acres in Philadelphia's Fairmount Park. Most were awestruck by the massive Corliss steam engine that anchored the exhibition, the largest such engine ever built, standing nearly seventy feet high, weighing 650 tons, and powering all the machines in the exhibition's Machinery Hall. Attendees witnessed the wonders of technology in other ways too: they watched printing presses run off copies of the New York papers, which published editions from the exhibition floor; they were introduced to the typewriter and a mechanical calculator; and they were fascinated when inventor Alexander Graham Bell demonstrated his telephone. Only two months earlier, Bell had uttered the words to his partner, "Mr. Watson—come here—I want to see you," and Watson had heard him through the device handset, proof that the invention had worked. In that moment at his Boston workshop, Bell had advanced the evolution of mass communications well beyond Samuel Morse's telegraph, invented thirty-two years earlier; Bell's famous words had supplanted Morse's first telegraph message—"What hath

God wrought?"—as the iconic description of modern and rapid human communications.

After opening ceremonies, attendance at the exposition dipped somewhat, averaging about 20,000 each day during the early weeks. But as word spread across the country of the marvels in Philadelphia, interest and attendance picked up. Americans were enthusiastic, proud, and eager to make the pilgrimage to the city where so much of the nation's heritage and history had taken shape.

This excitement reached a fever pitch as the "day of days," the centennial Fourth of July, approached.

BY THE TIME RICHARD HENRY LEE read the Declaration from the reviewing stand in Independence Square on July 4, the tens of thousands of visitors who had converged on Philadelphia had enjoyed several days of commemorations. Businesses and stores had been closed since Saturday, July 1, when dignitaries offered speeches and good wishes to the crowd. Several private celebrations were held on Sunday; public festivities were limited due to the Sabbath. On Monday, thousands more visitors arrived, mostly by train, and Philadelphia was pulsating with excitement. That night, 5,000 veterans led a magnificent torchlight procession, nearly 15,000 marchers strong and seven miles long, through the city to Independence Hall.

On the morning of the Fourth, more than half a million people watched a second procession wind through city streets, pass under an enormous archway last used during Lafayette's visit in 1824, and approach the reviewing stand near Independence Hall.

After silencing the throng, Lee began his public reading. One hundred years earlier, from virtually the same spot upon which they now stood, John Adams, Thomas Jefferson, Benjamin Franklin, Caesar Rodney, John Hancock, and other brave delegates had risked so much to create a new nation. The original engrossed document that each of these men had signed, the document that had nearly been destroyed during the War of 1812, had been entrusted by President Grant to

Philadelphia's mayor, William S. Stokley, for display at the Centennial Exhibition.

The reality of the Declaration's physical condition quickly became apparent to visitors and journalists alike. It was certainly now treated with more care than in previous years. It was "framed and glazed for protection" and then deposited in a fireproof safe "especially designed for both preservation and convenient display," according to the *Public Ledger.* "When the outer doors of the safe were opened, the parchment was visible behind a heavy plate-glass inner door; the doors were closed at night." But the public display also revealed the Declaration's physical flaws; the Centennial Exposition was a celebration of American progress, but the country's founding document was deteriorating badly. Its lengthy exposure to sunlight and smoke from fireplaces, and perhaps the wet-press process that it had been subjected to earlier in the century, had left the Declaration "faded and time-worn" and "age-dimmed." Although the text was "fully legible," the signatures were "so pale as to be only dimly discernible in the strongest light." Worse, while some were readable, "some are wholly invisible, the spaces which contained them presenting only a blank."

Richard Henry Lee had electrified the crowd with his reading of the Declaration—he held it aloft when he finished and was greeted with "cheer after cheer"—but even the account of his performance noted that Lee clung to "the faded and crumbling manuscript, held together by a simple frame."

Colonel Frank Etting, chairman of the Committee on the Restoration of Independence Hall and of the National Centennial Commemoration, found the Declaration's condition deplorable and depressing, and was struck by the irony that age, light, and atmosphere had done something the British could not do.

"Yonder parchment . . . scarce bears trace of the signatures," Etting lamented, "the execution of which made fifty-six names imperishable."

*

THE DECLARATION'S HIGHLY VISIBLE display at the centennial celebration initially served as a wake-up call; by late summer, the document's physical condition had become a matter of public concern.

Thousands of Americans had viewed the document; countless others had read about its deteriorated state in newspapers and other publications. On August 3, Congress responded, adopting a joint resolution "that a commission, consisting of the Secretary of the Interior, the Secretary of the Smithsonian Institution, and the Librarian of Congress be empowered to . . . resort to such means as will most effectually restore the writing of the original manuscript of the Declaration of Independence—with the signatures appended thereto."

The resolution had actually been proposed the previous January but had stalled in Congress. The time line is important considering that in April—a month before the Declaration's sojourn to Philadelphia— William J. Canby, an employee of the Washington Gas Light Company, believed he had a solution to restoring the Declaration to its former glory. In a letter to the Library of Congress, Canby declared himself as the right man for the job. "I have over thirty years experience in handling the pen upon parchment, and in that time, as an expert, have engrossed hundreds of ornamental, special documents." Once establishing his credentials, Canby offered his recommendation: "The only feasible plan is to replenish the original with a supply of ink, which has been destroyed by the action of light and time, with an ink well known to be, for all practical purposes, imperishable."

Canby's suggestion seems to have fallen on deaf ears—likely a good outcome for the future of the Declaration—as the special commission took no action on the parchment itself. Despite initial resolve to improve the Declaration's physical condition after the centennial, bureaucratic inertia stalled any meaningful efforts to tackle the job for the next two decades. However, with the approval of President Grant, the Declaration was moved from the Patent Office into the new fireproof building that now housed the State, War, and Navy departments (which later became the Old Executive Office Building). In early March 1877, the Declaration was mounted in an open cabinet in the State Department library—still exposed to light—where it would be exhibited for the next seventeen years. Officials seemed unconcerned with the irony that, within a so-called fireproof building, smoking was allowed in the library and the room contained an open fireplace located just a short distance from the Declaration.

But the Declaration's travels are filled with such ironies—its new home proved far safer than its previous domicile. The Patent Office was gutted by fire just a few months after the document was moved. Once again, the original engrossed and signed copy of the Declaration of Independence had narrowly escaped destruction.

NEGLECT, HOWEVER, WAS ANOTHER matter. Committees and commissions studied the Declaration, offered opinions, and made recommendations throughout the 1880s, but still it hung in the State Department library and nothing was done to improve its condition. Fading and parchment deterioration continued. Finally, in 1894, the State Department issued the following sober announcement: "The rapid fading of the text of the original Declaration of Independence and the deterioration of the parchment upon which it is engrossed, from exposure to light and lapse of time, render it impracticable for the Department longer to exhibit it or to handle it." Thus, State Department officials had reached an unfortunate decision: "For the secure preservation of its present condition, so far as may be possible, it has been carefully wrapped and placed in a steel case." The Declaration was removed from the case briefly in 1898 to produce a photograph for the *Ladies' Home Journal* and the parchment was described as "still in good legible condition," although "some of the signatures" were "necessarily blurred."

Five years after the photo appeared in the magazine, the secretary of state, John Hay—President Lincoln's former secretary—deeply concerned about the Declaration's physical condition, asked the National Academy of Sciences for help. The organization, established by Congress and signed into law by President Lincoln, consisted of scientific scholars who provided the nation with counsel on the issues of science and technology. Hay's April 1903 letter requested "such recommendations as may seem practicable. . . . touching [the Declaration's] preservation." He explained how the document had been kept out of the light, sealed between two pieces of glass, and locked in a steel safe. Still, despite these precautions, he was "unable to say that the text is not continuing to fade and the parchment to wrinkle and perhaps to break."

Ten days later, after examining the Declaration closely, the National Academy issued its report to Hay. "The instrument has suffered very seriously from the very harsh treatment to which it was exposed in the earlier years of the Republic," lamented Charles F. Chandler. "Folding and rolling have creased and broken the parchment." In addition, the wet-press process, which Chandler presumed occurred in the early 1820s to produce a facsimile, "removed a large portion of the ink." Moreover, Chandler reported, "exposure to the action of light for more than thirty years, while the instrument was placed on exhibition, has resulted in the fading of the ink, particularly in the signature[s]."

There was some good news. The academy's examination had uncovered no evidence of mold or other disintegrating agents, nor did it find evidence that further deterioration was in progress. Chandler and the committee were reluctant to apply any chemicals to the document to attempt to restore the ink, fearing such treatment would present a dangerous risk. Perhaps some ink could be restored, but chemicals could also result in "serious discoloration of the parchment." And for similar reasons, the committee warned that it was inadvisable for any "solution, such as collodion, paraffin, etc." to be applied in the misguided attempt to "strengthen the parchment or making it moisture proof."

IN ESSENCE, THE SCIENTIFIC experts were stumped.

"The present method of caring for the instrument seems to be the best that can be suggested," the academy report stated, not the conclusion Hay had sought, since that method meant that the Declaration was hidden from the American people who had grown to cherish it as the indisputable symbol of the freedoms they enjoyed. Indeed, said Chandler, that was exactly what the scientists were recommending. The Declaration "should be kept in the dark and as dry as possible, and never placed on exhibition."

Hay apparently heeded the National Academy's recommendation. A 1904 book about the Declaration alluded to the fact that the document had been "locked and sealed, by order of Secretary Hay" and, further, "is no longer shown to anyone except by his direction."

Hay's decision meant that at the dawn of the twentieth century, both the Declaration of Independence and the U.S. Constitution—the country's two most important founding documents—were sealed in cases, placed in drawers, no longer available for Americans to see, even out of sight and perhaps out of mind of the State Department employees entrusted with their safekeeping.

Both documents would remain under lock and key at the State Department for nearly two decades, before they were finally unveiled during a ceremony that attendees would describe as nothing less than extraordinary.

23

★

"Touch Any Aspect
of the Address,
and You
Touch a Mystery"

★

Robert Todd Lincoln was exasperated but polite when he wrote to John Nicolay's daughter, Helen, on November 6, 1908. "I venture to trouble you to ask," Abraham Lincoln's son began, "whether you know where the original manuscript of the Gettysburg Address is."

Robert Todd had been searching in vain for his father's speech in preparation for a number of activities that were being planned for the 100th anniversary of Abraham Lincoln's birth in 1909. The Gettysburg Address had last publicly surfaced in 1894, when John Nicolay had published an article about the speech and included a facsimile copy—Nicolay had also included a detailed comparison between Lincoln's battlefield copy and handwritten copies that he had prepared after comparing the Associated Press reports of the cemetery commemoration. Robert Todd Lincoln had originally given custody of the Lincoln papers to Hay and Nicolay as the two secretaries were researching their massive biography of the sixteenth president. When Hay died in 1905, his widow, Clara Hay, transferred the Lincoln papers to Robert Todd Lincoln, but the Gettysburg Address was not among them. "If in the course of further examinations it is found," Robert Todd wrote to Helen Nicolay, "it will be considered as belonging to you, but I have little hope of such good fortune."

Helen Nicolay replied with disappointing news: "I do not know where the original ms. of the Gettysburg Address is," she said. "It is a mystery that has puzzled and distressed me for a long time." But with Robert Todd's inquiry, it was time for Helen to unburden herself. "Now that you have asked me," she said, "I am going to tell you the whole story."

THE "WHOLE STORY" ABOUT the original manuscript of the Gettysburg Address is long, convoluted, filled with innuendo and accusations, enmeshed in arcana that scholars have sifted through for decades, and has been the subject of lengthy analyses and speculation by historians. At various points along the way, experts have raised serious questions about whether Nicolay or Hay misplaced or even stole copies of Lincoln's famous speech; or more accurately, whether they removed copies from Lincoln's papers before returning the papers to Robert Todd. Some of the controversy revolved around the question of whether Lincoln gave each of his secretaries a copy of the speech, whether he gave only Hay a copy, or whether his intention was to give neither a copy but to retain both the Battlefield copy and the handwritten copy he produced afterward. Years later, David Mearns, chief of the Manuscript Division of the Library of Congress, would observe of the controversy: "Touch any aspect of the address, and you touch a mystery."

In the end, both copies—which would become known as the Nicolay copy and the Hay copy—were found among John Hay's personal papers, including the second version, which wasn't discovered until late in November 1908, weeks after Robert Todd Lincoln had written to Helen Nicolay. Clara Hay discovered it among her late husband's papers, apparently after inquiries from Robert Todd. Historians believe that both documents originally had been part of Lincoln's papers, had been used for research by both secretaries, and thus wound up among Hay's personal papers.

After numerous letters, Hay's three children and Helen Nicolay ignored the essence of the controversy and agreed on a polite solution to the mystery of the Gettysburg Address. On April 11, 1916, they simultaneously donated to the Library of Congress four precious documents. The Hays donated both drafts of the Gettysburg Address and the draft of his inspirational second inaugural address. Helen Nicolay donated a memorandum that Lincoln had prepared on August 23, 1864, which stated that it seemed probable he would lose the upcoming election, in which case it would be his duty to cooperate with the president-elect to save the Union. (Lincoln sealed the document and after he won the election, read the memo to his cabinet.)

In its press release describing the donation, the Library of Congress noted that one of the copies of the Gettysburg Address was "held in his [Lincoln's] hand when he delivered it." George Herbert Putnam—who went by Herbert—could barely contain his excitement, calling the donation "the most precious individual documents that have been entrusted to me during the seventeen years that I have been in charge of the Library—priceless relics of one of the noblest figures in history."

Putnam, who had always advocated that the Library of Congress share its collections and gifts with the American public, added: "The papers will be put on exhibition for the benefit of the many thousands of people who come to visit the library."

February 28, 1924

THE GETTYSBURG ADDRESS CONTROVERSY had been long forgotten when, eight years later, a ceremony took place at the Library of Congress. The location was the second floor of the Great Hall, which visitors reached by ascending a grand staircase. There, between two pillars, stood a marble shrine that resembled an altar, consisting of a sturdy pedestal with a large display area across its top supporting a special cabinet with doors that could open and close. Small bronze eagles flanked the cabinet doors and on the gray-black marble above the shrine was inscribed: "The Declaration of Independence and the Constitution of the United States of America."

For Herbert Putnam, twenty-five years into his nearly forty-year tenure, this was a very special day. Irrepressible, authoritarian, a micromanager, and often combative, he had amassed substantial power during his reign at the Library of Congress. He had his sights on acquiring America's two most important documents from the State Department for more than two decades, since a 1903 congressional act that allowed an executive branch department to turn over to the Library of Congress books, maps, records, or other material the department no longer needed. Putnam had sought many records from the revolutionary and constitutional era, writing to the State Department in 1906 that the library not only was the appropriate steward for such documents, but it could better protect the records from fire or accident "to a degree not possible in an Executive Department or in a building of the character of the State." Such a consideration, he argued, became of "fresh and vivid importance" in view of the destruction of old Spanish records in the San Francisco earthquake and fire. Putnam's suggestion received a cool reception at the time.

The State Department balked at turning over most of its important papers, arguing, for example, that the papers of the Continental Congress were "essential to the continuity [and] completeness of the Archives of this Department, and cannot be transferred without serious injury thereto and inconvenience."

SEVERAL YEARS PASSED WITHOUT action, and World War I distracted officials from the State Department from making any major moves with their records. Putnam, too, was consumed with other issues, including the details of administering the Library of Congress and providing wartime requests for information.

Finally in 1920, Secretary of State Bainbridge Colby, concerned for the "care and preservation of the original Declaration of Independence, Constitution of the United States," and other critical documents, appointed a committee to recommend steps for the "permanent and effective preservation from deterioration and from danger from fire, or other form of destruction, of those documents of supreme value." Part of the committee's review would include how the documents could be safely displayed for the benefit of the "patriotic public." The committee examined the Declaration and, despite its deterioration, concluded that little additional harm could occur if the parchment was exhibited "between two sheets of glass, hermetically sealed at the edges, and exposed only to diffused light." The four sheets of the Constitution were in "excellent condition," the committee reported, and exposure to only diffused light would not adversely affect its condition. "Properly cared for," the report said, "[the four sheets] have as reasonable a prospect of life as the parchments of the middles ages, which have survived for centuries." Heavy glass, diffused light, sealed edges—both the Declaration and the Constitution could be safely displayed if these steps were taken.

The committee had one more recommendation: the State Department should send the two documents and many others to the Library of Congress for organization and display. State was simply not equipped to properly display the Declaration and the Constitution for the general public.

While nothing was done immediately, on September 28, 1921—after the Harding administration had assumed office—the new secretary of state, Charles Evans Hughes, prepared an executive order for the president to sign transferring the Declaration and the Constitution to the Library of Congress. Hughes traced the history and travels of both documents and then pointed out the benefits of relocating them: "The [Library of Congress] building is of modern fireproof construction; there is no fire in it; smoking is not allowed; it has exhibition halls which are always under guard." Further, making the documents accessible to the general public was a responsibility of the administration, Hughes noted, pointing out that when visitors traveled to Washington "there is no document which they desire to see so much as the Declaration of Independence."

President Harding signed and issued the order on September 29, calling for the "original engrossed Declaration of Independence and the original engrossed Constitution of the United States" to be transferred from the State Department to the Library of Congress. The following day, Hughes wrote to Putnam and announced that he was "prepared to turn the documents over to you when you are ready to receive them."

Putnam was more than eager. That very day he presented himself at the State Department in the library's Ford Model T mail wagon. He signed a receipt for the parchments, cushioned them on a pile of leather U.S. mail sacks, returned to the library and locked the Declaration and the Constitution in his office safe.

The wily bureaucrat, who had developed a keen political sense in his more than two decades at the library's helm, now turned his attention to a permanent home for America's founding documents. For that, he needed money.

PUTNAM WAS UP AGAINST the clock: the Bureau of the Budget was about to print department spending estimates for the coming year, and he had no time to secure blueprints, plans, or precise specifications for the structure that would house the Declaration and the Constitution. He knew they needed to be "fully safeguarded," given "distinction," and "open to inspection to the public at large." He consulted his building superintendent and, on his advice, requested $12,000 for the purpose of building a display for the two precious parchments. In early January 1922, Putnam told a congressional appropriations committee that with proper lighting and sturdiness, the documents could be protected and displayed, "and you could have something that every visitor to Washington would wish to tell about when he returned."

Those visitors would regard the display housing "with keen interest as a sort of shrine," he said.

Putnam was persuasive, and on March 20 Congress made the $12,000 "immediately available" for funding a "safe, permanent repository of appropriate design, within the Library of Congress building."

Designed by Francis H. Bacon (brother of Henry Bacon, architect of the Lincoln Memorial), the beautiful marble shrine certainly provided the place of dignity that Putnam had demanded. The cabinet's gold-plated bronze doors, for example, would remain swung back to display the Declaration when the library was open to the public. Both the Declaration and the Constitution cases would be covered with double panes of plate glass, with specially prepared gelatin films between the two plates to "exclude the actinic rays of light." Gustavus T. Kirby, formerly of the American Art Association, who had demonstrated "a most helpful interest in preserving the manuscripts from injurious light," had suggested the gelatin filters and would oversee their installation. The floor beneath the shrine was constructed of Greek marble, and surrounding the shrine would be a solid balustrade of Italian marble. From outside the balustrade, the documents would be clearly visible, and visitors who wanted a closer look could pass single-file inside. A twenty-four-hour detail of uniformed guards would protect the shrine from the "evil-disposed," Putnam reported.

AFTER NEARLY TWO YEARS of construction, the shrine was completed early in 1924 and dedicated on February 28 in the presence of President and Mrs. Coolidge, Secretary of State Hughes, and a contingent of congressional members.

Not a word was spoken at the dedication. In a remarkable moment—one that would later be called the "silent ceremony"—Putnam simply stood upon the desk portion of the shrine and fitted the Declaration to its frame, then arranged the leaves of the Constitution, closed the glass lid, and turned the locks. When finished, he faced the president and the members of Congress, and from the adjoining hall, the library staff began singing "America" (AKA "My Country 'Tis of Thee"). The dignitaries assembled at the shrine joined in and together the group completed two stanzas. With that, the ceremony ended "without a single utterance," save for the voices joined in song.

Putnam recalled later the import of the moment. It appeared to him that "the impression upon the audience proved the emotional potency of documents animate with great tradition."

Ironically, for all the lofty rhetoric and eloquent debate that had been part and parcel of the creation of the Declaration and the Constitution, the fact that they were now displayed for all Americans to see in a new permanent home had left ceremony attendees at a loss for words.

What none of the participants could have known in 1924 is that permanence is fleeting; in this case, the Declaration and the Constitution would remain on display in the Library of Congress for only the next seventeen years.

As was the case in 1814, the winds of war would force them out of Washington. They would return only after an American victory appeared imminent.

★ ★ ★

1944

★ ★ ★

24

★

"Nothing that Men Have Ever Made Surpasses Them"

★

September 19, 1944, Fort Knox, Kentucky, 3:35 p.m.

The provost marshal of Fort Knox, Major W. C. Hatfield, ordered the heavily armed convoy to move out. Slowly, the vehicles began rolling, led by Hatfield's car, whose occupants included a lieutenant and three rifle-carrying military policemen. Bringing up the rear was a Secret Service car. In the middle was a large truck guarded by a sergeant, two corporals, three privates, and several military policemen. Inside the truck were the containers that had been removed from the bullion depository vault a short time earlier.

The Declaration of Independence, the Constitution of the United States, and the Gettysburg Address were going home.

The Allied landings at Normandy—D-day—had occurred three months earlier and British and American troops were now pushing across Europe toward Germany. Months of hard fighting lay ahead in both Europe and the Pacific, but President Roosevelt, the Joint Chiefs, and the War Department had decided that bombings or sabotage on the U.S. mainland were now unlikely. It was time for the most valu-able of Library of Congress documents to return to Washington. Most of the other nearly 5,000 boxes had been moved during the previous two months. "They see no need," Archibald MacLeish wrote of mili-tary commanders, "to keep materials of this kind in the woods and hills any longer." MacLeish and his staff agreed; they were anxious for the documents to return to the library but had deferred to military lead-ers on the appropriate time.

The Library of Congress made no announcement of any kind, though MacLeish eventually lauded in his 1944 report the efforts of "those responsible for the transportation over the Blue Ridge and the Alleghenies of 4,789 cases of books and manuscripts valued in uncount-able millions of dollars."

The final transfer, the return of the documents from Fort Knox to Washington, was the most sensitive operation of all. Preparations at the bullion depository had been meticulous.

The convoy reached Louisville's 7th Street Station and entered through a rear entrance "without any public notice or knowledge." Agents placed the cases aboard a Pullman sleeper car—number 42— of the 5:30 p.m. Baltimore & Ohio train to Washington.

Harry Neal met the train and he and several other agents quickly removed the containers to an armored and guarded truck, which ar-rived at the Library of Congress annex just before noon. MacLeish met the documents and supervised their transfer to the vault. There, MacLeish, Alvin Kremer, Clapp, chief assistant librarian Luther Evans, and Reference Department director David Mearns opened the containers and examined the documents. "The contents were found to tally with the list previously given . . . and to be in good condition," Clapp noted, "whereupon they were immediately removed to the Librarian's safe."

MacLeish insisted that the Declaration and the Constitution be placed in their shrine so that the public could view them and to pub-licly memorialize the moment, declaring that the documents' return had "the same spiritual and intellectual symbolization for the people of this country that the return of the lights to London [after years of blackout] had for the people of London." On Sunday, October 1, 1944, the doors of the library were opened at 11:30 a.m. Beside the shrine stood a Marine guard of honor, which, in rotation, would be relieved in succeeding weeks by army and navy guards.

Secret Service agent Harry Neal, who had been invited by Mac-Leish, was one of those in attendance at the ceremony.

MacLeish wrote and spoke often about what the Declaration and Constitution represented, but at no time more passionately and evocatively than when he delivered his instructions to the Marines guarding the shrine. "Our nation differs from all others in this—that it was not created by geographic or by racial accident, but by the free choice of the human spirit, conceived and founded by men who chose to live under one form of government rather than under another," he said. "The sheets of vellum and the leaves of ancient paper in those cases which you guard are the very sheets and leaves on which [our] form of government [was] brought to being. Nothing that men have ever made surpasses them." It was appropriate that the documents should be guarded by men who fought against "the enemies of everything this Constitution and this Declaration stand for."

With that, the captain of the Marine band, in position nearby, raised his baton and the Great Hall resonated with the sounds of the national anthem.

ONCE THE DOCUMENTS WERE safely returned to the Library of Congress, MacLeish would tell lawmakers that the collaboration from the repositories that stored his library's collections was heartening, especially the cooperation his staff had received from Fort Knox personnel. "No mere words of gratitude can begin to express our sense of obligation to the officers of these various institutions," he said.

To this point, they had done their duty under the shroud of secrecy; it was forbidden under the "code of voluntary censorship and by military regulation" to acknowledge their contributions. But in his 1944 annual report, MacLeish wrote, "It is now possible to announce" which institutions had provided safe harbor for the documents. He described the specific buildings and rooms in which boxes were stored at the University of Virginia at Charlottesville, Washington and Lee, VMI, and Denison University. Their "patient and uncomplaining acceptance" of twenty-four-hour guards in their buildings and stacks of boxes in their halls spoke "eloquently of their generosity, their devotion, and—for no other word that is wholly expressive—their patriotism."

Perhaps the most remarkable and gratifying expression of patriotism was the fact that townspeople, librarians, custodians, shippers, domestic help, truck drivers, railroad personnel, and curious onlookers alike—in every case—maintained the secret about the largest single relocation of priceless documents, books, and artifacts in American history.

ARCHIBALD MACLEISH SUBMITTED HIS resignation on November 8, 1944, the day after an ailing President Roosevelt was elected to an unprecedented fourth term. MacLeish informed the president that his most important work was done—he had completed an administrative reorganization of the Library of Congress, and the exhausting and emotionally draining mission of securing and protecting the nation's most important documents had been successfully carried out. MacLeish was tired—tired of war and tired of Washington.

He expected that his days in the nation's capital were over, but Roosevelt had other plans. He nominated MacLeish to be assistant secretary of state for cultural and public affairs, where his first responsibility would be to persuade the American people on the concept of a United Nations. MacLeish concurred with Roosevelt that only through a strong United Nations could a lasting peace be maintained. After a contentious series of confirmation hearings in the Senate—MacLeish's left-wing leanings were objectionable to many conservatives—the former librarian reported to the State Department on December 19.

"I think it is thrilling that you are not leaving us," FDR wrote to Mac-
Leish. "The only trouble is that you jump from one mausoleum to the
other." In reply, MacLeish could not resist a pun, pointing out to the
president that "a rolling stone gathers no Mausoleum."

MacLeish's legacy was one of leadership and decisive action. He
was the "most articulate librarian we've ever had," noted Frederick
Goff, head of the Rare Books Division, and it did not hurt that he had
a direct line to the White House. Staffers were struck by his speed of
thought, movement, and expression. As a boss, MacLeish "wanted it
done now," said one library executive, and another noted that in reor-
ganizing the library and broadening its services, MacLeish "plunged
boldly ahead at a pace that few, if any, trained librarians would have
attempted." In addition to his streamlining of the library's operations,
his protection of the documents and his transformation of the library
to a war-time footing, MacLeish appointed the library's first woman
and first African American department directors.

After recounting MacLeish's achievements in the 1945 annual report, Luther Evans, who succeeded him, wrote: "In these, and in a
myriad of other ways, the brush of the comet gave a new dimension to
the Library. But the outstanding characteristic of that brilliant episode
is not the fact that so much was consummated in so short a time, but
rather that there is now so little to repent."

HARRY NEAL WOULD RISE through the ranks to become assistant
chief of the Secret Service before his retirement in 1957. Along the
way he prepared the service's budgets, wrote articles on counterfeiting, and—in what he called a "highlight day in my life"—stood next
to Harry Truman when the president signed a bill that officially defined the duties and powers of the U.S. Secret Service. It was Harry
Neal who believed that the service had to be given its own designation
to reflect its growing gravitas and responsibility—something it could
not achieve by being buried as a mere "division" within the Treasury
Department. Throughout his career, and during his retirement, he

dedicated himself to cultivating, preserving, and writing about the service's history. He wrote more than thirty books and was one of the founders and long-time editors of *The Pipeline*, the quarterly newsletter of former agents of the U.S. Secret Service.

His contributions to the Secret Service earned him the prestigious five-pointed gold badge—an exact replica of his sterling silver agent's badge—one of a handful that have been awarded in the 150-year history of the service. Hand-engraved at the Bureau of Engraving and Printing, the front of the badge is stamped with US in the center, the word SECRET above it and SERVICE below. The back of the badge is engraved with his years of service: HARRY E. NEAL, ASSISTANT CHIEF, 7-1-1926 TO 4-30-1957. The Secret Service honored Neal again when it dedicated its Exhibit Hall to him.

In the biography plaque that graces the room, the final sentence reads: "Until his death in 1993, he always spoke of his pride in being a member of the Secret Service and the ideals the agency represents."

To this day, Harry's children—Harry Jr. and Barbara—are honorary members of the 3,500-strong fraternity of former agents. When they attend Secret Service events, they are seated at reserved tables and introduced as dignitaries along with other VIPs. Harry Neal Jr., who is the steward of his father's gold star, normally stores it in a safe-deposit box, except when he and Barbara attend these functions. Then he brings the badge with him to honor the contributions and the memory of his father.

NEITHER ARCHIBALD MACLEISH NOR Harry Neal ever forgot the events of the 1940s.

In 1970, Neal wrote to MacLeish—now retired at Uphill Farm in Conway, Massachusetts—to convey his regards and reminisce about the heavy burden he felt during the transfer of documents to and from the Library of Congress. MacLeish expressed his gratitude for the letter and began his response: "I have never forgotten that momentous occasion and it is a pleasure to have an opportunity to send my thanks once more to the man who mastered the difficulties so brilliantly."

Then MacLeish added: "Whenever I think, now, of the terrifying responsibility of shipping the Constitution and the Declaration to Fort Knox, my appetite suffers for days. I am glad you remember it with the same emotions."

ARCHIBALD MACLEISH DIED ON April 20, 1982, seventeen days short of his ninetieth birthday, and was buried in a family plot at Pine Grove Cemetery in Conway. Later that month, at a memorial service at Harvard, one friend eulogized MacLeish as "one of the great Americans of our time." He mentioned the lyricism of MacLeish's poetry and the depth of his compassion, and though he did not specifically mention Archie's tenure as librarian of Congress, his language seemed appropriate for those wartime years, when MacLeish was responsible for protecting America's priceless documents.

Archibald MacLeish, his friend declared to the assembled mourners, represented "an imposing part of the landscape of this republic. . . . Where he stood and what he stood for will remain with us for the rest of our days."

★ ★ ★

1952

★ ★ ★

25

★

"They Are Not Important
As Manuscripts,
They Are Important
As THEMSELVES"

★

December 13, 1952, Washington, D.C.

The clock struck eleven on this Saturday morning, a signal to Brigadier General Stoyte O. Ross that the delicate transfer should begin.
With the crisp precision of a man accustomed to issuing orders, the
commanding general of the U.S. Air Force Headquarters Command
gave the signal. Twelve members of the U.S. Armed Forces Special
Police carried six pieces of priceless parchment in helium-filled glass
cases, enclosed in wooden crates, through a cordon of eighty-eight
servicewomen, who stood at attention down the Library of Congress
steps. At the bottom, an armored Marine Corps personnel carrier
awaited the cases.

The original engrossed Declaration of Independence and Constitution of the United States were leaving the care of the Library of Congress and, after years of bureaucratic wrangling and often contentious

foot-dragging, were headed to their new and permanent home at the National Archives.

Pennsylvania Avenue had been—and would be—the site of many parades, marches, and processions, but the resplendence and pomp that accompanied this ceremony was a sight to remember. When the six boxes—containing the Declaration, plus the four leaves of the Constitution and its separate transmittal letter from the Federal Convention to Congress—reached the bottom of the library steps, military personnel carefully placed them on mattresses inside the personnel carrier. Once stored, the carrier started to move, accompanied by a color guard, ceremonial troops, the U.S. Army Band, the U.S. Air Force Drum and Bugle Corps, two light tanks, servicemen carrying submachine guns, and a motorcycle escort—a parade down Pennsylvania and Constitution avenues to the National Archives building. Along the way, U.S. Army, Navy, Coast Guard, Marine, and Air Force personnel lined both sides of the street.

At 11:35, General Ross and the twelve special policemen arrived at the National Archives and carried the containers up the steps, where the U.S. archivist, Wayne Grover, formally took custody of America's two most important founding documents. They would finally be displayed at the National Archives, along with their sister document, the Bill of Rights, which the archives had held in its custody since 1938.

Grover had waited a long time for this moment; in fact, he had been the driving force behind making it happen.

SOME OF THE MOST important deals in American history have had their general structure hammered out over lunch, and the agreement between the National Archives and the Library of Congress to finally transfer the Declaration and the Constitution to the archives was no exception.

In September 1951, the Library of Congress hosted a ceremony, attended by President Harry S. Truman and other dignitaries, to celebrate what was called the "permanent" encasement of the Declaration and Constitution in helium-filled cases. It was a frustrating day for Wayne Grover, who had been appointed archivist of the United States in 1948. He reported later that it was impossible to "go on indefinitely with ceremonies which gave the impression that the documents would remain everlastingly in the Library of Congress." Since 1933, there had been numerous unsuccessful attempts to relocate the documents to the National Archives, though officials had expressed the will and inclination to move them. On February 20 of that year, at the laying of the cornerstone of the National Archives, President Herbert Hoover dedicated the building and announced: "There will be aggregated here the most sacred documents of our history—the originals of the Declaration of Independence and of the Constitution of the United States."

Because of that presidential declaration, the archives built special cases in the exhibition hall to someday display the original documents, along with patriotic murals to accompany the founding documents. Since then, a combination of turf battles, political gamesmanship, world war, governmental inertia, legal machinations, and recalcitrance on the part of key players had prevented the transfer from occurring.

With a new Librarian of Congress, Luther Evans, taking the helm after MacLeish's resignation, Wayne Grover detected renewed interest by the library in relocating the Declaration and the Constitution. At the September 1951 ceremony, Evans escorted President Truman to his car, and as he returned to his office, he passed Grover on the stairs. Evans stopped and said, "Wayne, the next ceremony for these documents will be when they're transferred to the National Archives."

With Evans making the first move, Grover took the opening. The next day, he invited Evans to lunch to discuss the entire issue, and the two agreed to meet at the Cosmos Club about a month later.

In the meantime, Grover turned to his staff for information.

GROVER ASKED THAD PAGE, head of the National Archives' Legislative and Fiscal Records Branch, to gather background material on the legal status of the Declaration and the Constitution, including their transfer to the Library of Congress, and their possible future move to the archives. Next, he asked preservation chemist Arthur E. Kimberley to compare the safety of the documents in the Library of Congress with their possible level of safety at the National Archives.

He received the answers he expected.

Page submitted two lengthy memos, the gist of which said that the transfer was in accordance with the Federal Records Act of 1950, which provided that all "federal records" not in current use for research, law-making, or other reasons, should go to the National Archives for storage or display purposes. The Declaration and the Constitution certainly fell into this category. (In fact, this was the main reason that Archibald MacLeish later explained why he did not think the Library of Congress was the right place for the documents. "They are not important as manuscripts, they are important as *themselves*," he declared. "Not to use; to look at." For that reason, they belonged in the National Archives.)

Kimberley's report on safety and potential threats to the documents was perhaps more compelling. The chief chemist pointed out that the "unique character" of the two documents and their "peculiar relationship to the morale of the United States" made their preservation and protection "imperative . . . against any contingency whatever." He noted that the Declaration was currently fastened to a second-story exterior wall "of an old masonry building," while the Constitution was displayed in a floor case within a dozen feet of the same wall. "In the event of a sudden bombing, or other shock, little or no protection could be expected from the present structure." In addition, virtually no protection was afforded against fire. In the event of a calamity, the Declaration and the Constitution would have to be immediately removed from the Library of Congress premises, "which would expose them to all the hazards of hasty handling, especially in view of the fragile nature of the glass cases." Further, there was no close temperature control at the library—whereas the entire archives were air-conditioned—meaning the parchments "are continually expanding or contracting as the temperature rises and falls." Such movement against the glass protective plate "cannot fail to cause damage with the passage of time."

Consider the alternative scenario: transferring the two documents to the archives in the rotunda that was designed for them. The Declaration would be mounted on a retractable steel frame that would allow it to be exhibited and, when retracted, "would carry it into an insulated steel blast shield much as one slides a letter into its envelope." In addition, at closing time or in a sudden emergency, "a steel panel carrying the documents could be rotated downward . . . and then lowered into a blast shield." Moreover, inserting the documents into the blast shield would be accomplished mechanically, "thus eliminating undesirable manual transfers." The same protections would shield the documents from fire and, in tandem with the archives' air-conditioning, guard them against abnormal temperature variations.

Kimberley was not shy in his conclusion: "Architecturally, there can be no comparison between the two exhibit sites, for the present scene of exhibition is an obvious makeshift while the recommended place [the National Archives] was designed as a setting for these gems."

The reports were good enough for Wayne Grover. Armed with legal and safety data from his experts, he was ready for lunch with Luther Evans.

AT THE COSMOS CLUB, Evans and Grover shared a table near the fireplace, but their lunch generated little heat. Both men shared a fundamental belief that the Declaration of Independence and the Constitution of the United States belonged in the National Archives.

Grover—whose strengths included his persuasive one-on-one skills, a superb sense of timing, an affinity for people, and a deep belief in the mission of archivists—did the bulk of the talking, sharing his reports and making his case. The "only business" of the Declaration and the Constitution was to be on exhibit, he pointed out, and even Evans admitted that the National Archives had better exhibition facilities and better protection capabilities. Grover said that, "sooner or later," the document would have to be transferred, that Evans was "a generous soul heading a great institution," and that the Library of Congress would remain great even without the two founding documents. Evans concurred and also acknowledged that, under the Federal Records Act, he could not justify keeping the Declaration and the Constitution by claiming they were needed for "current business" at the Library of Congress.

By the end of lunch, Evans had agreed to the transfer, but he was concerned about political protocol. The two executives might be legally permitted to make the transfer, but Evans wanted them to consult with the president and congressional leaders. In addition, he wanted it stressed—for both the public and his own staff's sake—that he was under legal obligation to transfer the documents to the archives. Grover agreed with the approach Evans outlined.

Over the next several months, Grover and Evans collaborated—even conspired—to build a rock-solid and unassailable legal, moral, practical, and national security argument to transfer the documents from the Library of Congress to the National Archives. Grover was the primary driver of the effort, but without Evans's cautiously enthusiastic support, the transfer likely would have been thwarted for years to come.

GROVER ASSURED EVANS AND other officials in numerous written communiqués that the decision to move the documents was on solid legal grounds, but he focused most of his energy on two other arguments: the American people's right to view the documents in the institution constructed for that purpose, including the morale boost this would provide; and, especially, the far greater physical protections the documents would receive at the National Archives.

With the United States at war again—this time in Korea—with World War II and the atomic bombs still fresh in the country's memory, with cold war tensions heightening between the United States and the Soviet Union, fear of an attack on Washington again factored into the collective consciousness of the people most responsible for securing America's priceless records. Even though an attack was not imminent, Grover continued to build on the security arguments that chemist Arthur Kimberley had highlighted in his report.

"The National Archives building is the most invulnerable building to shock, blast, and bombing in Washington," Grover wrote to Evans in a January 1952 memo. Indeed, the archives was referred to as "Fort Archives" during World War II for the quality of its construction. Grover even quoted the opinion of an army engineer who believed that "barring a very near miss or an explosion at ground zero, we [the Archives] should come through an atomic attack in fairly good shape."

Such protections made the archives the natural home for the Declaration of Independence and the Constitution, as did the matter of "public morale," in Grover's view. "It is desirable and necessary to keep the document on display . . . until some overt act takes place which would signal the outbreak of a large-scale war." According to Grover, the overt act could be "a bomb dropped on Washington." Barring such a catastrophe, the documents belonged where the American people could most easily and safely view them. "The National Archives of the United States will never be complete without the records of the Continental Congress and the Constitutional Convention," Grover contended, of which the Declaration and the Constitution were the most critical components.

Grover made similar arguments to the White House and Congress, training his rhetoric mostly on Senator Theodore Green, chairman of the Joint Committee on the Library. "These two documents, together with the Bill of Rights . . . already in our custody, are the most basic of our official records, and certainly belong with other official archives of the United States Government," he wrote to Green. He urged him and the committee to support "the Librarian of Congress and myself in our mutual desire to see this transfer accomplished."

True to his word, librarian Luther Evans fulfilled his pledge to support the transfer. He wrote a letter to Green listing the items he wanted to present to the committee at its April 30, 1952, meeting. Item 2 was "Transfer of certain documents to the National Archives," to which he attached Grover's letters and his own letter to Senator Green.

He wrote that the Declaration and the Constitution could be better preserved in the National Archives; they were not needed in the Library of Congress and they should be relocated.

If the congressional committee concurred, he would transfer them.

★

26

"The National Archives Will Not Forget"

★

Evans went to the Committee hearing alone—he knew that many of his colleagues at the Library of Congress were overtly resistant to the idea of transferring the documents. They believed that the library's prestige and reputation would be irreparably harmed without its two preeminent parchments.

The committee voted unanimously to direct the librarian to transfer the documents to the archives, but Evans requested a stronger resolution. He wanted the committee to "instruct or order" him to make the transfer—he needed the political cover both for the external record and to protect his flank from internal library staffers. The committee granted his wish. The *Congressional Record* of May 1 reads that congressmen "ordered the transfer of the Declaration of Independence and the Constitution to the National Archives."

In the *Information Bulletin* for the Library of Congress for May 5, 1952, Evans wrote that the transfer was required "according to the routine application of the statutes concerning the records of the U.S.

Government." Although it was an "emotional wrench to surrender the custody of the principal documents of American liberty, logic and law require it," he said. "We can only join Dr. Wayne C. Grover, the Archivist of the United States, and his staff, in celebrating the occasion."

WITH THE FORMALITIES COMPLETED, Grover and Evans simply needed to agree on scheduling, logistics, preparing the shrine, notifying the press and the public, and organizing the ceremony that would commemorate the transfer. Both men were quite pleased with themselves and their efforts. "I don't know what history will say about our friendly collusion," Evans wrote to Grover on May 5, "but I can tell you that I feel darned broad-minded and just a wee bit righteous— something like a fellow who gave up his gal to an ugly clumsy younger brother who wasn't very good at finding gals of his own." Two days later, he sent Grover the formal and official letter declaring that he was "ready to transfer to you . . . the collections of records of the Continental Congress and the Constitutional Convention now in custody of the Library of Congress."

Grover, too, responded to Evans in a playful manner: "I hereby give you permission to use the line about an 'ugly clumsy younger brother' at all future professional gatherings we jointly attend. It's a marvelous line and I guess I can bear up under it." He added, however: "But what a price to pay for a couple of old pieces of parchment!" He turned serious in the same letter and assured Evans that "history is going to say good things about you. It startled my colleagues here somewhat that a man heading a great and powerful institution should be so reasonable and generous." Evans's behavior, however, came as no surprise to Grover. "I never was in doubt as to what you would do," the archivist assured the librarian.

Grover concluded his May 15 letter by reverting to humor even as he cited the author of the Declaration: "Jefferson wanted on his tombstone that he wrote the Declaration. I want on mine that I saw it safely enshrined in the Archives of the United States." And then he said to

Evans: "If you'll be satisfied with a footnote on a tombstone, I will certainly see to it that the source is properly cited."

Later in the summer, the two men exchanged poetry about their successful collusion to transfer the documents. Evans wrote first in limerick form:

> There once was an agency rich
> Whose head had a terrible itch
> To take all records over.
> His name it was Grover,
> A two-fisted son-of-a-bitch

Not to be outdone, Grover responded with his own brand of humor:

> I have read your effusions;
> I bleed with remorse
> No further contusions
> Will come from this source.
>
> But to label us "rich"
> Is outright deception.
> Better limit the pitch
> To unimmaculate conception.

Joking aside, for Grover and Evans the transfer of the original Declaration and the Constitution was serious and important business. Both men felt strongly that the founding documents belonged in the people's archives, that the more Americans who could view them—under secure and protective conditions—the more deeply the citizenry would appreciate the country's founding and its democracy.

ONE OTHER FACTOR LIKELY convinced Grover and Evans that the National Archives was the place for the Declaration and the Constitution.

Had they any doubts, both men would have been convinced of Americans' affection for historical documents by their reactions a few years earlier to the nationwide travels of the Freedom Train.

For sixteen remarkable months during 1947–1949, the train, which carried 127 of the most important documents in American history—though neither the engrossed and signed Declaration nor the engrossed and signed Constitution—crisscrossed the country, covering 37,000 miles and 326 cities in all forty-eight states of the time, the only train ever to travel in every state, a feat that required the Freedom Train to use the tracks of fifty-two different railroads. Along the way, more than 3 million Americans waited hours in line to view documents such as the Bill of Rights, Jefferson's original rough draft of the Declaration, Thomas Paine's pamphlet *Common Sense*, Lincoln's manuscript copy of the Gettysburg Address, the Emancipation Proclamation, the original manuscript of "The Star-Spangled Banner," and the Mayflower Compact. Included were more than twenty World War II documents, among them Hitler's last will and testament, the surrender documents signed by both Germany and Japan, and Emperor Hirohito's statement to the Japanese people at war's end.

The brainchild of National Archives' assistant director of public information William Coblenz, who sold his idea to his superiors and President Truman, the Freedom Train project was underwritten by the American Heritage Foundation and supported enthusiastically by the national archivist, Solon Buck, Luther Evans, and others such as business magnate Henry Ford II, publisher William Randolph Hearst, and songwriter Irving Berlin, who wrote an original tune for the Freedom Train.

The train began its journey in Philadelphia on September 17, 1947, the 160th anniversary of the signing of the Constitution. During its tour, hundreds of newspapers covered its stops and interviewed Americans who flocked in droves to tour the three Pullman cars filled with historical documents. *Reader's Digest* reprinted 3.5 million copies of an article on the Bill of Rights that were distributed to visitors to the Freedom Train, and *Look* magazine published 775,000 copies of an illustrated thirty-two-page booklet entitled *Our American Heritage*, which described the major documents aboard the Freedom Train. A detachment of Marines traveled aboard the train and guarded the documents around the clock.

From the beginning, the train's journey was a rousing success—Americans simply could not get enough of the Freedom Train, dubbed the "Spirit of 1776," and the documents it carried aboard. Peak daily attendance during the tour exceeded 14,000 and the attendance low of just over 6,000 people occurred during a fierce snowstorm. In New York City, the line started at Grand Central Station and covered fifteen blocks, with people standing four abreast. In Cleveland, thousands stood in a serpentine line for four to five hours to board the train. Nearly half the population of Burlington, Vermont, turned out to greet the train, including 10,000 people in a single day; and thousands more congregated in a park in Green Bay, Wisconsin, to sign the Freedom Pledge Scroll that accompanied the train. In Boston, teachers adjourned classes as thousands of schoolchildren flocked to South Station to visit the Freedom Train. A two-hour parade, attended by an estimated 250,000 people, marked the train's arrival in Dover, Delaware; in Elizabeth, New Jersey, thousands gathered in a rainstorm, huddled beneath umbrellas, to greet the train upon its arrival.

The one-millionth visitor was a sixteen-year-old Oklahoma girl who traveled sixty miles in a blizzard to see the exhibit.

Although 10:00 a.m. was the standard opening time for the train's exhibits, lines in most cities began forming before dawn. In California, a thirteen-year-old boy got up at 2:00 a.m. to get in line early. Winston Luck, an African American from Chicago, left his job at 4:00 a.m. "to see the documents that stand for freedom." As people moved from car to car, from document to document, most did so with a sense of reverence and emotion.

Marines reported that the World War II exhibits were most popular, but many documents left people with "tears in their eyes." R. W. Stempfel confessed: "You got a deep emotional feeling as you go through the cars. I can't explain it, but it's wonderful." Another visitor said: "They are really our moral background—The whole thing should make everyone more conscious of freedom and what it means." Nor was it only visitors who felt the spiritual aura of the train. One *New York Times* writer described what it was like: "Inside, one has the feeling he is in church. The only light is the soft fluorescent glow reflected from the lighted documents. Parents shush their children and little school boys take off their caps without being told. People speak in low-guarded tones used by tourists in ancient cathedrals."

The American Heritage Foundation did its best to maintain the spirit of the exhibit amidst racial tensions, particularly in the South. When the mayor of Memphis announced in November 1947 that the viewing day would be divided in half, six hours each for whites and blacks separately, the foundation canceled the train's exhibit. The foundation also withdrew the train from Birmingham when city officials demanded two separate lines of visitors that would merge at the train's entrance. After the Birmingham cancellation, no other city attempted to segregate visitors, although Selma, Alabama, withdrew its request to have the train visit.

After visiting cities and small towns, the Freedom Train's tour ended officially on January 22, 1949, during President Truman's inauguration week in Washington, D.C. More than 100,000 Washingtonians visited the train in the nation's capital.

There was little doubt that the Freedom Train's tour had captured the imaginations of Americans and reawakened them to the value of the documents that defined their history. In February 1949, Dwight D. Eisenhower, heroic World War II general and future president, wrote to the American Heritage Foundation, praising it for "instilling into the American people an increased consciousness of our manifold heritage." Such an achievement, he added, "has been one of the outstanding and most satisfying phenomena of the postwar period."

When the Freedom Train concluded its sojourn in 1949, Wayne Grover had succeeded Solon Buck as chief archivist. Shortly thereafter, Grover and Luther Evans began their quest to transfer the Declaration and the Constitution to the National Archives. Both documents were considered too valuable to accompany the Freedom Train on its odyssey across the United States.

Still, both men knew—in light of the exuberant response of the American people to the train's contents—that placing the parchments in a permanent home, for all to see, would best illustrate their contributions and importance to the nation's heritage.

BY 1952, THOUGH, NOT everyone was pleased about the transfer of the Declaration and the Constitution. Of the library staffers upset about the move, David Mearns was particularly bitter. Mearns, who had been part of the team that secured the founding documents for their trip to Fort Knox in 1941, was asked by Evans to write two or three pages about the transfer for the library's annual report. Mearns wrote almost seven pages, an emotional essay he called "Forever Is Twenty-Eight Years," the length of time the Library of Congress had possessed the Declaration and the Constitution.

Despite his dismay when he first heard that the documents would move to the National Archives, Mearns concluded that fighting the transfer was futile: "The retired but retained records of the Government must be entrusted to the National Archives. Retired! Retained! They will never retire. They must always be retained. But they will be removed."

A crestfallen Mearns added: "To have been host—even to have been host by sufferance—to these imperishable records has been to enjoy a transient prestige which the Library is unlikely ever to enjoy again."

Mearns was wrong about the Library of Congress's status—it still held (and holds) the original copies of the Gettysburg Address and countless other vital documents—but correct that his institution would never again be responsible for protecting and displaying parchments so priceless.

★

27

"Symbols of
a Power that
Can Move
the World"

★

December 15, 1952

No one would ever officially declare it so, but there is little doubt that December 15, 1952, the 161st anniversary of the ratification of the Bill of Rights, was the most important day in the history of the National Archives.

Two days after the Declaration of Independence and the Constitution had arrived from the Library of Congress, the nation's original founding documents were permanently enshrined in their new home in a moving ceremony marked by pageantry, solemnity, military precision, and an inspirational address by President Truman. Fred M. Vinson, chief justice of the United States, presided over the ceremony, which was attended by more than 100 national civic, patriotic, religious, labor, business, educational, and veterans groups.

After introductions and the invocation, the governor of Delaware,

Elbert Carvel, stepped to the podium; a black drape covered the Charters of Freedom in the shrine behind him. Delaware had been the first state to ratify the Constitution; thus, he had the honor of leading the roll call of states. One by one their names were called, in the order in which they had ratified the Constitution or were admitted to the Union. As each state was called, a servicewoman carrying the state's flag entered the exhibition hall and remained at attention as they circled the hall.

With the flags held high, President Truman delivered the main address, the Charters behind him, still draped, when he began speaking at 10:30 a.m. "The Declaration, the Constitution, and the Bill of Rights are now assembled in one place for display and safekeeping," he said. "Here, so far as humanly possible, they will be protected from disaster and from the ravages of time." The speech was one of Truman's last official acts as president—Dwight D. Eisenhower, who had been elected in November, would take office in 1953—and the president rose to the occasion. Truman captured the seriousness and significance of the moment, the responsibility that had been placed in the hands of those responsible for the documents' safety and security, and the meaning of those documents in the nation's past, present, and future. "We venerate these documents not because they are old, not because they are valuable historical relics," Truman said, "but because they still have meaning to us."

The Bill of Rights, he noted, was "the only document in the world that protects the citizen against his Government," and 161 years after the first ten amendments to the Constitution were adopted, they still were "pointing the way to greater freedom and greater opportunities for human happiness." The Constitution set forth "our idea of government," and it was paired with the Declaration of Independence, which "expresses our idea of man." The core principles were clear and simple: "We believe that man should be free. And these documents establish a system under which men can be free and set up a framework to protect and expand that freedom."

*

TRUMAN DETAILED THE DISPLAY and storage measures that the National Archives would undertake, "every device that modern science has invented to protect and preserve them." The hall had been constructed to exhibit the documents, the vault beneath to protect them, and from their glass cases, "we have excluded everything that might harm them, even the air itself." Such efforts were honorable, President Truman said, and something in which America could take pride.

But all the efforts were for naught if the Declaration and the Constitution were enshrined only in the archives building and nowhere else. If that were the case, then the enshrining ceremony would be little more than a "magnificent burial," the documents "no better than mummies in glass cases . . . that could in time become idols whose worship would be a grim mockery of true faith."

No, Truman warned, Americans could not allow such a fate for its founding documents. "The Constitution and the Declaration of Independence can live only as long as they are enshrined in our hearts and minds," Truman declared. Only under these circumstances "can they remain symbols of a power that can move the world." Indeed, he added, it may be hard to believe that liberty could ever be lost in America, "but it can be lost, and it will be, if the time ever comes when these documents are regarded not as the supreme expression of our profound belief, but merely as curiosities in glass cases."

The current generation, the president added, needed to be the stewards of freedom, responsible for preserving and extending "popular liberty." Whether they would do so was a "very serious" and "very old" question. "The men who signed the Declaration faced it," he said. "So did those who wrote the Constitution. But each succeeding generation has faced it and so far each succeeding generation has answered it in the affirmative. I am sure that our generation will give the same affirmative answer."

What America was accomplishing today, Truman asserted, was "placing before the eyes of many generations to come the symbols of a living faith." And then: "Like the sight of the flag in the 'dawn's early light,' the sight of these symbols will lift up their hearts, so they will go out of this building helped and strengthened and inspired."

WHEN TRUMAN HAD FINISHED, Senator Theodore Green, whose committee had approved the transfer, traced the history of the documents. When he had finished, Wayne Grover and Luther Evans, appropriately enough, parted the drapes. The Declaration of Independence, the Constitution, and the Bill of Rights were unveiled, finally exhibited together in one place. The audience responded with enthusiastic applause.

Chief Justice Vinson offered a few closing remarks, the House chaplain gave the benediction, and the U.S. Marine Corps Orchestra played its rendition of "The Star-Spangled Banner." President Truman was escorted out, and the forty-eight flag bearers marched out of the rotunda behind him.

AS THE GUESTS FILED OUT, as their eyes caught sight of the three engrossed documents now on display, did any of them consider how the precious parchments had come to be, how they had endured, and what they meant to America's present and future?

Did any know about Caesar Rodney's midnight ride from Dover to Philadelphia on the eve of the independence vote in 1776? Or John Adams's courage and indefatigable insistence that declaring independence was the colonies' only hope to live as free men? Or Jefferson's magnificent and timeless draft that defined the unalienable rights of life, liberty, and the pursuit of happiness, concepts that had become seared into America's consciousness and national identity?

Did the 1952 audience pause and wonder about Timothy Matlack's laborious effort to engross the Declaration with the flourish, dignity, panache, and gravitas befitting the nation's founding document?

Did they wonder about the anxiety the signers felt as they queued up on August 2, 1776, to ink their names on a parchment that the British Crown viewed as treasonous?

As the crowd exited the National Archives rotunda in 1952, did the Constitutional Convention of 1787 enter their minds? Had they studied in high school history class the story of the "miracle" in Philadelphia that occurred during the most inspirational summer in American history, and did they call those lessons to mind now?

Perhaps they knew of James Madison's bold and imaginative vision, his relentless energy, and his meticulous record keeping that gave us our most complete account of the creation of the Constitution. Perhaps they had read about the quiet, dignified, and masterful leadership of George Washington, the wisdom of Franklin, or the poetry of Gouverneur Morris as he proclaimed to the world that the Federal Convention was speaking on behalf of "we the people." And what of the dissenters—George Mason and Patrick Henry, among others—whose vociferous objections eventually led to the adoption of the Bill of Rights, which President Truman had proclaimed moments earlier as the most important document of all?

Did the 1952 audience wonder about those who took extraordinary measures to save the documents now ensconced in their permanent shrines or protect the records that brought the documents to life? Of Stephen Pleasonton's quick action to remove the Declaration and the Constitution to a farmhouse in Virginia just before the British burned Washington? Of Dolley Madison's courageous vigil in the White House before escaping with her husband's notes of the 1787 Constitutional Convention and other important papers? Did any recall the recently revealed accounts of Archibald MacLeish's leadership to protect the documents during World War II and Harry Neal's steady hand in ensuring that the parchments arrived at Fort Knox safely? Or the effort required to relocate and to protect from potential enemy attack 5,000 additional boxes of documents that collectively contained the essence of America's history?

And what of the man who had virtually single-handedly reinvigorated and redefined the Declaration, the Constitution, and the promise of equality in America more than eighty years after the new nation declared independence? Abraham Lincoln's Gettysburg Address was not part of the enshrinement ceremony at the National Archives on this day in 1952; because his two-minute address was never engrossed, its lack of calligraphic flourish likely prevented it from being displayed in a magnificent shrine. It was still one of the most prized possessions of the Library of Congress. But did any thoughtful members of the crowd departing the National Archives ponder Lincoln's love for and reliance on the Declaration and the Constitution for his guidance and inspiration? Or consider the Gettysburg Address's connection to the founding documents, its contribution to the ongoing struggle for American liberty, and its spawning of a second American revolution that would broaden forever those included in the proposition that all men were created equal?

Maybe all of this would be too much to ask of the audience exiting the National Archives in December 1952. Current events may have assumed more prominence in their minds: Americans were still fighting in Korea, a World War II hero had been elected president in November, and Christmas was just a few days away.

It was enough, perhaps, that President Truman's ringing speech in the rotunda had impressed and moved them, that the roll call of states and the flag-bearing servicewomen had signified the intense importance of the moment, and that the parting of the drape and uncovering of the documents by Luther Evans and Wayne Grover had captured the dramatic essence of an unprecedented event.

But as the departing crowd recounted the ceremony, glanced once more at the Declaration, the Constitution, and the Bill of Rights, it would *not* be too much to ask whether they had read the inscription on the inside page of their program booklet. This one simple sentence would have helped them grasp how 1776, 1787, 1814, 1826, 1863, 1941, and virtually every other year in American history linked to the historic 1952 enshrinement ceremony, and even more important, how the

Declaration and the Constitution linked to their own lives, their own liberty, their own sacred honor—and the ongoing fortunes of the United States of America.

The inscription read simply:

"The heritage of the past is the seed that brings forth the harvest of the future."

Epilogue

★

Even in his wildest dreams in 1776 about the importance of his work, even if his estimable friend Thomas Jefferson watched over his shoulder as he engrossed the Declaration of Independence, Timothy Matlack could never have conceived that, more than 200 years later, his work would undergo such scrutiny; that his craftsmanship would be examined and assessed by professional conservators using such instruments as binocular microscopes, electronic imaging, and fiberoptic lighting.

It would have been far beyond Matlack's ability to comprehend that the National Archives—now the National Archives and Records Administration—had expended $3 million to design a monitoring system employing sophisticated technology "to assess the state of preservation . . . with specific attention to changes in readability from ink-flaking, ink-fading, off-setting of ink to glass, changes in document dimensions, and enlargement of existing tears and holes." The Charters Monitoring System, installed in 1985 in a contract with the Jet Propulsion Laboratory at the California Institute of Technology, through the National Aeronautics and Space Administration, used electronic imaging technology similar to that of NASA's space telescope and computer analysis akin to the type used to interpret data from space probes.

Stephen Pleasonton, who in 1814 had stuffed the Declaration and the Constitution into a coarse linen bag for safekeeping, and Archibald MacLeish, who in 1941 had shipped them in sealed cases to Fort Knox, would have envied the documents' protective vault beneath the rotunda at the National Archives in the second half of the twentieth century. Twenty-two feet below the floor of the exhibit hall was a fifty-five-ton vault of steel and reinforced concrete, seven feet long, five feet wide, and six feet high. Each night for years, the Declaration, the Constitution, and the Bill of Rights were lowered into the vault by electrically operated scissor jacks. Once the documents were safely inside, massive interlocking leaves of metal and concrete closed over the vault.

And all of them—Matlack, Pleasonton, MacLeish, and so many other protectors of these documents—would have been astounded if they could know that at the start of the twenty-first century, the National Archives would team up with scientists and technical experts from the National Institute of Technology to conduct major conservation treatments and design and build state-of-the-art reencasements for the Declaration, the Constitution, and the Bill of Rights, thereby hermetically sealing and protecting the documents for years to come.

The Charters of Freedom, the nation's founding documents with their timeless message of liberty, equality, self-governance, and the rights of the people, are now ready to endure and continue to inspire Americans far into the future.

GENUINE TECHNOLOGICAL MODERNITY CAME to the National Archives in 1985 with the installation of the Charters Monitoring System, which can detect any loss of readability caused by ink flaking, offsetting of ink to glass, changes in document dimensions, and ink fading.

The impressive system was capable of recording in fine detail one-inch-square areas of the documents, and later retaking the pictures in exactly the same places and under the same conditions of lighting and reflectivity. Essentially, the system was designed to take a "fingerprint" of the exact state of the Charters of Freedom at any given moment and to match the current condition with earlier recordings. In the years that followed, conservators rescanned patches of the parchments and compared them pixel by pixel to the baseline image, looking for changes.

By 1996, after more than 125 scans, the ink on the documents was holding up well; restorers noticed just one "insecure flake of ink" on a raised ridge of the transmittal page of the Constitution—the letter George Washington signed turning the new Constitution over from the Federal Convention to the Congress.

However, the encasements that held the priceless documents, which had first been built in 1951, were problematic. Experts detected crystals and liquid droplets on the glass surfaces, indicating "progressive glass deterioration" and a change of relative humidity inside the encasements that could potentially damage the documents. There was no need for panic, no "imminent danger" from the condition of the encasements, emphasized Norbert S. Baer, a New York University conservationist and head of the archives committee that examined the documents. Still, he concluded, "it is a problem that won't get better without some level of intervention."

Baer's committee recommended changes to the way the documents were displayed and protected. For example, only two of the five leaves of the Constitution were on display—the remaining three leaves remained in the vault beneath the rotunda—because the archives did not have sufficient space in the exhibition hall. Shouldn't the public be able to view the entire document when they visited Washington? Members were also concerned that the vibrations as the charters were lowered by scissor jack into the vault could cause the documents to rub against the inside pane of glass.

The recommendation of Baer and his team went beyond their original mission: it was not only time to reexamine, reencase, and redisplay the Charters of Freedom but also to redesign the rotunda itself.

In 1995, Norvell M. Jones, the archives' chief of preservation policy, agreed: "These are virtual icons to the people of the United

States and accessibility is a priority for the National Archives. When you come to Washington, it is one of the things you must see."

ON THE DAY AFTER the Fourth of July, 2001, the National Archives closed the rotunda and exhibit hall for massive top-to-bottom renovations, and simultaneously began its painstaking reencasement project for the Declaration of Independence, the Constitution, and the Bill of Rights.

There was no room for error and no manual that instructed conservators on how to open the cases that had been sealed for fifty years; thus, the experts opened first the encasement that held the transmittal letter of the Constitution. The page signed by Washington was valuable, but if there was any encasement that conservation staff could test and refine their opening and preservation techniques on, this was it; if a mistake occurred, better that it be with the case holding the transmittal letter rather than those holding the four pages of the Constitution, or the Declaration of Independence or Bill of Rights.

According to a National Archives report, conservators made a tiny puncture in the seal to extract and analyze interior gas and determine what percentage of helium remained inside; they were pleased to find that the original encasements had functioned well. They used a sharp blade to enlarge the pinprick hole and allow the insertion of a larger tool that would carefully slice through the soldered lead seal. When that was completed, they lifted away the glass that had covered the parchment for fifty years, taking great care to ensure that the parchment did not adhere to the glass, and also to confirm that no flecks of ink had attached themselves to the inner surface of the glass that had been in direct contact with the parchment. Once removed from the seal, conservators were able to examine, measure, and photograph the document without layers of glass in between, a process that began with the transmittal letter and continued with the other charters.

As they worked, restorers noted that the condition of the documents offered clues to their journey over the years. The Bill of Rights, though it had been stored flat for almost a century, still contained horizontal and vertical creases from being folded. The Declaration had fold lines and horizontal creases that showed evidence of rolling; it also had a band around the edges that confirmed it had been glued to its base in the early twentieth century. The Constitution did not show evidence of folding, but it had adhesive strokes on the backs of the parchments, indicating that the leaves had been glued to a backing. Conservators then began the task of cleaning the documents, introducing humidity to relax the parchment skins fully and making unobtrusive repairs.

Afterward, the charters were placed in larger encasements, constructed of an aluminum base, a titanium frame, and laminated tempered glass. The new encasements accommodated all six pages of the charters for public display (minus the transmittal letter), removed pages from direct vertical placement, and eliminated contact of the parchment with the glass. Each case contained inert gas, was kept at 40 percent relative humidity, and was surrounded with a stable temperature of 67 degrees Fahrenheit. To protect the documents from insects or microbes, the cases were airtight. In addition, the encasement design included a pair of sapphire windows at the top edge that permitted a light beam to travel a path below the document platform, "reflected by precisely positioned mirrors," in the words of the archives. Using optical instruments that can detect absorption of light in the exiting light beam, conservators could detect any environmental changes that occurred inside the encasements.

It was an amazing technological system designed to protect the documents that Stephen Pleasonton had once hidden in the corner of an abandoned farmhouse and Archibald MacLeish had shipped to Fort Knox. As Pleasonton and MacLeish had taken the initiative to save and protect the documents in 1814 and 1941, their twenty-first-century successors were doing the same.

THE NATIONAL ARCHIVES FINISHED its renovation project in 2003. Physical, accessibility, lighting, and environmental improvements abounded, but perhaps the most important change was that, for the first time, all four pages of the Constitution could be exhibited and viewed.

Appropriate then, that the rededication and reopening ceremony was held on September 17, 2003, the 216th anniversary of the adoption of the Constitution. "In this Rotunda are the most cherished material possessions of a great and good nation," President George W. Bush said. "By this rededication, we showed our deep respect for the first principles of our republic, and our lasting gratitude to those first citizens of the United States of America." Further, President Bush noted that the ideas embodied in the Charters of Freedom are not America's alone. "America owns the Declaration of Independence and the Constitution," he said, "but the ideals they proclaim belong to all mankind."

Then the Archivist of the United States, John W. Carlin, noted that people visited the National Archives and viewed the charters "not just because they are historical documents, but because they are a living part" of American society and traditions. "Every day we celebrate the freedom first declared in the Declaration of Independence," he said. "Every day our government is an example to the world of democratic government laid out in the Constitution. And every day our people exercise the liberties set down in the Bill of Rights."

Once again, Carlin noted, Americans could enter the archives and "read the very parchments that our Founding Fathers signed in giving birth to our democracy."

CHANGE DID NOT JUST come to the National Archives during the renovation and reencasement project, but to America itself. Less than two months after the Declaration, the Constitution, and the Bill of Rights were removed for restoration, the United States suffered the worst terrorist attack in its history.

Like virtually every institution in the country, the National Archives implemented tightened and highly secretive security procedures in the aftermath of September 11, 2001. There are plans and backup plans to protect America's priceless documents, but archives officials remain understandably tight-lipped about any and all of them. "No discussion about security," said the current Archivist of the United States, David S. Ferriero. "Part of the security plan is not talking about the security plan."

EXACTLY WHY DO MORE than 1 million people each year file through the National Archives rotunda to view the Charters of Freedom?

The answer is probably best embodied in John Carlin's observations at the 2003 rededication ceremony—these documents are a "living part" of America's way of life, and have been since their creation. They have stood the test of time and today are as relevant and integral to American democracy as they ever have been. Time and again, the United States and its people find ways to memorialize and enshrine them. George Washington's copy of the Constitution was on display aboard the Freedom Train that traveled across the country in 1975–1976 to mark the nation's bicentennial, replicating—and perhaps improving upon—the first Freedom Train's odyssey. More than 4 million people have visited the National Constitution Center in Philadelphia since it opened its doors—fittingly, on July 4, 2003—just two blocks from Independence Hall: an entire museum devoted to America's governing document.

Virtually every modern political debate breathes life into our most important documents—every critical issue rests upon the principles they embody. And because Americans are reminded of them at every turn nearly every day, their intrinsic value holds a revered place in the nation's consciousness.

The concepts of "life, liberty, and the pursuit of happiness" and "all men are created equal," enshrined in the Declaration, are embedded in American law, the American psyche, and American aspirations.

The Constitution's system of separation of powers and checks and balances are on display every time a newscaster wonders, "Will Congress have the votes to override a presidential veto?" or "Will the Supreme Court find the new law constitutional?" or "Who will gain control of the Senate in the next election?" The powerful three-word introduction to the preamble, "We the People," defines the very essence of the American way of life—the power to govern is granted *only* by the governed.

And the Bill of Rights—the first document ever that expressly enumerates the rights that a government is *forbidden* to usurp—encapsulates the individual freedoms Americans cherish most, guard most zealously, and even debate most vigorously. Indeed, it is this last that makes the Bill of Rights so vibrant and its historical precedents so meaningful: individual liberties often bump up against societal needs and desires, and to settle those arguments—or at least to advance them—professional and amateur advocates and opponents often turn to the intent of the founders and the framers for guidance.

The fact is, the history of the documents *is* the history of America—and it is a remarkable history, indeed. In an age of cynicism, these documents remind us not only of the promise of America but of the fulfillment of that promise in so many ways.

Moreover, it is the documents themselves that provide the inspiration, the moral underpinnings, and the practical means to right wrongs that do exist. The "more perfect union" that Gouverneur Morris so eloquently describes in his preamble to the Constitution was aspirational in 1787 and continues to be so today. America, like all nations, wrestles with issues of injustice and unfairness—"men are not angels," as Madison pointed out, so such struggles will never cease—but as it constantly strives to improve, the documents, with their core values and messages of freedom and equality, provide clear directional guideposts. The answers are there if only we look for them.

At his core, Abraham Lincoln knew all of this. On his watch, the nation fought a bloody Civil War to redress its most egregious wrong—slavery—left unaddressed by its founding documents. After reuniting, America continued to function as a nation using the same core documents—albeit with an amended Constitution—as its foundation, its governing blueprint, and its moral compass. It was Lincoln's Gettysburg Address that provided the inspiring words and philosophical framework that ultimately helped bind the nation's wounds—the Great Emancipator knew well that a redefinition of the precepts contained in the Declaration, not the document's destruction, held the key to the nation's long-term future after slavery; that an amended Constitution, not a scrapped one, would ensure that a government "of the people, by the people, for the people, shall not perish from the earth."

AMERICANS TODAY GRASP THESE principles as they file through the National Archives shrine, viewing the founding documents under low light and the watchful gaze of security guards, speaking in low tones, straining to view the faded signatures on the Declaration of Independence and pausing to read the articles of the Constitution. Their innate understanding of the value of the mounted and displayed parchments in the shrine make these Americans one and the same with Thomas Jefferson, George Washington, Benjamin Franklin, John and Abigail Adams, James and Dolley Madison, Stephen Pleasonton, Abraham Lincoln, Harry Neal, Archibald MacLeish, and hundreds of others who helped create, protect, and preserve America's priceless documents for future generations.

The documents are the mirror to our national heritage and the blueprint of our national identity.

For two centuries, others have protected them well. The responsibility to keep them safe, and preserve them always, now falls to us.

Bibliographic Essay

One of the most exciting parts about researching *American Treasures* was the opportunity to examine a vast and rich array of primary and secondary sources that, for all intents and purposes, provide the connective tissue for virtually the entire time line of American history.

The theme that continued to emerge throughout my research was that America's precious documents are so intrinsic to, and interwoven with, the nation's identity and consciousness that their history helps illuminate the country's priorities, struggles, and successes; in so many ways, the documents themselves define the American journey. Because of their impact upon the nation's collective experience, the Declaration of Independence, the Constitution, the Gettysburg Address, and many other documents often have been written about and described in reverential and spiritual tones. And such references influence our nomenclature in current times. It is no accident that the exhibit area at the National Archives is referred to as a "shrine" or that historian Pauline Maier's insightful book about the creation of the Declaration is entitled *American Scripture*.

As I've done in my previous books, below I provide an extensive and wide-ranging list of primary and secondary sources, and for certain ones, I include a brief explanation of how I used them in the narrative and why they were important. I have grouped them into chronological and topical categories for easy reference and understanding, based upon the many favorable comments readers have shared with me about this approach.

While the World War II portions of the story appear throughout the braided narrative, I have grouped those sources in chronological order; thus they appear later in this bibliographic essay. I'm also pleased to note that in some cases—particularly the narrative about World War II and the relocation of documents from Washington, D.C., and in the transfer of the Charters of Freedom from the Library of Congress to the National Archives—many sources have either never, or rarely, been used before.

Of course, the ultimate primary-source documents, which I read multiple times during the research, were the Declaration of Independence, the Constitution (including the Bill of Rights), and the Gettysburg Address. The texts are worth reading and rereading for the simplicity of their language and the power of their ideas.

A final note: when an author writes about the grand sweep of American history, a certain level of selectivity needs to occur when amassing sources, particularly secondary sources. There is no way to read or refer to all of the great books written about the various momentous time periods described in this book—for example, the revolutionary and constitutional eras, the War of 1812, Lincoln and the Civil War, and World War II. The books and articles I list below are but a fraction of the thousands written, but in my view, they are among the best and most important, and they provided me with invaluable material for this work.

1776: The Creation of the Declaration of Independence

Primary Sources

Some of the most important sources from this time period are available digitally, and I referenced them often. The *Journals of the Continental Congress*, held by the Library of Congress (LC), is the best example, accessed at http://memory.loc.gov/ammem/amlaw/lwjc.html. The journals incorporate the proceedings of the First Continental Congress (which met from September 5 to October 26, 1774) and the Second Continental Congress (which ran from May 10, 1775 to March 2, 1789). The journals are the records of the daily proceedings of the Congress, kept by the office of its secretary, Charles Thomson. They were printed contemporaneously in different editions and in several subsequent reprint editions (the LC published the complete edition from 1904 to 1937 under the title

Journals of the Continental Congress 1774–1789, and subtitled *Edited from the Original Records in the Library of Congress by Gaillard Hunt, Chief, Division of Manuscripts*).

It is important to note that these editions did not include the "secret journals," or confidential records of the Congress, which were not published until 1821. Those journals, in multiple volumes, are entitled *Secret Journals of the Acts and Proceedings of Congress* and subtitled *From the First Meeting Thereof to the Dissolution of the Confederation, by the Adoption of the Constitution of the United States.* They carry the notation "Published under the direction of the President of the United States, conformably to Resolution of Congress of March 27, 1812, and April 21, 1820" (Boston: Printed and Published by Thomas B. Wait, 1821), and are available in e-book form at https://archive.org/details/secret journalsof03unit.

Needless to say, these records were indispensable to telling the story of the creation of the Declaration of Independence, but because the official records were so sparse, I needed much more to round out the narrative. Among the most critical sources were:

- *Letters of Members of the Continental Congress,* edited by Edmund C. Burnett (Washington, D.C.: Carnegie Institution of Washington, 1921), a priceless collection of letters to and from Philadelphia in which delegates share so much of their thinking with colleagues and friends in the days and weeks leading up to July 1–4, 1776, and then express their views on their accomplishments after the Declaration was adopted.
- The Adams Family Papers: An Electronic Archive, compiled and produced by the Massachusetts Historical Society, a treasure trove that I accessed frequently at www.masshist.org /digitaladams/archive. This amazing collection includes correspondence between John and Abigail Adams, the diary of John Adams, and the autobiography of John Adams. If you're so inclined to visit, allow yourself ample time: it is easy to get lost in these records.
- The Papers of Thomas Jefferson, compiled by Princeton University (https://jeffersonpapers.princeton.edu) and also as part

of the Avalon Project at the Lillian Goldman Law Library at Yale Law School (http://avalon.law.yale.edu/subjectmenus /jeffpap.asp). I also made extensive use of Thomas Jefferson's *Writings*, edited by Merrill D. Peterson (New York: Library of America, 1984), which includes the Declaration author's autobiography, numerous public papers, addresses, messages, letters, his "A Summary View of the Rights of British America" and "Notes of the State of Virginia," and other miscellaneous writings.

- *The Papers of Benjamin Franklin,* sponsored by the American Philosophical Society and Yale University, with the magnificent digital edition prepared by the Packard Humanities Institute. I accessed it frequently at http://franklinpapers.org/franklin/. The collection allows you to browse by date, name, and subject matter, and its ease of use almost guarantees that you will spend hours each time you visit.

- *The Letters of Richard Henry Lee, Volume 1, 1762–1778,* collected and edited by James Curtis Ballagh at Johns Hopkins University (New York: Macmillan Company, 1911), had some valuable insights into the man who offered the resolution for American independence.

- *Letters to and from Caesar Rodney, 1756–1784,* edited by George Herbert Ryden at the University of Delaware for the Historical Society of Delaware (Philadelphia: University of Pennsylvania Press, 1933), provides an in-depth look into the Delaware delegate who made the overnight ride from Dover to Philadelphia in time to cast the vote for independence on July 2, 1776. The letters also offer insights into Rodney's physical maladies, which affected him for much of his life, including his disfiguring facial cancer. His letters to his brother, Thomas, are particularly revealing and poignant. I gleaned additional material on Rodney and his ride from the booklet published in accompaniment with the unveiling of his statue in Dover on October 30, 1889, entitled: *Proceedings of the Unveiling of the Monument to Caesar Rodney and the Oration Deliv-*

ered on the Occasion by Thomas F. Bayard at Dover Delaware (Wilmington: Delaware Printing Company, 1889).

• Founders Online: Correspondence and Other Writings of Six Major Shapers of the United States (accessed frequently at http://founders.archives.gov/) includes an extensive and valuable collection of papers from, to, and about John Adams, Benjamin Franklin, Thomas Jefferson, James Madison, George Washington, and Alexander Hamilton (and even includes a couple of entries from John Quincy Adams's diary). The collection boasts more than 167,000 searchable documents and shows the value of online records when used properly.

• John Adams's recollections of the creation of the Declaration of Independence years after the fact are recounted by Timothy Pickering during an Independence Day oration in Salem, Massachusetts, on July 4, 1823; the text of Pickering's remarks is contained in *Colonel Pickering's Observations, Introductory to Reading the Declaration of Independence, at Salem, July 4, 1823* (Salem, MA: Warwick Palfray, 1823).

Other primary sources for this period included:

• *Life in Early Philadelphia: Documents from the Revolutionary and Early National Periods,* edited by Billy G. Smith (University Park, PA: Penn State University Press, 1995), a collection of primary-source documents that provides a window into Philadelphia during this era. I used several of these to paint the picture of the city in the book's Declaration and Constitution sections.

• *The John Dunlap Broadside: The First Printing of the Declaration of Independence,* by Frederick R. Goff (Washington: Library of Congress, 1976), a study of the first printing of the nation's founding document. Goff was engaged by the Library of Congress to examine as many of the surviving copies as he could assemble in the library during May 1975. Of the twenty-one surviving copies, seventeen were brought together at that time from all over the United States, the first time so many had been gathered at one place. Goff offers a detailed explanation of his examination—including his methodology—and his findings, and includes photographs of each copy.

• *Sources and Documents Illustrating the American Revolution, 1764–1788, and the Formation of the Federal Constitution,* 2nd ed., selected and edited by Samuel Eliot Morrison (Harvard: 1929), which contains a valuable introduction by the great historian and approximately seventy-five documents from the era.

• On June 30, 2000, Strom Thurmond, the senator from South Carolina (now deceased) read into the Congressional Record an oration entitled, "Remembering the Sacrifices Made for Freedom." As the nation approached the Fourth of July, Senator Thurmond urged Americans to remember the sacrifices the Declaration signers made in 1776. He asked "unanimous consent" (and received it) to have printed in the record an article by historian T. R. Fehrenbach entitled "What Happened to the Men Who Signed the Declaration of Independence?" I list it in the Primary Source section because of its inclusion in the Congressional Record. Fehrenbach published a book in 1968 (updated in 2000) entitled: *Greatness to Spare: The Heroic Sacrifices of the Men Who Signed the Declaration of Independence.*

• Last, but certainly not least, some scholars may quibble with including this volume under primary sources, but I would strenuously argue otherwise. John H. Hazelton's *The Declaration of Independence: Its History* (New York: Dodd, Mead, 1906) is a book that includes observations from its author, but its greatest value is the prodigious amount of work Hazelton did in amassing a compilation of primary-source documents from many different quarters on all aspects of the Declaration: the debates, the drafting, the signing, and the impact of the document afterward. This volume is filled with letters, diary entries, official journal records, quotes, and other primary documents. It is impossible to consider writing about the Declaration of Independence without consulting Hazelton's book. Through his labors,

Hazelton saved so many other researchers enormous amounts of time, and for this reason, I include his work among my primary sources.

Secondary Sources
Articles, Booklets, and Unpublished Works

Both the Library of Congress and the National Archives have sponsored numerous articles and booklets about the Declaration of Independence. Among those I found most helpful was a booklet produced as part of the Milestone Documents in the National Archives series entitled *The Declaration of Independence: A History* (Washington: National Archives and Records Administration, 1992), an excellent summary of the Declaration's creation and travels. I also examined Stephen E. Lucas's "The Stylistic Artistry of the Declaration of Independence" (www.archives.gov /exhibits/charters/declaration_style.html, accessed December 20, 2012); and "Travels of the Declaration of Independence: A Time Line" (www .archives.gov/exhibits/charters/treasure/declaration_travels.html). From the Library of Congress perspective, I found valuable John Y. Cole's "The Library and the Declaration: LC Has Long History with Founding Document," published in the Library of Congress Information Bulletin in August 1997.

Declaration scholar Julian P. Boyd puts forth an interesting theory of a "lost" version of the famous document in his article "The Declaration of Independence: The Mystery of the Lost Original," published in the *Pennsylvania Magazine of History and Biography*, October 1976. I found the seventeen-page piece most helpful for its excellent background on the Declaration's creation and the quotes from founders. I also found intriguing the following: Mellen Chamberlain's paper for the November 1884 *Proceedings of the Massachusetts Historical Society* entitled "The Authentication of the Declaration of Independence, July 4, 1776," which was published in 1885 (Cambridge: John Wilson and Son); William F. Dana's "The Declaration of Independence," published in the *Harvard Law Review* in January 1900 (vol. 13, no. 5); and Heather A. Phillips's "Safety and Happiness: The Paradox of the Declaration of Independence," published online by *Archiving Early America* at www.earlyamerica.com/review /2007summerfall/preserving-documents.html. The article, which I accessed several times, discusses the back-and-forth struggle by Americans to preserve the Declaration on the one hand and display it for all to see on the other.

For an excellent discussion on the hardships suffered by the signers of the Declaration of Independence, see William Hogeland's "Suicide Pact: 56 Men Put their Lives on the Line by Signing the Declaration of Independence," published in *American History* magazine in August 2013.

For more on the indefatigable and heroic midnight rider, Caesar Rodney, I was aided by Ann Decker's graduate thesis at Lehigh University (December 2005) entitled "The Coalition of the Two Brothers: Caesar and Thomas Rodney and the Making of the American Revolution in Delaware," a fine piece of research and writing.

For an excellent discussion on Declaration engrosser Timothy Matlack, I examined a paper entitled "Col. Timothy Matlack: Patriot and Soldier," by Dr. A. M. Stackhouse, read before the Gloucester County Historical Society at the Old Tavern House in Haddonfield, New Jersey (read on April 14, 1908, and privately printed in 1910).

For information on Rhode Island's Stephen Hopkins, including his famous quote, "My hands tremble but my heart does not," I referred to a booklet published in 1918 by the Merchants National Bank of Providence to commemorate Providence's centenary entitled *Old Providence: A Collection of Facts and Traditions Relating to Various Buildings and Sites of Historic Interest in Providence.*

Books

Works by some of America's finest historians provided me with valuable background and insights into the founders themselves and the process of creating the Declaration of Independence.

As previously mentioned, Pauline Maier's *American Scripture: Making the Declaration of Independence* (New York: Vintage Books, 1997) was indispensable, as was John H. Hazelton's *The Declaration of Independence: Its History* (which I included in the Primary Sources section). Others included Carl L. Becker's *The Declaration of Independence: A Study in the History of Political Ideas* (New York: Vintage Books edition, 1958), and Julian Boyd's in-depth analysis, *The Declaration of Independence: The Evolution of the Text* (Princeton, NJ: Princeton University Press, 1945), which contains a foreword by former Librarian of Congress (and Declaration protector) Archibald MacLeish.

I'm also grateful to excellent biographers who brought the founders to life and, I hope, helped me to do so. These include: Walter Isaacson's colorful *Benjamin Franklin: An American Life* (New York: Simon & Schuster, 2003); H. W. Brands's *The First American: The Life and Times of Benjamin Franklin* (New York: Doubleday, 2000); David McCullough's gripping *John Adams* (New York: Simon & Schuster, 2001); and Jon Meacham's extraordinary *Thomas Jefferson: The Art of Power* (New York: Random House, 2012). I also spent time with the first volume of Dumas Malone's classic six-volume biography of Thomas Jefferson, entitled *Jefferson the Virginian* (Boston: Little, Brown, 1948).

Other books that provided me with insights and ideas from the founders, and background and analysis about the Declaration itself, included (in alphabetical order by author): Danielle Allen, *Our Declaration: A Reading of the Declaration of Independence in Defense of Equality* (New York: Liveright, 2014); Roberdeau Buchanan, *Genealogy of the McKean Family of Pennsylvania* (Lancaster, PA: Inquirer Printing Company, 1890); James MacGregor Burns, *The Vineyard of Liberty* (New York: Alfred A. Knopf, 1982); William P. Frank, *Caesar Rodney, Patriot: Delaware's Hero for All Times and All Seasons* (Dover: Delaware American Revolution Bicentennial Commission, 1975); Harry Clinton Green and Mary Wolcott Green, *Wives of the Signers: The Women Behind the Declaration of Independence* (Aledo, TX: Wallbuilder Press, 1997); John Fitzpatrick, *The Spirit of the Revolution* (Boston: Houghton Mifflin, 1924); and Jack Kelly, *Band of Giants: The Amateur Soldiers Who Won America's Independence* (New York: Palgrave Macmillan, 2014).

I also referred to Denise Kiernan and Joseph D'Agnese, *Signing Their Lives Away: The Fame and Misfortune of the Men Who Signed the Declaration of Independence* (Philadelphia: Quirk Books, 2009); A. J. Languth, *Patriots: The Men Who Started the American Revolution* (New York: Touchstone, 1988); Richard Henry Lee (grandson of the founder), *Memoir of the Life of Richard Henry Lee and His Correspondence* (Philadelphia: William Brown, 1825); Charlene Mires, *Independence Hall in American Memory* (Philadelphia: University of Pennsylvania Press,

2002); David MuCullough, *1776* (New York: Simon & Schuster, 2005); John Sanderson, Robert Waln, and Henry Dilworth Gilpin, *Biography of the Signers to the Declaration of Independence* (Philadelphia: R. W. Pomeroy, 1827); Larry Schweikart and Michael Allen, *A Patriot's History of the United States* (New York: Penguin Group, 2004); and Gordon Wood, *The Creation of the American Republic, 1776–1787* (New York: W. W. Norton, 1972).

1787–1791: The Creation of the United States Constitution

Primary Sources

James Madison unquestionably was the lifeblood of the United States Constitution, so it's best to start with sources that helped me understand the Virginian who fought tirelessly for a strong national government and authored a large number of *The Federalist Papers* that helped convince states to ratify the new Constitution.

The Library of Congress has amassed a wonderful collection entitled The James Madison Papers, 1723–1836 (www.loc.gov/collections/james -madison-papers/, to which I referred frequently). It contains more than 12,000 items that span Madison's public life, including letters, personal notes, legal and financial documents, drafts of correspondence and legislation, and an autobiography. Here, researchers can view actual letters, written in a neat, compact hand, from the man who became known as the Father of the Constitution. Of course, the collection includes his notes from the 1787 Constitutional Convention and writings about his pivotal role in the 1788 Virginia ratification convention. Correspondence in the collection includes letters to and from John Adams, John Quincy Adams, Elbridge Gerry, Alexander Hamilton, Thomas Jefferson, Dolley Madison, George Mason, James Monroe, Edmund Randolph, and George Washington. In addition, it contains extensive correspondence between President Madison and his secretary of war, James Armstrong, during the War of 1812.

Other Madison primary sources I referred to included: *The Writings of James Madison,* edited by Gaillard Hunt (New York: Putnam, 1900–1910); *The Papers of James Madison, Purchased by Order of Congress*, published under the direction of Henry D. Gilpin by Langree and O'Sullivan in 1840, which includes his reports of debates of the Constitutional Convention, and later republished as *Letters and Other Writings of James Madison in Four Volumes* (Philadelphia: J. B. Lippincott, 1867); *James Madison's Notes of Debates in the Federal Convention of 1787 and Their Relation to a More Perfect Society of Nations*, by James Brown Scott, a U.S. delegate to the Second Hague Peace Conference (New York: Oxford University Press, 1918); and *Notes on the Debates in the Federal Convention*, published online by the Avalon Project at the Lillian Goldman Law Library at Yale Law School (http://avalon.law.yale.edu/subjectmenus/jeffpap.asp).

As for other sources for the Constitutional Convention, the Yale Avalon Project's *Notes* contains valuable information, as do the indispensable *The Records of the Federal Convention of 1787*, revised edition, edited by Max Farrand (New Haven, CT: Yale University Press, 1937, reprinted 1966); and the *Supplement to Max Farrand's The Records of the Federal Convention of 1787*, edited by James H. Hutson (New Haven, CT: Yale University Press, 1987).

For George Washington's thoughts and feelings about the Federal Convention and other matters, I consulted frequently The George Washington Papers at the Library of Congress (http://memory.loc.gov/ammem/gwhtml.gwhome.html), the largest collection of original Washington documents in the world, with more than 65,000 items (along with so many presidential papers, it was part of the massive relocation effort by the library after the Pearl Harbor attacks). It includes correspondence, letter books, diaries, journals, military records, and other reports accumulated by Washington between 1741 and 1799. I also consulted often *The Papers of George Washington Digital Edition* from the University of Virginia Press (http://rotunda.upress/virginia.edu/founders/gewn.html), which includes his complete diaries; the University of Virginia's *Papers of George Washington: The Complete Correspondence* (http://gwpapers.virginia.edu); and the National Archives' comprehensive Founders Online series, Correspondence and Other Writings of Six Major Shapers of the United States (http://founders.archives.gov).

For the debates on ratification of the Constitution and the ensuing debates on the Bill of Rights, I consulted the Madison and Hamilton records already cited, and also relied on the following:

- *The Federalist* (also known as *The Federalist Papers*), by Alexander Hamilton, James Madison, and John Jay, Papers No. 1–85, October 27, 1787–May 28, 1788, arranged, edited, and annotated by Jacob E. Cooke (Limited Edition, The Franklin Library: Franklin Center, Penn., 1977).
- *The Documentary History of the Ratification of the Constitution,* edited by Merrill Jensen, John P. Kaminski, et al. (Madison, WI: State Historical Society of Wisconsin, 1976–). Volume 2 (1976) contains the ratification debate in Pennsylvania; volumes 8–10 (1988, 1990, 1993) contain the crucial debates in Virginia; and a subseries called *Commentaries on the Constitution: Public and Private*, contain the day-to-day debate about the Constitution that took place on a regional or national level in newspapers, pamphlets, magazines, and public and private correspondence from diplomats.
- *The Documentary History of the First Federal Elections, 1788–1790*, edited by Merrill Jensen, Robert A. Becker, and Gordon DenBoer (Madison: University of Wisconsin Press, 1976–1989).
- *The Documentary History of the First Federal Congress of the United States of America*, edited by Linda Grant DePauw, Charlene Bangs Bickford, Helen E. Veit, and Kenneth R. Bowling (Baltimore and London: Johns Hopkins University Press, 1972–1996).
- The Constitution Society, a private nonprofit organization, offers extensive primary-source documents, including comprehensive debates on the state ratification conventions at www .constitution.org/elliott.htm.), which I consulted frequently.
- The Massachusetts Historical Society offers primary-source documents on the state's ratification convention in its collection entitled Massachusetts Considers Ratifying the U.S. Constitution (www.masshist.org/features/mass-raitification# TOCanchor1); TeachingAmericanHistory.org also offers ratification primary sources at http://teachingamericanhistory .org/ratification).

- The National Archives offers documents about the Constitution, the Federal Convention, and ratification at www.archives.gov/nationalarchivesexperience/constitution.html.
- I found Massachusetts's Mercy Otis Warren's writings opposing the Constitution in Michael P. Johnson's *Reading the American Past: Volume 1: To 1877* (Boston: Bedford/St. Martin's, 2012).
- Francis Hopkinson provided a thorough first-hand account of the Grand Federal Procession in Philadelphia in 1788; see "An Account of the Grand Federal Procession Performed at Philadelphia on Friday, the 4th of July 1788," in *The Miscellaneous Essays and Occasional Writings of Francis Hopkinson, Esq.*, vol. 2 (Philadelphia: T. Dobson, 1792), pp. 349–422.

Secondary Sources
Articles, Booklets, and Unpublished Works

As they did for the Declaration of Independence, both the Library of Congress and the National Archives have sponsored numerous articles and booklets about the Constitution. Among those I found most helpful were Arthur Plotnik's "The Odyssey of the Constitution," in *Celebrating the Constitution: A Bicentennial Retrospective*, a commemorative issue of *Prologue*, the quarterly publication of the National Archives edited by Timothy Walch (Washington, D.C.: 1988); the National Archives "A More Perfect Union: The Creation of the U.S. Constitution," at www.archives.gov/exhibits/charters/constitutionhistory.html, which is based on the introduction, by Roger A. Burns, to *A More Perfect Union: The Creation of the United States Constitution*, authored by the National Archives and Records Service (Washington, D.C.: National Archives Trust Fund Board, 1978); and Henry Bain's "Errors in the Constitution—Typographical and Congressional," published in *Prologue* 44, no. 2 (2012).

In addition, while the Constitution was at Fort Knox, Library of Congress executives David Mearns and Verner Clapp published a booklet entitled *The Constitution of the United States: An Account of Its Travels Since September 17, 1787* (Washington, D.C.: Library of Congress, 1942); the pair updated the booklet in 1952 and included the text of the

Constitution. Both versions end with the "silent ceremony" after the Library of Congress accessed the document in 1924.

Other important articles about the Constitutional Convention that I referenced include: A. E. Dick Howard, "The Constitutional Convention of 1787," in *Historians on America: Decisions That Made a Difference* (U.S. Department of State, Bureau of International Information Programs, 2007); Jack N. Rakove, "The Great Compromise: Drafting the American Constitution," *History Today* 37 (1987); Christopher Wolfe, "On Understanding the Constitutional Convention of 1787," *Journal of Politics*, 39 (1977); Colleen Sheehan, "James Madison: Father of the Constitution," in the Heritage Foundation's *First Principles: Foundational Concepts to Guide Politics and Policy*, No. 8 (April 8, 2013); David Brian Robertson, "Madison's Opponents and Constitutional Design," *American Political Science Review* 46 (1986); and Michael Coenen, "The Significance of Signatures: Why the Framers Signed the Constitution and What They Meant by Doing So," *Yale Law Journal* 119, no. 5 (March 2010).

I found immensely helpful the Lehrman Institute's "The Making of the United States Constitution," an exemplary sixty-page narrative of the events of the summer of 1787, complete with many primary-source quotes (http://lehrmaninstitute.or/history/constitution.asp, consulted frequently).

For information about the preamble's author, Gouverneur Morris, I examined Richard Brookhiser, "The Forgotten Founding Father," *City Journal* (Spring 2002); John K. Bush, "Gouverneur Morris," *America's Forgotten Founders*, 2nd ed., edited by Gary L. Gregg II and Mark David Hall (Wilmington, DE: ISI Books, 2014); and Scott Bomboy, "The Man Who Wrote the Words 'We the People,'" written for the National Constitution Center's blog and posted on January 31, 2014 (http://blog.constitutioncenter.org/2014/01/the-man-who-actually-wrote-the-words-we-the-people/).

Ron Soodalter asks whether George Washington overstepped the bounds of the presidency by asking Americans to give thanks to God for the new Constitution; see "For All the Great and Various Favors," *American History* (December 2014).

Books

I believe that any research on the Constitutional Convention would be lacking—certainly mine would have been—without consulting the following three books: Max Farrand, *The Framing of the Constitution of the United States* (New Haven: Yale University Press, 1913), an early work that presents an overview of the convention based on primary sources; Catherine Drinker Bowen, *Miracle at Philadelphia: The Story of the Constitutional Convention, May to September 1787* (Boston: Little, Brown, 1966), the classic narrative study of the events in Philadelphia; and Richard Beeman, *Plain, Honest Men: The Making of the American Constitution* (New York: Random House, 2009), a wonderful account of the drama, the debates, and the motives of delegates during the Constitutional Convention.

I also found valuable Andrew C. McLaughlin's *The Confederation and the Constitution, 1783–1789* (New York: Crowell-Collier, 1962), and Gerry and Janet Souter's *The Constitution: The Story of the Creation and Adaptation of the Most Important Document in the History of the United States of America* (San Diego, CA: Thunder Bay Press, 2013). For interesting anecdotes on all of the delegates, I found helpful Denise Kiernan's and Joseph D'Agnese's follow-up work to the Declaration book, this one entitled *Signing Their Rights Away: The Fame and Misfortune of the Men Who Signed the United States Constitution* (Philadelphia: Quirk Books, 2011).

Books on James Madison's life that I found valuable were Lynne Cheney's thorough and excellent biography, *James Madison: A Life Reconsidered* (New York: Viking, 2014); Ralph Louis Ketcham's complete *James Madison: A Biography* (Charlottesville: University of Virginia Press, 1990); Jack N. Rakove's readable *James Madison and the Creation of the American Republic* (New York: HarperCollins, 1990); and Robert A. Rutland's *James Madison: The Founding Father* (New York: Macmillan, 1987).

Of the hundreds of books written about George Washington (many focusing on his revolutionary military career or his presidency), I found these works most helpful in understanding his role at the Constitutional Convention: Edward J. Larson, *The Return of George Washington: 1783–1789* (New York: William Morrow, 2014); Richard Brookhiser,

Founding Father: Rediscovering George Washington (New York: Free Press, 1996); and Joseph J. Ellis, *His Excellency: George Washington* (New York: Alfred A. Knopf, 2004).

For Benjamin Franklin's role at the convention, I once again consulted the previously cited Isaacson's *Benjamin Franklin: An American Life* and Brands's *The First American: The Life and Times of Benjamin Franklin*.

Books that I consulted on preamble author and Constitution polisher Gouverneur Morris include: Richard Brookhiser, *Gentleman Revolutionary: Gouverneur Morris—the Rake Who Wrote the Constitution* (New York: Free Press, 2003); William Howard Adams, *Gouverneur Morris: An Independent Life* (New Haven: Yale University Press, 2003); and Melanie Randolph Miller, *An Incautious Man: The Life of Gouverneur Morris* (Wilmington, DE: ISI Books, 2008).

For information about the Grand Federal Procession on July 4, 1788, I consulted Len Travers's *Celebrating the Fourth: Independence Day and the Rites of Nationalism in the Early Republic* (Amherst: University of Massachusetts Press, 1997); and Diana Karter Appelbaum's *The Glorious Fourth: An American Holiday, An American History* (New York: Facts of File Books, 1989).

I consulted many fine works about post–Constitutional Convention events, including the state ratification process, the writing of *The Federalist*, and the adoption of the Bill of Rights. Among the books I found valuable and highly recommend: Pauline Maier's dramatic *Ratification: The People Debate the Constitution, 1787–1788* (New York: Simon & Schuster, 2010); Jay Winik's sweeping history, *The Great Upheaval: America and the Birth of the Modern World, 1788–1800* (New York: Harper Collins, 2007), which describes how events in America influenced the French Revolution and Catherine the Great's Russia; Michael J. Meyerson's *Liberty's Blueprint: How Madison and Hamilton Wrote the Federalist Papers, Defined the Constitution, and Made Democracy Safe for the World* (New York: Perseus Book Group, 2008); and Chris DeRose's *Founding Rivals, Madison vs. Monroe: The Bill of Rights and the Election That Saved a Nation* (Washington, D.C.: Regnery Publishing, 2011), a thorough examination of the 1789 election in which Madison and Monroe ran against each other for Congress and how the outcome—Madison's victory—helped ensure the passage of the Bill of Rights.

In addition, I found two books helpful when researching the all-important Virginia ratification process. These were W. Asbury Christian's *Richmond: Her Past and Present* (Richmond, VA: L. H. Jenkins, 1912); and Hugh Blair Grigsby's sweeping *The History of the Virginia Federal Convention of 1788 with Some Account of the Eminent Virginians of That Era Who Were Members of the Body* (Richmond, VA: Virginia Historical Society, 1891).

1814: The Burning of Washington

Primary Sources

To tell the remarkable story of the British invasion and near destruction of Washington, D.C., while James Madison was president, I made extensive use of the previously cited *The James Madison Papers, 1723–1836* (collected by the Library of Congress) and *The Writings of James Madison* (edited by Gaillard Hunt). In addition, I consulted many of Dolley Madison's writings in *The Selected Letters of Dolley Payne Madison*, edited by David B. Mattern and Holly C. Shulman (Charlottesville: University of Virginia Press, 2003); *Memoirs and Letters of Dolly* [sic] *Madison, wife of James Madison, President of the United States*, edited by her grandniece, Lucia B. Cutts (Boston: Houghton Mifflin, 1888). Several of Dolley's writings are also contained within The James Madison Papers, 1723–1836 from the database The Founding Era Collection, "The Dolley Madison Digital Edition, Correspondence and Related Documents, First Lady Years, 4 March 1809–3 March 1817."

To learn about James Monroe's efforts to scout British troop movements and protect the country's founding documents, I relied on *The Writings of James Monroe: Including a Collection of His Public and Private Papers and Correspondence Now for the First Time Printed, Volume 5, 1807–1816*, edited by Stanislaus Murray Hamilton (New York: Putnam, 1901). In addition, there is Monroe–Madison correspondence in Madison's papers and in *American State Papers: Documents, Legislative and Executive, of the Congress of the United States, March 3, 1789–March 3,*

1819, Class V, Military Affairs, vol. 1. (Contained in this collection is Monroe's warning to Madison: "You had better remove the records.")

Stephen Pleasonton wrote a letter to Brigadier General William Winder on August 7, 1848, describing his role in relocating the Declaration and other vital papers. The letter is found in John C. Hildt's "Letters Relating from the Capture of Washington," in *South Atlantic Quarterly* 6 (1907): 58–65. This collection also contains the anonymous letter to President Madison from a "friend to the United States of America," warning of the impending attack on Washington, plus several letters from James Monroe to President Madison detailing the movement of British troops in Maryland and around Washington. The Pleasonton-Winder letter is also contained in "How the Declaration Was Saved," *Century Illustrated Monthly Magazine* 10 (1886): 633–635. Pleasonton also recounted his service to America in a letter to James Buchanan on February 7, 1853. It is contained in the *James Buchanan and Harriet Lane Johnston Papers, 1825–1887*, Manuscripts Division, Library of Congress, Box 2, Reel 2.

There is a rich collection of letters and documents on the Battle of Bladensburg and the attack on Washington in *The Naval War of 1812: A Documentary History,* vol. 3, *1814–1815*, Michael J. Crawford, editor (Washington: Naval Historical Center, Department of the Navy, 2002). In addition, several riveting letters on these topics are contained in "Commodore Joshua Barney's Official Report of the Battle of Bladensburg," August 29, 1814, contained in *Select Committee Papers and Reports* (National Archives, Record Group 233). In addition, the Report on the Removal of Powder from the Navy Yard at the Time of the British Invasion of Washington, 1814 (National Archives RG 45/350) also contains extensive information about the dramatic events taking place in Washington in August 1814.

The U.S. Capitol Visitor Center contains copies of letters related to this period, including the correspondence to Patrick Magruder, clerk of the House of Representatives, from S. Burch and J. T. Frost (September 15, 1814), in which the two clerks provide their account of the difficulties in attempting to obtain carts to save the House records. The letter can be found at www.visitthecapitol.gov/exhibitions/more-perfect-union -congress-and-war-1812-part-1/knowledge/war-1812-congress

-investigates?page=3#. Senate Clerk Lewis Machen, who along with messenger Tobias Simpson, managed to save a number of Senate records from the burning of Washington, described his efforts in a letter to Senator William C. Rives, written on September 12, 1836, more than twenty years after the fact. His dramatic recollection can be found in its original form at www.senate.gov/artandhistory/history/resources /pdf/MachenLetter1836.pdf, or in transcript form at www.senate.gov /artandhistory/history/common/generic/letterfrommanchentorives.hm.

I found additional information about the Leesburg farm where Pleasonton relocated the Declaration and the Constitution when the owners of the property applied for nomination to the National Register of Historic Places (U.S. Department of the Interior, National Park Service, National Register of History Places, May 20, 1975). In the form, owners Mr. and Mrs. Frank R. Coughlan note: "The interesting cellar vault is believed to be where the papers were hidden."

Secondary Sources
Articles, Booklets, and Unpublished Works

I referred to several excellent contemporaneous newspaper accounts of the events in Washington in August 1814 as recorded in the *National Intelligencer*. Specifically, I gleaned information from front-page accounts on August 30, August 31, September 7, and September 9 of that year.

White House History, the journal of the White House Historical Association, devotes its entire Fall 1998 issue to "The Burning of the White House During the War of 1812." The issue contains several articles from historians on all aspects of the British invasion, including an overview of events, Dolley Madison's efforts to save her husband's papers, and eyewitness accounts of the burning. I found helpful the account of events by Thomas Fleming in "How Dolley Madison Saved the Day," *Smithsonian Magazine*, March 2010. The National Archives also posted an online account entitled "The Burning of Washington," in anticipation of the 200th anniversary of the British attack (posted on August 18, 2014, at http:// blogs.archives.gov/prologue/?p=13456).

American History devoted a large section of its October 2014 issue to the events of August 1814, including the bombardment of Fort McHenry and Francis Scott Key's writing of "The Star-Spangled Banner." These articles included Marc Leepson's "The Second American Revolution," Don Hawkins's "Rare First-Hand View of the Battle of Bladensburg," and Leepson's "'Our Good Frank's Patriotic Song': Francis Scott Key, the Battle of Baltimore, and 'The Star-Spangled Banner.'" In addition, *American History* published an excellent account of the meaning of the War of 1812 to Americans in "Oh Say Can you see . . . ? How the War of 1812 Gave Us Something Worth Fighting For" (June 2013).

After Stephen Pleasonton's career as a State Department clerk, he went on to become the man in charge of America's lighthouses. His career, including an account of his heroic efforts to save the Declaration and the Constitution, are chronicled by *Lighthouse Digest* in an online story entitled "The Lighthouse Man Who Saved America's History," a story that first appeared in the July 2001 print edition of *Lighthouse Digest Magazine*. The piece can be found at www.lighthousedigest.com/digest/StoryPage .cfm?StoryKey=1056.

As part of Maryland's bicentennial commemoration of the War of 1812, the Maryland State Highway Administration's archaeologists partnered with state, county, and federal agencies to locate, survey, and excavate War of 1812 battlefields, encampments, routes, etc. The War of 1812 Archaeology website posted an account on November 22, 2013, of Dolley Madison's route after she fled the White House entitled "Dolley's Difficult Run." It can be found at http://warof1812archaeology.blogspot.com/2013 /11/dolleys-difficult-run.html.

Books

In addition to previously cited biographies of James Madison, I found the following helpful for Dolley Madison's efforts during this perilous time: Catherine Allgor, *A Perfect Union: Dolley Madison and the Creation of the American Nation* (New York: Henry Holt, 2007); Richard N. Cote, *Strength and Honor: The Life of Dolley Madison* (Mt. Pleasant, SC: Corinthian Books, 2004); and Hugh Howard, *Mr. and Mrs. Madison's War: American's First Couple and the Second War of Independence* (New York: Bloomsbury Press, 2012).

For an overview of the destruction of Washington, I relied heavily on Anthony S. Pitch's dramatic *The Burning of Washington: The British Invasion of 1814* (Annapolis, MD: Naval Institute Press, 1998); and A. J.

Langguth's excellent *Union 1812: The Americans Who Fought the Second War of Independence* (New York: Simon & Schuster, 2006).

Other books that I consulted include: Carole Herrick, *August 24, 1814: Washington in Flames* (Falls Church, VA: Higher Education Publishing, 2005); Donald R. Hickey, *The War of 1812: A Forgotten Conflict* (Urbana: University of Illinois Press, 1990); Walter Lord, *The Dawn's Early Light* (New York: W. W. Norton, 1972); and Steve Vogel's gripping *Through the Perilous Fight: Six Weeks That Saved the Nation* (New York: Random House, 2013).

1826–1860: America's Golden Jubilee and Years Following

Primary Sources

For a comprehensive look at John Quincy Adams, and to help me construct the scenes in which he was prominent, I consulted several sources. These included:

- The Massachusetts Historical Society's The Diaries of John Quincy Adams: A Digital Collection, which contains fifty-one volumes of Adams's diaries, part of the Adams Family Papers. Adams began keeping his diary at the age of twelve (1779) and continued until shortly before his death in 1848. I looked specifically at volumes 30 to 37 (covering the years 1816 to 1828).
- The *Memoirs of John Quincy Adams, Comprising Portions of His Diary from 1795 to 1848,* vol. 7, edited by Charles Francis Adams (Philadelphia: J. B. Lippincott, 1875).
- The *Writings of John Quincy Adams,* vols. 6–7, edited by Worthington Chauncey Ford (New York: Macmillan, 1913–1917).
- John Quincy Adams's famous July 4, 1821, oration to Congress ("She goes not abroad in search of monsters to destroy") while he was secretary of state is found in many locations online; I relied on the official printed version entitled "An Address Delivered at the Request of the Committee of Arrangements for Celebrating the Anniversary of Independence at the City of Washington on the Fourth of July 1821 upon the Occasion of

Reading the Declaration of Independence by John Quincy Adams" (Cambridge, MA: Harvard, 1821).

The letters from the five renowned Americans declining Roger C. Weightman's invitation to the July 4, 1826, jubilee—including the last letter written by Thomas Jefferson—can be found in *Records of the Columbia Historical Society of Washington, D.C.*, vol. 22, edited by John B. Larner (Washington, D.C.: Columbia Historical Society, 1919).

A source rich in content and style was John A. Shaw's *Eulogy of John Adams and Thomas Jefferson, Delivered August 2, 1826, by the Request of the Inhabitants of Bridgewater* (Taunton, MA: Samuel W. Mortimer, 1826). The lengthy oration—twenty manuscript pages—occurred on the fiftieth anniversary of the Declaration's signing.

Secondary Sources
Articles, Booklets, and Unpublished Works

For the best and most thorough periodical account of America's fiftieth-year celebration, please see L. H. Butterfield, "The Jubilee of Independence, July 4, 1826," in *The Virginia Magazine of History and Biography* 61, no. 2 (April 1953): 119–140. Butterfield was the director of the Institute of Early American History and Culture at Williamsburg, and the article was originally delivered as the annual address to the Virginia Historical Society at its meeting on January 19, 1953. Butterfield cites numerous 1826 newspaper accounts in his article.

In addition to the many sources already cited on the history of the Declaration—the original and its derivatives—I also found helpful Catherine Nicholson's "The Stone Engraving: Icon of the Declaration," in *Prologue* 35, no. 3 (Fall 2003), accessible at www.archives.gov/publications/prologue/2003/fall/stone-engraving.html.

For an analysis of John Quincy Adams's 1821 "monsters to destroy" speech and how it pertains to our foreign policy today, see Charles Edel, "John Quincy Adams and American Foreign Policy in a Revolutionary Era," *E-Notes*, published by the Foreign Policy Research Institute, February 2013, and accessible at www.fpri.org/articles/2013/02/john-quincy-adams-and-american-foreign-policy-revolutionary-era.

The Secretary of State Office of the Historian publishes biographies of all secretaries, including Timothy Pickering. I consulted the Pickering biographical sketch for background at https://history.state.gov /departmenthistory/people/pickering-timothy.

The *National Intelligencer* published several stories on Dolley Madison's funeral in July 1849. I examined these as part of the Dolley Madison Project at the University of Virginia, accessible at www2.vcdh .virginia.edu/madison/.

Books

In addition to several books already cited, I found the following volumes helpful for this section: Fred Kaplan's *John Quincy Adams: American Visionary* (New York: HarperCollins, 2014); Andrew Burstein's compelling *America's Jubilee: How in 1826 a Generation Remembered Fifty Years of Independence* (New York: Alfred A. Knopf, 2001); and—for an outstanding and thorough history of America during this period—Daniel Walker Howe's *What Hath God Wrought: The Transformation of America, 1815–1848* (New York: Oxford University Press, 2007).

1860–1924: Creating the Gettysburg Address, America's Centennial, The Documents Move to the Library of Congress

Primary Sources

Again, thanks to the wonders of technology, the Library of Congress has digitized the Abraham Lincoln Papers, a superb collection consisting of some 20,000 documents and available at http://memory.loc.gov/ammem /alhtml/malhome.html. The collection is organized into three "general correspondence" series that include incoming and outgoing correspondence and enclosures, drafts of speeches, notes, and other printed material—it is a true research treasure. Included in this collection are the Nicolay and Hay copies of the Gettysburg Address; Edwin M. Stanton's letter to Lincoln about arrangements for the trip to Gettysburg; Edward Everett's letter to Lincoln complimenting the president for his words at Gettysburg; and several pieces of correspondence related to interested parties seeking copies of Lincoln's address in late 1863 and 1864. I accessed this collection frequently.

There are also a number of primary-source documents at the Cornell

University online project The Lincoln Presidency: Last Full Measure of
Devotion, available at http://rmc.library.cornell.edu/lincoln/index.html.
And, Cornell's outstanding Samuel J. May Anti-Slavery Collection (ac-
cessible at http://digital.library.cornell.edu/m/mayantislavery/), also
contains numerous documents related to Gettysburg. For example, Edward
Everett's lengthy keynote speech, entitled "An Oration Delivered on the
Battlefield of Gettysburg (November 19, 1863) at the Consecration of the
Cemetery," is available in its entirety.

In addition, I made use of *The Collected Works of Abraham Lincoln*,
edited by Roy P. Basler et al. (New Brunswick, NJ: Rutgers University
Press, 1953)—the first major scholarly effort to collect and publish the
complete writings of the sixteenth president—and made available in
electronic form through the efforts of The Abraham Lincoln Association
in Springfield, Illinois, at http://quod.lib.umich.edu/l/lincoln/.

I also found helpful *Abraham Lincoln's Speeches and Writings,
1859–1865*, edited by Don E. Fehrenbacher (New York: Library of America, 1989), a collection of Lincoln's speeches, letters, presidential messages, proclamations, and miscellaneous writings.

Lincoln's secretary, John G. Nicolay, offered his thorough first-hand
account of the events of November 1863 more than thirty years after the
fact in "Abraham Lincoln's Gettysburg Address," published in a popular
quarterly, *The Century* 47, no. 4 (February 1894).

An interesting collection of primary documents is contained in *Lincoln
As I Knew Him: Gossip, Tributes & Revelations from His Best Friends
and Worst Enemies*, edited by Harold Holzer (Chapel Hill, NC: Algon-
quin Books, 1999).

A collection of primary sources and letters on the 1876 Centennial
Exhibition can be found in James Dabney McCabe's *The Illustrated
History of the Centennial Exhibition Held in Commemoration of the
One-Hundredth Anniversary of American Independence* (Philadelphia: National Publishing Company, 1876). The title page description
foretells much of the contents of the collection, including "With a full description of the great buildings and all the objects of interest exhibited in
them," "biographies of the leading members of the Centennial Commission," a "complete description of the City of Philadelphia," and "embellished with over 300 fine engravings of buildings and scenes of the

Great Exhibition." I also found helpful the *Visitor's Guide to the Centennial Exhibition and Philadelphia, May 10th to November 10th, 1876* (Philadelphia: J. B. Lippincott, 1876), authorized by the Centennial Board of Finance, and billed as "The Only Guide-Book Sold on the Exhibition Grounds."

I developed the narrative about the controversy surrounding the "missing" Gettysburg Address and subsequent donations to the Library of Congress through several different primary sources, including: "Some Correspondence Regarding a Missing Copy of the Gettysburg Address," in *Lincoln Lore*, part 1, no. 1437 (November 1957); the John Hay Papers, the John G. Nicolay Papers, and the Ainsworth Rand Spofford Papers at the Library of Congress; and the Library of Congress collection entitled Lincoln, Abraham—Gettysburg Address, 1909–1923, Administrative Case File, Manuscript Division. In addition, the *Library of Congress Annual Report of 1916* offers a brief overview of the Gettysburg Address donation.

There are numerous secondary accounts of the "silent ceremony," when the Declaration and Constitution were placed into the Library of Congress shrine in 1924; the primary sources I consulted included the Herbert Putnam Papers, 1783–1958 in the Library of Congress and *Report of the Librarian of Congress for the Fiscal Year Ending June 30, 1924* (Washington, DC: Government Printing Office, 1924).

Secondary Sources
Articles, Booklets, and Unpublished Works

For two good articles about Abraham Lincoln's reverence for the founding fathers and the founding documents, I referenced the Lehrman Institute's online site Mr. Lincoln and the Founders for the following pieces: Lewis Lehrman's "Mr. Lincoln and the Declaration," available at www.mrlincolnandthefounders.org/inside.asp?ID=1&subjectID=1; and Richard Behn's "Mr. Lincoln's Commitment to the Founders," available at www.mrlincolnandthefounders.org/inside.asp?ID=3&subjectID=2.

For a fine analysis of the scene at Gettysburg and the impact of Lincoln's words, see Glenn LaFantasie, "Lincoln and the Gettysburg Awakening" in the *Journal of the Abraham Lincoln Association* 16, no. 1 (Winter 1995): 73–89. A short but effective recap of the Gettysburg

Address can be found at EyeWitnesstoHistory.com entitled "Lincoln's Gettysburg Address," a 2005 article available at www.eyewitnesstohistory .com/pfgtsburgaddress.htm.

Walter Nugent wrote a strong and helpful analysis on the Centennial of 1876 in "The American People and the Centennial of 1876" for the *Indiana Magazine of History* 75, no. 1 (1979): 53–69. I also found helpful Dennis T. Lawson's "Centennial Exhibition of 1876," in *Historic Pennsylvania Leaflet No. 30* (Harrisburg: Pennsylvania Historical and Museum Commission, 1969). *The New York Times* reprinted a *Harper's Weekly* cartoon from May 20, 1876, and included an analysis of the Centennial in its *On This Day* online series entitled "Columbia Welcoming the Nations," found at www.nytimes.com/learning/general/onthisday/harp /0520.html.

The most thorough secondary treatment of the "missing" Gettysburg Address is Martin P. Johnson's "Who Stole the Gettysburg Address?" in the *Journal of the Abraham Lincoln Association* 24, no. 2 (2003) (Board of Trustees of the University of Illinois). In addition, David Mearns, former chief of the Manuscript Division at the Library of Congress, wrote about the subject at "Unknown at This Address," in *Lincoln and the Gettysburg Address: Commemorative Papers*, edited by Allen Nevins (Urbana: University of Illinois Press, 1964).

The Washington Post ran a short story when the Gettysburg Address was donated to the Library of Congress on April 16, 1916, entitled "Give Lincoln Manuscripts: C. L. Hay and Miss Nicolay Present Documents to Government."

The "silent ceremony" that took place in 1924 when the Declaration and the Constitution were moved to the Library of Congress is recounted in numerous sources already cited, and also in "The Library and the Declaration: LC Has Long History with Founding Document," in the *Library of Congress Information Bulletin*, August 1997.

Books

It is often said that only Jesus, Shakespeare, and John F. Kennedy have had more written about them than Abraham Lincoln. Each generation, hundreds of books are written about the Great Emancipator. I relied on but a fraction, but I consider them among the best.

I found Richard Brookhiser's *Founders' Son: A Life of Abraham Lincoln* (New York: Basic Books, 2014) invaluable in analyzing how the founders influenced Lincoln and why Lincoln revered the Declaration of Independence and the Constitution. Among the best general biographies on Lincoln that I consulted are David Herbert Donald's masterful *Lincoln* (New York: Simon & Schuster, 1995); Benjamin P. Thomas's *Abraham Lincoln* (New York, Alfred A. Knopf, 1952); and Phillip Shaw Paludan's *The Presidency of Abraham Lincoln* (Lawrence: University Press of Kansas, 1994).

For fine accounts of Lincoln and the Gettysburg Address, I recommend Garry Willis's *Lincoln at Gettysburg: The Words that Remade America* (New York: Simon & Schuster, 1992); and Martin P. Johnson's *Writing the Gettysburg Address* (Lawrence: University of Kansas Press, 2013). For recountings of the battle itself, I consulted Stephen W. Sears's *Gettysburg* (Boston and New York: Houghton Mifflin Company, 2003); and James McPherson's classic *Battle Cry of Freedom: The Civil War Era* (New York: Oxford University Press, 1988).

I found helpful Joshua Zeitz's *Lincoln's Boys: John Hay, John Nicolay, and the War for Lincoln's Image* (New York: Penguin Books, 2014), a thorough and lively look into Lincoln's official secretaries, who enjoyed more access, witnessed more history, and knew Lincoln better than anyone outside of his immediate family. They took seriously their role as the gatekeepers of Lincoln's legacy.

For a colorful account on the Centennial of 1876, see the *Library of Universal History: Containing a Record of the Human Race from the Earliest Historical Period to the Present Time* by Israel Smith Clare and Moses Coit Tyler (New York: R. S. Peale and J. A. Hill, 1897). The piece appears in the section entitled "Recent History of the United States."

Good information about the Gettysburg Address donations to the Library of Congress appears in David C. Mearns, *The Lincoln Papers: The Story of the Collection with Selections to July 4, 1861*, 2 vols. (New York: Doubleday, 1948).

For a recount of the "silent ceremony" and the Library of Congress itself, I consulted Lucy Salamanca's *Fortress of Freedom: The Story of the Library of Congress* (New York: J. B. Lippincott, 1942). Salamanca was head of the Inquiry and General Research Section of the Legislative Reference Service at the Library of Congress.

For a good general account of the time period covered in this section, I consulted Paul Johnson's *A History of the American People* (New York: Harper Collins, 1997). I also consulted this volume for other sections of *American Treasures*.

1939–1945, World War II: To Fort Knox and Elsewhere

Primary Sources

The primary-source material about the Library of Congress's relocation of the Charters of Freedom to Fort Knox, and thousands of other documents to inland repositories, is voluminous, but before this book, virtually untapped. I was grateful to make use of sources that only a handful of other historians and researchers have even perused.

First, a number of letters, photos of the evacuation, lists of collections to be evacuated, and reports from Library of Congress division heads were included in the Library of Congress Archives, Central Files Series, Boxes 342, 731, 733, 734, 735, 736, and 737, Library of Congress, Manuscript Division; from the American Council of Learned Society Records (ACLS Records) General Office File Series, 1919–1951, Boxes D10, D11, D12; and from The Archibald MacLeish Papers, Library of Congress, Manuscript Division, Washington, D.C., including: "Correspondence 1907–1981," Boxes 6, 11, 16, and 19; and "Additions, 1926–1981," Box 58 Notebooks, 1933–1955 (eight volumes).

The National Archives and Records Administration (NARA) also contains numerous documents on the relocation of the Charters of Freedom, the protection of documents, and related events in Record Group 64, *Records of the National Archives and Records Administration*; Record Group 87 and *The Records of the Secret Service*; Record Group 187, Records of the *National Resources Planning Board*. Fort Knox material is included in NARA Record Group 319, *Records of the Army Staff*, and Record Group 87, *Records of the Adjutant General's Office*.

The U.S. Secret Service provided me with biographies and other documents on the agents involved in the transfer and a collection of primary

sources—mainly from the Library of Congress and National Archives—
on the transfer of documents to Fort Knox.

In addition, more information about the document transfers and the
work of the Library of Congress during wartime can be found in the *U.S.
Library of Congress: Annual Report of the Librarian of Congress* for the
years 1940–1946 (Washington, D.C., Library of Congress in all cases).

For excellent primary-source information on the protection of rec-
ords see *The Protection of Cultural Resources Against the Hazards of War:
A Preliminary Handbook*, published by the National Resources Planning
Board, Committee on Conservation of Cultural Resources (Washington:
National Resources Planning Board, 1942); and *The Care of Records in a
National Emergency*, a bulletin of the National Archives, no. 3., December
1941.

In addition, Archibald MacLeish spoke and wrote extensively about
the mission of libraries to protect records and act as wartime stewards of
records and information. Among the best sources were (all by MacLeish):
"The Library of Congress Protects Its Collections," in the American Library
Association *Bulletin* 36, no. 2, part 1 (February 1942); "Libraries in the
Contemporary Crisis," an address delivered at the Carnegie Institute in
Pittsburgh, Pennsylvania, on Founders' Day, October 19, 1939 (Wash-
ington, D.C.: Government Printing Office, 1939); and "The Librarian
and the Democratic Process," a paper delivered on May 31, 1940, at the
American Library Association's general session in Cincinnati, Ohio. Mac-
Leish also wrote about these topics in several book collections of essays
and papers, including: *A Time to Speak: The Selected Prose of Archibald
MacLeish* (Boston: Houghton Mifflin, 1941); *A Time to Act: Selected
Addresses of Archibald MacLeish* (Boston: Houghton Mifflin, 1943);
*Champion of a Cause: Essays and Addresses on Librarianship by
Archibald MacLeish*, compiled by Eva M. Goldschmidt (Chicago:
American Library Association, 1971); and *Archibald MacLeish: Re-
flections*, edited by Bernard A. Drabek and Helen E. Ellis (Amherst:
University of Massachusetts Press, 1986). Several letters that offered
insight into MacLeish's character were included in *Letters of Archibald
MacLeish, 1907 to 1982*, edited by R. H. Winnick (Boston: Houghton
Mifflin, 1983).

While he was chief assistant librarian of the Library of Congress,

Luther H. Evans wrote a script for broadcast called "The Library of Congress Goes to War," broadcast on April 29, 1942, and found at http://memory.loc.gov/service/mss/mff/003/003023/0001.gif; and an essay called "The Library of Congress and the War" on May 30, 1942, found at http://memory.loc.gov/cgi-bin/ampage.

The family of Harry E. Neal generously provided me with a number of his private documents and correspondence, including correspondence with MacLeish, photos, and a lengthy unpublished autobiography (and accompanying notes) that Neal entitled *A Lucky Life*.

For information about the Library of Congress taking possession of the Magna Carta, I was grateful to consult *Magna Carta: The Lincoln Cathedral Copy Exhibited in the Library of Congress, Some Notes Prepared by David C. Mearns and Verner W. Clapp* (Washington, DC: Government Printing Office, 1939); and Archibald MacLeish's remarks on November 28, 1939, entitled "Deposit of the Magna Carta in the Library of Congress," and accessed at http://memory.loc.gov/service/mss/mff/003/003004/0001.gif.

President Franklin Delano Roosevelt's December 8, 1941, "date of infamy" speech is found in many locations. For a look at FDR's handwritten transcript, go to www.archives.gov/education/lessons/day-of-infamy/. For Winston Churchill's address to Congress on December 26, 1941, I accessed www.ibiblio.org/pha/policy/1941/411226a.html. In addition, Churchill's own magnificent history, *The Second World War*, provided me with his thoughts, both on Pearl Harbor in *The Grand Alliance*, vol. 3 (Boston: Houghton Mifflin, 1950), and on German attacks on London in *Their Finest Hour*, vol. 2 (Boston: Houghton Mifflin, 1949).

The National Archives provided me with copies of the Jefferson Memorial dedication program, entitled "Program of Exercises Attending the Declaration of the Thomas Jefferson Memorial, The Tidal Basin, West Potomac Park, Washington, Tuesday, April 13, 1943." FDR's dedication speech can be found at www.presidency.ucsb.edu/ws/?pid=16383.

For an interesting first-hand account of World War II in Washington, D.C., I consulted *Wartime Washington: The Secret OSS Journal of James Grafton Rogers, 1942–1943*, edited by Thomas Troy (Frederick, MD: University Publications of America, 1987).

Secondary Sources
Articles, Booklets, and Unpublished Works

I referenced many articles related to Archibald MacLeish's selection as Librarian of Congress and his philosophy once he assumed the job. Many of these cited primary sources in their footnotes and endnotes, which augmented my own use of primary sources. In alphabetical order by author, these included: David Barber, "Archibald MacLeish's Life and Career," *American National Biography*, edited by John A. Garraty and Mark C. Carnes (New York: Oxford University Press, 1999); Nancy L. Benco, "Archibald MacLeish: The Poet Librarian," *Quarterly Journal of the Library of Congress* 33, no. 3 (July 1976); Peter Buitenhuis, "Prelude to War: The Interventionist Propaganda of Archibald MacLeish, Robert E. Sherwood, and John Steinbeck," *Canadian Review of American Studies* 26, no. 1 (Winter 1996); Eva Goldschmidt, "Archibald MacLeish: Librarian of Congress," *College & Research Libraries* (January 1969); Betty Schwartz, "The Role of the American Library Association in the Selection of Archibald MacLeish as Librarian of Congress," *Journal of Library History (1974–1987)* 9, no. 3 (July 1974); Eleanor M. Sickels, "Archibald MacLeish and American Democracy," *American Literature* 15, no. 3 (November 1943); Frederick J. Stielow, "Librarian Warriors and Rapprochement: Carl Milam, Archibald MacLeish, and World War II," *Libraries and Culture* 25, no. 4 (Fall 1990); Dennis Thomison "FDR, the ALA, and Mr. MacLeish: The Selection of the Librarian of Congress, 1939," *Library Quarterly* 42, no. 4 (October 1972); and Sydney Weinberg, "What to Tell America: The Writers' Quarrel in the Office of War Information," *Journal of American History*. 55, no. 1 (June 1968).

I consulted numerous articles on the wartime atmosphere in Washington, D.C., both before and after Pearl Harbor. In alphabetical order by author, these included: Jane Aikin, "Preparing for a National Emergency: The Committee on Cultural Resources, 1939–1944," *Library Quarterly* 77, no. 3 (July 2007); John Y. Cole, "The Library of Congress and the Democratic Spirit," *Libraries & Democracy: The Cornerstones of Liberty*, edited by Nancy Kranich (Chicago: American Library Association, 2001); Douglas Cox, "National Archives and International Conflicts: The Society of American Archivists and War," *American Archivist* 74 (Fall–Winter 2011); Anne Bruner Eales, "Fort Archives: The National

Archives Goes to War," *Prologue* 35, no. 2 (Summer 2003); Jerrold Orne, "The Library of Congress Prepares for Emergencies," *ALA Bulletin* 35, no. 6 (June 1941); Kathy Peiss, "Cultural Policy in the Time of War: The American Response to Endangered Books in World War II," *Library Trends* 55, no. 3 (Winter 2007); and Brett Spenser, "Preparing for an Air Attack: Libraries and American Air Raid Defense During World War II," *Libraries & the Cultural Record* 43, no. 2 (2008).

For background and illustrative purposes, I consulted several articles on the universities to which the Library of Congress transferred documents after the Pearl Harbor attacks. These included Melissa Cragin's article on Foster Mohrhardt, who served as the librarian at Washington and Lee University for eight years, beginning in 1938. It is entitled "Foster Mohrhardt: Connecting the Traditional World of Libraries and the Emerging World of Information Science," *Library Trends* 52, no. 4 (Spring 2004). In addition, I found helpful a paper by Geoffrey Corey Harmon, "A Brief History of the Washington and Lee University Library, 1938–2003" (master's thesis, School of Information and Library Science, University of North Carolina at Chapel Hill, 2009). The Denison University website contains a story by Ginger Moore entitled "Documents Stored Here Returned to Washington," available at www.denison.edu /library/research/documentsstoredherereturnedt.html. The piece cites as its source the *Denisonian*, November 10, 1944. For the University of Virginia perspective, I consulted Jennings L. Wagoner and Robert L. Baxter Jr., "Higher Education Goes to War: The University of Virginia's Response to World War II," *Virginia Magazine of History and Biography* 100, no. 3 (July 1992): 399–428. In addition, I found helpful Lawrence Thompson's more contemporaneous account, entitled "The Role of the University Library in the War Effort, with Special Reference to the Midwest," *College and Research Libraries* (December 1942): 11–16.

For information on the Magna Carta held in the United States for safekeeping, I consulted Carl. L. Meyer, "Magna Carta in America," *American Bar Association Journal* 26, no. 1 (January 1940); and John Pullinger and Robert R. Newlen, "Parliamentary Libraries Celebrate the 800th Anniversary of the Magna Carta," a paper submitted for the World Library and Information Congress Assembly in Helsinki in 2012.

Robert Penn Warren, who served as editor of the *Library of Con-

gress Quarterly Journal of Current Acquisitions, told for the first time the story of the transfer of the Charters of Freedom to Fort Knox in an illustrated feature story in the November 1944 issue of the publication. The *Chicago Tribune* ran several stories in early 1937 on the relocation of gold bullion to the Fort Knox depository, including: "U.S. Armored Trains Preparing to Move Four Billions [*sic*] in Gold" (January 11, 1937); "Move Millions in Gold to New Treasure House" (January 13, 1937); "120 Millions [*sic*] in U.S. Gold Sent out of New York (January 19, 1937); "Hide 200 Million in Gold as Army of Guards Looks On" (January 14, 1937); and "U.S. Gold Again Buried, This Time in Vaults" (January 24, 1937). Secrecy still shrouds Fort Knox in many ways; however, a good history of the fort and the depository appears on the Fort Knox website at www.knox.army .mil/history.asp. In addition, the U.S. Department of the Treasury includes information about the bullion depository at www.treasury.gov /about/education/Pages/fort-knox.aspx.

Other articles I consulted for this period included the *New York Times* article on the bombing of Buckingham Palace, headlined "Five German Bombs Hit Buckingham Palace in Day and Night of Air Terror; Lords Also Hit; R.A.F. Pounds Nazi Bases; Italy Masses Troops," published on September 14, 1940; Malcolm Freiberg, "All's Well That Ends Well: A Twentieth-Century Battle over the Declaration of Independence," *Massachusetts Historical Review* 1 (1999); and the National Gallery of Art, "A Guide to Research Resources Relating to World War II" (1999).

Books

The literature on World War II, of course, is voluminous. The books I cite here are a few that helped me shape the braided narrative for *American Treasures*.

A complete biography of Archibald MacLeish was written by Scott Donaldson and entitled *Archibald MacLeish: An American Life* (Boston: Houghton Mifflin, 1992).

For books about potential attacks on America during World War II, see (in alphabetical order by author): James P. Duffy, *Target America: Hitler's Plan to Attack the United States* (Guilford, CT: Lyons Press, 2004); Manfred Griehl, *Luftwaffe over America: The Secret Plans to Bomb the United States in World War II* (London: Greenhill Books,

2004); Robert C. Mikesh, *Japan's World War II Balloon Bomb Attacks on North America* (Washington, D.C.: Smithsonian Institution Scholarly Press, 1973); my own *Due to Enemy Action: The True World War II Story of the USS Eagle 56* (Guilford, CT: Lyons Press, 2005); *Clint Richmond's Fetch the Devil: The Sierra Diablo Murders and Nazi Espionage in America* (Lebanon, NH: ForeEdge, 2014); and Harold Everett Wessman and William Allen Rose, *Aerial Bombardment Protection* (New York: Wiley, 1942).

There are also several fine books about the home front during World War II. The two I relied on most heavily were Doris Kearns Goodwin, *No Ordinary Time: Franklin and Eleanor Roosevelt and the Home Front in World War II* (New York: Simon & Schuster, 1994), and Craig Shirley, *1941: 31 Days That Changed America and Saved the World* (Nashville, TN: Thomas Nelson, 2011). Others I relied on included (in alphabetical order by author): David Brinkley, *Washington Goes to War: The Extraordinary Story of the Transformation of a City and a Nation* (New York: Alfred A. Knopf, 1988); Lorraine Diehl, *Over Here! New York City During World War II* (Washington, DC: Smithsonian, 2010); Scott Hart, *Washington at War: 1941–1945* (Englewood Cliffs, NJ: Prentice-Hall, 1970); and Richard Lingeman, *Don't You Know There's a War On? The American Home Front 1941–1945* (New York: Putnam, 1970).

I read Walter S. Bowen's and Harry E. Neal's book *The United States Secret Service* (New York: Chilton Company, 1960) for a good summary on the organization that Harry Neal loved.

For works on Pearl Harbor—itself a major area of World War II literature—I relied on Steven M. Gillon, *Pearl Harbor: FDR Leads the Nation into War* (New York: Basic Books, 2011); and Stanley Weintraub, *Pearl Harbor Christmas: A World at War, December 1941* (New York: Da Capo, 2011).

An excellent work on the early days of American intelligence is former CIA analyst Thomas F. Troy's *Donovan and the CIA: A History of the Establishment of the Central Intelligence Agency* (Frederick, MD: University Publications of America, 1981).

Michael O'Malley's *Face Value: The Entwined Histories of Money and Race in America* (Chicago: University of Chicago Press, 2012) contains an interesting discussion of Fort Knox and the Roosevelt administration's efforts to portray it as an impregnable fortress to protect the nation's money supply.

Other works that I consulted for this section included (alphabetical by author): Dick Camp, *Shadow Warriors: The Untold Stories of American Special Operations During WWII* (Minneapolis, MN: Zenith Press, 2013); Robert M. Edsel, *The Monuments Men: Allied Heroes, Nazi Thieves, and the Greatest Treasure Hunt in History* (New York: Center Street, 2009); David Edward Finley, *A Standard of Excellence: Andrew W. Mellon Founds the National Gallery of Art at Washington* (Washington: Smithsonian Institution Scholarly Press, 1973); Donald R. McCoy, *The National Archives: America's Ministry of Documents 1934–1968* (Chapel Hill: University of North Carolina Press, 1978); and Gertrude Dana Parlier, *Pursuits of War: The People of Charlottesville and Albemarle County, Virginia, in the Second World War* (Charlottesville, VA: Albemarle Historical Society, 1948).

1952 and Beyond: Onto the National Archives

Primary Sources

The National Archives holds extensive correspondence and information on the discussions between Luther Evans and Wayne Grover to transfer the Charters of Freedom from the Library of Congress to the National Archives. These are found in Record Group 64 (1932–1998), Case Files, 052-144, Box 79. The documents include letters between the two, memos and official circulars, Grover's memo that summarizes discussions with Evans, and reports from archives staffers to Grover on the transfer. Also included is the program from the enshrinement ceremony, entitled "Ceremonies on the Occasion of the Enshrining of the Declaration of Independence and the Constitution of the United States of America and the Bill of Rights" (December 15, 1952).

In addition, information about the transfer of documents is included in the *Annual Report of the Librarian of Congress for the Fiscal Year Ending June 30, 1953* (Washington, D.C.: Library of Congress, 1954). President Harry Truman's speech at the ceremony can be found at the Harry S. Truman Library & Museum and is available online at http://trumanlibrary.org/calendar/viewpapers.php?pid=2012.

The National Archives also holds voluminous records on the Freedom Train, which probably deserves a book in itself. These are contained in the American Heritage Foundation files at Collection AHF, A1 27120X, file "Freedom Train Correspondence 1947–1951," Box 4. The documents include reports of the Freedom Train Committee, information about the construction of the train, correspondence on how the documents would be protected, and news on the train's travels around the country. The previously mentioned RG 64 also contains information about the Freedom Train.

Secondary Sources
Articles, Booklets, and Unpublished Works

Milton Gustafson of the National Archives wrote a piece entitled "Travels of the Charters of Freedom" in *Prologue* 34, no. 4 (Winter 2002), which details the journey of the Declaration and the Constitution from their creation and includes the transfer from the Library of Congress to the National Archives. Gustafson had previously written a more thorough and lengthy story on the 1952 transfer, entitled "The Empty Shrine: The Transfer of the Declaration of Independence and the Constitution to the National Archives," in *American Archivist* 39, no. 3 (July 1976).

Greg Bradsher wrote an excellent piece on Wayne Grover called "Shaping the National Archives: Longest-Serving Archivist Wayne Grover Steered Agency During Critical Years," in *Prologue* 41, no. 4 (Winter 2009).

Bradsher also posted a story about the Freedom Train on the National Archives blog on September 14, 2012, entitled "The Travels of the Bill of Rights, Emancipation Proclamation, and Other National Archives Holdings on the Freedom Train, 1947–49," which can be accessed at http://blogs.archives.gov/TextMessage/2012/09/14/the-travels-of -the-bill-of-rights-emancipation-proclamation-and-other-national -archives-holdings-on-the-freedom-train-1947–1949/. The most extensive photo display of the Freedom Train's trek across all forty-eight states was captured in *National Geographic* issue of October 1949. In addition, I referred to Stuart J. Little, "The Freedom Train: Citizenship and Postwar Political Culture 1946–1949," *American Studies* 34 (1993). Finally, the Lincoln Highway National Museum and Archives in Galion, Ohio, contains online information about the Freedom Train that can be accessed at www.lincoln-highway-museum.org/FT/TF-Index.html.

Books

The most helpful book for this section was the official book of the Freedom Train entitled *Heritage of Freedom: The History and Significance of the Basic Documents of American Liberty*, by Frank Monaghan (Princeton, NJ: Princeton University Press, 1947). The book not only catalogues the documents that traveled aboard the Freedom Train, but offers excellent analyses of the history and significance of each.

Epilogue

Primary Sources

On the issue of preservation, I consulted *Preservation of the Declaration of Independence and the Constitution of the United States*, a report by the National Bureau of Standards to the Library of Congress (National Bureau of Standards Circular 505, July 2, 1951). I also found helpful the *Report of the Ad-hoc Charters Committee of the National Archives Advisory Committee on Preservation* (August 3, 1982), which helped lead to the Charters Monitoring System.

In addition, I found helpful two reports to the National Archives from the Jet Propulsion Library at the California Institute of Technology: "Conceptual Design of a Monitoring System for the Charters of Freedom" (numerous authors, March 15, 1984); and Edward A. Miller's "Final Report: System to Assess the State of Preservation of the Charters of Freedom: System Analysis and Performance of the NARA Charters Monitoring System" (December 31, 1989). Finally, I found interesting National Institute of Standards and Technology Charles R. Tilford's "Monitoring the United States Charters of Freedom," a paper delivered at the 2004 National Conference of Standards Laboratories.

Secondary Sources
Articles, Booklets, and Unpublished Works

The National Archives published information about the Charters of Freedom reencasement project at www.archives.gov/press/press-kits

/charters.html. These include photos, fact sheets, and renovation information. I also found these helpful: Catherine Nicholson and Mary Lynn Ritzenthaler, "The Declaration of Independence, the United States Constitution and the Bill of Rights: Scientific Basis and Practice of Encasement," in *Art on Paper*, edited by Judith Rayner, Joanna M. Kosek, and Birthe Christensen (London: Archetype Books, 2005); and Nicholson and Ritzenhaler, "A New Era Begins for the Charters of Freedom in the National Archives," *Prologue* 35, no. 3 (Fall 2003). In the same publication, Richard Biondo writes "A Top-to-Bottom Renovation for the National Archives Building." In *Prologue* 35, no 4 (Winter 2003), a non-bylined piece ran entitled "The Rotunda for the Charters of Freedom Reopens at the National Archives." The Charters of Freedom reencasement project photo gallery can be viewed at www.archives.gov/press/press-kits/charters-photos/index.html.

In addition, I consulted the work of Kenneth E. Harris and Susan E. Schur, "A Brief History of Preservation and Conservation at the Library of Congress," in the Library of Congress *Preservation Directorate* (October 2006), accessible at www.loc.gov/preservation. I also consulted the previously cited Plotnik's "The Odyssey of the Constitution."

Finally for this section, out of chronological order but a fitting tribute to the author who made the custody of the Declaration of Independence a core part of his professional life, I consulted Verner Clapp's "The Declaration of Independence: A Case Study in Preservation," in *Special Libraries* 62, no. 12 (December 1971): 503–508.

Miscellaneous

A small number of sources did not fit neatly into previous sections. These include the following secondary sources:

Articles, Booklets, and Unpublished Works

The State Department published an article through its Office of the Historian entitled "Buildings of the Department of State: Public Buildings West of the White House, May 1801–August, 1814," accessed at https://history.state.gov/departmenthistory/buildings/section22.

For information about Washington, D.C., in its earliest years, I con-

sulted "The Vision of Pierre L'Enfant: A City to Inspire, A Plan to Preserve," by Glen Worthington, a paper prepared for the Georgetown
University Law Center's Historic Preservation Seminar (Spring Term,
2005).

For general Library of Congress history, see "Jefferson's Legacy: A
Brief History of the Library of Congress," published at http://infousa.state
.gov/government/braches/loc.html. Also see John C. L. Andreassen, "Archives in the Library of Congress," in *American Archivist* 12, no. 1 (January
1949); and Jane A. Rosenberg, "Foundation for Service: The 1896 Hearings on the Library of Congress," Journal of Library History *(1974–1987)*
12, no. 1 (Winter 1986).

Books

I consulted the following books for general research (alphabetical by
author): William J. Bennett, *Our Sacred Honor: Words of Advice from the
Founders in Stories, Letters, Poems, and Speeches* (New York: Simon &
Schuster, 1997); Dr. John B. Ellis, *The Sights and Secrets of the National
Capital: A Work Descriptive of Washington City and All Its Various
Phases* (New York: U.S. Publishing Company, 1869); Paul Johnson, *A His-
tory of the American People,* previously cited; Patty Reinert Mason, *The
National Archives Building: Temple of American History* (Washington,
D.C.: Foundation of the National Archives, 2009); Ainsworth R. Spofford,
editor, *American Almanac: A Treasury of Facts for the Year 1880* (New
York: American News Company, 1880); Christopher L. Webber, *Give Me
Liberty: Speakers and Speeches that Have Shaped America* (New York:
Pegasus Books, 2014); and Gordon S. Wood, *The Purpose of the Past: Re-
flections on the Uses of History* (New York, Penguin Press, 2008).

Acknowledgments

This is my sixth book, and for the sixth time I'm deeply grateful to and heartened by the number of people who have taken the time and energy to assist me and make my work better. I appreciate the contributions of everyone who has taken this journey through American history with me. *American Treasures* would not have been possible without their help.

Before I get to them, I want to give thanks first to you, loyal readers, because you make this book and all books possible. I've always been humbled by your support—I love receiving your emails, enjoy talking with you at presentations and signings, and appreciate the interest you show in my work. I have been honored to meet and shake hands with thousands of you. No author could ask for more.

I would like to thank David Ferriero, Archivist of the United States, who first met with me in the early stages of this project at his National Archives office in Washington, D.C., and offered his encouragement and full support from the start. He asked Jessie Kratz, Historian of the National Archives, to work with me, and Jessie has been a true partner throughout, digging for (sometimes obscure) records when I've asked, answering my repeated questions, and offering guidance and counsel on archives documents and processes. If Jessie's professionalism is indicative of the rest of the staff at the National Archives, there is little doubt that the Declaration of Independence, the Constitution, and the Bill of Rights are in great hands. I'd also like to thank Tom Eisinger, Senior Archivist with the Center for Legislative Archives at the National Archives, for his assistance during the research.

Researcher Jessica Kaplan has my great thanks for uncovering hundreds of pages of documents at the Library of Congress, including many of the Archibald MacLeish papers and the memos and correspondence related to the relocation of precious documents during World War II. She is a smart and determined researcher with great instincts.

U.S. Secret Service Archivist Mike Sampson was engaging and helpful from our first conversation, providing me with numerous documents pertaining to his organization's role in the relocation of documents to Fort Knox a few weeks after Pearl Harbor. He also made available many of Harry Neal's records. Edwin M. Donovan, the Secret Service's deputy assistant director in the Office of Government and Public Affairs, also assisted with making available documents, photos, and biographical sketches of agents involved in the 1941 transfer.

I am deeply grateful to Harry Neal Jr., who talked extensively about his dad's stellar Secret Service record and provided me with Harry Neal's unpublished autobiography and numerous other records that were important to my research. Harry is proud beyond words of his father, not just for his professional accomplishments but because Harry Sr. found time to be a "wonderful, loving, caring, teaching dad" to his children. I regret not having the opportunity to meet the man responsible for managing the transfer of documents from the Library of Congress to Fort Knox on December 26, 1941.

I am always honored and thankful for the contributions and support of so many friends and family members whose interest and encouragement inspire my work. They all make me a better author, but it's impossible to list them all. For now, I would like to mention four very special people for everything they've done.

My friend Brian Cashman used his experience as a former military investigator to uncover background information and interesting details about Fort Knox. I am grateful for his friendship and his constant support of my work.

My dear friend Paula Hoyt once again shared her many editing gifts and proofreading skills to make this book better, and graciously lends her ear and her talent to me all year long. She is the architect and overall manager of my website (www.stephenpuleo.com) and my author Facebook page (www.facebook.com/stephenpuleoauthor), both of which many readers have complimented. She offers valuable suggestions, ideas, and insights that improve my work in so many ways; even with all that, I am most grateful for her continuous encouragement, unwavering support, and loyal friendship.

Since we met in college forty years ago, I have been blessed with the friendship of Ellen Keefe, whose contributions to my life are too numerous to count and too deep to measure. On the writing side, she assists me with research; edits my manuscripts; champions my books to friends, families, and colleagues; and possesses a love of history that makes idea sharing a pleasure. Most important of all, her bedrock friendship with, and love for, my wife Kate and me are among those timeless joys that we cherish most.

For the second consecutive book, I was honored to work with my niece, Rachel Brevich, who holds a degree in history and who again lent her considerable research skills to one of my projects. She has been involved with *American Treasures* from the outset. Rachel did initial research at the National Archives several years ago, before this book was even a full-fledged idea, where she discovered critical records related to the relocation of documents from the Library of Congress during World War II. More recently, she visited the archives to meet with staff members and archivists, unearth additional documents, and interview a conservator on the nature of her work. She did it all with her usual initiative, thoroughness, cheerfulness, attention to both the big picture and the details, and knack for finding more than I asked for. She is a fine researcher, a wonderful niece, and one of the most thoughtful people I know. I'm immensely proud of Rachel and her work.

I'm grateful to the team, past and present, at St. Martin's Press for their support of this project. Former editor Matt Martz sharpened my original proposal and helped reshape the book's direction and broaden its scope. My current editor, Tim Bartlett, has been enthusiastic about the project since taking it on in its very early stages and has been a pleasure to work with. A passionate editor helps improve a book for readers—I'm thankful Tim has improved *American Treasures*. Claire Lampen, former editorial assistant at St. Martin's, was supportive, responsive, and a pleasure to work with throughout this project, and Annabella Hochschild picked up the baton and impressed me with her enthusiasm and professionalism.

I find myself resorting to the cliché "Where has the time gone?" when I think about the fact that my agent, Joy Tutela, and I have been a team for more than fifteen years and that *American Treasures* is our sixth book together. Her passion and enthusiasm for my first book, *Dark Tide*, launched my author journey, and she has since remained steadfast in her encouragement, guidance, and loyalty. She is the consummate pro, and I'm honored that she has believed in me from day one. What an adventure! Thanks for being the best, Joy.

My mom, Rose Puleo, provided her constant interest, support, and love throughout the writing of this book, as she has done throughout my life. I greatly missed my dad (as I do every day) and thought about him each time I sat down to write—he loved getting updates on my word count and celebrating with a bear hug when a book was finished. I feel his comforting presence always. I will never be able to thank my parents for all they have done.

I save my final and most profound thanks for my wife and best friend, Kate, who thirty-six years ago made me the happiest man in the world and continues to do so today. We are true partners in so many things, including book writing. I am forever asking Kate to serve as a sounding board for ideas and she always offers thoughtful insights. She reads and edits my manuscripts and provides excellent suggestions on ways to improve my writing and the flow of the narrative. Her helpful and generous nature doesn't end with her contributions to me—she is forever assisting others with her time and talent. She constantly offers her gifts as an educator to children and their families, and her wellspring of contagious optimism makes those around her (including me) feel like anything is possible. I am proud of her for many different reasons and I am inspired daily by her strength, her smile, and her soul. This book's dedication to her is drawn from one of my favorite poems, "At Nightfall," by Charles Hanson Towne, which begins: "I need so much the quiet of your love / After the day's loud strife; / I need your calm all other things above / After the stress of life." My thanks to you, Kate, for the deep peace and quiet strength your love brings to our life.

Index